The Reception of Continental Ideas in the Common Law World 1820 - 1920

Comparative Studies
in Continental and Anglo-American Legal History
Vergleichende Untersuchungen zur kontinentaleuropäischen
und anglo-amerikanischen Rechtsgeschichte

Herausgegeben von

Prof. Dr. Dr. h. c. mult. Helmut Coing

und

Prof. Dr. Dr. h. c. Knut Wolfgang Nörr

Band 13

The Reception of Continental Ideas in the Common Law World 1820-1920

Edited by

Mathias Reimann

Duncker & Humblot · Berlin

Gedruckt mit Unterstützung der Gerda Henkel Stiftung, Düsseldorf

Die Deutsche Bibliothek – CIP-Einheitsaufnahme

The **reception of continental ideas in the common law world** :
1820 - 1920 / ed. by Mathias Reimann. — Berlin :
Duncker und Humblot, 1993
(Comparative studies in continental and Anglo-American
legal history ; Bd. 13)
ISBN 3-428-07682-6
NE: Reimann, Mathias [Hrsg.]; GT

Druck: Berliner Buchdruckerei Union GmbH, Berlin
Printed in Germany

ISSN 0935-1167
ISBN 3-428-07682-6

Inhaltsverzeichnis

Introduction: Patterns of Reception

The traditional view that the two great Western legal systems, the civil and the common law, developed in virtual isolation from each other is quickly being eroded. The influence of the medieval Roman scholars on English law, the role of continental doctrine in seventeenth and eighteenth century English jurisprudence, and the importance of civilian practice in the English courts have already been explored. Slowly but steadily, these and other connections between civil and common law are becoming general knowledge among legal historians.

The traditional view is still widely held, however, with respect to the nineteenth and early twentieth century. It is telling that even first-rate legal historians who are keenly aware of the historical interrelationship between the two systems can suddenly conceive of "absolute barriers between Continental law and the common law"[1]. The persistence of the traditional view with respect to the nineteenth century is probably due to the particular importance of this time period for the definition of the two systems. For better or worse, comparatists continue to define the common and the civil law mainly by contrasting case law and codification. This contrast was stark (only) between the first modern codes and the rise of the welfare state. Thus, this time period is the classical era of the antithesis between judgemade law and systematic legislation. In that era, the common and the civil law look so clearly like polar opposites that mutual influences are particularly hard to imagine. Only as the twentieth century progressed and as modern social and regulatory legislation blurred the traditional contrast, so it seems, the two systems began to converge.

Astonishing as it may be to many legal historians and comparatists, the exchange of ideas between the civil and the common law culture was lively and fruitful even during the heydey of case law and codification. Some Anglo-American scholars, among them several contributors to this volume, have recently begun to explore this exchange. There are now about two dozen articles in this area. But they are only a modest beginning.

Concrete information is still very sparse. Some aspects of the interrelationship between continental and common law in the nineteenth and early twentieth centuries have been thoroughly researched, aptly described, and lucidly analyzed,

---

[1] *R. Helmholz,* Continental Law and Common Law: Historical Strangers or Companions: 1990 Duke L. J. 1207, at 1209; see also *J. Dawson,* The Oracles of the Law (Ann Arbor 1968), p. 505.

but about many other important aspects nothing of value has yet been published. Moreover, the existing knowledge is not widely diffused[2]. This is particularly true for the Continent. While in England and the United States at least some expertise has been developed, most Continental comparatists and legal historians are by and large unaware of any modern connections between civil and comon law. This may in part be due to the lack of access to the Anglo-American publications about the topic.

Therefore, this volume should serve two goals. It should supply further pieces of knowledge about the modern interrelationship between the civil and the common law cultures, and it should help to disseminate this knowledge among a wider audience, especially in Europe. The intention behind the various contributions is not to deny the great disparity between the two legal systems in the nineteenth and early twentieth centuries, but to qualify this disparity by "continuing a tradition which has looked to the connecting, rather than to the deviding elements of the two great legal families"[3].

Needless to say, comprehensive coverage of the topic is neither possible nor desired within this framework. On the contrary, by presenting a diversity of subjects and approaches, this volume should illustrate the richness and promise of the topic as an area of research and instigate further studies by both Anglo-American and Continental scholars.

However, the contributions were not collected randomly buth rather according to specific parameters. Clarifying these parameters will enable the reader better to appreciate the scope and limits of this volume.

On the one hand, the topic was broadly conceived, as the title indicates. The studies do no focus primarily on legal rules but more on legal cultures in general. Hence the essays deal with "Continental" ideas from many parts of the civil law tradition, ranging from classical Roman law to French concepts of codification and German jurisprudence. And hence the volume considers "Anglo-American Law" in the sense of the legal world of both England and the United States, a world which was much more of a cultural unit before World War I than it is today. Furthermore, the "Ideas" discussed do not only consist of legal concepts or rules but also incorporate other elements of a legal culture as well — actors and their roles, sources and their significance, legal thought and its impact.

On the other hand, two limitations have been set. First, the timeframe was limited roughly to the century between 1820 and 1920. It thus by and large excludes the earliest nineteenth century as well as the post-World War I period,

[2] The standard works on legal history, Anglo-American and Continental alike, contain very little, if any, information about these connections.

[3] Vorwort der Herausgeber in *H. Coing / K. W. Nörr,* Englische und kontinentale Rechtsgeschichte: ein Forschungsprojekt (Berlin 1985); the translation from the German is mine.

both of which present issues so different from the ones addressed here that they are better explored separately[4]. Second, the contributions deal only with the influence of Continental ideas on the Anglo-American legal culture, not vice versa.

Even within these limits the scope and diversity of the contributions is bewildering. They are presented in roughly chronological order according to their subject matter. This is not only because in historiography there is a preference for chronology. More importantly, the chronological arrangment captures a particularly essential feature of the fate of Continental ideas in Anglo-American law — it illuminates the change of focus over time. In the first half of the nineteenth century, the common lawyers were interested in the civil law in a broad sense, then mostly represented by the Roman and French variety. In later decades, they quickly directed their attention almost exclusively towards German ideas. Here again, one can observe a change in emphasis. In the postbellum period, Anglo-American jurists focused mainly on the German historical school and its successor, conceptual jurisprudence. As the century turned, they became more interested in the next, sociologically oriented generation of German jurisprudence, which helped to lead them towards twentieth century legal thought.

Turning to the earlier period first, we find that before the middle of the nineteenth century, Continental ideas had a greater influence in the United States than in England[5]. This was no accident. England boasted a legal culture that had been firmly established for more than half a millenium, and most English lawyers had little inclination to borrow ideas from the European continent. In the United States, by contrast, an indigenous legal system was still in the making. Around 1820 the die was cast against a wholesale adoption of the civil law and in favor of following the common law path, but this does not mean that American lawyers slavishly adhered to English precedent. Civilian ideas were still attractive for several reasons — the prestige of Roman law, the novelty of many questions for which English law provided no immmediate answer, and the elegance of the French codes — to name just a few. The contributions of Michael Hoeflich, Alan Watson, and David Clark deal with this earlier period, addressing the

---

[4] Before 1820, they include particularly the politically charged debate about the respective virtues of civil and common law in the early decades of the American republic, i. e. before Kent and Story, and the impact of continental ideas on English agendas of legal reform. After World War I, the previously intense contacts between common and civil lawyers were much diminished. The impact of emigrant jurists in the 1930s and 1940s and the exchanges between the Anglo-American and Continental legal systems after World War II require studies in their own right.

[5] This does not mean that English lawyers were as hostile to continental learning as is frequently believed. Even in the earlier nineteenth century, English jurists often discussed continental ideas; see *M. Graziadei,* Changing images of the Law in XIX Century English Legal Thought (in this volume); see also *B. Simpson,* Innovation in Nineteenth Century Contract Law, 91 L.Q.R. 247 (1975).

attraction of the Roman law, the utility of civilian doctrine as an additional source of answers, and the issue of codification in turn.

The Roman law was especially cultivated in the old American South. There, the widespread admiration for its systematic elegance and the civilian (namely French or Spanish) background of many southern states combined with the southern ideal of broad, classical, gentlemanly education to vest Roman law with high prestige. Michael Hoeflich tells the story of three jurists, Francis Lieber, Hugh Swinton Legaré, and James Murdoch Walker, who made South Carolina a center of Roman and civil law in the antebellum period. While these scholars did not wish to replace American common with European Roman law, they eagerly pursued the enrichment of the common law through selective borrowing from the civilian sources. More importantly, they and others also built bridges between the legal cultures of the old and the new worlds. Especially Lieber, a German emigrant, funtioned as an intermediary between the Anglo-American and the Continental legal communities, establishing contacts between scholars like Story and Mittermaier. With the Civil War and the subjugation of the South by the victorious North, this aspect of the southern culture perished along with so many others.

Civilian learning also intrigued jurists in the American North. Legal giants like James Kent and Joseph Story, whose multivolume treatises laid the foundations for an indigenous American common law, were versed in Roman and civilian ideas. Kent in particular enjoys the reputation for having introduced large amounts of civilian doctrine into American law as a judge and chancellor as well as the author of his famous "Commentaries on American Law" (1826-1830). Kent's writings are replete with citations to Roman law (particularly Justinian's Institutes, the Digest, and the Codex), the French codes (mainly the *Code civil*), and the works of prominent civilian jurists (Pothier, Emerigon, Domat, Heineccius, Pufendorf, Grotius, etc.). How important, Alan Watson asks heretically, were these civilian sources really for Kent in his endeavor to solve doctrinal issues? Watson's meticulous analysis of Kent's writings as a judge and as a scholar leads him to a curious conclusion: despite a multitude of citations, Kent does not really employ civilian ideas for the development of American law. Virtually all of his references are superfluous because he could have relied on common law authority just as well, and often more easily. While Kent by and large had a good grasp of Continental ideas, he sometimes made egregious mistakes in using them. In short, Kent mostly employed civilian sources as window dressing, and often in a very sloppy manner. To be sure, the use of exotic authority for decorative purposes and the concomittant commission of errors is far from unusual among lawyers. Nonetheless, Watson's article hits home hard: it destroys one myth — that Kent enriched American law through his civilian learning — and implicitly challenges another — that there was a great need for civilian doctrine in the formative period of American law. Of course, the question then remains why Kent went through the trouble of referring to Continental sources at all. Perhaps, Watson surmises, it really helped (as Kent had claimed) to sell his decisions to his colleagues, who were impressed by the prestige of the foreign authorities although they understood little or nothing of them.

This prestige of the civil law was largely due to the impression that the European codifications, especially the French codes, made in the early and mid-nineteenth century United States. Throughout the century, codification was an issue in the new world, and the American codification movement scored some, albeit limited, practical successes. Its greatest hour came when New York codified its law of civil procedure in 1848, providing an influential example followed by many other states and thus revolutionizing the American law of civil procedure. Certainly, this codification (and others like it), many observers believe, must be based on European models. This conclusion seems to be bolstered by looking at the man behind the New York code. David Dudley Field, America's most ardent advocate for, and outright symbol of, codification, was fascinated by the European culture, spoke French, and travelled to the Continent with great frequency. Thus, it is tempting to conclude that his ideas about codification stemmed directly from Europe, especially from France. David Clark wanted to know for sure. In his essay, he undertakes the amazingly difficult task of tracing the origins of Field's ideas, and finds that things are not so clear at all. Clark concludes that Field seems to have borrowed significant elements from the civil law tradition, from the idea to the form and substance of codification. He also finds, however, that the civilian influence was transmitted primarily through Louisiana and especially its 1825 Code of Procedure, although European (mainly French) examples provided support. The idea and structure of Field's code in particular, probably did not stem directly from Europe but from Louisiana whose codes were in turn influenced by French and Spanish ideas. This is also true for some of Field's key concepts, such as the single form of action and simplified fact pleading. In sum, Continental thought was only one, albeit important source. Again, civilian ideology and systematization played a greater role than civilian legal rules.

The second half of the nineteenth century became what has been called the period of "classical" thought in Anglo-American law[6]. The old procedural structure of the common law, the medieval forms of action, were abandoned in both England and America and were gradually replaced by modern, substantive categories. Legal history was separated from positive law and became a pursuit in its own right. Moreover, law, at long last, turned into an academic discipline studied in the universities, no longer an affair of judges and legislators alone, but from then on a concern of professional academics as well. These changes required considerable reorientation, and many common lawyers sought guidance

---

[6] See e. g. *T. C. Grey,* Langdell's Orthodoxy, 45 U. Pitt. L. Rev. 1 (1983).

in the civil law culture. By then their attention was no longer directed primarily to classical Roman law, the 18th century civilians, or the French codes. In the postbellum period, Anglo-American jurists focused on Germany, where historical school and *Pandektenwissenschaft* had refined legal science to a high degree. The common lawyers looked to it for new ideas in legal doctrine, orientation in legal history, and patterns of legal academia. These are the topics addressed in the next four articles in this volume.

The role of German legal doctrine is discussed by two contributors from an institution with a longstanding relationship with the German legal culture, the University of California at Berkeley.

Stefan Riesenfeld traces the impact of a multitude of German ideas on the United States and identifies the major channels of transmission over several generations of American scholars, from Francis Lieber and John Chipman Gray to Roscoe Pound and, well into our own century, Karl Llewellyn. He addresses three areas of influence in particular. First, American jurists adopted a variety of German doctrinal concepts, such as the idea of a legal transaction *(Rechtsgeschäft)*, the notion of a declaration of intention *(Willenserklärung)*, the analysis of contract in terms of offer and acceptance *(Angebot und Annahme)*, the distinction between obligation and disposition *(Verpflichtung und Verfügung)*, and the doctrine of the failure of presupposed conditions *(Wegfall der Geschäftsgrundlage)*, to name just a few. Second, Riesenfeld emphasizes the German influence on American legal method, the most prominent example being the balancing of interest approach to the resolution of legal controversies. Finally he refers to the adoption of institutions such as social security and cooperatives; while the German influence on Anglo-American notions of social security has already been studied[7], the impact of German concepts of cooperatives on America is not yet completely explored. The picture that emerges evidences selective borrowing by American jurists from German legal science in a large variety of important instances.

Why did such borrowing take place? Certainly, sometimes the exporting and the importing cultures had similar doctrinal needs, and a solution already proven to work in one could be expected to work in the other as well. Still, the reasons were not always so straightforward. The borrowing process sometimes entailed fundamental changes in the meaning of a concept, for example when export and import served different functions in their respective environments. Richard Buxbaum gives a peculiar example by tracing the history of the *Kux,* a legal curiosity originating in fifteenth century Germany, in modern American corporate law. The *Kux* was a share in a mineral exploitation enterprise, and since the amount of capital needed was often initially uncertain, the shareholder had to add capital

---

[7] For England, see *E. P. Hennock,* British Social Insurance and German Precedents: The Case of Social Insurance 1880 - 1914 (1987).

in response to "rolling" subscription calls — in other words, the value of the share was open-ended. This concept became interesting to American corporate lawyers when they toyed with the idea of no-par stock around the turn of the century. When the *Kux* was reincarnated as no-par stock in the United States, though, its function was completely different from that in its first, German life. The introduction of no-par stock was meant to destroy the shareholders' illusion that a share was "worth" its par value — a purpose completely alien to the German *Kux*. Ironically, the concept of no-par stock was discussed (and rejected) in Germany in the 1920s as an original American idea in what Buxbaum calls a "reverse flow of concepts". "Bux on Kux" not only proffers an entertaining story, but also shows that Anglo-American references to civilian concepts sometimes simply amounted to the proverbial "pouring of new wine into old bottles".

The adoption of Continental concepts was not unproblematic for the Anglo-American jurists either, because the borrowing from civilian sources was intimately connected with the disturbing issue of the common law's uniqueness. Michele Graziadei tells the captivating story of the common lawyers' struggle with the issue of the origin of their own tradition, and of its relation with the civil law, by exploring the changes in the treatment of fundamental doctrines (trust, contract, bailment, etc.). From a fashionable but uncertain Romanism which dawned in the first half of the century, the pendulum swung to extreme Germanism in the latter part of the century, when the exploration of the common law past came under the spell of German legal historiography. Thus, in the last third of the century, the belief in a Romanist source for every English rule gave way to the conviction that the common law had nothing to do with the civilian tradition but was rooted in the Teutonic forests. As a consequence, the use of civilian doctrine to understand the common law was then regarded with suspicion. English jurists no longer considered civilian ideas as beneficial for the development of common law thinking, but began to regard them as alien matter likely not to enlighten but to confuse the common law mind. Finally, it was Maitland around the turn of the century who emphasized the elements which were distinctive of the English tradition vis à vis the Continental legal experience, thus laying the foundations for modern English historiography, and for many comparative studies. Graziadei's essay is a tour de force through a chapter of intellectual history and shows how much the common lawyers' attitudes towards their own legal tradition were subject to change over time, and how these changes responded to impulses linked to continental legal thought.

The Continental ideas that fascinated common lawyers were not limited to doctrinal concepts and legal history. They also encompassed images and roles of actors in the legal system. Being a creature of bench and bar, the common law culture obviously had no need to learn from Continental judges or attorneys, and English and American legislators had ample political experience. Yet, the common law systems had distinctly lacked one class of legal actors — legal academics. Leaders in the civil law tradition since the middle ages, professional legal scholars were virtually non-existent in the common law realm until well into the nineteenth century. Only in the postbellum-period did they begin to appear, especially in America with the rise of the modern law schools. Given the prestige the civilian tradition enjoyed in the Anglo-American world, it is no wonder that the newly emerging common law scholars saw role models in their firmly established Continental brethren. They looked particularly to their German colleagues, whose elegant systematization of legal concepts and whose historical research they deeply admired. The last of the four articles about the "classical period" analyzes the model function of German legal academica for the nascent Anglo-American professoriate. Emulating the learning, function, and academic status of their German counterparts, the new generation of common law scholars turned law into an academic discipline for the first time in common law history. This meant that the Anglo-American legal culture moved a considerable step closer to the Continental tradition, and it greatly facilitated the communication between the two systems.

As the nineteenth century drew to its close, and particularly after 1900, the Anglo-American attention to Continental ideas began to shift once again. The change was neither rapid nor complete but rather a gradual shift of emphasis. Interest in German scholarship remained dominant. Yet, as the common lawyers made progress in reworking their own substantive law, their fascination with civilian doctrinal concepts waned. As Anglo-American legal historiography approached maturity, German scholarship carried less weight. And as American and English law professors became professional scholars, the German academic model became dispensable. In the meantime, however, jurisprudence slowly came to the fore. Formalism and laissez faire-attitudes came under attack as new views of law and society began to emerge. Searching for theories adequate to modern industrial society, Anglo-American scholars again turned to Continental, and particularly to German ideas. The last two articles in this volume address the role of German legal and political theory in American thought. In terms of their time-frame, these contributions still deal with the "classical period", but in terms of their subject matter they point beyond it, far into the developments in our own century. Taken together they present a striking contrast between ideas that were enthusiastically embraced by American scholars, and others that, surprisingly, were not.

In the decades between 1880 und 1920, the historical and analytical forms of jurisprudence, hitherto dominant in America and rooted in the ideas of Austin, Maine, Savigny, and others, were gradually replaced by sociological theories of law. Some of the ingredients for the new approaches came from domestic soil, particularly Holmes' powerful ideas and the emerging philosophy of pragmatism. However, significant elements were imported from the old world. James Herget analyzes the impact of German thought on American jurisprudence. On the

European side, he focuses on the most important legal theorist of that period, Rudolf von Ihering and on the schools of thought stimulated by his ideas, the jurisprudence of interests, the free school of law, and modern legal sociology. He also looks to figures in the backgrond, like sociologists Gumplowicz, Simmel, and Ratzenhofer. On the American side, obviously Roscoe Pound was the principal transmitter of German ideas which he employed to build his sociological jurisprudence. Herget discusses other scholars as well, namely John Chipman Gray, political scientist Arthur F. Bentley, and sociologist Albion Small, who were also imbued with German thought. Despite the undeniable power of these influences, though, modern American jurisprudence was not simply a restatement of German ideas. In the hands of their recipients, their substance was transformed and combined with other elements, ultimately to form Legal Realism which was destined to dominate twentieth century American jurisprudence. Still, Herget concludes, Realism had essentially been anticipated in Germany a quarter of a century before its birth in America.

Again, one must not lightly conclude that enthusiasm for Continental ideas in nineteenth and early twentieth century America was all-embracing. There were clear, though not always easily explainable, limits to the American receptivity. James Whitman gives an example where reception unexpectedly failed. Venturing into the borderland between legal, social, and political theory, he describes the fortune of corporatist ideas in Germany and the United States. Much discussed in Germany by scholars like Albert Schäffle and Adolf Wagner and favored by Bismarck, corporatism was a powerful element of late nineteenth century German social thought. German social thought in turn dominated the minds of American scholars, many of whom had studied in Germany. Yet, while they imported German ideas with excitement and in great numbers, these scholars lacked all enthusiam for corporatist notions. Why did corporatism make no headway in America? Whitman proffers tentative but perceptive explanations that point to the differences between the political and social environments of Germany and the United States. The dominant factor was probably the contrast between the American commitment to individualism and the German desire, quite prevalent at least at the time, to transcend individual identity. Although (or because) Whitman deals with an instance of nonreception, his essay intimates two important points. Understanding the reasons for the failures of reception is just as important as, and perhaps more enlightening than, explaining its successes. And in order to understand either, we must be ready to look beyond the horizon of law to the cultural predispositions on which the reception of ideas is contingent.

Drawing a small number of general conclusions from the large quantity of particular topics discussed in all these articles is impossible without oversimplification. Nonetheless, a few guideposts are in order lest the reader be left adrift in a sea of detail. These should be taken not as authoritative interpretations but rather as tentative suggestions.

Three rather general obersavations, likely to meet with widespread approval, can be stated very briefly. First, Continental ideas were received by the common law culture throughout the nineteenth and early twentieth centuries in significant number and in a multitude of contexts, ranging from substantive rules to professional roles and from narrow concepts to broad jurisprudential theories. Second, this reception took on a variety of forms and was driven by many motives, from deliberate borrowing for specific purposes (innovation, persuasion, rationalization, etc.) to semi-conscious, slow infiltration of the common law tradition without strictly defined goals. Third, this reception was not an even and predictable process but a phenomenon full of oddities and surprises, as particularly the contributions of Watson, Buxbaum, and Whitman illustrate.

Beyond these observations, one may hazard three further points that are potentially more controversial. They concern the protagonists, the substance, and the manner of the reception. Considering them together leads to a final note of caution.

The leading protagonists of the reception were legal academics. Admittedly, this is not true without exception. Kent, Legaré, Field and some others not mentioned in this volume were primarily pracitioners, but even these men had considerable scholarly ambitions, and after the Civil War, academics clearly dominated the field. It is possible that this academic predominance is a misconception resulting from the myopic view of the authors in this volume who see the world too much through their own, academic eyes. Yet, there is reason to doubt that a team of practitioners would find equally strong European influence transmitted by judges and attorneys. Most likely, academics did play the leading role in the transmission of Continental ideas to the common law world. After all, they were the professional group most inclined to look beyond their own horizons to other cultures, especially at a time when international legal practice was negligible compared to today. Scholars were not always more cosmopolitan than practitioners, but they had more leisure, and curiosity was part of their job.

Whatever its reasons, this academic predominance affected the substance of the reception. Scholars borrow for scholarly, not for practical purposes. They are not primarily interested in the immediate practical utility of an idea; instead, their interests tend to range more broadly. It is noteworthy that the general prestige, the ideology, and the broad jurisprudential theories of the civil law culture played at least as prominent a role as concrete legal rules and concepts. To be sure, such rules and concepts often enjoyed the common lawyer's interest, as particularly Riesenfeld and Buxbaum demonstrate. The southern Romanists and Chancellor Kent, though, invoked Continental learning not because it offered better law but because it was vested with the aura of antiquity and the prestige of the natural law treatises. The new scholars at Harvard and codifier David Dudley Field looked to Europe not for its legal rules but for the fame of its academic culture and for its ideology of codification. John Chipman Gray and

Roscoe Pound were much less interested in German private law doctrine than in Jhering's and Ehrlich's sociological approaches.

Finally, the manner in which Anglo-American jurists borrowed from the civilian culture was always highly selective. Whether they venerated the Roman law, referred to French scholarship, emulated German role models, authored codes, or adopted rules and concepts, they were not interested in any sort of wholesale reception of Continental ideas, but only in picking and choosing what they deemed useful. Many common lawyers deeply admired the civilian legal culture, and some considered it superior to their own, but they never forgot that they were common lawyers and rarely wanted to be anything else[8]. This distinguishes even civil law enthusiasts like Kent or Legaré and Germanophiles like Pound or Llewellyn markedly from the Continental jurists who had once abandoned their indigenous legal culture and adopted another one, the Roman law, instead.

These observations on the leaders, substance, and style of the reception recommend caution in evaluating the overall significance of Continental ideas for Anglo-American law in the nineteenth and early twentieth centuries. In light of the quantity and diversity of borrowing displayed in this collection, it is easy to overestimate its importance. Reflection on who borrowed what and how can help to maintain the proper perspective.

Since most of the borrowing was done by academics, we must remind ourselves that influence on academic thought is one thing, but that impact on legal practice is quite another. While scholars eventually transmit their ideas to legal practice through their teaching and writing, this transmission is by and large diffuse, often weak, and sometimes fails altogether. This is particularly true in a legal system dominated not by the scholar but by the judge. Moreover, since these scholars were at least as interested in the prestige and ideology of the civil law as in its actual substance, we must take into account that much of their attention was not even focused on practical utility but on theoretical enrichment and ideological support. Lastly, since they borrowed elements of Continental learning very selectively, we should not overlook that much of the established substance of the common law remained completely unaffected.

All this does not mean that the civilian influence was unimportant or negligible. It simply means that we must not unthinkingly equate the Continental impact on the Anglo-American legal culture portrayed in this volume with civilian influence on the common law in action. Instead, we should admit that while we are beginning to understand the impact of Continental learning on Anglo-American scholarship, we know comparatively little about the civilian impact on common law practice. Particularly in that area, much remains to be done.

---

8 To be sure, there were exceptions, for example Lieber in America who never thought of himself as a common lawyer, or Austin in England who would have liked to be a civilian scholar, but these exceptions were few and prove the rule.

The contributors wish to thank the general editors of the series, Professors Knut Wolfgang Nörr and Helmut Coing, for initiating the project, as well as Rechtsreferendar Dieter Waibel of the Forschungsstelle für internationale Privatrechtsgeschichte in Tübingen for preparing the manuscript. We are also much indebted to the Gerda Henkel Stiftung for the generous financial support and the unimpeded way in which it was provided.

The remaining eight authors dedicate this volume to the ninth *Stefan Riesenfeld*. In fact, this is a dedication to two persons at the same time: First, to Professor Riesenfeld, who is a living symbol of Continental ideas in Anglo-American law. Formerly a student of Windscheid's disciple Kipp, later an acquaintance of Llewellyn and a student of Pound, he has taught and written on both continents for way over half a century. Second, to "Steve", as he is known to his friends, who was the good spirit of the authors' conferences in Berkeley / California and Lancaster / England with his insights, wit, and humor.

Mathias Reimann

MICHAEL H. HOEFLICH*

Roman and Civil Law in the Anglo-American World Before 1850: Lieber, Legaré and Walker, Roman Lawyers in the Old South

In 1870, an essayist began his review of the *Writings of Hugh Swinton Legaré* with this lament:

> The great names of the South are dying out. For want of an adequate record, men, whose genius the whole country honored in their lifetime, are beginning to sink into obscurity.[1]

In the first half of the nineteenth century, there flourished a brilliant and distinctive legal culture in the Southern United States. While the Northern tradition tended to center around concepts of "practical virtue" and was relatively narrowly focused upon the more technical aspects of law, in the South lawyers were also men of broad culture, following more in the path, perhaps, of Thomas Jefferson, the great polymath,[2] than Theophilus Parsons, the brilliant but intellectually ascetic Massachusetts judge.[3]

The South led the way, for instance, in legal education. George Wythe at the College of William & Mary was the first full-time law professor in the United States.[4] This model was followed at other universities.[5] Law schools were established and continued successfully at Transylvania University in Lexington, Kentucky and at Tulane in New Orleans, among others.[6] Southern lawyers were founders of and contributors to major literary journals such as the *Southern*

* I want to thank *Goney Freider* for her assistance in footnoting this piece.

1 Hugh Swinton Legaré, The Southern Review (1870), 123. *Michael O'Brien*, Rethinking the South (Baltimore and London: John Hopkins University Press, 1988), 24.

2 See *Noble E. Cunningham, Jr.*, In Pursuit of Reason — The Life of Thomas Jefferson (Baton Rouge and London: Louisiana State University Press, 1987).

3 On Theophilus Partons, see *Isaac Parker*, A Sketch of the Character of the Late Chief Justice Parsons (Boston, 1813).

4 *Robert Bevier Kirtland*, George Wythe: Lawyer, Revolutionary, Judge, diss., University of Michigan, 1983 (New York and London: Garland Publishing, 1986), 115.

5 See, the recent articles of Paul Carrington; *Carrington*, The Revolutionary Idea of University Legal Education, 31 Wm. & Mary L. Rev. (1990) 527; *Carrington*, Teaching Law in the Antebellum Northwest, 23 Univ. Toledo L. Rev. 3 (1991).

6 On Transylvania's Law School, see, *Kerr*, Transylvania's Law Department, Americana, vol. 31 (1937), 3 ff.; see, also, *Carrington*, Arts. Cit., n. 5, above.

Review and the *Southern Literary Messenger*.[7] Several built great libraries and became patrons of the arts and of letters.[8] They studied not only in the South, but in the North at Harvard, for instance, and abroad in England, Scotland, and on the European continent.[9] Brilliant legal centers existed at Charleston and in New Orleans.[10] And the political questions of the day, such as nullification and secession, called forth the best legal minds into the fields of constitutional law and political theory. Thus, it is particularly unfortunate that as the antebellum Southern tradition died out and the historiography of the period became obsessed with analyzing the influence of slavery, the full vitality and breadth of this tradition have been so utterly forgotten.[11]

It has been common, generally, to speak of American legal development in virtually complete isolation from the intellectual traditions of Europe during the nineteenth century.[12] It is as if the extensive contacts between the Founding Fathers of the American Republic and the great lawyers, philosophers, and statesman of Enlightenment Europe were simply broken off and forgotten after 1800.

To take this narrow historiographical position is to ignore completely the extensive interaction between Civil law and Common law ideas in the United States during the nineteenth century in the works of American Common law jurists and to ignore, as well, the extensive contacts between American and European scholars and jurists.[13] Interest in Continental legal scholarship and

---

7 The Southern Review was published quarterly beginning in February 1828. As a scholarly journal it contained poetry, book reviews and articles on law, science, mathematics, history, language, medicine, and other topics of interest. Chief contributors included T. C. Wallace, Robert Hayne, Thomas Cooper and the editors Stephen Elliot and associate Hugh Swinton Legaré. The last volume of the Review was published in February 1832.

The Southern Literary Messenger was a magazine published for the Virginia Historical and Philosophical Society, starting in August 1834. It was a monthly production which included travelogues, famous works, book reviews, poetry, articles on varied topics of interest and information and events of the Society. Chief contributors included Edgar Allan Poe, Lydia Sigourney, Oliver Oldschool and W. Gilmore Simms. T. W. White was replaced as an editor by R. Thompson in 1848. The last volume of the Messenger was published in 1864.

See *Calhoun*, Literary Magazines in the Old South, The History of Southern Literature, ed. Rubin (Baton Rouge and London: Louisiana State University Press, 1985).

8 See *M. O'Brien*, Rethinking the South. See also *Michael O'Brien*, ed., All Clever Men, Who Make Their Ways (Fayetteville: University of Arkansas Press, 1982).

9 See *M. O'Brien*, ed., Intellectual Life in Antebellum Charleston (Knoxville: University of Tennessee Press, 1986). See also *E. Merton Coulter*, College Life in the Old South, fwd. Thomas Dyer (1928; Athens: University of Georgia Press, 1983), pp. 181-182.

10 *Michael O'Brien*, A Character of Hugh Legaré (Knoxville: University of Tennessee Press, 1985).

11 I have dealt with this Southern tradition also in a different format. See *M. H. Hoeflich*, Roman Law in American Legal Culture, Tulane L. Rev., vol. 66, No. 6 (1992).

12 See *Lawrence F. Friedman*, A History of American Law, 2nd ed. (New York: Simon and Schuster, 1985).

practice was vigorous throughout the early nineteenth century. The influence of Continental legal learning was especially notable in the antebellum South. European scholarship was an important part of the Southern legal tradition just as European literature formed a major part of the Southern literary public's reading matters.[14] Southern lawyers trained abroad and were in close contact with Europeans. Roman and Civil law scholarship reached a high level among Southern lawyers and jurists in the Common law jurisdictions of the South during the antebellum period in, for example, Virginia and South Carolina, as well as in those with Civil law traditions such as Louisiana and Texas.

One circle of "civilians" that has received very little attention is that which grew up around Charleston and Columbia, South Carolina. This group, in particular, stands as an example of the highest intellectual attainments reached by antebellum American lawyers. They rivaled their Northern colleagues, Story, Kent, and DuPonceau, in both knowledge and influence. The three principal members of this circle were Francis Lieber,[15] Hugh Swinton Legaré,[16] and James Murdock Walker.[17] All were South Carolinians, two by birth, one by adoption. Hugh Swinton Legaré was born in Charleston in 1797; James Walker was born in Charleston in 1813; Francis Lieber was born in Berlin in 1800 but emigrated first to the Northeastern United States in 1827 and then to Columbia, South Carolina in 1835. Legaré and Walker were both practicing lawyers as well as government servants. Walker was a South Carolina state legislator; Legaré served as American charge d'affaires in Belgium, as well as United States Attorney-General and Secretary of State *pro tem* in 1842-3. Lieber held the chair of constitutional history at South Carolina College in Columbia for two decades. In 1857 he left South Carlolina for Columbia University School of Law in New York and there held the second chair in law under Theodore Dwight.[18]

---

[13] *M. H. Hoeflich,* Savigny and his Anglo-American Disciples, The American Journal of Comparative Law 37 (1989): pp. 17-37.

M. H. Hoeflich, Transatlantic Friendships and The German Influence on American Law in the First Half of the Nineteenth Century, The American Journal of Comparative Law 35 (1987): pp. 599-611.

[14] See *Carl Holliday,* A History of Southern Literature (1906; Port Washington, New York: Kennikat Press, 1969).

[15] On Lieber, see *Frank Freidel,* Francis Lieber, Nineteenth-Century Liberal (Baton Rouge: Louisiana State University Press, 1947); see also *Thomas Sergeant Perry,* The Life and Letters of Francis Lieber (Boston, 1882).

[16] On Legaré, see *Rhea,* Hugh Swinton Legaré, a Charleston Intellectual (Chapel Hill: The University of North Carolina Press, 1934); see also *Michael O'Brien,* A Character of Hugh Legaré (Knoxville: University of Tennessee Press, 1985). Legaré's major writings are collected along with a memoir by his sister (of which the original is in the Caroliniana collection), in Legaré, The Writings of Hugh Swinton Legaré, Mary Legaré ed. and intro. (Charleston, 1846).

[17] On Walker, see *John Belton O'Neall,* James M. Walker, Biographical Sketches of the Bench and Bar of South Carolina (Charleston, 1859).

[18] *Freidel,* p. 366.

Walker, Lieber, and Legaré were all prolific authors. Walker wrote three books: *An Inquiry into the Use and Authority of Roman Jurisprudence in the Law Concerning Real Estate* (1850);[19] *A Theory of the Common Law* (1852)[20] (which is actually a study in comparative legal history and a disquisition on the relationship between Roman law andCommon law); and *A Tract on Government* (1845) (which he published anonymously).[21] Lieber, too, wrote a number of books including his *Legal and Political Hermeneutics,*[22] the *Manual of Political Ethics,*[23] and his *Civil Liberty.*[24] The *Legal and Political Hermeneutics,* the most prominent of his works, has been characterized by the late Arthur Schiller as the first American attempt to establish a set of "canons" of legal interpretation.[25] Although not explicitly a Civilian or Romanist work, Lieber's text drew principally upon Roman legal sources and the principles of the new German School of biblical criticism for its inspiration and its models in developing hermeneutic rules. Legaré authored no books, but he was a co-founder of and a frequent contributor to the *Southern Review* as well as an occasional contributor to its forerunner, the *North American Review,* both of which were widely read literary magazines on the model of such European journals as the *Edinburgh Review,* and contained substantial amounts of legal material.[26] All three men were passionately involved not only with Roman and Civil law but also with Classical and European culture in their writing.

Lieber, the German émigré, never abandoned his connections with Germany, even as he fully embraced his new country.[27] His correspondence reveals a wide circle of scholarly and personal friendships with both leading European as well as American jurists. This circle, as previously mentioned, included American lawyers such as Kent and Story and Europeans such as the Swiss, Bluntschli and the German, Mittermaier.[28] Lieber's wide professional and social acquaintance may be attributable in part to his peripatetic career. He began by journeying from Germany to Italy in the household of Gottfried Niebuhr, the classical historian,[29] and, after a brief stay in England, found his way to Boston for several

---

19 James Murdock Walker, An Inquiry into the Use andAuthority of Roman Jurisprudence in the Law Concerning Real Estate (Charleston, S. C., 1850).

20 James Murdock Walker, A Theory of the Common Law (Boston 1852).

21 James Murdock Walker, Tract on Government (Boston, 1853).

22 Francis Lieber, Legal and Political Hermeneutics (Boston 1839).

23 Francis Lieber, Manual of Political Ethics (Boston, 1838; 2nd ed. rev. Philadelphia, 1875).

24 Francis Lieber, On Civil Liberty and Self-Government (Philadelphia, 1859).

25 *Arthur Schiller,* Roman Interpretation and Anglo-American Interpretation and Construction, Virginia Law Review 27 (1940-1): pp. 733-768.

26 Ballantyne & Hughes began printing the Edinburgh Review in Oct. 1802. The Review ran until Oct. 1929.

27 *Hoeflich,* Transatlantic, pp. 602-606.

28 *Freidel,* pp. 98, 118-119, 161.

29 *Freidel,* vii, pp. 35-40.

years where he founded a swimming school,[30] then to Philadelphia,[31] where he worked on penology and prison reform and, finally, to Columbia, South Carolina where he took up a professorship.[32] In part, too, his wide acquaintance undoubtedly derived from his own efforts to cultivate powerful and important men such as Story, Kent, and Mittermaier in order to further his professional career.[33] Lieber had the advantage in this both of his German university training and extensive travels, and his willingnes to pursue those he felt could aid him professionally.[34].

Indeed, Lieber served as an intermediary for European legal culture in two related ways. First, of course, through the nearly half-century of his career in the United States, Lieber incorporated Roman and Civil law ideas into his writing and teaching and provided a corpus of work which helped to popularize this incorporation. Second, Lieber acted as a personal intermediary between German and American jurists. For instance, Lieber introduced Joseph Story to Carl Joseph Anton Mittermaier at a crucial time in both their careers.[35] Story had just taken the Dane Professorship and was embarked on the ambitious project of writing his several *Commentaries* on various topics in American law. Mittermaier and Lieber helped Story to acquire current German scholarship on these topics (such as conflicts-of-laws) and ensured that Story's writings would bekome known on the European continent.[36] Reciprocally, Story aided Mittermaier in his major project at this time, publication of the *Kritische Zeitschrift für Rechtswissenschaft und Gesetzgebung des Auslandes*. Story contributed a specially written article on American law to Mittermaier's new journal and joined its board of editors.[37] In all of this, Lieber's role as an intermediary was crucial.

Legaré's birth and early education were wholly domestic, but, after graduation from South Carolina College, he resolved to study abroad.[38] It would seem, from later correspondence, that his initial desire was to go to Germany to study law.[39] This, however, was thwarted by the then unstable political situation on the Continent. Instead, in 1818 Legaré matriculated as a student at Edinburgh University in the Department of Civil Law.[40] At this time the Edinburgh faculty boasted

---

30 *Freidel*, pp. 57-58.

31 *Freidel*, pp. 98-102.

32 *Freidel*, p. 115.

33 *Hoeflich*, Transatlantic, pp. 602-606.

34 *Hoeflich*, Transatlantic, pp. 602-606.

35 *Hoeflich*, Transatlantic, pp. 602-606.

36 *Hoeflich*, Transatlantic, pp. 603-604.

37 *Hoeflich*, Transatlantic, pp. 606.

38 *Hoeflich*, Transatlantic, pp. 603. See also Huntington Library Lieber Papers Ms. LI3255 cited in *Nadelmann*, Joseph Story's Sketch of American Law, American Journal of Comparative Law 3 (1954): 4.

39 *Rhea*, pp. 1-45.

40 *Rhea*, p. 48.

two professors who would have been of interest to a young American law student. Irving was professor of Civil Law and offered two courses on Civilian subjects.[41] The first was an introductory course in Roman law based upon the text of Justinian's *Institutes*. The second, the more advanced course, analyzed Justinian's *Digest* and jurists' law. Both courses consisted of lectures based, in large part, on the works of Heineccius, a leading eighteenth century German commentator. Also, then lecturing at Edinburgh in the philosophy faculty, was Dugald Stewart, the first volume of whose *Elements of the Philosophy of the Human Mind* had appeared in 1792.[42] Stewart was a student of Reid and Adam Ferguson and his philosophical work was firmly in the tradition of the Scottish Enlightenment.[43] Therefore, much of it was concerned with law as one of the "human sciences" and a philosophical approach to law and morality.

The year at Edinburgh had a major impact on Legaré. It was apparently during this year that he first acquired his love of Roman and Civil law. As his sister wrote:

> ... now, in its wide and regular principles, the accumulation of such long applied learning and ability, it rose upon his sight as a great and noble science, capable of being brought to enlighten, as had never yet been done, the narrower and more dogmatic methods of our inherited jurisprudence. Its exacter and more elegant vehicle and authors, and its close connection with his favorite bodies of literature and history served also, no doubt, greatly to allure him. It became henceforth, therefore, one of his regular studies, especially as mixing so much with another — that of law, natural and national; and finally grew (as we shall see) to be one of his chief attainments, with a view to a very lofty and bold juridical purpose."[44]

Legaré's stay in Edinburgh was not to be his only foray abroad, however. He returned to the Continent in 1832, after having achieved professional success at the South Carolina Bar, to become United States charge d'affaires in Brussels.[45] In spite of ill health and a constant shortage of money, he found the time, the energy, and the funds to travel widely on the Continent.[46] He travelled especially in Germany, to seek out books and to meet and study with Friedrich Carl von Savigny, desiring to learn as much as he could about Savigny's "historical school", to which he later claimed allegiance.[47]

James Murdock Walker was born in Charleston in 1813.[48] His father was a Scotsman, his mother a native of Charleston. He was educated at Charleston and

---

41 *Rhea*, p. 51.

42 Legaré, Writings xlv. *Rhea*, p. 54.

43 See *Dugald Stewart*, Elements of the Philosophy of the Human Mind, vol. 1 (London, 1792).

44 *George Davie*, The Democratic Intellect (1961; Edinburgh: The Edinburgh University Press, 1982), p. 147.

45 Legaré, Writings, xlv.

46 *Rhea*, pp. 131 - 155.

47 Legaré, Writings, lxi.

48 *O'Neall*, p. 574.

then at South Carolina College in Columbia from which he graduated in 1830. After college he returned to Charleston where he studied law with Mitchell King, a leading pracitioner and doyen of the Carleston Bar, and was called to the Bar in 1834. Apparently, he had a successful practice and also concurrently served several terms in the state legislature. Although his professional and social life was centered in Charleston, both by birth and parentage and because of the extremely cosmopolitan nature of Charleston itself during this period, he was exposed to a substantial dose of Continental and Classical culture and learning, which shows clearly in his written works.[49]

Of course, exposure to European culture does not automatically give rise to an interest in Civil law, nor does it make those who are so exposed into experts on Roman and Civil law. Lieber, Legaré, and Walker, nevertheless, all showed not only a high regard for Continental legal learning in their writings, but also showed substantial expertise in this field. To author books and articles such as theirs, it is clear that they not only needed some training in Civilian and Roman legal scholarship, as Legaré, for instance, obtained in Edinburgh, but that they also needed language skills and access to substantial library holdings on Roman and Civil law.

Of the three men, Lieber seems to have been the best endowed linguistically, speaking not only English but German and French, and reading the classical languages.[50] Legaré apparently did not learn German until 1833, but after this had German, French and the classical languages.[51] Again, Walker's background is the most obscure, although he clearly read Latin. Thus, all three could read some classical and European sources when they were available. And, in the antebellum South, they were available.

Many American law libraries (and some general libraries) in the first half of the nineteenth century had substantial holdings in Civil law and Roman law. For instance, Harvard had an excellent collection through the generosity of one of its alumni, Samuel Livermore.[52] It was Livermore's library which formed the

---

49 *O'Neall*, p. 574-575.

50 Lieber was raised in Prussia during the time of the Napoleonic occupation. Therefore, it is understandable that he spoke German and French. As for his knowledge of the classical languages and his linguistic ability, see *Freidel*, pp. 178-182.

51 As mentioned in Rhea, Legaré was also learned in Italian, Spanish and Portuguese (pg. 40). However, it is important to note that although the number of languages with which Legaré was familiar was large, the quality of his linguistic ability was less than Lieber's.

52 Samuel Livermore was born on Aug. 25, 1786 in Concord, N. H. After graduating from Harvard College in 1804, he was accepted to the bar in Essex County, where he worked as a lawyer for many years. Livermore authored a variety of works, his key point calling attention to the works of medieval authors. Livermore died on July 11, 1833 in Florence, Alabama while travelling. For further information and references, see *Dumas Malone*, ed., The Dictionary of American Biography, vol. 11 (New York: Charles Scribner's Sons, 1933), p. 308.

nucleus of Joseph Story's working collection when he was writing his *Commentaries*. It is here, again, that the breadth of the Southern legal and literary tradition was to play an important role. Books on Roman and Civil law were not difficult to find in the antebellum South. In South Carolina, two libraries, in particular, were rich in these holdings and were used by the "Civilian Circle" of Lieber, Legaré, and Walker.

The library of South Carolina College was not a large library, but its collection was cosmopolitan and well chosen, including a number of the most important books on Roman, Civil, and Natural law.[53] Amongst the Civil law holdings were introductory texts such as Jean Domat's *Les Loix Civiles dans leur Ordre Naturel* and Thomas Wood's *Institutes of the Civil Law.*[54] There was a copy of Brown's lectures on the Civil law, as well.[55] Grotius, Pufendorf, Rutherforth, Martens, and Burlamaqui were all represented in the Natural law section.[56] The library had copies, also, of Delolme and Flowers on the French constitution, Beccaria on criminal law, and Goguet on the *Origin of Laws.*[57] The library had in addition a copy of Gibbon's *Decline and Fall of the Roman Empire,* the fortyfourth chapter of which was a standard introductory text for Roman law studies during the early nineteenth century, both in the United States as well as on the Continent.[58] And, quite naturally, the library had an extensive collection of Cicero's works, both in the original Latin and in English translation. Cicero, like Gibbon, was seen as a principal literary source for Roman law and legal oratory in the ninteteenth century. The College library at Columbia was available to all three men. Furthermore, both Walker and Legaré had access to the Charleston Bar Library. This, though a working lawyer's library, also apparently had Civil law holdings. For instance, Walker used the Bar library's copy of Duck's *De Usu et Auctoritate Juris Civilis in Anglia* a leading Anglo-Romanist treatise, in writing his 1850 monograph on the Roman law of real property.[59] All three also had their own private libraries to consult. Of these, the best known to us, from its privately printed catalogue, is Legaré's. The catalogue lists 143 Latin titles, 77 Greek titles, 53 French titles, 61 German titles, 9 Italian titles, 36 English titles, as well as Italian, French, Spanish, Hebrew, and Portuguese dictionaries and reference works.[60] The vast majority of the non-English books — excluding

---

53 Catalogue of Books Belonging to the South Carolina Library (Columbia, 1807).

54 Catalogue of the South Carolina Library.

55 Catalogue of the South Carolina Library.

56 Catalogue of the South Carolina Library.

57 Catalogue of the South Carolina Library.

58 See, *M. H. Hoeflich,* Edward Gibbon, Roman Lawyer, American Journal of Comparative Law (1992).

59 See Duck, De Usu et Authoritate Juris Civilis Romanorum Per Dominia Principum Christianorum (London 1665). See also *Coquillette,* The Civilian Writers of Doctor's Commons, London (Berlin: Duncker & Humblot, 1988, p. 161 - 165). Walker, An Inquiry, p. 47.

Greek — are Roman and Civilian legal texts. The remainder tend to be editions of classical authors and commentaries thereon. Among these titles were not only most of the major editions of primary Roman law texts from the seventeenth and eighteenth centuries, representing the humanist legal-textual tradition, but also all of the major humanist Roman legal commentators on the Continent from Cujas to Heineccius to Savigny.[61] Legaré's library was also very strong in the modern Civilians and Pandectists and included the works of Pothier, Cooper, Barbeyrac, Hugo, Grimm, Eichhorn, and Dirksen.[62] Legaré's Civil law collection was better than that in the Library of Congress, as judged by its 1812 catalogue,[63] and than the Livermore library, which was donated to Harvard, used, as notes, by Joseph Story in writing his *Commentaries,* and which was donated and became the foundation of the Harvard Law School libraries.[64] While the total number of Civilian volumes owned by Legaré was less than that owned by Harvard's at that time.[65] In short, Legaré's library went far beyond the norm for both private and public law libraries during this period, and provided a perfect base from which to work.

But the background, training, and resources available to Lieber, Legaré, and Walker do not reveal the extent to which their Circle was so significant. To understand this it is necessary to analyze their writings and document the extent to which their writings were known to the literate public.

Lieber's main Romanist work is his *Legal and Political Hermeneutics,* first published in book form at Boston in 1839.[66] The book is an attempt to systematize and rationalize the confused doctrine regarding proper interpretive principles to be applied in reading legal documents. The text has a number of notable features. First, it is systematic. Lieber attempts to develop legal interpretation into a science based upon broadly applicable hermeneutic rules. At the time he was writing hermeneutic method amongst the Common lawyers was in a primitive state. Commonly accepted rules of interpretation were available as to specific types of legal texts, e. g., wills, but no serious attempts had been made to establish universally applicable rules of interpretation. This task Lieber set himself in the

---

60 There are two printed catalogues of Hugh Legaré's library: Catalogue of the Library of the Hon. Hugh Legaré (Washington, 1843) which appears to have been prepared by his executors immediately after his death and Catalogue of the Rare & Valuable Private Library of the Late Hon. H. S. Legaré (Washington, 1848) which was prepared by an auction house. Copies of both are at the Caroliniana Library at the University of South Carolina, Columbia S. C.

61 Library of the Hon.; Private Library of the Late Hon.

62 Library of the Hon.; Private Library of the Late Hon.

63 The 1812 Catalogue of the Library of Congress, a Facsimile (Washington City, 1812; Washington D. C.: Library of Congress, 1982).

64 See, also, p. 26, n. 54.

65 Library of the Law School of Harvard University (Cambridge, 1826).

66 See, above, p. 22, n. 22.

Hermeneutics. He analyzes the types of verbal ambiguities a reader may encounter, classifies them according to cause, and then establishes principles for resolution of those ambiguities. To draw a specific example of Lieber's use of Roman and Civilian sources, one might, for instance, note Lieber's discussion of the proper interpretation to be placed upon a statement made in contradistinction to a superior authority external to the text in question.[67] Lieber argues that such a statement made contrary to a higher authority must be interpreted as legally null and void. It can have no validity *ab initio,* since it is, by definition, impermissible. In supporting this proposition which, itself, follows the general logic of interpretation, Lieber looks to two Roman legal passages for support and confirmation, the first from Justinian's *Code,* the second from an argument of Papinian contained in Book 50 of Justinian's *Digest.*[68] Even more interesting, Lieber goes on to connect this hermeneutic principle based upon Roman law to the American practice of judicial review of legislation raising constitutional issues.[69] In short, Lieber not only utilizes Roman legal principles to illustrate his own hermeneutic rules, but goes on to analyze American legal principles in light thereof. In fact, the *Legal and Political Hermeneutics* demonstrates throughout not only Lieber's extensive knowledge of Roman and Civilian sources, but also his ability to utilize principles contained in these systems in analyzing Anglo-American law. This aspect of his work is particularly significant, for it meant that the *Legal and Political Hermeneutics* could be extremely useful to working lawyers and jurists and not just to scholars and antiquaries. Lieber's approach to Roman and Civil law in the *Hermeneutics* is neither antiquarian nor historical. Rather, Lieber used examples from these legal systems for comparative and illustrative purposes. Since he was attempting to develop a *universally* useful method of interpretation and construction applicable to all legal texts, the ability to show that a particular principle of interpretation or construction was valid not only for Anglo-American law, but also for Roman and Civil law, was crucial. In effect, by showing that a particular principle of interpretation was accepted as valid in a number of legal systems, Lieber was able to confirm precisely that universal aspect of his hermeneutical method which he aimed for. Thus, for instance, Lieber cited not only Roman and Civil law, but also, in one instance, Chinese law, as described in George Staunton's *Penal Code of China.*[70] In utilizing Roman and Civil law as a basis for comparison Lieber put himself into a solid tradition. Story, for instance, also drew from these sources for comparison.[71] Story, however, used the Roman and Civil law sources to demonstrate the validity of Common law substantive rules or to supplement the Common law when a particular substantive law rule

---

67 Lieber, Hermeneutics, p. 135.

68 Lieber, Hermeneutics, p. 162.

69 Lieber, Hermeneutics, p. 162.

70 *George Staunton,* Ta Tsing Leu Lee, trans. (London, 1810). Originally published in Peking, in Chinese.

71 *M. H. Hoeflich,* Ciceronian Ethic.

was lacking. Lieber uses the Roman and Civil law materials in a rather different way. In part, he does use them to affirm the validity of a particular Anglo-American rule, but he goes beyond this. He attempts really to show that the particular rules of interpretation are almost like Natural law rules, underlying *all* legal hermeneutics regardless of the system being examined. Story uses the comparative material experientially; another system, i. e., the Roman, uses a particular rule and, therefore, that rule has the imprimatur of history and experience. Lieber's use of the comparative material is less historical, less like Story before him and Maine after him, and more in keeping with the Natural law tradition.

In addition to the *Hermeneutics* Lieber also wrote extensively on political theory, international law, and the laws of war.[72] In these, too, especially in his writings on international law, Lieber showed himself knowledgeable in Roman law.[73] This was unavoidable, since international law until the late nineteenth century was firmly grounded in the Natural law tradition, which itself, through the writings of scholars such as Pufendorf and Grotius, was heavily dependent on the Roman legal tradition.[74] Here, again, we see Lieber introducing Continental legal materials into domestic American jurisprudence. Of course, Lieber was far from a pioneer in this. Traditionally, several specific legal areas had required any practitioner to have some acquaintance with Roman and Civil law materials. Admiralty, itself considered a subtopic of the "law of nature and nations," the nineteenth century version of international law, required such knowledge.[75] Lieber, in his lectures on international law, displayed a wide-ranging knowledge of the early modern writers on the law of nature and nations as well as a more than passing acquaintance with the Roman sources upon which these writings depended. In this way, then, Lieber not only demonstrated his own expertise in the areas, but also helped to further its incorporation into the mainstream of American legal thought.

Hugh Legaré's expertise as a Romanist shows most clearly in an essay he wrote for the *Southern Review* entitled "The Origin, History and Influence of Roman Legislation,"[76] although it is clearly present in other essays as well, such

---

[72] *Freidel,* pp. 432-435.

[73] See, for instance, the unpublished manuscripts of Francis Lieber's Lectures on International Law, found in the Columbia University Library, Lieber Archives 1863-1864.

[74] See Pufendorf, Of the Law of Nature and Nations, trans. Kennet & Carew, 8 vols. (London, 1729).

See also Hugo Grotius, The Rights of War and Peace (Du Juri Belli et Pacis, trans. A. C. Campbell (Westport, Conn.: Hyperion Press 1979).

[75] See, generally, *Grant Gilmore & Charles L. Black,* The Law of Admiralty (Brooklyn: The Foundation Press, Inc., 1957).

[76] Legaré, The Origin, History and Influence of Roman Legislation, Writings of Hugh Swinton Legaré 1, pp. 502-558.

as his reviews of Kent's *Commentaries,*[77] and d'Aguesseau's work,[78] and his article on the concept of codification.[79] The long essay on Roman legislation is, in form, a review of five books: Hugo's *Lehrbuch eines civilistischen Cursus,* Story's *Commentaries on the Conflict of Laws,* Haubold's *Institutiones Juris Romani Privati Historico Dogmaticarum Lineamenta,* Heffter's edition of Gaius' *Institutes* (based upon Angelo Mai's publication of the newly discovered Verona Ms. of the *Institutes*), and Schrader's new edition of the *Corpus Juris Civilis.*[80] The review is a stunning *tour de force* of contemporary Civilian learning. Legaré shows a breadth and profundity of Civilian and Roman scholarship the match for which it is difficult to find in the antebellum period, even among such learned contemporaries as Story, Livingston, and DuPonceau. Ranging from a discussion of the history of early Rome and the problems of reconstructing the earliest Roman code, the *Twelve Tables,* through to an analysis of the impact of the new philology pioneered by Bentley and the German school upon nineteenth century editions of the principal Roman law texts, each page reveals enormous learning and a highly developed sensitivity to the sources. The essay ultimately dwells upon two specific points, however: (1) the health of Roman law studies both in Europe and the United States, and (2) the utility of Roman law both to the modern Civilian and to the American lawyer. As to the first point, Legaré focuses upon a statement of Henry Hallam, a noted nineteenth century British historian, who argued that knowledge of and interest in Roman law was fading into obscurity.[81] Hallam was an exceptionally popular and prolific author of the period. He was especially well known for his *Constitutional History of England.*[82] In another work, his *History of the Middle Ages,*[83] Hallam commented upon the end of the Roman legal tradition. Legaré was enraged at this seeming calumny aimed at the great nineteenth century Civilians and leaped to the rescue. He cites Hugo, Savigny, Niebhur, Eichhorn, Dirksen, and Schrader as examples of the continuing strength of Romanist studies on the Continent:

> ... at no former period was there ever more order and activity displayed in the study of the civil law on the continent of Europe than at this very time ... The great jurisconsults of the present day to equal zeal add more knowledge, that is,

[77] Legaré, Kent's Commentaries, Writings of Hugh Swinton Legaré 2, pp. 102-141.

[78] Legaré, D'Aguesseau, Writings of Hugh Swinton Legaré 2, pp. 559-598.

[79] Legaré, Codification, Writings of Hugh Swinton Legaré 2, pp. 482-501.

[80] *Gustav Hugo,* Lehrbuch eines civilistischen Cursus (Berlin, 1835).
Joseph Story, Commentaries on the Conflicts of Laws (Boston, 1834).
Christian Gottlieb Haubold, Institutiones Juris Romani Privati Historico-Dogmaticarum Lineamenta (Lipseae, 1826).
Gaius Jurisconsulti Institutionum, ed. Heffter (Berolini, 1827).
Corpus Juris Civilis, ed. Heinrich Schrader (Berolini, 1832).

[81] Legaré, Origin, p. 502.

[82] *Henry Hallam,* Constitutional History of England, 3 vols. (Boston, 1829).

[83] *Henry Hallam,* History of Europe during the Middle Ages, rev. ed., 3 vols. (New York, 1899).

more exact and available knowledge, a penetration more refined and distinguishing, and, above all, views of the construction of society, and of the principles, the spirit, and the influence of legislation, comparably more profound, comprehensive, and packed.[84]

Certainly, Legaré's virtuoso displays of Romanist and Civilian learning in print placed him within the ranks of those he cited against Hallam. Indeed, at the time of his death in 1843, amidst the busy schedule of a lawyer and statesmen, Legaré was at work translating into English one of the major seventeenth century systematic Civilian treatises, that of Heineccius.[85]

As to the second point, the universal utility of substantive Roman law, Legaré's comments are even more interesting and significant. In this essay Legaré poses the question: "[w]as there anything in the original character of the Roman law, that fitted it to become thus universally applicable, or by what causes, and through what process, was it ultimately so?"[86] To this question Legaré gave a two-part answer. First, it was clear to him that Roman law had indeed become universally applicable in the Western legal tradition. He noted that:

... infinitely the largest and most important portion of it — that relating to *Meum* and *tuum* — is suitable not only to other countries, but to all other countries — that it is as applicable at Boston as at Paris, and has served equally to guide the legislation of Napoleon and to enlighten the judgment of Story.[87]

At another point in this essay Legaré elaborates further on this theme. In effect, Legaré attributed the widespread utility of Roman and Civil law to their systematic and rational natures. In was this "philosophical" aspect of Roman and Civil law that so appealed to Legaré. For instance, Legaré cites a leading textbook writer of the day, Fearne; Fearne's treatise on property law was, by Legaré's period, one of the classics of English land law.[88] Indeed, Legaré admits that it was "generally considered ... one of the most lucid and satisfactory treatises in the library of an English lawyer."[89] Yet, for Legaré, Fearne's book was unsatisfactory; it is too complex, unsystematic, and "prolix".[90] To Legaré, Fearne is like other English textbook writers. He "carefully collects all the decided cases" and "critically distinguishes the circumstances that ought to affect their authority as law."[91] They provide "safe guides" for "counselors or their clients."[92]

84 Legaré, Origin, p. 504.

85 *Joseph Story,* Tribute to Mr. Legaré, Boston Daily Advertiser (30 June 1843). A copy of the original newspaper article can be found in the South Carolina Library.

86 Legaré, Origin, p. 524.

87 Legaré, Origin, p. 525.

88 *Charles Fearne,* An Essay on the Learning of Contingent Remainders and Executory Devises (London, 1772).

89 Legaré, Origin, p. 517.

90 Legaré, Origin, p. 517.

91 Legaré, Origin, p. 517.

92 Legaré, Origin, p. 517.

They do not provide, however, "a scientific distribution of their subject, of genus or species, class or category."[93] They do not provide useable principles, for "the principle of a rule is seldom stated as a theorem."[94] As a result, when particular facts of a newly arising case "in which the file affords no precedent" come up, the judge is compelled to look elsewhere, for these textbooks give no assistance.[95]

To this sorry state of Anglo-American affairs, Legaré contrasts Civilian and Civilian inspired texts. He praises Gaius, the Roman jurist, for his *elegantia juris.*[96] He praises Pothier, the French Civilian, as well.[97] And, significantly, he also praises Mr. Justice Story *as a Civilian.*[98] He commends the reader to compare Story's *Commmentaries on Equity* to Maddox's *Chancery,* the one a paragon of system and rationality, the other firmly in the traditional, and unsystematic, mold.[99]

Professor Peter Stein has noted that Legaré saw Roman Law, especially the Roman notion of *ius gentium,* as representative of what every advanced legal system would develop into.[100] Thus, Legaré would appear to have seen Roman Law as a model and source for substantive principles as well, as a disembodied system which had reached a high point of historical development of much value to all lawyers and legislators as a quarry for substantive law. For Legaré, the Roman legal tradition represented century upon century of legal development. Roman and Civilian jurists, according to Legaré, drew "their materials from a longer and more diversified experience than the English lawyers."[101] The Civilians had encountered substantive law questions not yet raised in Anglo-American jurisprudence. He cites, for instance, the problem of apportioning rights of use among two states separated by a river. Such a question had long ago been raised in the Romanist tradition and could be found discussed in Struve's *Corpus Juris Germanici.* In Legaré's opinion, when such matter arose in Anglo-American jurisprudence, the Civilian and Roman sources ought to be searched, rather than attempting to fashion solutions *de novo* wholly within the insular Common law tradition.[102] More than his contemporaries, perhaps, even than those like Joseph Story who were Romanists themselves, Legaré was willing to embrace Roman and Civilian legal method and substantive principles as a fundamental basis for

---

93 Legaré, Origin, p. 517.

94 Legaré, Origin, p. 517.

95 Legaré, Origin, p. 517.

96 Legaré, Origin, p. 515.

97 Legaré, Origin, p. 522.

98 Legaré, Origin, p. 517.

99 Legaré, Origin, p. 518.

100 See *Peter Stein,* The Attraction of the Civil Law in Post Revolutionary America, The Character and Influence of the Roman Civil Law Historical Essays (London and Ronceverte: Hambledon Press, 1988).

101 Legaré, Origin, p. 518.

102 Legaré, Origin, p. 518.

Anglo-American law. More than most of his contemporaries, as well, he had the intellectual background and temperament to do so successfully.

One ought not make a mistake here, however. While Legaré admired Roman law both for its systematic and philosophical elegance as well as for the richness of its substantive law tradition, he did not advocate a wholesale reception of Roman or Civil law in the United States as a replacement for Common law. On the contrary, Legaré, like Story, was an accomplished Common lawyer who was quite willing to criticize Roman or Civilian rules and prefer Common law rules.[103] Indeed, while much of his *Southern Review* essay on Kent's Commentaries may be read as a paean to the Civil law,[104] in his later essay for the same journal on codification he was quite willing to dispense with a Civilian or Roman notion as ill-considered and antithetical to the Common law spirit.[105] Legaré, like virtually all of the Anglo-American jurists of the period from 1800 to 1860, wanted to enrich the Common law through selective use of Roman and Civil law sources and enjoyed the study of the more philosophically sophisticated Roman and Civilian systems, but never wanted to see the Civil law triumph over the Common law in the Anglo-American world.

James Murdock Walker is the most obscure in his personal history of the three men discussed herein, but his writings tell us much about his mind, if not about him as a man. He published three books, all of which dwell substantially on Roman law and all of which show a high level of expertise in the subject. One book, the *Inquiry into the Use and Authority of Roman Jurisprudence in the Law Concerning Real Estate*, published in 1850, is explicitly a work on substantive Roman Law.[106] Two others, *The Theory of the Common Law*, published at Boston in 1852,[107] the *Tract on Government*, published anonymously at Boston in 1853,[108] utilize Roman law for their underpinnings. In the *Inquiry* Walker set himself the task of examining the origins of Common law property rules, especially the law of remainders, and the relation of these Common law rules to the Roman law. The *Inquiry* is, in fact, one of the earliest American contributions to the debate amongst legal historians as to whether substantive Roman law was ever received into the Anglo-American tradition.[109] Walker's argument is directed specifically to then contemporary legal historians, such as the Englishman Reeves who, in his *History of English Law*, argued that Roman law had no influence upon the development of the Common law, even in the period before the reign

---

103 Legaré, Origin, p. 511.

104 See Legaré, Kent's Commentaries, n. 78, above.

105 See Legaré, Codification, n. 80, above.

106 See, p. 22, n. 19, above.

107 See, p. 22, n. 20, above.

108 See, p. 22, n. 21, above.

109 It predates the seminal work on this subject of Roscoe Pound by more than fifty years.

of Edward II.[110] In this, his first, short book, Walker attempted to refute Reeves' theories. He notes of them:

> ... that this opinion is not only unfounded in fact, but that it has also had detrimental effects upon the cultivation of the law as a science.[111]

It was Walker's opinion — common amongst those who argued that some form of reception of Roman rules *had* taken place — that the denial that a reception had occurred permitted Common law lawyers and judges to refuse to utilize Roman or Civilian rules even on a selective basis since their use — in this anti-reception view — would be alien to the Common law tradition. In effect, Walker argued that the legal historical argument was of more than scholarly concern, for it was being used to justify contemporary refusals to reform the Common law through the use of Roman and Civilian ideas.

Walker's second book, the *Theory of the Common Law,* has, unfortunately, been ignored by virtually all legal historians, even those interested in Roman and Civil law. This is sad, though understandable, because the book presents a complex and lenghty (but fascinating) continuation of Walker's investigations begun in the *Inquiry* and carries them into contemporary jurisprudence. It is, in form, an attempt to explicate "the science of law," to analyse those "rules of human conduct which are universally recognized as obligatory."[112] As such, it is very similar to the already contemporary work of the English legal philosopher John Austin in his *Lectures on Jurisprudence.*[113] Like Austin, Walker argued that Roman and Civil law could be properly used as the basis for a scientific examination of Common law jurisprudence. In so doing he echoed not only Austin, but his countryman Legaré. Walker says:

> An indispensable instrument in the investigation of all scientific truth is method. Science cannot exist without it. Now our juridical writers altogether neglect it ... It is in this respect that the Roman has so great an advantage over the Common law. The universal error of our juridical writers is in supposing that, even in those countries over which the Civil Law presides, it is valued chiefly for its doctrines. The reverse is the truth ... The legal literature of no other people [the Romans] can show a casuistry so thoroughly spiritual, where the matter of fact only seems designed to corporealize and exhibit the spirit.

Building on this insight, Walker undertakes to organize the Common law of real property as outlined in the *Theory* on the lines of Roman Law. In fact, the book is largely, as already noted, an attack on Fearne's *Remainders,* the leading property law treatise of its period and a work which Legaré, too, had condemned.[114] Walker's book is an attempt to "Romanize" the Common law of

---

110 See *John Reeves,* History of English Law, 5 vol. (London, 1814-1829).

111 Walker, Inquiry, p. 8.

112 Walker, Theory, p. 1.

113 See, *John Austin,* Lectures on Jurisprudence, ed. Campbell (Jersey City, 1869).

114 Walker, Theory, pp. 3-4.

property into a coherent and rational system. In doing so, Walker displays a wide-ranging knowledge of both the Roman and Civilian primary sources and the commentators thereon. Finally, undoubtedly under the influence of his Romanist reading, Walker displays an intolerance towards the writ system and Common law formulas and a bias in favor of "scientific legal principles". He says:

> It is manifest that formulas do not commend themselves to the natural reason of mankind, and therefore cannot become the property of humanity. They are the mere husks of the law ... [I]f the law be merely an unconnected series of decisions and statutes, its use may remain, though its dignity as a science be lost. Reason must yield its supremacy to memory, and the *Cantor Formularum* is the greatest of lawyers.[115]

In taking this position against the mindless use of writs and in favor of "scientific jurisprudence," Walker takes his place next to Daniel Mayes of Transylvania College as a precursor of the Langdellian reform movement of the 1870's.[116]

The picture that emerges, therefore, from this brief history of Lieber, Legaré, and Walker is one of a circle of talented and learned lawyers centered around Charleston and Columbia, South Carolina, interested in and writing about Roman and Civil law.

The final question I will address concerns the effect that such Roman and Civilian learning had on other American lawyers of the period and legal development thereafter. In doing so, I recognize the difficulty of determining intellectual influence, if one is searching for an absolute showing of a causal connection between two events. Instead of attempting to make a *post hoc, ergo propter hoc* argument, I will try to show only that the efforts of Lieber, Legaré, and Walker were neither unknown to contemporaries nor accomplished in a vacuum with no connection to the larger society. Finally, I will conclude by suggesting that these three Roman lawyers of the Old South were not the only members of their profession involved in such Romanist and Civilian studies.

Lieber's works had a wide distribution in his lifetime. His works on political theory and on international law were well-known. Indeed, during the Civil War he became an advisor to the Union on military law.[117] Unfortunately, it would seem that the *Legal and Political Hermeneutics* probably was one of his least-known works.[118]Nevertheless, it was far from unknown. Certainly Lieber's *Hermeneutics* was known to his wide circle of friends and scholarly acquaintances.

---

[115] Walker, Theory, pp. 129-130.

[116] See, *Daniel Mayes,* An Address to the Students of Law in Transylvania University, The Gladsome Light of Jurisprudence, ed. Michael H. Hoeflich (New York: Greenwood Press, 1988), p. 145-164.

[117] On Lieber's participation during the Civil war, see *Freidel,* pp. 317-359.

[118] There is little evidence of wide spread distribution of *Hermeneutics* in either private or public libraries.

The book itself was dedicated to Chancellor Kent. Lieber himself gave a copy to Justice Joseph Story. Other notable lawyers and editors of his acquaintance were Edward Everett, the editor of the *North American Review,* Edward Livingston, the force behind the *Louisiana Code of 1825,* Rufus Choate, Charles Sumner and a host of other leaders of the American Bar.[119] All, presumably, read the

[119] Edward Everett was born in Dorchester, Mass. on April 11, 1794. He graduated from Harvard in 1811 and received his PhD from Göttingen in 1817. While he was a chair of Greek literature at Harvard in 1819, he also edited the North American Review. The power of his oration, however, soon swept him into Congress where he served for five terms to leave only to become the Governor of Massachusetts for four terms. After his governorship, he became president of Harvard from 1846-1849. In 1852, Everett served his 6th term in Congress. While there, Congress grappled with issues pursuant to slavery. Although it was known that Everett was ardently opposed to slavery, his absence during a major vote ruined him politically, and soon after he resigned from his office. During the Civil War, Everett continued doing what he did best — public speaking and calling for Northerners to support the patriotic cause. Everett was a strong Unionist and his lectures remained forever patriotic. Everett died on Jan. 15, 1865. See *Edward Everett,* Orations and Speeches on Various Occasions, 4 vols. (Boston, 1853-1868). For more information and references, see *Dumas Malone,* ed., Everett, Edward, Dictionary of American Biography, vol. 6 (New York: Charles Scribner's Sons, 1931), pp. 223-226.

Edward Livingston was born in Cleremont, N.Y., on May 28, 1764. He graduated from Princeton in 1781 and then studied law at the office of John Lansing along with Alexander Hamilton, James Kent and Aaron Burr. He was accepted to the bar in 1785 and practiced law until he was elected to Congress in 1794. While in Congress Livingston voted to ratify the Constitution, and a bill for relief for American seamen impressed or abandoned in foreign lands. Livingston left the political stage to appointment as an U.S. State Attorney for N.Y. and the Mayor of N.Y. He did both until 1803 when he contracted yellow fever. Once recovered, he moved to New Orleans, practiced law and worked on compensation for land taken by the government. During the 1812 war he worked as an aide-de-camp, military sec., interpreter and confidential advisor to General Andrew Jackson. In 1820, he was elected to the State Legislature and was commissioned to work on a revision to the penal code, a topic of interest from his former days in the U.S. Congress. Although this code was never adopted, it brought him recognition. In 1822 he represented Louisiana in the House of Rep. and in 1828 he represented Louisiana in the Senate, where he presented a revision for the system of penal laws in the U.S. In 1831 he was appointed as Sec. of State, where his most important work was in securing a treaty with France. Two years later, he became a foreign minister in France and retired in 1835, only to return to Washington to work with the President on relations with France. Livingston died on May 23, 1836. For information on his work, see *Edward Livingston,* The Complete Works of Edward Livingston on Criminal Jurisprudence, 2 vols. (New York, 1873). See also *Dumas Malone,* ed., Dictionary of American Biography, vol. 11 (New York: Charles Scribner's Sons, 1933), p. 309.

Rufus Choate was born on Oct. 1, 1799 on Hog Island. He graduated from Dartmouth College in 1819 and was admitted to the Massachusetts court of common pleas in Sept. 1822 and to the Supreme Judicial court in Nov. 1825. In the same year, he was elected to the lower house of the Massachusetts General Court. Two years later he was elected as a state senator. He remained as a state senator until he resigned in 1832 to return to his profession of choice, private lawyer. He remained in the political scene, however, and helped create the Whig party and then was asked to rejoin the Senate. Once he completed the term in 1845, he returned to private practice and remained there, eventually becoming, as found in a letter from Sumner to Lieber, "the leader of our bar." Choate died on July 13, 1859. For more information and references to his works, see *Dumas*

work. Lieber was not above self-promotion, either. In October of 1840, for instance, he sent a copy of the *Hermeneutics* to C. A. J. Mittermaier, apparently in the hopes that this German jurist would review it for a learned journal, as he had done with Justice Story's *Commentaries on the Conflict of Laws* in the *Kritische Zeitschrift.*[120] It was, in fact, reviewed favorably in a number of widely published journals. Indeed, in 1840, after the publication of the *Legal and Political Hermeneutics,* Lieber wrote to his wife of his hope that he might soon obtain a chair in international law at another (presumably Northern) university.[121] Lieber's short volume, so dependent on Continental thinking, appears to have been well-known, therefore, to a number of important contemporary lawyers and politicians and as such undoubtedly had some influence. Indeed, the *Hermeneutics* sold well enough to justify revision and reprinting. A revised edition was planned in the early 1860's, but failed to materialize because of the death of the reviser.[122] Finally, in 1880, a posthumous revised edition was published.[123] Certainly, the *Hermeneutics* found its way into many American law libraries of the period. A copy was even listed as being in the collection of the California State Library at Sacramento in the 1857 catalogue issued by that institution.[124] Robert Cover has characterized the *Hermeneutics* as the most coherent single exposition of the legal establisment's view of the interpretative process to be found in the antebellum period.[125] Considering the book's foreign law content and comparative approach, that is saying a great deal about the spread of Roman and Civil law ideas during this period and about Lieber's role in that process.

Malone, ed., Choate, Rufus, Dictionary of American Biography, vol. 4 (New York: Charles Scribner's Sons), 1930, p.p. 86-90.

Charles Sumner was born on Jan. 6, 1811 in Boston Massachusetts. He graduated from the Harvard Law School in 1833, where he was a pupil of Joseph Story. A staunch abolitionist, he made and broke many friendships with his unbending views. He became a Senator in 1851 and worked against slavery, giving many speeches which attacked the South directly. His views were so strong, that when asked if he would uphold the Constitution and return a fugitive slave, he said "No." In 1861, he was appointed chairman on the Committee of foreign relations, but was demoted by Pres. Grant due to personal disagreements. Still, he worked diligently on equal and civil rights during and after the Civil War. He died on March 11, 1874. For more information and references, see *Dumas Malone,* ed., Sumner, Charles, Dictionary of American Biography, vol. 18 (New York: Charles Scribner's Sons, 1936), pp. 208-214.

120 Lieber to Mittermaier, October, 1840, Ms. Lieber Papers, Caroliniana, Univ. of South Carolina.

121 Lieber to his wife, Matilda, on 20 March 1840, Ms. Lieber Papers, Caroliniana, Univ. of South Carolina.

122 W. G. Hammond, preface, Legal and Political Hermeneutics, by Francis Lieber (St. Louis, 1880), iii.

123 Francis Lieber, Legal and Political Hermeneutics, ed. W. G. Hammond (St. Louis, 1880).

124 California State Library Catalogue (Sacramento, 1857).

125 See, *Robert M. Cover,* Justice Accused: Antislavery and the Judicial Process (New Haven: Yale University Press, 1975).

Legaré's articles in the *Southern Review* may well have had an even greater diffusion than did Lieber's book. Legaré's intent in his *Southern Review* articles was to provide information for educating gentlemen. One of the preeminent interests, if not preoccupations, of the antebellum Southern gentleman was Classical civilization.[126] The best part of Classical civilization, Legaré thought, was its legal system. The extent to which this type of essay on Classical civilization, so well done by Legaré, influenced the professional behavior both of lawyers and non-lawyers, however, is hard to estimate precisely. Perry Miller and Robert Ferguson have both suggested that Classical literature influenced contemporary legal-oratorical styles in both the courts and the legislatures.[127] Certainly, Legaré himself avowed that he followed a Roman model in his practice. When asked about his success at the Bar, he responded:

> ... in general, sir, I practice upon the old Roman plan; and, like Cicero's, my clients pay me what they like — that is, often nothing at all.[128]

And, of course, Legaré's essays, too, were read by jurists. For instance, in a letter of 13 October 1839, Francis Lieber wrote of reading Legaré's "excellent article on Roman law" and James Murdock Walker, in his *Inquiry,* bracketed Legaré with Kent and Story as a leading American jurist.[129]

Nor was Legaré's role in diffusing Roman legal knowledge limited to his writings. Where Lieber utilized Roman and Civil law texts for comparative and illustrative purposes in his writings and lectures, Legaré used these sources as legal authorities not only in his writings but also in his court appearances. As Attorney-General in 1842, Legaré represented the United States before the Supreme Court twelve times. The majority of these cases involved disputed land grants in territories formerly under French or Spanish rule. Thus, the legal issues involved were often Roman or Civilian in origin. Of the three men discussed herein, Legaré was most able, seemingly, to incorporate Roman and Civilian principles directly into American law. Both men, of course, thereby helped to spread knowledge or Roman and Civil law and both, also, utilized Roman and Civil law to try to reform some aspects of the Anglo-American legal tradition. Legaré's arguments before the Supreme Court in those twelve cases, apparently, helped to do so, at least in a small way. Certainly, they impressed one justice in this way. In a lecture reported in the *Boston Daily Advertiser* in 1843, Justice Story recalled Legaré for his law students. He said:

> I had looked to see him accomplish what he was so well fitted to do — what I know was the darling object of his pure attention — to engraft the civil law upon

[126] See, *Robert A. Ferguson,* Law and Letters in American Culture (Cambridge: Harvard University Press, 1984).

[127] See, *Robert Ferguson,* Law and Letters. *Perry Miller,* The Life of the Mind in America (San Diego, New York and London: Harcourt Brace Jovanovich, 1965).

[128] Legaré, Writings, lv.

[129] Walker, Inquiry, p. 46.

the jurisprudence of this country, and thereby to expand the common law to greater usefulness and a wider adaptation to the progress of society ... he ... devoted himself ... to the study of the civil law, with a view to make it subservient to the great object of his life — the expansion of the common law, and the forcing into it the enlarged and liberal principles and just morality of the Roman jurisprudence. This object he seemed about to accomplish; for his arguments before the Supreme Court were crowded with the principles of the Roman law, wrought into the texture of the common law with great success. In every sentence that I heard, I was struck with this union of the two systems.[130]

An essayist writing in the *Southern Review* in 1870 echoed Justice Story's comments. Legaré, he said, wanted to achieve:

... the gradual infusion of a large portion of the spirit and philosophy of the Civil law, and even of its forms and process, into the more common system of jurisprudence.[131]

James Murdock Walker's influence is the most difficult to assess, since we know so little about him and since his books are infrequently mentioned in contemporary sources. We may presume that *The Theory of the Common Law,* simply by virtue of its publication by Little-Brown at Boston, had more diffusion than his privately printed *Inquiry*. Neither book seems to have been widely reviewed or noticed, however. The *Inquiry,* nonetheless, was the subject of a substantial review in the *Southern Quarterly Review* in 1851.[132] The reviewer was greatly impressed with the book and recommended it to his readers. He praised Walker in glowing terms:

It must appear, from what has been said, that in the present absence of English translations of works on the civil law, he renders a valuable service to the cause of jurisprudence, who, like Mr. Walker, devotes himself to the labour of tracing the analogies of the older and new systems, and importing a knowledge of the truthful doctrines of the former.[133]

There is, also, one extremely interesting aspect of Walker's other book, *The Tract on Government,* published anonymously in 1853, that merits mention. The *Tract* is a work on political theory rather than law specifically, but like both the *Inquiry* and the *Theory,* the *Tract* bases much of its argument on Roman models. Most interesting about the *Tract* is that it takes the position that the dissolution of the Union, argued for so fervently by the South Carolina secessionists, would be disastrous. Indeed, if one looks at the political stance of all three men, Lieber, Legaré, and Walker, all were allied with J. L. Pettigru, the leading anti-secessionist member of the Charleston Bar.[134] Could it be that their knowledge of Roman

---

130 *Joseph Story,* Tribute, p. 31, n. 85, above.

131 Hugh Swinton Legaré, The Southern Review (1870), p. 138.

132 P., An Inquiry into Roman Jurisprudence, Southern Quarterly Review 3 (April 1851), p. 544.

133 Ibid.

134 J. L. Petigru was born on May 10, 1789 in Abbeville District, South Carolina. He was admitted to the Bar in 1812, and elected solicitor in 1816. In 1819, he moved to

law and Roman history may have had some effect on their politics? Could Walker's political position against secession in the *Tract* reflect this influence of Roman models? Could their knowledge of the dolorous effects of civil war on the Roman Republic have made them so staunchly defend the American Republic? This is, indeed, an interesting point for speculation.

In concluding this survey of the South Carolina "circle" of Romanists, it is necessary to make it clear that while Francis Lieber, Hugh Swinton Legaré, and James Murdock Walker were notable "Romanists" in the antebellum South, they were far from alone in their interests. Indeed, quite the contrary was true. The pages of Southern literary magazines of the antebellum period frequently contained articles on Roman and Civil law and often contained reviews of foreign books on these subjects as well. Obviously, the Classical world appealed to the Southern gentleman. Lawyers in the South were, quintessentially, gentlemen. Thus, it is not surprising at all that we find articles on Roman and Civil law sprinkled through the pages of the *Southern Literary Messenger* and the *Southern Quarterly Review,* next to reviews of fiction, notes on science, and poems such as "To My Own Little Girl" and "Moses Smiting the Rock."[135] And while most of these notices and reviews concerning Roman and Civil law are brief and somewhat superficial, several approach a level of expertise, if not equal to Lieber's or Legaré's, or even Walker's, respectable nonetheless. For instance, in the *Southern Literary Messenger* for 1842 there is a long article by "a lawyer of North Carolina" on the Civil law. In many respects this article is reminiscent of Legaré's essays in the *Southern Review.*[136] It, too, begins with a discussion of Hallam and attempts to disprove his theories. This article, moreover, criticizes the Common law for its lack of a principled foundation and system:

> Though the Common Law arrogate to itself all that is beautiful and perfect in reason, its advocates may ransack philosophy, in order to find an established principle applicable to every rule therein expressed; yet to the contemplator of that venerable structure, it too often appears, when surveying the patchwork resorted to, to prevent conveyances in mortmain, and the many unexpected resources which the Statute of Uses introduced, that very much of this law is the result of accident. So compli-

---

Charleston to join in partnership with James Hamilton, and three years later was elected Attorney General, and remained so until 1830, when he excepted a position as a state representative. By 1832, he was the leader of the Union party, but his dislike of politics swayed him to return to his private practice. Petigru was against secession, but favored the South's rights to hold slaves, himself owning a few. Much of his property was destroyed during the war, his own life ending on March 9, 1863. For further information and references, see *Dumas Malone,* ed., Dictionary of American Biography, vol. 14 (New York: Charles Scribner's Sons, 1934), p. 514-515.

135 *Mrs. E. J. Eames,* To My Own Little Girl, Southern Literary Messenger 8 (April 1842), p. 255.

N. C. Brooks, Moses Smiting the Rock, Southern Literary Messenger 3 (1837), p. 25.

136 A Lawyer of North Carolina, The Civil Law, Southern Literary Messengers 8 (April 1842), p. 249-255.

cated is the stern and inflexible system, that the introduction of a new regulation has often conflicted with standing rules of laws; and the application of a remedy has been perverted by the finesse of ingenious men, to the creation of still sorer evils than those it was intended to correct.[137]

And, like Legaré, the anonymous "lawyer of North Carolina" held that the principles of Roman law were of universal validity and that, Montesquieu's dictum that laws "are peculiarly adapted to the particular nations which gave them birth" was totally inapplicable here:

From the mouth of the Tiber to that of the Mississippi, the Civil law may be traced through multifarious nations of various governments, exercising over the whole its healthful and genial influence. It is as admirably adapted to those nations, where the mandate of the King is heard and obeyed with fear and trembling, as to those where all other authority is drowned in the voice of the people. Instead of being exclusively and inseparably connected with a city whose glory is fast fading from the earth, the Roman Law has become blended with the fate of many people; and its existence is coupled with its existence of nations that are yet in the vigor of youth. What revolution in the social organization of the world will be sufficiently great to exterminate a law that is so generally disseminated, and so admirably adapted to the necessities of the human race.[138]

Indeed, so far had Roman and Civil law studies made their way into the Southern legal consciousness during the antebellum period that they are found, too, in a plan for an ideal "legal university" published in the 1837 volume of the *Southern Literary Messenger.*[139]

It must be remembered that in 1837 university-affiliated law schools were rarities. Harvard and Transylvania were among the few.[140] But it was also a time of experimentation in legal education. Benjamin Butler, then the Attorney-General of the United States, was just beginning his attempt to start a new law school in New York City.[141] Thus, this 1837 essay was both reflective of its time's

---

137 The Civil Law, n. 137, above, at p. 249.

138 The Civil Law, n. 137, above, at p. 253.

139 Anon., Study of the Law, Southern Literary Messenger, vol. 3 (1837), pp. 30 ff. rptd., in The Gladsome Light of Jurisprudence, ed., *Michael H. Hoeflich* (New York: Greenwood Press, 1988), pp. 201-213.

140 On Harvard, see *Charles Warren,* History of the Harvard Law School, 2 vols. (New York: Lewis Publishing Company, 1908; New York: Da Capo Press, 1970).

On Transylvania, see *Kerr,* Transylvania University's Law Department, Americana 31 (1937), p. 3.

141 Benjamin Butler was born on Dec. 14, 1795 in Columbia County, New York. Admitted to the Bar in 1817, he then joined the law office of Martin Van Buren. In 1821 he was elected as district attorney in Albany, and in 1827 he was elected into the state legislature until 1833, when he declined both a position in the U.S. Senate and Justice in the New York Supreme Court. He did however accept the position as Attorney General for his friend, Vice-President Van Buren and Pres. Jackson. After his position as Attorney-General, he remained mostly as an U.S. attorney in New York, although in 1838 he organized the law school in New York University and remained there as the

views but also experimental in its proposals. The essay begins with a critique of the then common form of legal education, apprenticeship in a law office. It moves on to discus the proposal of the establishment of a "law university."[142] The students in preparing for this university would first be required to learn Latin and become skilled in mathematics. The faculty of the university would consist of professor of logic, rhetoric, moral philosophy, history and historical jurisprudence, and of Civil law, as well as of the various Common law subjets. The justification for having a professor of Civil law (and instruction in that subject) is particularly revealing. Civil law, according to the anonymous essayist, is:

> "... as regards contract (a comprehensive title in the law) ... 'fons et principum,' and which though not law here by enactment, involved and elucidates the principles of justice so fully, so clearly, so justly, and has furnished so large a portion of the basis of the law of all civilized nations, that he who is well skilled in its teachings shall have little more of general principles to learn."[143]

Thus, Lieber, Legaré, and Walker should be viewed as but a sampling of lawyers who represented and embodied the significance of the Roman and Civil law tradition in the legal culture of the antebellum South. One could as easily have discussed other important Southern lawyers who possessed both interest and expertise in Roman and Civil law during this period. One might have mentioned Chancellor George Wythe of Virginia, for instance, whose writings and decisions are replete with Roman law, as Hamilton Bryson has demonstrated.[144] Or one might mention William Cooper, a Tennessee lawyer who was instrumental in the codification of Tennessee law, in fact becoming Chief Justice of the Tennessee Supreme Court, who travelled widely on the Continent in the 1860's, studied equity in London, and wrote on Roman law in the *Southern Review.* Or one might mention Benjamin Porter, born in Charleston in 1808, who became the Supreme court Reporter for the State of Alabama, and succeeded where Legaré failed in translating the works of the German Romanist Heineccius into English. Or, finally, one might mention Brigadier General Albert Pike of the Army of the Confederate States of America, Commissioner for Indian Affairs for the Confederacy, who, amidst the grapeshot of Civil War battles is reported to have translated into English the entirety of the *Corpus Juris Civilis,* as a means of relaxation.

---

head professor. Butler died in Paris form Bright's disease on Nov. 8, 1858. For further information and references, see *Allen Johnson,* ed., Dictionary of American Biography, vol. 3 (New York: Charles Scribner's Sons, 1929), pp. 356-357.

See *Benjamin Butler,* Plan for the Organization of a Law Faculty in the University of the City of New York (New York, 1835). Reprinted in *M. H. Hoeflich,* ed., The Gladsome Light of Jurisprudence (New York: Greenwood Press, 1988), pp. 165-182.

142 Art. Cit., n. 139, above.

143 Art. Cit., n. 139, above.

144 See, *W. Hamilton Bryson,* The Use of Roman Law in Virginia Court, Amer. Jour. Leg. Hist., vol. 28, pp. 135-146 (1984).

In conclusion, one may make several observations about Roman and Civil law and its influence on antebellum southern lawyers and legal scholars. First, the Southern ideal of the lawyer as a classically educated gentleman aided in Roman and Civil law's acceptance into the Southern legal tradition. Similarly the attraction of Continental literature and philosophy — especially German — naturally inclined the best Southern legal scholars towards Roman and Civil law, and process which was aided by the frequency with which such Southerners travelled on the Continent or brought Continental scholars to the South. The popularity of literary magazines in the South during this period further aided this process, for they provided an outlet for Southern lawyers literary efforts, often focused on European or Roman legal subjects.

Of course, Roman and Civil law also were attractive to Southerners for intellectual reasons. Roman law was the law of a great Republic and the republican tradition was then strong in the South. Roman and Civil law were seen as more systematic and philosophically sophisticated than the Common law, a perception common both in the South and in the North, as well. Roman and Civil law also could provide historically tested substantive rules where such were needed. And, naturally, Roman and Civil law appeared particularly appropriate for study in the South, even in Common law jurisdictions, because several of the Southern states, Louisiana, Arkansas, Florida, Texas had either once been or still remained under civilian based legal systems. Thus it was that the tradition of Roman and Civil law studies flourished in the antebellum South until the Civil War destroyed this tradition along with so many others.

ALAN WATSON

Chancellor Kent's Use of Foreign Law

James Kent (1763-1847) was pivotal in American law, and his importance can scarcely be exaggerated. He is famous for, among other things, introducing much foreign law into the U.S. and it is his use of foreign law that is the subject of this paper. I will not examine Kent's influence on the course of the law whether in New York or in South Carolina,[1] nor will I consider the state of the law when he became Chief Justice of New York or the impact of his *Commentaries on American Law*. Rather I will examine only his citations of foreign, other than English,[2] law, to determine the extent of his knowledge, the appropriateness of his citations, and his accuracy of understanding. Then I wish to establish the need or purpose of such citation. Was there an absence of authority in England and the U.S., or was English authority inappropriate, or were the foreign citations particularly persuasive, or were they nothing more than decoration?

For convenience, Kent's work will be examined for three historical stages. We will first consider his judgments from 1804 to 1814 when he was Chief Justice of New York; secondly his judgments from 1814 to 1823 when he was Chancellor and then his *Commentaries on American Law,* first published between 1826 and 1830.

I.

During the period when he was Chief Justice of New York, Kent referred to Roman and subsequent European law relatively infrequently, but in total the references come to a goodly number.[3] Of the more recent writers, Robert Pothier[4]

---

[1] See e.g. *J. T. Horton,* James Kent, A Study in Conservatism (New York, 1969), p. 211 n. 28.

[2] For Kent's use of English law see now *D. W. Raack,* To Preserve the Best Fruits: The Legal Thought of Chancellor James Kent, 33 American Journal of Legal History (1989), pp. 320 ff.

[3] Even before he became Chief Justice, Kent was referring to Roman law: e.g. *Hunn v. Bowne,* 2 Caines 38 (1804) at 44. The proposition for which he cites D.19.1.1.13 seems accurate but the text is not relevant. Since he uses a different form of citation for D.41.1.9.6 it is possible he was not directly using the Digest. He also was citing Scots law. In what follows, I shall not refer to his use of Scots law, which was usually through John Erskine, Institute of the Law of Scotland (1773), but sometimes using Thomas Craig, Jus Feudale (1655).

is by far the one most often cited, though as time goes by Kent cites ever more writers. From the beginning, though, others such as Domat are also cited. The foreign authorities are usually, though not always accurately, stated; but, rather frequently, the citation of the foreign author gives an inaccurate reference.[5] Usually, there was ample authority in English and U.S. law for the decision rendered, and the foreign law was not needed. For Kent's use of English law it is important to remember that the New York Constitution, art. 1 § 14, enacted that such parts of the common law as formed part of the law of the colony should continue the law of the state, subject to alterations made by the New York legislature.

An instructive example of Kent's approach occurs in one of the earliest cases[6] where Justinian's *Code* 8.45.6, his *Digest* 19.1.11.2 and 21.2 are cited for the proposition that in Roman law an adequate price in sale implies warranty of title. In fact, warranty of title was not a Roman concept as Roman law did not require a seller to transfer ownership. But the texts are the ones concerned with the Roman equivalent, the seller's guarantee that the buyer's legal posession would not be disturbed. For this, adequacy of price was not a relevant issue. Kent goes on to state: "But whatever may be our opinions on the point, as an abstract question, or whatever may be the decisions of the civil law, or the feudal and municipal law of other countries, we must decide this question by the common law of England." On this account, the references to Roman law should, in any event, be superfluous.

In the case of *Walden v. LeRoy* which he heard shortly thereafter,[7] he correctly cites the French writer, B. M. Emérigon, as sharing the opinion of English law on general average, and he correctly distinguishes *D.*14.2.6. Again, in *Ludlow v. Bowne*[8] he correctly states that Roman and French law were different from

4 Roman legal texts are directly cited in: 2 Caines, 191, 266; 3 Caines, 114; 1 Johns. 17, 115; 2 Johns. 55, 459; 3 Johns. 341; 4 Johns. 97; 5 Johns. 57, 245; 6 Johns. 170, 184; 7 Johns. 17, 475, 504; 8 Johns. 252, 295, 312; 9 Johns. 14 f., 518; 10 Johns. 10, 103, 159; 11 Johns. 31.

Pothier (1699-1772) is cited in: 3 Caines, 194; 1 Johns. 17, 114, 480; 2 Johns. 334, 356, 401, 459; 3 Johns. 329, 520 f.; 5 Johns. 56, 267, 307; 6 Johns. 159, 170, 184; 7 Johns. 62, 475; 8 Johns. 212 f., 216, 435; 9 Johns. 139; 10 Johns. 84, 461; 11 Johns. 60.

Emérigon (1716-1785) is cited in: 2 Caines, 266; 3 Caines, 194; 1 Johns. 114, 249; 5 Johns. 307; 7 Johns. 426, 475, 529; 8 Johns. 248, 277; 10 Johns. 9, 235.

Others, including Vinnius, Heineccius, J. Voet, Perezius, Grotius and Bynkershoek are cited in: 3 Caines, 114; 1 Johns. 248, 481 f., 2 Johns. 74, 334; 3 Johns. 329, 340 f., 520 f.; 5 Johns. 245, 267, 307; 7 Johns. 475, 505 f., 8 Johns. 212 f., 295, 9 Johns. 14 f., 58; 10 Johns. 10, 103, 159, 185.

5 It is not always possible to be certain. Some works, such as Pothier, Traité des Obligations, were numbered differently in different editions.

6 *Frost v. Raymond,* 2 Caines, 188 (1804) at p. 191.

7 2 Caines, 263 (1805), at p. 266; cf. *McBride v. Marine Insurance Co.,* 7 Johns. 431 (1811) at p. 433.

8 1 Johns. 1 (1806) at p. 17; cf. 2 Johns. (1806) 52 at 55.

English law, and his use of Justinian and Pothier is accurate. At times, very occasionally, when there is no English case, civilian doctrine is expressly followed.[9] At the close of his period as Chief Justice the civilian references are much more complex than they were at the beginning.

It is instructive to take one year of reports to show how Kent used Roman and continental sources. I have chosen 8 Johnson (1811) because Kent claimed to have written all the judgments of the court that year.[10]

In *Case v. Potter,*[11] Pothier, *Traité des Obligations,* §§ 719, 813, is cited for the proposition that in countries where writings of a party are permitted in support of his own claim, the oath of that party is required to give effect to the writings. Section 719 (which is § 754 in later editions) ist relevant, but § 813 is not. Section 719 does show that Dumoulin did require an oath in supplementation, but Kent should also have cited § 720 (§ 755) which shows that Boiceau could be satisfied with something less. The issue is of importance for Kent, because he claims "we have no authority to require or admit the oath of the party." He thus rather manipulates French law to exclude it.

In *Watkinson v. Laughton,*[12] Kent correctly stated the doctrine of Pothier[13] which he says "is a sufficient authority for the rule, if there be no adjudged case or settled practice (and we know of none to the contrary)." Significantly, he adds "especially as the rule is in furtherance of the general policy of the marine law."

In *Gracie v. New York Insurance Co.,*[14] Emérigon[15] was not followed as being contrary to English law. In *Powell v. Smith,* Justinian's *Institutes* 4.14.4 is cited as additional support for a well-established rule.[16] And Emérigon[17] was used in the same way in *Hallet v. Columbian Insurance Company.*[18] The references to *D.* 1.10.2 and Cicero, *De Legibus,* book 2, in *The People v. Ruggles*[19] are purely rhetorical. In *Barker v. Phoenix Insurance Co.* there is a very general, accurate and unnecessary reference to the *Digest* title in the *lex Rhodia de iactu.*[20] In *Putnam v. Wiley,*[21] he refers to Pothier[22] for the proposition that a lessee of

---

9 *Mumford v. Commercial Insurance Co.*, 5 Johns. 262 (1810), at p. 267.

10 William Kent, Memoirs and Letters of James Kent (Boston, 1898), p. 118.

11 211 at pp. 212 f.

12 213 at p. 216.

13 Traité de la Charte-Partie, §§ 33, 35. The doctrine is really contained in §§ 27-48.

14 237 at p. 248.

15 Traité des assurances et des contrats à la grosse (1783), 1, pp. 467, 472.

16 249 at p. 252.

17 Assurances, 1, p. 370.

18 272 at p. 277.

19 290 at p. 295.

20 307 at p. 312.

21 432 at p. 435.

22 Traité de la Proprieté §§ 33, 34, 35.

animals would be the owner of offspring born during the continuance of the lease. The proposition of law is accurate for Pothier, but not for the rationale attributed to him by Kent that the lessee "becomes temporary proprietor of the animals."

During Kent's tenure of this office, his fellow justices did not cite such foreign authorities, with the possible significant exception on one occasion of Livingston who in an opinion dissenting from Kent and the other justices, relies heavily on Emérigon, and through him, on numerous other jurists, and says: "If there be any foreign author who thinks differently, his *dictum* will not be found to be supported by the best and more ancient writers on the law of insurance."[23] One such foreign author expressly mentioned by Livingston was Ricard on whom Kent much relies. It is noteworthy that Kent attempts a more precise delineation of the scope of the relevant *Digest* text (14.2.6). The point at issue was whether, if a ship was forced into a port for refitting following tempest damage, the seamen's wages and provisions fell under general average. Kent favored the positive side of the question which he said was still open under English law. *D*.14.2.6 runs:

> The mast and riggings of a ship which had been caught in a storm were struck by lightning and burnt. After putting into Hippo where it was equipped with temporary riggings, the ship proceedes to Ostia with its cargo safe. The question was raised whether the cargo owners should contribute for the damage of the ship. He (Julian) replied they need not; for the expenditure was incurred more to equip the ship than to save the cargo.

Kent regarded the text as not relevant because of the reason given for Julian's decision. Thus, on this approach, for Kent, the seamen's wages and provisions would be more to save the cargo than equip the ship. The text seems to me to support the position of Livingston.[24]

Kent wrote in a well-known letter:

> Between that time and 1804 I rode my share of circuits, attended all the terms, and was never absent, and was always ready in every case by the day. I read in that time Valin and Emerigon, and completely abridged the latter, and made copious digests of all the English law reports and treatises as they came out. I made much use of the *Corpus Juris*, and as the judges (Livingston excepted) knew nothing of French or civil law, I had immense advantage over them. I could generally put my brethren to rout and carry my point by my mysterious wand of French and civil law. The judges were Republicans and very kindly disposed to everything that was French, and this enabled me, without exciting any alarm or jealousy, to make free use of such authorities and thereby enrich our commercial law.[25]

---

23 *Walden v. LeRoy*, at 272.

24 Livingston might also have referred to D.14.2.2.1; h.t. 5 pr.

25 W. Kent, Memoirs, p. 117.

It seems to me that despite this letter, all in all, one cannot say that Chief Justice Kent altered the direction of the law by his use of Roman and continental doctrines.

II.

Kent's approach did not much change when he became Chancellor, although the references to Roman and continental legal materials do become rather more extensive. He cites writers who were not used, or not much used, by him before. References to French codes make their appearance. J. Voet who was being cited near the end of Kent's reign as Chief Justice is given considerably more prominence. Nonetheless, the only non-English works referred to are still those written in Latin or French.[26]

Such foreign sources are again usually relied on to support existing English or American authority and on that account are mere window dressing.[27] And again, there is a similar carelessness in citation.[28]

---

[26] The cases I consider relevant, all from the New York Chancery Reports are: from 1814; *State of Connecticut v. Jackson*, 13; *Simpson v. Hart*, 89; *Betts v. Betts*, 194; from 1815; *Williamson v. Parisien*, 387; *Cheesebrough v. Millard*, 408; *Stevens v. Cooper*, 413; *Williamson v. Williamson*, 385; *Dunscomb v. Dunscomb*, 505; *Shotwell v. Murray*, 510; *Manning v. Manning*, 526; *Schieffelin v. Stewart*, 619; from 1816; *Peck v. Ellis*, 129; *Gardner v. Village of Newburgh*, 161; from 1817; *Underhill v. Van Cortlandt*, 236; *Barrow v. Rhinelander*, 119; *Gray v. Murray*, 166; *Decouche v. Savetier*, 189; from 1818; *Duncan v. Lyon*, 350; *Reade v. Livingston*, 479; *McMenomy v. Murray*, 433; from 1819; *in re Daniel Washburn*, 105; *Hayes v. Ward*, 121; *Wightman v. Wightman*, 340; *Moore v. Lyttle*, 182; *Barrere v. Barrere*, 185; *Searle v. Scovell*, 217; from 1820; *Campbell v. Mesier*, 332; *Brower v. Fisher*, 437; *Holmes v. Remsen*, 459; *Van Veghten v. Van Veghten*, 500; *Brush v. Wilkins*, 505; *Campbell v. Macomb*, 531; from 1821; *Van Alst v. Hunter*, 145; from 1822; *Seymour v. Delancey*, 220; *Neilson v. McDonald*, 200; *Kirby v. Taylor*, 240; from 1823; *Ellis v. Craig*, 5; *Walton v. Walton*, 256.

[27] See *Manning v. Manning*, 526 (1815) at p. 532 f.; *Duncan v. Lyon*, 351 (1818) at p. 359; *Reade v. Livingston*, 481 (1818) at pp. 506 f.; *Hayes v. Ward*, 123 (1819) at p. 130; *Campbell v. Macomb*, 534 (1820) at pp. 538 ff.; *Neilson v. McDonald*, 210 (1822) at p. 212; *Kirby v. Taylor*, 242 (1822) at p. 252; *Williamson v. Parisien*, 389 (1815) at p. 393; *King v. Baldwin*, 554 (1817) at p. 563; *Riggs v. Murray*, 565 (1817) at p. 577; *Searle v. Scovell*, 218 (1819) at pp. 226 f.; *Connecticut v. Jackson*, 13 (1814) at p. 95; *Betts v. Betts*, 197 (1814) at p. 149; *Chessebrough v. Millard*, 409 (1815) at p. 413; *Dunscomb v. Dunscomb's Execs.*, 508 (1815) at p. 511; *Schieffelin v. Stewart*, 620 (1815) at 628; *Gardner v. Newburgh*, 162 (1816) at pp. 166 f.; *Underhill v. Van Cortlandt*, 339 (1817) at pp. 368 f.; *Gray v. Murray*, 167 (1817) at pp. 180 f.; *In re Washburn*, 106 (1819) at p. 109; *Wightman v. Wightman*, 343 (1819) at pp. 349 f.; *Barrere v. Barrere*, 187 (1819) at pp. 181 f.; *Van Veghten v. Van Veghten*, 501 (1820) at p. 503; *Brush v. Wilkins*, 506 (1820) at pp. 510 f.; *Van Alst v. Hunter*, 148 (1821) at pp. 158 f., 161; *Seymour v. Delancey*, 222 (1822) at p. 232; *Walton v. Walton*, 258 (1823) at pp. 262 f.; *Stevens v. Cooper*, 425 (1815) at p. 431; *Peck v. Ellis*, 131 (1816) at pp. 137 ff. (Roman law followed, Pothier rejected); *Campbell v. Mesier*, 334 (1820) at pp. 339 ff.

[28] *Reade v. Livingston*, 481 (1818) at p. 507; *Brower v. Fisher*, 441 (1820) at p. 444; *Hayes v. Ward*, 123 (1819) at p. 130 (under no. 496).

Some cases require particular attention. In *Williamson v. Williamson,* when there was no relevant English or American authority for lapse of time being a bar to divorce for adultery, Roman and French divorce law was used to bolster the general common law rule that long acquiescence bars an action for civil injury. It is to be noted, however, that the specific foreign doctrine that the acquiescence in adultery had to be persisted in for five years was not accepted.[29]

In *Manning v. Manning,*[30] the issue was whether or not executors or trustees were entitled to compensation for their services. The English rule was that they were not, but some states had ruled differently. Kent declared:

> But this practice cannot be received here as authority, however respectable the source; for it is not founded upon any different construction of the English law, but upon local usages or statutes, which have confessedly changed the English rule. I am not responsible for the justice of that rule. I only declare the law as I find it to be settled; and if the rule was admitted to be, according to the language of one of the southern chancery cases, "a monstrous rule," I should not feel myself at liberty to say, as that case does, "so far as I can go I shall blot it out forever." *Miller v. Beverley,* 4 Hen. & Munf. 415-419, per *Chancellor* Taylor. It is the province of the legislative and not of the judicial power to change the law; and our constitution has auspiciously declared that the common law of England (in which I include, of course, the equity system) "shall continue the law of this State, subject to such alterations and provisions as the Legislature of this State shall, from time to time, make concerning the same." Nor does the rule strike me as so very unjust or singular and extraordinary.

And this opinion, supporting the acceptance of English law, was bolstered by citing Roman and continental law to the same effect. Here the foreign references may have been useful, given the then unpopularity of things English, in persuading the other judges not to follow the practice of other U.S. states:[31] all the more so since Kent is exaggerating the status of English law.[32] Art. 1 § 14 of the New York constitution preserved as law only such parts of the common law as formed part of the colony of New York on 19 April, 1777. But it should be noted that Kent is actively praising English law; the Constitution, he says, "auspiciously" accepted English law.

Manning v. Manning is also important as showing the respect Kent felt for English law, and was willing to express.

> The rule there must be the rule here; for I take this occasion to observe that I consider myself bound by those principles which were known and established as law in the courts of equity in England at the time of the institution of this court; and I shall certainly not presume to strike into any new path, with visionary schemes of innovation and improvement; *via antiqua via est tuta.* It would no doubt be at

29 487 (1815) at p. 492.

30 527 (1815) at 534.

31 For hostility then to English law see *Raack,* Best Fruits, pp. 333 ff.

32 Admittedly not in a way that would affect the judgment here.

times very convenient, and perhaps a cover for ignorance or indolence or prejudice, to disregard all English decisions as of no authority, and to set up as a standard my own notions of right and wrong. But I can do no such thing. I am called to the severer and more humble duty of laborious examination and study. It was Lord Bacon, who laid it down as the duty of a judge to draw his learning from books, and not from his own head.[33]

[I]t may be laid down as a certain truth, that the English system of equity jurisprudence forms an important and very essential branch of that "common law" which was recognized in the Constitution of this State. If it were not so, this court would be a dangerous tribunal, with undefined descretion, and without either science or authority to guide it. The English decisions are undoubtedly the most authentic evidence of the English common law; and the dignity of independence of our courts is no more affected by adopting these decisions than in adopting the English language; or than the independence of France or Holland is wounded by following, as they do, the civil code of the ancient Romans.[34]

Valuable use was made by Kent of Justinianian and subsequent continental (and Scottish) law in *Hayes v. Ward.*[35] He observed that before Justinian, as in English law, the creditor could proceed against the surety before applying to the principal. This was changed by *Novella* 4.1 of 535 A.D. to protect the surety, and this was followed by states such as France, Holland and Scotland. He uses this foreign law to show that such protection of the surety was reasonable:

A rule of such general adoption shows that there is nothing in it inconsistent with the relative rights and duties of principal and surety, and that it accords with a common sense of justice and the natural equity of mankind.

He does not pretend to lay down any such general rule for New York, but he uses the foreign law to support an exception to protect the surety in the particular circumstances of this case.

It was established law in England that a person who was deaf and dumb was not on that account to be judged an idiot. In *Brower v. Fisher,*[36] Kent supposed that the rules (as he claims) of Roman law that a person born deaf and dumb was incapable of making a will and was a person to whom a guardian or curator was appointed, were perhaps based on a presumption, in the first instance, that every such person was incompetent. He then uses this "reasonable presumption" in holding that a plaintiff who brought a commission of lunacy against a person who was born deaf and dumb was not acting vexatiously.[37] Kent's treatment is very odd. In Roman law a person who was deaf and dumb was not, on that account, subject to a guardian or curator. And guardians and curators were very different legal persons. Under Justinian, persons who were deaf and dumb could

---

33 At pp. 529 f.

34 A. p. 531.

35 123 (1819) at p. 133.

36 441 (1820) at p. 444.

37 The case concerned the matter of costs.

generally make wills. The previous Roman disability resulted because will making was based on the oral *mancipatio,* and deaf and dumb persons could not use that ceremony because of its orality, since they could not speak or hear what was said. There was no presumption of imbecility. Kent gives as his authorities: "Inst. 1, 2, 12, 3, 23, 24; Ferniere, *h.t.;* Ferrier and Vinnius, *h.t.*" The reference to Justinian's *Institutes* (on which the others depend) is an impossible one and the correct reference is to J.2.12.3 where the law is not as Kent states it. Ferniere and Ferrier are presumably Ferière. And Vinnius on J.2.12.3 states expressly the correct Roman reason for deaf and dumb persons' previous incapacity to make wills. This, of course, is not what Kent presumes it to be. It appears plausible from all this that Kent did not here check his sources but was relying on (faulty) memory — or worse.[38]

Finally, in *Ellis v. Craig* where there was no direct authority, civilians were cited to show that their doctrines were inapplicable to the case.[39]

III.

In his *Commentaries,* Kent continues to cite Roman and continental law. Indeed, he increases, expands and enriches his use of foreign materials. He has elegant disquisitions on, say, French law even when he has no intention of influencing American law.[40] A notable feature of volume one is his extended treatment of the law of nations with frequent references to such international giants as Vattel, Grotius, Pufendorf and Bynkershoek. That volume also ends with an impressive description of Roman law until the time of Justinian, ample testimony to his high regard of that system. Much of his history is culled from J. V. Gravina (1664-1718), *De ortu et progressu juris civilis, De jure naturali, gentium et XII tabularum,* and *De romano imperio.* From an early point in volume two[41] he begins to cite C.-B.-M. Toullier who thereafter is a favorite of his. Presumably he did not previously have access to this writer whose *Droit civil français suivant l'ordre du Code* first appeared from 1812-1818.

But as with his judgments, his statement of the American law is soundly based on English and American cases and statutes. French and other law is not used to develop American law or to point it in a new directon. At times, again, his references are inaccurate, and one is forced to wonder whether he has always consulted the sources hi cites.

---

38 He could assume that Ferrière and Vinnius would say something *à propos* in the Institutes text.

39 7 (1823), at pp. 12 f.

40 See e.g. 2, pp. 80 n.b., 87, 103 n.d.

41 P. 43 n.b.

In what follows I have chosen to examine in some detail two topics where his approach most seems to be faulty, namely the water rights of riparian owners and his general treatment of contracts.

Water rights: Of the rights of riparian owner, Kent says:

> Every proprietor of lands on the banks of a river has naturally an equal right to the use of the water which flows in the stream adjacent to his lands, as it was wont to run, *(currere solebat)* without diminution or alteration. No proprietor has a right to use the water, to the prejudice of other proprietors, above or below him, unless he has a prior right to divert it, or a title to some exclusive enjoyment. He has no property in the water itself, but a simple usufruct while it passes along. *Aqua currit et debet currere,* is the language of the law. Though he may use the water while it runs over his land, he cannot unreasonably detain it, or give it another direction, and he must return it to its ordinary channel when it leaves his estate. Without the consent of the adjoining proprietors he cannot divert or diminish the quantity of water, which would otherwise descend to the proprietors below, nor throw the water back upon the proprietors above, without a grant, or an uninterrupted enjoyment of twenty years, which is evidence of it.[b] This is the clear and settled general doctrine on the subject, and all the difficulty that arises consists in the application.[42]

At his footnote b he cites in support several English and American cases, and prefixes to them: "*Dig.* 39.3,4 and 10. Pothier, Traité du Contrat de Société, second app. No. 236, 237." Scholarly references to the *Digest* have usually three or four parts. The first tells us which of the fifty books of the *Digest* contains the text, the second gives the title or chapter of the particular book. The third gives the actual *lex* or law, and the fourth, when there is a fourth, sets out the appropriate fragment of the law. In this instance something is wrong with Kent's citation. *D*.39.3. is the relevant Digest title, *De aqua et aquae pluviae arcendae,* 'Water, and the action to ward off rain water.' But 39.3.4 has five fragments and 39.3.10 has three, and one should expect the appropriate fragments to be identified. In fact, none of the fragments is directly relevant.[43] But help comes from Pothier. In article 236 of his second appendix he cites "L.1. §§ 3,5,7 *eod. tit.*" The citation is to the 'same title' as previously cited, that is *D*.39.3., so the full reference is to *D*.39.3.1.3,5,7. But for a further point he has *"eod. L § 4"*, that is, fragment 4 of the same *lex,* that is *D*.39.3.1.4. And in article 237 he cites *"eod. L. § 10"*, that is *D*.39.3.1.10. *D*.39.3.1.4 and *D*.39.3.1.10 are in fact texts that would be relevant for Kent. Kent, it thus appears, has taken his *Digest* references at second hand from the articles he cites from Pothier. Pothier's mode of citation, which until recently was the standard mode, has misled Kent who cannot have looked up the *Digest.*

---

42 Commentaries, 2, pp. 353 f.

43 The texts will be found in the original Latin and English translation in Digest of Justinian edit. by T. Mommsen, P. Krueger and A. Watson, 3 (Philadelphia, 1985), pp. 398 ff.

Even more surprising, neither the *Digest* passages nor the articles of Pothier really give the law as stated by Kent. For the Roman jurists and for Pothier, a landowner could diminish, divert or use up the supply of water to a neighbor: what he was not allowed to do was increase the supply of water in a way that could cause harm to his neighbor's land.[44]

In contrast, the English and American cases support Kent to the full.[45] Thus, even if the law of Rome and in Pothier had been as described by Kent there would have been no need for the references to them.

Slightly further on, Kent reports:

> But *de minimis non curat lex,* and a right of action by the proprietor below would not necessarily flow from such consequences, but would depend upon the nature and extent of the complaint or injury, and the manner of using the water. All that the law requires of the party, by or over whose land a stream passes, is, that he should use the water in a reasonable manner, and so as not to destroy, or render useless, or materially diminish, or affect the application of the water by the proprietors below on the stream. He must not shut the gates of his dams and detain the water unreasonably, or let it off in unusual quantities to the annoyance of his neighbour. Pothier lays down the rule very strictly, that the owner of the upper stream must not raise the water by dams, so as to make it fall with more abundance and rapidity than it would naturally do, and injure the proprietor below. But this rule must not be construed literally, for that would be to deny all valuable use of the water to the riparian proprietors. It must be subjected to the qualifications which have been mentioned, otherwise rivers and streams of water would become utterly useless, either for manufacturing or agricultural purposes. The just and equitable principle is given in the Roman law: — *Sic enim debere quem meliorem agrum suum facere, ne vicini deteriorem faciat.*[22]

In this instance, too, the American cases cited at footnote *a* amply support Kent's propositions. The passage of Pothier reads:

> It is on this principle that the action for the warding off of rain water *(aquae pluviae arcendae)* was founded.
>
> This action lies, on the part of the owner or possessor of the lower land against his neighbor who owns or possesses the higher land wherever the possessor of the higher land by means of some work he has done on his land, collects together the waters which descend from it, hence causing them to descend into the lower land

44 See *A. Watson,* Transformation of American Property Law: A Comparative Law Approach, 24 Georgia Law Review (1990), pp. 163 ff. at pp. 176 ff.

45 *Brown v. Best,* 1 Wills Rep. 174 (England): see especially pp. 174 ff.; *Bealey v. Shaw,* 6 East's Rep. 208 (England): especially p. 214 f.; *Wright v. Howard,* 1 Simon & Stuart 190 (England): especially p. 203; *Gardner v. Village of Newburgh,* 2 Johns. Ch. Rep. 161 (N. Y.), especially p. 614: *Belknap v. Belknap,* 2 Johns. Ch. Rep. 463 (N. Y.): contains implicit support but is not a good statement of the law; *Merrit v. Parker,* 1 Coxe's N. J. Rep. (N. J.); *Tyler v. Wilkinson,* 24 F. Case. 472 (No. 14, 312): especially p. 474. See already, *T. E. Lauer,* The Common Law Background of the Riparian Doctrine, 28 Missouri Law Review (1963), pp. 60 ff.

> with more abundance and rapidity than they would naturally descend, and thus cause him some loss.
>
> But when the waters flow naturally from the higher to the lower land, the possessor of the lower land has no complaint; for in this case it is not the possessor of the higher land who causes the descent, but the nature of the land: "If the water naturally descends, the action does not lie.": *D*.39.3.1.10; "It is not the water but the nature of the place that causes the injury."; *D*.39.3.1.14.
>
> The possessor of the lower land also cannot complain of furrows that the possessor of the higher land has made there when the furrows are only the ordinary furrows which are necessary for plowing his field: *D*.39.3.13,5,7.
>
> But he cannot make them either deeper or more sloping than is necessary, though in making them in this way he improves his land, for he cannot improve his property to the detriment of his neighbor: "For one ought to improve one's land in such a way that it does not make a neighbor's land worse.": *D*.39.3.1.4.

It would seem that Kent misunderstands or misrepresents Pothier. Pothier, who is following the Roman jurists, is to be construed literally: any increase in the quantity or speed of the water flowing onto a lower proprietor's land and which causes damage will give rise to an action.[46] Moreover, this is so when the work done is anything other than ordinary plowing: even when the furrows are deeper or more on a slope than is necessary, the owner of the lower land will have an action. Kent's notion that riparian owners could make reasonable use of the water just did not apply for Pothier or in Roman law. And it must not be forgotten because of the context in which Kent refers to Pothier, that for Pothier as for the Roman jurists, the riparian owner had a remedy only when a neighbor increased the flow of water, not also when he diminished it.

The "just and equitable principle" of Roman law that he quotes appeared in *D*.39.3.1.4 in a limited context: that ditches should not be dug to flow in one channel in such a way that they could injure a neighbor's land. The quotation appears in Pothier and could have been taken from him.[47] Given his faulty references, there is no reason to suppose that Kent actually consulted the *Digest*.

Kent's footnote 'b' reads: "The *Code Napoleon*, No. 640, 641, 643, 644 establishes the same just rules in the use of running waters." Actually, the articles cited are scarcely helpful. Art. 640 basically gives the law that we have seen in Pothier and at Rome. Art. 641 rules that the owner of land in which a spring arises may use it as he wishes unless a lower proprietor has acquired rights by prescription. Art. 643 enacts that the same owner in whose land a spring arises may not divert it when it supplies the inhabitants of a commune, village or hamlet, but he may claim an indemnity if the inhabitants have not acquired use by prescription. Art. 644 is, however, relevant:

---

[46] Though, naturally *De minimis non curat lex* would apply.

[47] Société, 2nd app. § 236.

> He whose property borders on running water, other than that which is declared a dependence on the public domain by article 538 under the title *On the distinction of things,* may use it in its passage for the irrigation of his property.
>
> He whose estate is crossed by such water may even use it during the time it crosses the land but with the duty of restoring it to its ordinary channel at the boundary of his land.

It is not clear how far this gives the law set out by Kent. Nothing indicates that the superior proprietor may not substantially diminish the flow of water to his neighbor, and the first paragraph talks only of irrigation, not also of using the water for manufacturing purposes.

Kent might possibly have referred to art. 645 which he does not cite:

> If a dispute arises between proprietors to whom such waters may be useful, the courts, in pronouncing their judgment, must reconcile the interest of agriculture with the respect due to property; and in all cases particular and local regulations on the course and use of waters must be observed.

This is more relevant than any of the articles of the *code civil* cited here by Kent with the exception of art. 644, but again the law in it seems to relate — even more clearly — only to agricultural purposes.

Thus, of the four articles of the *code civil* cited for water rights for neighboring proprietors, three are scarcely relevant at all, and the remaining one is not wholly in line with Kent's propositions. Moreover, an article not cited is as much to the point for Kent as the last of those he refers to. The problem for us is to explain Kent's usage here. I have found no definite answer, but we can, I believe, exclude the possibility that his reference followed directly upon an examination of the relevant articles of the *code.* There are two serious possibilities. Either he took the citations from some unnamed intermediary source, or he took them from notes he had made on a previous occasion when his concern was not quite the same. He could have made use of the articles in the *code civil* on the water rights or riparian owners when dealing, as Chancellor, with the case of *Gardner v. Village* of Newburgh in 1816.[48]

Oddly perhaps, it is in this context that Kent (and before him Story in *Tyler v. Wilkinson*[49]) is given most credit for using French authorities to develop American law. For instance, Samuel C. Wiel reports:

> Kent is found using in his Commentaries the words of the Code Napoléon, and in elaborating upon them his leading citations are to the Code Napoléon, the Digest of Justinian, the Codex of Justinian, and the works of Pothier, of Toullier, and of Merlin.
>
> His text is an unconcealed commentary upon the civil law, discussing the rule of Pothier and adapting "the just and equitable principle given in the Roman law" at

48 2 Johns. Ch. Rep. 161 (N. Y.).

49 4 Mason, 397. Fed. Cas. No. 14, 312 (1827).

one place incorporating bodily a passage from the Roman Institutes, and closing the exposition of the subject with the following note: "The Code Napoléon, n. 640, 641, 643, 644, establishes the same just rules in the use uf running water," referring to the rules he has set forth in the text of his Commentaries.[50]

T. E. Lauer properly stresses the common law background of the riparian doctrine but even he says:

> In 1825 the common law contained the seeds of the reasonable use test; the development across the centuries had been in the direction of a flexible legal standard which would enable the greatest beneficial use of watercourses. Story and Kent were unquestionably conversant with the common law background. It is true, of course, that in constructing the riparian doctrine they drew heavily upon the Code Napoleon and Roman law. But at most the continental legal system can be assigned only a paternal role in the conception of the American riparian doctrine. The gestation of the doctrine occurred within the matrix of the common law, over centuries of judicial experience and growth.[51]

This still gives too much credit to the *code civil* and Roman law.

Contracts: Kent does not devote a section to the law of contracts in general, but at the beginning of his treatment of sale he has a few general pages. At an early point he claims:

> A contract valid by the law of the place where it is made, is valid every where *jure gentium,* and on that broad foundation all contracts were introduced.[a] If it were otherwise, the citizens of one nation could not contract, or carry on commerce in the territories of another. The neccessities of commerce require, that acts valid where made, should be recognised in other countries, provided they be not contrary to the independence of nations, and do not proceed from the public power.[b][52]

His notes are:

> [a] *Inst. 1.2.2. ex hoc jure gentium, omnes pene contractus introducti sunt.*
>
> [b] This principle of public law, says Toullier, Droit Civil, tome 10.117. is well explained and enforced by M. Bayard, in the *Nouvelle Collection de Jurisprudence,* tome 9.p. 759 and which he untertook in conjunction with M. Camus.

The passage cited from the *Institutes* does not at all justify Kent's proposition that a contract valid where it is made is valid everywhere. Justinian is there distinguishing the law of nature *(ius naturale),* the law of all peoples *(ius gentium)* and the law of a state *(ius civile),* and he declares that *ius gentium* is common to all people and that contracts arise from this *ius gentium.* There is nothing to justify the deduction from this that a contract valid where it is made is valid everywhere. Even more to the point, Kent has overlooked *pene,* 'almost'; that

---

50 *Waters:* American Law and French Authority, 33 Harvard Law Review (1919), pp. 133 at pp. 137 f.

51 Common Law Background, p. 107.

52 P. 364.

is the quotation from the *Institutes* says: "from that *ius gentium almost* all of the contracts were introduced." The earliest Roman contract, *stipulatio,* was at first restricted in its use to citizens, hence it was part of the *ius civile,* not the *ius gentium.*[53] This fact turns Kent's use of the quotation into nonsense. But Kent has taken the Roman text from Toullier at paragraph 79:

> In the contracts made before notaries in foreign lands, the private will of the parties concords with the public power: one forms the obligation, the other makes it executory. In our ordonnance the legislator thus separates the work of the public power from the work of the will of the parties: it destroys the one and preserves the other. He means the obligation not to be executory in France: but at the same time he intends that it have the role of *simple promises.*[54]

At the end of the passage quoted, Toullier has a footnote that begins:

> *Simple promises.* Even when one of the parties is unable to sign, for the law makes no distinction. The authenticated act made before foreign notaries between two parties who do not know how to sign, or of whom only one does not know how to do so, has no less validity in France as a simple promise. This is a principle founded in the law of nations *(ius gentium)* and is established by the unanimous consent of all nations, even tacitly and without an express written treaty, for the common utility of all people: *'through force of circumstances and human necessity'*; J.1.2.2.
>
> *'From this law of nations came almost all the contracts, as sale, hire, partnership, deposit, loan and innumerable others.'*
>
> If it was otherwise, the citizens of one nation could not contract, nor consequently enter into any commerce, in the territory of another nation. It was therefore agreed, *'by the tacit agreement of peoples'* that "if the contracts are clothed in the conditions necessary for authentication in the place where they were made, they carry their authentication in every country in the world." This is a point of doctrine well developed by M. Bayard in the *Nouvelle Collection de Jurisprudence* that he undertook with M. Camus.

Then follows in Toullier a long quotation from Bayard. At paragraphs 77 to 79 Toullier is making a complex point. The French ordonnance of 1629, he claims, drew a distinction with regard to foreign contracts: it sustains them in so far as they depend on the will of the parties, but annuls them in France in so far as they are attached to the foreign power. Thus, with regard to contracts made abroad before notaries, there is a concurrence between the public power and the will of the parties. The public power attributes legal effect to the notarial formalities and renders the agreement executory; the will of the parties creates the obligation. The ordonnance destroys that part of the arrangement that depends on the foreign power, but it sustains that part the depends on the will of the parties, hence the contract has the force of a simple promise.

---

[53] See e.g. *J. A. C. Thomas,* Textbook of Roman Law (Amsterdam, 1970), p. 259.
[54] 10, § 79 (p. 103 in the fourth, Belgian, edition of 1824).

Toullier is best understood in terms of a French conception of obligation which goes back before the *code civil,* but has an impact even thereafter. For Pothier, obligations are imperfect or perfect. An imperfect obligation is a duty owed only to God and which cannot be exacted by any individual. Perfect obligations give those with whom we have contracted the right to demand performance. Perfect obligations are of two types: those that form a *vinculum iuris,* a civil obligation that will be enforced in court; and those that form a *solius aequitatis vinculum,* a natural obligation, that gives the promisee the right in the forum of conscience to demand performance.[55] On this analysis, the foreign contract before a notary that is described by Toullier is a perfect natural obligation. Even after the *code civil* a perfect natural obligation is not without effect at civil law. Thus, a preexisting natural obligation that is followed by an act recognizing it which, however, is lacking in the formalities needed for a binding civil law obligation, will create a full civil law obligation.

But Toullier's footnote is a little odd. The first paragraph is in harmony with his text, but then the quotation from J.1.2.2 is just as irrelevant for Toullier — even worse — than it is for Kent. The remainder of the note quoted here relating to Camus actually contradicts Toullier's own text. In contrast to Toullier, Camus gives the proposition of law that Kent cites Toullier for, namely that a contract valid where it is made is valid everywhere.

To return to the qualification in the final sentence quoted from Kent: "... provided they be not contrary to the independence of nations, and do not proceed from the public power." Though it is not easy to know what Kent precisely means, since he adds nothing in explanation, there would seem to be here a misunderstanding of Toullier. 'Proceeding from the public power' seems to refer to Toullier's point about particular formalities established by the law of the land, but Toullier has nothing corresponding to the first part of the qualification. Rather, Kent's own words here indicate that for him the whole qualification is to the effect that a contract made abroad which is the object of foreign political endeavors does not share in the universal validity of foreign made contracts.

Kent next proceeds to discuss *consideration* in contract. He says:

> It is essential to the validity of a contract, that it be made by parties competent to contract, and be founded on a sufficient consideration. There must be something given in exchange, something that is mutual, or something which is the inducement to the contract; and it must be a thing which is lawful, and competent in value to sustain the assumption. A contract without a consideration is a *nudum pactum,* and not binding; and this maxim of the common law was taken from the civil law, in which the doctrine of consideration is treated with an air of scholastic subtlety.[c] Whether the agreement be verbal, or in writing, it is still a *nude pact,* and will not support an action if a consideration be wanting.[56]

---

[55] Traité des obligations, article preliminaire.

[56] 2, pp. 364 f.

His footnote 'c' (which is alone relevant) runs:

> *Dig.* 19.5.5. Sir William Blackstone in his Commentaries, vol. ii, 444 has borrowed and explained the distinctions in the Pandects upon the four species of contracts, of *do ut des, do ut facias, facio ut des,* and *facio ut facias.*

Kent's description of Roman law in his text could not be more wrong. Developed Roman law did not have a system of contract law but a system of contracts, and some of these contracts were, of necessity, gratuitous: loan for use *(commodatum),* deposit *(depositum),* mandate *(mandatum).* If a reward in money was specified for a loan for use, deposit or mandate, that contract did not emerge but hire *(locatio conductio)* did. If a non-monetary counter prestation was agreed on, no contract would come into being. Again, the *stipulatio,* a formal promise to give or do something, was unilateral. Of course, a *stipulatio* might be given because of some performance or promise of performance by the promisee, but such performance was not legally linked to the *stipulatio,* and was, indeed, quite irrelevant for the validity and enforcement alike of the first *stipulatio.* Then, the action on loan for consumption *(mutuum)* lay only for the return of the exact equivalent of what was given, not also for interest. Not that interest on a loan was illegal, buth the action on *mutuum* was not available for it. If interest was promised by a *stipulatio* connected with a *mutuum,* an action lay on the stipulatio. So it makes no sense to suppose that the contract of *mutuum* required consideration.[57]

Kent's footnote 'c' is as erroneous as the description of Roman law in his text. In *D.*19.5.5 the jurist Paul was not claiming that the four types of agreement, "I give that you give, I give that you do, I do that you give, and I do that you do," exhaust the categories of contracts, and that contracts therefore had to be bilateral and involve a *quid pro quo.* His point was that where performance by one party followed such a bilateral agreement, that party would have a right to an action against the other. This was the case, in Paul's view, even when the agreement fell outside the scope of any of the recognized Roman contracts.

Once again it is as if Kent had no personal familiarity with Roman law. He has taken the reference from Blackstone, whose use of the text is, as we shall see, very different. Blackstone's treatment of consideration is more complex, and Kent fails to do it justice, Blackstone claims: "The civilians hold, that in all contracts, either express or implied, there must be something given in exchange, something that is mutual or reciprocal." For this statement he does not cite Roman law but J. V. Gravina (1664-1718) *De Ortu et Progressu Juris Civilis,* 2.12, "Exchange is contained in all contracts, nominate or innominate." But Blackstone in his turn seems to mistreat Gravina whose point was probably not the same as his own. The context is important. The title of Gravina's chapter 10 is entitled, 'On the Origin of Human Society', chapter 11 'On the Law of

---

57 For the Roman system of contracts see e.g. *Thomas,* Textbook, pp. 225 ff.

Nations and the Origin of Commerce', chapter 12 (with which we are concerned) 'On Exchange, an Element of all Contracts' and chapter 13 'On the Law of Peace'.

Gravina ist concerned with the primary place of *permutatio,* barter or exchange, in the rise of contract or commerce. But he is not talking of *permutatio* as the oldest enforceable contract. Others, including sale, were centuries earlier at Rome.[58] His concern is not so much technical aspects of law, but the centrality of reciprocity in the development of contractual relationships. He is well aware that Roman law did not require a tangible reciprocity for the validity of a contract. Thus, for *commodatum,* loan for use, which had to be gratuitous, he sees the reciprocity in the gratitude of the borrower towards the lender. Indeed, he goes so far as to treat gift, *donatio,* among the reciprocal contracts, again on the basis of the donee's gratitude to the donor. Gravina's notion of reciprocity is that as a matter of fact reciprocity is involved in all contracts. But the reciprocity need not in law exist within the bounds of the one contract under discussion. The sentence of Blackstone is ambiguous. It could be making Gravina's point: namely, in fact, when a contract exists there is reciprocity. Or it could be saying that no contract is valid unless there is a *quid pro quo.* The latter is the sense in which Kent understands Blackstone, and it does not represent civilian doctrine.

For Blackstone there has to be sufficient consideration for a valid contract. This sufficient consideration is either a valuable or good consideration. A good consideration is that of blood or natural affection between near relatives, and this type of contract may be set aside when it is in fraud of creditors. Valuable consideration is a reciprocity within the contract. Blackstone subsequently says "These valuable considerations are divided by the civilians into four species," and he refers to *D.*19.5.5. The reference may mislead since that text was not really concerned with the recognized Roman contracts. Still, what Blackstone writes is accurate in that, in so far as valuable consideration was needed for a civilian contract, it would fall within one of these types.

But Kent does not make Blackstone's distinction between good and valuable consideration (though at one point he uses the term valuable consideration). This in turn makes his reliance on Blackstone for civilian doctrine into abject nonsense. Surprisingly, Kent, who made so much use of Gravina in the final chapter of his volume one, appears not to have consulted him. There remains a problem. Kent, one would think, knew too much Roman law to believe his own account.

IV.

To conclude. Both in his judgments and in his *Commentaries* James Kent founds his opinion on the usually solid basis of existing English and American

---

58 See e.g. *Thomas,* Textbook, p. 312.

law. He shows not the slightest reluctance to cite English cases as authority, despite what may have been the political climate of his time. Indeed, he frequently relies on English cases dating from after 19 April 1777 which should have been no authority in New York. Despite numerous citations, Kent does not really use Roman, French or other continental law to develop law in America. Many of his citations are mere window dressing when there was already sufficient English or American authority. Nonetheless, one cannot exclude the possibility that his use of foreign law sometimes persuaded his colleagues to accept his opinion. Kent usually shows a firm knowledge of the foreign law he uses. But he sometimes cites works that he has either not consulted or, at least, not on that occasion. And it is possible for him at times to make almost unbelievably egregious mistakes.

DAVID S. CLARK*

The Civil Law Influence on David Dudley Field's Code of Civil Procedure

Why might we not have *comparative law,* to place the legal systems of different countries and ages side by side, that the lawyer may profit by the history of the world? He is, perhaps, the only man of science who does not look beyond his own commonwealth, and to whom the history of other countries is as a sealed book.[1]

David Dudley Field

One of the leitmotive in American legal history is the tension between the goals of order and flexibility.[2] This leitmotiv was personified in the second half of the 19th century by the ongoing debates between David Dudley Field (1805-1894) and James Carter (1827-1905) about the desirability of codifying American common law.[3]

---

* Professor of Law, The University of Tulsa. I wish to thank my colleagues in the working group "The Reception of Continental Ideas in 19th Century Anglo-American Legal Thought," especially the organizer Mathias Reimann, for valuable suggestions useful in preparing this article.

Literature cited in abbreviated form: *Charles M. Cook,* The American Codification Movement: A Study of Antebellum Legal Reform (1981); *Daun van Ee,* David Dudley Field and the Reconstruction of the Law (1974, reprint 1986); David Dudley Field, Introduction to the Completed Civil Code (1865), in 1 Field Papers 323 (cited: Field, Civil Code); *Henry M. Field,* The Life of David Dudley Field (1898); *Henry G. McMahon,* The Proposed Louisiana Code of Practice: A Synthesis of Anglo-American and Continental Civil Procedure, 14 La. L. Rev. 36 (1953); 1-3 Speeches, Arguments, and Miscellaneous Papers of David Dudley Field (A. P. Sprague ed. 1884) (cited: Field Papers); *Stephen N. Subrin,* David Dudley Field and the Field Code: A Historical Analysis of an Earlier Procedural Vision, 6 Law & Hist. Rev. 311 (1988).

1 Field, Study and Practice of the Law (1844), in 1 Field Papers 484, 491.

2 The pejorative terms rigidity and chaos capture part of the tune.

3 *Mathias Reimann,* The Historical School Against Codification: Savigny, Carter, and the Defeat of the New York Civil Code, 37 Am. J. Comp. L. 95, 98-107 (1989); see Field, Codification of Our Common Law: A Short Reply to a Long Essay (1884), in 2 Field Papers 494-502; Field, Codification Once More, 40 Albany L. J. 464 (1889), in 3 Field Papers 411-22. See also infra text at n. 88.

Field expressed his views on the flexibility issue:

"A still further objection to the expediency of a code is its supposed inflexibility. Expressed in formal propositions, and couched in positive terms, it is not as flexible, say the objectors, as the common law. This is the objection most insisted upon by those who oppose a code, and it should, therefore, receive the most careful consideration. It may be first observed, that flexibility, in its ordinary sense, is one of the worst

Kermit Hall, in his introductory text on the history of American law, expresses the conventional view about the importance of codification in that history and the influence of the civil law tradition.

> The civil law tradition contributed only modestly to the origins of American law. In the nineteenth and twentieth centuries American law reformers, however, repeatedly invoked the concept of codification — of a rational, written body of rules for all to see — as a way of imposing order on the unruly common law.[4]

Hall recognizes that David Field was the 19th century's most persistent advocate for codification.[5] The aim of this article is to reconsider the civil law influence on Field and particularly on his Code of Civil Procedure.[6]

---

qualities which a law can have, or rather that it is inconsistent with the idea of law. As the law is a rule of property and of conduct, it should be fixed . . .
Another way of stating the objection is to say that, while the common law is expansive, a code does not expand or adapt itself to the expanding exigencies of society. A different phrase for the same idea is, that the common law is elastic and accommodating, and that a code will be the opposite. Now, to say that a law is expansive, elastic, or accommodating, is as much as to say that it is no law at all. The real significance of the objection, if it has any significance, is, that it is better to let the Judges make the law as they go along, than to have the lawgiver make it beforehand . . .
It is possible that the idea of flexibility in one form, and inflexibility in the other, has arisen from not sufficiently attending to the distinction between general and partial rules. It may be perfectly safe to lay down a certain general rule, but not at all safe to undertake the enumeration of all the particulars to which the rule may be applied. A code which should attempt to do the latter would fail, not because it would be inflexible, but because it would be defective . . .
If by flexibility be meant susceptibility of progression, then it may be affirmed with confidence, that a code, upon the theory on which this is framed, not only adapts itself to the present wants of society better than the existing common law, but that it contains within itself, in a greater degree, the elements of future progress . . .
Nothing is more conspicuous in the history of jurisprudence than the tenacity with which the Judges of America and England, unlike those of Continental Europe, have adhered to precedents, even though the reason for them has ceased, and their mischiefs have become palpable."
Field, Civil Code 330-34.

4 *Kermit L. Hall,* The Magic Mirror: Law in American History 10 (1989); see id at 126-27.

5 Id. 127. Field summarized the benefits of codification:
"Assuming that it is possible to have a body of written law in a convenient form, and in scientific order, containing the materials and framed in the manner already described, what benefits will it confer? In the first place, it will enable the lawyer to dispense with a great number of the books which now incumber the shelves of his library. In the next place, it will thus save a vast amount of labor, now forced upon lawyers and judges, in searching through the reports, examining and collecting cases, and drawing inferences from the decisions, and so far facilitate the dispatch of business in the Courts. In the third place, it will afford an opportunity for settling, by legislative enactment, many disputed questions, which the Courts have never been able to settle. In the fourth place, it will enable the Legislature to effect reforms in different branches of the law, which can only be effected by simultaneous and comprehensive legislation . . . In the fifth place, the publication of a code will diffuse among the people a more general and accurate knowledge of their rights and duties than can be obtained in any

Field's greatest success came as the pivotal member of the New York Commission on Practice and Pleadings, which submitted its draft 391 section Code of Civil Procedure to the legislature in 1848.[7] The Code was enacted that year, and together with revisions and amendments proposed by the Commission and adopted in 1849, became the final 473 section New York Code of Civil Procedure.[8] The Commission drafted a longer version in 1849, including a criminal procedure code and evidence rules, but the legislature rejected it.[9] The Code's influence, nevertheless, in one of these three versions, was deep and wide. First, it was revolutionary since it abolished the English feudal writ and bill system of pleading, replacing it with a single civil action guided by "code" pleading. And it implemented the merger of law and equity, a distinction that was a source of great confusion and delay. Second, other states adopted the Code. Missouri began when it enacted the 1848 version in 1849. David Field's brother, Stephen — later to become a United States Supreme Court justice — persuaded the California legislature to enact in 1851 a procedure code based on the 1850 model. By 1873 more than half the American states and territories had embraced civil procedure codes based on one of the New York models or on the California model.[10]

In this article I investigate the degree to which the civil law tradition influenced David Field's Code of Civil Procedure. This I do on three levels. First, the ideology of codification. From where or whom did Field come to believe the

---

> other manner ... If in Holland, or in Germany, or France, a civil code has been found beneficial, much more is it likely to be beneficial to us."

Field, Civil Code 336-37.

6 For the substantial civilian influence on Field's Civil Code, see *Rodolfo Batiza,* Sources of the Field Civil Code: The Civil Law Influences on a Common Law Code, 60 Tulane L. Rev. 799 (1986); *William B. Fisch,* The Dakota Civil Code: Notes for an Uncelebrated Centennial, 43 N.D. L. Rev. 485, 503-16 (1967). See also *Friedrich K. Juenger,* David Dudley Field's Contribution to the Conflict of Laws, in Liber Memorialis François Laurent, 1810-1887, at 837 (Johan Erauw et al. eds. 1989). Edward Livingston's criminal code, prepared for Louisiana, influenced Field's Code of Criminal Procedure. Ee 43.

7 First Report of the Commissioners on Practice and Pleadings: Code of Procedure (29 Feb. 1848) (cited: Field, First Report, for those passages written by Field; see 1 Field Papers 262).

8 Second Report of the Commissioners on Practice and Pleadings: Code of Procedure (29 Jan. 1849); 1849 New York Laws 613-705 (chap. 438).

9 The amended code adopted in New York was originally called the "Code of Procedure." The commissioners' fifth and final report to the legislature, dated December 31, 1849 and published in 1850, included two documents: the "Code of Civil Procedure" and the "Code of Criminal Procedure." *Milred V. Coe & Lewis W. Morse,* Chronology of the Development of the David Dudley Field Code, 27 Cornell L. Q. 238, 241-43 (1942).

10 David Dudley Field, Reasons for the Adoption of the Codes (1873), in 1 Field Papers 361, 365; see *Charles M. Hepburn,* The Historical Development of Code Pleading in America and England 91-111, 114-50 (1897).

idea that a code would be the appropriate vehicle by which to reform the law of procedure? Second, the form of codification. Here I consider the method of division in the Field Code, and the use of "scientific" categories and definitions. Third, the substance of codification. Were central ideas and actual sections in the Field Code directly borrowed from a civilian code of Civil procedure? To answer these questions, I focus on the French Code of Civil Procedure (1806) and the Louisiana Code of Practice (1825).

I. The Ideology of Codification

After about 1820 a general American law reform movement appeared that was both more vital and comprehensive than earlier episodic and localized efforts to improve the law.[11] Lawyers were concerned with at least four problems in the American legal system.

First, legal source materials were growing too fast and were too diverse. Joseph Story's (1779-1845) address "Progress of Jurisprudence" to the Suffolk Bar in 1821 illustrated both points. He counted about 150 volumes of American case law (probably closer to 170 volumes in fact) and feared that its growth was "a fearful calamity, which threatens us of being buried alive, not in the catacombs, but in the labyrinths of the law."[12] Story also worried about the independent development of the common law in 24 states, drawing many rules further and further from a common standard. Although case law comprised perhaps 90 percent of the state law in 1820, legislation was also significant and growing in importance: 157 volumes of state statutes (excluding session law pamphlets) had been published since 1800.[13]

Related to the concern about legal prolificacy and lack of doctrinal uniformity was a second problem of what to do with English law. Under the Blackstonian legal tradition many jurists continued to conceive of the common law as a general body of jurisprudence intended to endure. Transcendent legal principles, encapsulated in English cases, encouraged the idea of a national jurisprudence. But each state made its own determination of the viability of English law for its society.[14] Many judges had an instrumental conception of law. They ignored English precedent and formulated doctrine with the self-conscious goal of social change.[15] In some quarters English law was roundly criticized as unnecessarily

---

11 *Cook* 69.

12 Id. 48-50; Joseph Story, Progress of Jurisprudence, in Miscellaneous Writings of Joseph Story 212, 237 (William W. Story ed. 1852), quoted in *Cook* 49.

13 *Cook* 49-50.

14 Id. 53-55.

15 *Morton J. Horwitz,* The Emergence of an Instrumental Conception of American Law, 1780-1820, in Law in American History 287, 317, 326 (Donald Fleming & Bernard Bailyn eds. 1971).

mysterious and uncertain, and poorly suited to fit American legal needs. The most influential example was William Sampson's famous 1823 "Anniversary Discourse" before the New York Historical Society.[16] Sampson (1764-1836), an exiled Irish patriot, denounced the common law as "Norman subtleties" and "Saxon barbarity," and called for the enactment of a code.[17]

A third problem debated in the 1820s dealt with the institutional role of the judiciary in a common law system. Some lawyers condemned judge-made law as capricious. Edward Livingston (1764-1836), a New Yorker who moved to Louisiana in 1804, believed that judges had too much discretion and had to be restrained by definite written laws.[18]

A fourth problem involved the feasibility of interpreting American statutes. Critics complained that legislatures drafted many laws too hastily, so that they were too wordy or too poorly organized to be intelligible.[19]

The widespread perception of defects in American law in the 1820s led to a notion of law reform through codification. Charles Cook states: "Codification,

---

16 William Sampson, An Anniversary Discourse Delivered before the Historical Society of New York, on Sat., Dec. 6, 1823; Showing the Origin, Progress, Antiquities, Curiosities, and Nature of the Common Law (1824), also in Sampson's Discourse, and Correspondence with Various Learned Jurists upon the History of the Law 3 (Pishey Thompson ed. 1826); see *Cook* 58.

17 *Perry Miller,* The Life of the Mind in America: From the Revolution to the Civil War 107, 246 (1965).

18 Edward Livingston, 1 The Complete Works of Edward Livingston on Criminal Jurisprudence 91, 181, 187, 411 (1873, reprint 1968); *William B. Hatcher,* Edward Livingston: Jeffersonian Republican and Jacksonian Democrat 272, 287. Livingston wrote:

> "[The common law consists] of unwritten rules, promulgated by the judges ... of uncertain authority ... to be followed, according to some writers, however unjust or absurd; and, according to others, to be modified by the principles of *reason* and the *divine law,* that is to say, by the caprice or the bigotry, or the enthusiasm of the judge."

Livingston (supra) 91, quoted in *Mitchell Franklin,* Concerning the Historic Importance of Edward Livingston, 11 Tulane L. Rev. 163, 187 (1937).

19 *Cook* 61-62. David Field later responded to the problem of indeterminacy:

> "Another objection to the expediency of a code is its supposed uncertainty. The argument is this: In the attempt to be systematic and concise, you must of necessity leave the language open to different interpretations. Now, it is quite true that, as a word has often various meanings and a change in the structure of a sentence may suggest different ideas, it is difficult to frame a section that may not be tortured into a meaning unlike that which its framers attached to it. But it is a great mistake to consider this true only of the concise propositions of a code. Diffuseness is not a helper to clearness. The longest judicial opinions are generally the least precise and the least comprehended. As a long document is usually more obscure than a short one; as a statute of many sections is commonly less understood than one of a few; as many words tend to confusion rather than enlightenment; so a single propositon, carefully expressed and made as concise as possible, is more likely to be precise and suspectible of one meaning only, than if the same idea were put into a different form and a greater number of words."

Field, Civil Code 329-30.

as promoted in antebellum America, was, by and large, a lawyer's reform designed to remedy ills that practitioners and judges observed in the legal environment. The foot soldiers as well as the generals of the codification movement were recruited from the law guild."[20] The generals, however, were not comfortable with theory or legal philosophy. There was no American Jeremy Bentham. The American generals, including Field and Livingston, were practical men who learned their law from experience.

Experience dictated that if the codifiers were going to convince their colleagues of the merits of reform through codification, they would have to draw upon examples from other countries. Most early interest fell on the French substantive codes. Both the Penal Code and the Commercial Code were translated into English in 1811.[21] David Hoffman (1791 - 1878), Henry Dwight Sedgwick (1785 - 1831), and Joseph Story all favored the French methodology of expressing the law as exemplified in the *Code Napoléon* (1804).[22] The French achievement of codification, complete and timely, seemed to provide the single greatest source of tangible inspiration for American codifiers. Although some writers referred to Justinian's *Corpus juris civilis,* this compilation was simply too remote from American reality to serve as an effective model for law reform. The French codes, in addition, directly affected codification efforts in Louisiana.[23] The Louisiana codes, in turn, particularly the Louisiana Civil Code (1825) and the Code of Practice (1825), reaffirmed the French examples and both were available to common law jurisdictions in English.

Jeremy Bentham (1748 - 1832) is sometimes mentioned as a source of inspiration for American codifiers. His actual influence, however, is difficult to assess. First, Bentham never actually drafted a code. Second, his "speculations," as a philosopher, were often labeled "visionary" and therefore unworkable and even dangerous. Third, few reformers credited Bentham as a source of their ideas and proposals for reform. Edward Livingston, however, was a notable exception.[24]

Livingston had been a member of Congress, as well as district attorney and mayor of New York City. In 1804 he moved to the Louisiana Territory and established a successful law practice in New Orleans. Livingston became a

---

20 *Cook* 70.

21 Penal Code of the French Empire, 2 Am. Rev. Hist. & Pol. 1 - 69 (app. 1811); John Rodman, Commercial Code of the French Empire Translated for the American Review (1811); see *Cook* 71.

22 Hoffman, Legal Outlines (1829); [Sedgwick], The Common Law, 19 No. Am. Rev. 411, 435 (1824); Story (supra n. 12) 238; see *Cook* 71 - 73, 106; *Roscoe Pound,* David Dudley Field: An Appraisal, in David Dudley Field: Centenary Essays 3, 8 - 9 (Alison Reppy ed. 1949).

23 *Cook* 74.

24 Id. 74 - 75, 80, 166 - 67; see letter from Livingston to Bentham (1 July 1830), in Jeremy Bentham, 11 The Works of Jeremy Bentham 51 (John Bowring ed., 1st ed. 1843, reprint 1962).

disciple of Bentham through his reading of Etienne Dumont's three volume edition of *Traités de legislation civile et pénale* (1802), which was created from Bentham's unpublished papers. In addition, Livingston was learned in the civil law systems of France and Spain.

Livingston's first effort at law reform in Louisiana was to draft a concise statute regulating civil procedure, which the legislature adopted in 1805. Derived from his knowledge of civil law systems and his reading of Bentham, it consisted of 22 sections.[25] The Louisiana Practice Act of 1805 was primarily based on Spanish procedure, which emphasized a simplified form of pleading by petition (demanda) and answer (respuesta). The *Siete Partidas* (1256-1265) stated: "The very commencement and foundation of every lawsuit in which judgment should be rendered is when the parties come into it by complaint and answer before a judge."[26] Similarities to Anglo-American chancery practice can be attributed to the common Romano-canonical influences on both chancery and Spanish procedure.[27] Louisiana had the Spanish system of granting all remedies in a single judicial system; there was no rigid distinction between law and equity.

The idea of codification for American law reformers came from a number of sources. Americans were pragmatic in temperament, so that the possibility of a wholesale importation of a code — as in some Latin American nations after their wars of independence — was unlikely. Codifiers rather improvised their own idea of codification by borrowing selectively, as to form and as to content. Charles Cook concludes: "the codification movement was quite compatible with the essentially conservative nature of the American law reform tradition."[28]

The general American interest in codification in the 1820s was particularly focused in New York. The state's population had tripled between 1800 and 1820

---

[25] Practice Act of 1805, Acts of the Legislative Council of the Territory of Orleans of 1805, chap. XXVI (10 Apr. 1805); *Hatcher* (supra n. 18) 225; *Peter J. King*, Utilitarian Jurisprudence in America: The Influence of Bentham and Austin on American Legal Thought in the Nineteenth Century 4-5, 270-72 (1986). Livingston later described his civil procedure statute to Bentham: "A simple system was submitted, based upon the plan of requiring each party to state, in intelligible language, the cause of the complaint and the grounds of the defense." Letter from Livingston to Bentham (supra n. 24) 52, quoted in *King* (supra) 272.

[26] Las Siete Partidas (Samuel Parsons Scott trans. 1931). Part. 3, title 10, law 3, at 623. See Field's statement, infra n. 74, and his interest in Louisiana pleading, infra n. 51.

[27] *Agnes v. Judice*, 3 Martin (O. S.) 182, 185-86 (La. 1813); *McMahon* 42-46. The Practice Act made two major changes to the Spanish procedure used in Louisiana. First, it authorized trial by jury. And second, it required available witnesses to testify in open court, which led to the English practice of direct and cross-examination of witnesses. *McMahon* 43, 45-46. The importance of the jury was reduced when the Louisiana Supreme Court followed the civilian practice of full appellate review of factual issues. *Abat v. Doliolle*, 4 Martin (O. S.) 316 (La. 1816); *Martineau v. Hooper*, 8 Martin (O. S.) 699 (La. 1820); see *McMahon* 49.

[28] *Cook* 80; see id. 83.

and New York was clearly becoming the nation's premier commercial center. Law seemed to expand at a similar rate. Between 1799 and 1823, 30 volumes of common law decisions and seven volumes of chancery decisions were published. The annual session law pamphlets contained between 300 and 500 pages. Besides the proliferation of legal rules, the state's litigation rate more than doubled in the decade up to 1821. These factors, together with the legal intricacies of procedure and the many delays, pushed discontent to the point where William Sampson's 1823 discourse mobilized demand for legal reform through codification. The most significant direct influence on the ensuing debate from another jurisdiction came from Louisiana. Reformers induced the *New York Review* and *Atheneum Magazine* to reprint the letters of Charles Watts, a former New York lawyer practicing in Louisiana and a zealous convert to codification.[29]

In this milieu David Field began his law apprenticeship in 1825 in the New York City law office of Henry and Robert Sedgwick. Henry Dwight Sedgwick in 1822 had published *The English Practice,* a stinging critique of English law.[30] Two years later he wrote that a written code was the remedy for the defects William Sampson had identified. "The laws should be as simple as is consistent with the multiple relations of society, . . . they should be intelligible, that they may be understood."[31] Field was admitted to the bar in 1828 and became Henry Sedgwick's law partner.[32]

The law reformers' push for codification, however, fell short and resulted in only a half success: statutory revision. The New York legislature in 1824 turned its attention to this issue by appointing three revisers. In 1825 it passed an act giving the revisers broad authority to redevelop New York (and incorporated British) statute law, but not to tamper with the common law. This preclusion so concerned New York's most outspoken codifier, William Sampson, that he suggested that the task was impossible and that the job would have to be redone.[33] The revisers began with an outline based on the divisions found in William Blackstone's *Commentaries.*[34] Henry Wheaton (1785 - 1848), one of the revisers,

---

29 Id. 131 - 32, 134 - 36. For Sampson's discourse, see supra text at nn. 16 - 17.

30 Sedgwick, The English Practice (1822); see *Cook* 133 - 34; Ee 11 - 14. See also supra text and n. 22.

31 Sedgwick (supra n. 22) 430, 438 - 39.

32 *H. Field* 37 - 38. As a commissioner to reform the procedural law of New York, Field wrote:

> "In a country where the people are sovereign, where they elect all officers, even the Judges themselves, where education is nearly universal, it was not long possible to keep the practice of the Courts enveloped in mystery.
>
> The Commissioners have never lost sight of these considerations. In aiming at directness and efficiency they have aimed also at diffusing a knowledge of legal proceedings, and there is, they trust, nothing in this code which any person of ordinary intelligence and education can not understand."

Final Report of the Practice Commission (31 Dec. 1849), in 1 Field Papers 291 - 92.

33 *Cook,* 136 - 37, 141 - 43; see *Sampson,* (supra n. 16), 62, 65.

called the plan a *projet*, which would allocate the statutes into five divisions: (1) internal administration and civil polity; (2) property, domestic relations, and private rights; (3) courts and civil procedure; (4) criminal law; and (5) public laws of a local and miscellaneous nature.[35]

When the revisers submitted their work on the first two parts to the legislature in 1826, it was clear that the ideology of codification colored their product. The divisions ultimately adopted in 1827 and 1828 for the Revised Statutes consisted of four parts, divided into chapters, titles, articles, and sections.[36] In part I on territorial divisions, internal administration, and civil polity, the statutes were thoroughly rewritten in simple language so that ordinary citizens or laypersons who were civil officers could understand their responsibilities. In part II on property, wills and estates, and domestic relations, alternatively, the revisers had promised to tread lightly, aware that alteration in phraseology could alter long-standing judicial decisions on property and other private law matters. Nevertheless, many changes were made, including rules based on what common law judges had decided. The revisers altered rules on expectant estates, powers, trusts, and ejectment, and they abolished the rule in Shelley's case.[37]

The revisers' reforms were, on the whole, judicious. They labored in an environment where a majority of the bench and bar opposed codification. They did not attempt to build a new structure based on a theoretical or imported model. However, they did some borrowing. Contemplating their work on penal law, which was incorporated into part IV on crimes, criminal procedure and prisons, the revisers referred to "the great experiment now making in Louisiana [Livingston's criminal code] under the auspices of an accomplished jurist, a native of this state."[38] In the end, though, the revisers achieved what most members of the legal profession supported, the idea that law should be clearly stated and systematically ordered. The New York legislature agreed when it adopted the three volumes of Revised Statutes, most sections of which went into effect on January 1, 1830. But the heart of the common law — cases — remained essentially intact. Opponents of change, furthermore, understood that the common law continued to exist as a big brother to the statutes, particularly since the latter had to be interpreted by courts.[39]

---

34 William Blackstone, Commentaries on the Laws of England, 4 vols. (1765 - 1769) was divided into the following four books: (1) rights of persons (including rights in public relations); (2) rights of things; (3) private wrongs (courts and civil procedure); and (4) public wrongs (crimes and criminal procedure).

35 *Cook* 143 - 44.

36 The Revised Statutes of the State of New York, 3 vols. (1st ed. 1829 - 1830); see 1 id. xi-xiv (1836 ed.).

37 1 - 2 id.; *Cook* 144 - 45, 149 - 50. The property law rule in Shelley's Case is found in 1 Coke Reports 93b (King's Bench 1581).

38 Report from the Commissioners Appointed to Revise the Laws of the State of New York 8 (1826), quoted in *Cook* 145; see *Cook* 151 - 52.

Part III of the 1830 Revised Statutes, entitled "An act concerning courts and ministers of justice, and proceedings in civil cases," consisted of 2,547 sections. The plan of organization was derived from William Tidd's (1760-1847) treatise on English practice.[40] According to the revisers, their goal in this part was "to prevent multiplicity of suits; to avoid fictitious, useless, and protracted forms; and to save unnecessary expense."[41] The enacted reforms included: (1) authorization for the chancellor to impose fines in the chancery court for unnecessarily verbose bills, answers, and other papers; (2) the requirement of security for injunctions; (3) permission for a defendant to rejoin several matters to a plaintiff's replication; (4) extension of chancery discovery powers to the supreme court in aid of a defendant's defense; and (5) simplification and reduction of bail in civil cases.[42] In spite of these reforms, critics from the bar and general public continued to complain about the confusion, costs, and delay associated with unchanged English pleading, the cumbersome structure and rules of trial and appellate courts, and the division between law and equity courts itself.[43] There were three editions of the Revised Statutes prior to Field's Code of Procedure: the first in 1829-1830, the second in 1835-1836, and the third in 1846-1848.[44]

The inability of the Revised Statutes to quiet discontent about court structure and procedure encouraged New York governors, beginning in 1834, to urgently request that the legislature implement further reform. David Field entered the fray in 1839 and for nearly 50 years pursued law reform, and especially codification, in New York.[45] What brought Field to believe that codification was the

---

[39] 2 Revised Statutes xiv (1836); *Cook* 151-52. The revisers described their reform in the preface to the first edition of the Revised Statutes:

> "The public statutes of this state, in force at the time of this revision, constitute the basis of the work, and have generally been incorporated in it, although their original form has seldom been preserved. For the purpose of simplifying their language, supplying their omissions, and remedying other defects; and above all, of presenting them in the systematic arrangement which was the great object of the legislature, it became indispensable to break up their long and sometimes complicated sections ... In numerous instances, also, the rules of the common law have been reduced to a written text, and inserted in their proper place in connection with the statutory provisions on the subject to which they relate; whilst in other instances those rules have been enlarged, modified or varied, the more fully to conform them to the nature of our government, and the habits and exigencies of the people."

1 Revised Statutes xi (1836).

[40] William Tidd, 1-2 The Practice of the Court of King's Bench in Personal Actions: With References to Cases of Practice in the Court of Common Pleas (1st American ed. 1807).

[41] 1826 Report (supra n. 38), quoted in *John T. Fitzpatrick,* Procedural Codes of the State of New York, 17 Law Libr. J. 12, 13 (1924).

[42] *Fitzpatrick* (supra n. 41) 13-14.

[43] *Cook* 185-86.

[44] McKinney's Consolidated Laws of New York Annotated: 1 Statutes ix, n. 3 (1971).

[45] See letter from Field to Gulian C. Verplanck, New York state senator (26 Dec. 1839), in 1 Field Papers 219-23.

correct solution to the problems of New York's legal system? Henry Field, David Field's biographer, listed three sources for David Field's exposure to ideas about codification: (1) reading the codes and writings of Edward Livingston, (2) reading William Sampson's "Anniversary Discourse"; and (3) associating with his law partner Henry Sedgwick.[46]

In addition, Field traveled in Europe for 14 months during 1836-1837 after the death of his wife and daughter. Searching for models useful in improving the chaotic American law he had experienced, he observed and compared the English and continental legal systems. Since childhood Field admired the order and rigorous logic of mathematics and science, and later wished to extend it to law. Having studied French and Spanish in 1824, he sneered at Anglophiles who were unable to read foreign languages. His travel to France, Italy, Germany, and other lands reinforced his respect for civil law systems and especially the French codes.[47]

Bentham was likely a minor influence on David Field. Bentham and his disciples, especially Sir Samuel Romilly (1757-1818), could have helped Field question the common law and to see the value of reform through statutes. But Field's concept of codification varied from the iconoclastic vision of Bentham, whose method was essentially deductive, based on first principles. Field was eclectic, retaining from the common law what was useful, borrowing from the civil law what appealed to his sense of justice and natural law, and synthesizing the rest. Field did not want to destroy the common law or to begin anew with utilitarian axioms; his goal was to preserve the existing law's essence by simplifying it and organizing it. Field believed that America was in the disorderly status of France before Napoleon or Byzantium before Justinian. Codes could establish order and make law intelligible for lawyer and layperson alike.[48]

---

46 *H. Field* 43-44; see *Cook* 188; *Ee* 14; *Subrin* 311, 352 n. 53.

47 *Ee* 4, 14-15, 18-19, 21; *H. Field,* 39-41. During his lifetime Field made 59 trips to Europe. *Alison Reppy,* The Field Codification concept, in David Dudley Field: Centenary Essays 17, 52 (Alison Reppy ed. 1949).

48 *King* (supra n. 25) 321, 323, 325; *Reppy* (supra n. 47) 18-19, 30; see Field, Civil Code 326; Field, First Report (supra n. 7), in 1 Field Papers 310. Field wrote about his vision of codification:

"Law ist the growth of time and circumstance. An original system of jurisprudence, founded upon mere theory, without reference to national characteristics, habits, traditions, and usages, would be a failure. The science of government and law is progressive; new regulations spring from necessity, or are suggested by experience, and the application of the rules of justice to human affairs is constantly modified by the changing circumstances of society ...

All the laws of a State arrange themselves under one or the other of two general divisions, substantive and remedial laws; or, in other words, the laws which contain the rules of property and conduct, and those which prescribe the mode of enforcing these rules. The latter division has been already brought into the Codes of Civil and Criminal Procedure, which were presented to the Legislature in 1850, by the Commissioners on Practice and Pleadings ...

When the codification is finished, there will remain no portion of the Revised Statutes

Field gave four reasons for codification. One, it supports the principle of separation of powers by reducing the role for judges in ex post facto lawmaking. Judges should resolve disputes according to pre-established law and not according to their arbitrary will. Two, it gives citizens, who are required to obey the laws, an opportunity to know what the laws are. Three, it brings greater certainty to the law, so that lawyers may function more efficiently. And four, the experience of history teaches that no people who have once exchanged case "guess" law for codes have ever turned back.[49]

The most important vehicle for Field's ideas about the codification and content of civil procedure rules probably came from the 1825 Louisiana Code of Procedure.[50] Field explicitly referred to the civil procedure of Louisiana in his writing, especially the fact that Louisiana pleadings consisted of only a petition and answer.[51] Edward Livingston, along with Louis Moreau Lislet (1767-1829) and Pierre Derbigny (1767-1829), drafted the Louisiana Code's *projet,* drawing from French, Spanish, and Roman civil law sources as well as the common law tradition. An eclectic code, the projet cited: Justinian's *Digesta, Codex,* and *Institutiones;* the Spanish *Siete Partidas* (1265), *Recopilación de las Indias* (1680), Juan de Hevia Bolaños's *Curia Philípica* (1767),[52] and José Febrero's *Adicionado* (1806-1808);[53] the French scholars Jean Domat (1625-1696) and Robert Pothier (1699-1772); Livingston's 1805 practice act, and other Louisiana statutes and supreme court decisions.[54] Both the projet and the 1825 Code were printed in English as well as French.

---

not included in it, or in the special laws mentioned in the analysis ... The whole of the third part of the Revised Statutes is already included in the reported complete Code of Civil Procedure ...

When the outline sketched in this analysis shall have been filled up, the Commissioners hope that there will be presented to the people of this State, in a condensed and convenient form, the great body of their laws — not the laws of England, nor the laws of France, nor yet the laws of Rome, but the laws of the foremost American Commonwealth, formed out of those which were brought in by our ancestors, and those which have sprung from the genius and the wants of our land."

Field, First Report (supra) 311, 313-14.

49 Field, Codification, 20 Am. L. Rev. 1 (1886), in 3 Field Papers 238, 239-41. Cf. Livingston's similar view on judicial caprice: supra text and n. 18.

50 *McMahon* 51.

51 E. g., Field, What Shall Be Done (infra n. 57) 232, 241-42, 250. See also Field, Comparative Jurisprudence of the English Peoples (1885), in 3 Field Papers 137, 143.

52 Hevia Bolaños, 1-2 Curia Philípica (1767) (vol. 1 treated lawyers, judges, and civil procedure).

53 Febrero, 1-7 Febrero adicionado, ó librería de escribanos: instruccíon teórico y práctica para principiantes (1806-1808).

54 *McMahon* 46-50. *John H. Tucker, Jr.,* Source Books of Louisiana Law: Part II — The Code of Practice, 7 Tulane L. Rev. 82, 84-87 (1932); A Republication of the Projet of the Code of Practice of Louisiana of 1825, in 2 Louisiana Legal Archives 1-180 (1937) (cited: Code of Practice Projet); see *Raphael J. Rabalais,* The Influence of Spanish Laws and Treatises on the Jurisprudence of Louisiana: 1762-1828, 42 La. L. Rev. 1485, 1491-1505 (1982). Robert Pothier, 1-2 Traité de la procédure civile (9th

Field saw in the 1840s that the legislature was unwilling to heed the governor's annual plea for procedural reform. In 1846 a constitutional convention provided an opportunity to break the political logjam. Field and others argued for judicial reorganization and the convention acted to abolish separate equity and law courts, merging their jurisdiction in the supreme court.[55] The distinct pleading and practice systems of equity and law, however, remained. Therefore, the convention directed in the new constitution that the legislature should indirectly carry out the reform of procedure by the "appointment of three Commissioners, whose duty it shall be to revise, reform, simplify, and abridge the rules and practice, pleadings, forms, and proceedings, of the courts of record of this State."[56]

After the 1846 constitution was ratified, Field wrote *What Shall Be Done with the Practice of the Courts?*[57] It urged a revolutionary change in New York procedure, abolishing the forms of action and implicitly following the model of codification.[58] Field's seeming radicalism precluded his initial appointment to the three member Commission on Practice and Pleadings. But given the spirit of general support for meaningful reform, the conservative commission member resigned and in 1847 Field was appointed in his place. Three like-minded commissioners now drafted in five months what the legislature enacted as the 1848 Code of Procedure.[59]

II. The Form of Codification

David Field had no British or other common law code of procedure to follow in drafting the New York Code. Part III of the New York Revised Statutes on courts and civil procedure, although helpful, did not go far enough in implementing the reforms that Field felt were necessary. William Fisch, drawing on the work of Robert Millar, has recently discussed the question of influence in terms of the following model. Traditional American common law courts, on the one hand, were seen as English (that is, feudal Germanic), dominated by the principles of rigid pleading, orality, and publicity. Equity courts, on the other hand, were

---

ed. 1776) was a commentary on the French Ordonnance civile pour la réformation de la justice (or Code Louis) of 1667, which formed the foundation for the 1806 Code de procédure civile. *Tucker* (supra) 85-86. For the role of Livingston, see supra text at nn. 18, 25, 54.

55 N. Y. Const. of 1846, art. XIV, § 8; David Dudley Field, Reorganization of the Judiciary (1846); see *H. Field* 46-47; *Cook* 189; *Ee* 31-32.

56 N. Y. Const. of 1846, art. VI, § 24.

57 David Dudley Field, What Shall Be Done with the Practice of the Courts? Shall It Be Wholly Reformed? Questions Addressed to Lawyers (1847), in 1 Field Papers 226-60.

58 "[I]t appears to me the wiser and safer plan, when we are about it, to make a radical reform; in short, to go back to first principles, break up the present system, and reconstruct a simple and natural scheme of legal procedure." Id. at 229.

59 *H. Field* 48-49; see *Cook* 190-91; *Ee* 33-35.

viewed as Romano-canonical, dominated by the opposite principles of flexibility between pleading and proof, documentation, and secrecy. The most important difference between the two types of practice was the use of a jury trial in common law courts. The existence of a jury forced common law actions into two distinct stages (pleading and proof), while these two elements were blended in equity procedure.[60]

Field believed that the procedures of both common law and equity courts were defective, though in different ways. Although neither Bentham nor Story favored merger of the two systems into a single court, the New York Constitution of 1846 had settled that matter and Field now urged completion of the merger process by adopting a uniform procedure for both types of lawsuits. For the pleading stage, Field drew primarily on the Romano-canonical system as illustrated by French and Spanish law. He clearly rejected verbose English and American equity pleading, which was expected to fully state the detailed contentions of the parties. For the proof stage, alternatively, Field preferred the common law jury, extending it even to equity cases. In part this was justified by efficiency, since the jury trial permitted a rapid examination of witnesses, and in part by justice, since Field distrusted the discretion of chancery judges.[61]

In short, the overall structure of the New York Code of Civil Procedure[62] was eclectic: parts of it were influenced by Romano-canonical procedure, reflected imperfectly in American equity courts, and parts were derived from common law procedure. I now consider the form of the Field Code in three dimensions as it relates to influence from the civil law tradition: (1) division of the code; (2) scientific categories; and (3) definitions.

First, the New York Code was divided into parts, titles, chapters, and sections. The initial division consisted of an introductory "General Definitions and Divisions," "Part I: Of the Courts of Justice, and Their Jurisdiction," and "Part II: Of Civil Actions." The introductory part had eight sections, part I had seven titles (only one of which used chapters) for a total of 60 sections, and part II had 15 titles (eight of which used chapters) for a total of 405 sections.

This method of classifying rules, using functional divisions of increasing specificity, was a great advance over the usual American technique, still found

60 *William B. Fisch,* The Influence of German Civil Procedural Thinking and of the ZPO in the United States, in: Das deutsche Zivilprozeßrecht und seine Ausstrahlung auf andere Rechtsordnungen 400, 403 (Walter J. Habscheid ed. 1991); *Robert Wyness Millar,* The Formative Principles of Civil Procedure, in A History of Continental Civil Procedure 3, 27-39 (Arthur Engelmann et al. eds. 1927).

61 *Fisch* (supra n. 60) 403-05; *Subrin* 336-38.

62 The version of the Field Code that I examine in this and the next part was adopted by the New York legislature in 1849. It was the final draft accepted in New York. It differed from the 1850 version in that it excluded evidence and criminal procedure and from the 1848 original since it added 82 sections for a total of 473 sections. See supra text and nn. 7-9.

today,[63] of alphabetically arranging divisions, many of which had limited utility and were used primarily as locations to store the legislature's annual output. To illustrate, part I of the Code concerned courts and their jurisdiction. Title I, "Of the Courts in General," was then followed by six titles treating specific courts in detail.

Consider further part II on civil actions. The order of the 15 titles more or less tracked the usual manner in which a lawyer would think about his case.

Title I: Their Form
Title II: Time of Commencing Them
Title III: Parties
Title IV: Place of Trial
Title V: Manner of Commencing Them
Title VI: Pleadings
Title VII: Provisional Remedies
Title VIII: Trial and Judgment
Title IX: Execution of the Judgment
Title X: Costs
Title XI: Appeals
Title XII: Miscellaneous Proceedings
Title XIII: Actions in Particular Cases
Title XIV: Existing Suits
Title XV: General Provisions

The use of functional divisions was further illustrated at the level of titles. Divisions that made sense to the Code's audience helped to demystify the law and in a democratic political system should give the rules more legitimacy. Examine title VI on pleadings.

Chapter I: Complaint
Chapter II: Demurrer
Chapter III: Answer
Chapter IV: Reply
Chapter V: General Rules
Chapter VI: Mistakes in Pleading and Amendments

Functional divisions to clarify legislative enactments, and the idea of codes itself, of course were part of the 19th century codification movement that we associate with the civil law tradition. The Field Code took the process for civil procedure a step beyond what was accomplished in part III of the New York Revised Statutes of 1830. The Revised Statutes' functional divisions — parts, chapters, titles, articles, and sections — were likely drawn from the existing terminology of the French and Louisiana codes. But the content of the headings

63 E. g., Illinois Revised Statutes, 148 chaps. (1979); Oklahoma Statutes 1981, 85 titles (1982).

was influenced more by Blackstone's *Commentaries* and Tidd's *Practice of the Court.*[64]

Examine the Louisiana Code of Practice (1825) and the French Code of Civil Procedure (1806). The Louisiana Code was divided into parts, titles, chapters, sections, subsections, and articles. The first four divisions tracked the New York Code. Greater subdivision may have been necessary for the Louisiana Code since it had 1,161 articles. It was divided into two parts like Field's Code — "Part I: Of Civil Actions," and "Part II: Of Procedure before the Courts" (De la Procédure devant les Tribunaux).[65] This reversed the New York order, but the two parts superficially followed the same conceptual division. A difference was that most of the rules regulating the flow of a first instance proceeding in Louisiana occurred in part II (title 1, chapters 2-11) rather than in the part "Civil Actions." The part "Procedure before the Courts," however, did include all the rules of jurisdiction as in New York. The Louisiana court structure (ordinary, probate, justice of the peace, supreme), furthermore, was substantially simpler than in New York, even after the 1846 merger of law and equity.

The Louisiana Code may also have influenced the breakdown in the New York Code for part II, titles I to XV treating civil actions. The match was only rough, as the following partial listing of New York titles shows, with the Louisiana counterpart on the right.

New York		*Louisiana*
I	Form	Part I, title I, chaps. 1-3
III	Parties	Id. chaps. 5-6
IV	Place	Id. chap. 4
V	Manner	Id.
VI	Pleadings	Part II, title I, chap. 2
VII	Provisional	Id.
VIII	Trial	Id. chap. 5
IX	Execution	Id. chap. 7
XI	Appeals	Id. chap. 6
XII	Miscellaneous	Id. chap. 11
XIII	Particular	Id. chaps. 8-9

The French Code was divided into parts, books, titles, sections, and articles. This division had fewer similarities to the New York Code than did the Louisiana Code. The French Code, however, for its 1,042 articles was separated into two

---

64 See supra text at nn. 35, 40.

65 The Louisiana Code of Practice was originally written in French and then translated into English. Occasionally I use my translation of a French term when it is more informative than the 1825 English translation provided for the entire Code. I derived article numbers for the 1825 Code from a comparative table for the Code and projet, in Code of Practice Projet (supra n. 54) app. B, 69-70.

parts — "Part I: Procedure before the Courts," and "Part II: Special Procedures." Although the French part I roughly paralleled in structure part II of the same name in Louisiana, there were significant differences between the French Code and both of the American procedural codes. First, Charles Seruzier, writing in 1845, stated that the plan for part I of the French Code was based on the following definition by Robert Pothier: "Civil Procedure is the totality of the rules by which one must file a claim, defend it, intervene, examine, judge, appeal judgments, and finally carry them out."[66] This definition excluded matters of court structure or jurisdiction, which in France were placed into an auxiliary code of judicial organization. This model of creating a special code or law was followed in most civil law countries, but was not used in either Louisiana or New York, which incorporated judicial organization and jurisdiction rules into their codes. Second, the French Code excluded rules about the nature of suits or the legal capacity of parties to sue or be sued, which were included in the American codes. Third, the naming of the 25 titles in part I, book II (First Instance Courts) of the French Code revealed a distinct tradition of procedure-emphasizing documents, judicial examination, and experts — that did not have a counterpart in Louisiana or New York.

The second factor related to form concerned the use of scientific categories. This was an attempt to reify notions about law so that they might have unquestioned validity. For Field, one of his principal goals in the New York Code was to mandate a single form of action (the civil action), abolish the writ system, and simplify pleadings. A few examples of reform categories appeared in the Code. "Remedies . . . are divided into, (1) Actions; (2) Special proceedings" (§ 1). "Actions are of two kinds. (1) Civil; (2) Criminal" (§ 4). "No other pleading shall be allowed than the complaint, answer, rely and demurrers" (§ 156). "Issues arise upon the pleadings, when a fact or conclusion of law is maintained by the one party and controverted by the other. They are of two kinds: (1) Of law; and (2) Of fact" (§ 248). "There shall be three kinds of execution; one against the property of the judgment debtor; another against his person; and the third to the delivery of the possession of real or personal property" (§ 286).

In contrast to the Louisiana Code, however, the use of conceptual categorization in New York was quite minimal and rudimentary. In Louisiana, much of part I on civil actions (123 articles) was concerned with the classification of actions, suits, and jurisdiction in different ways followed by definitions of the terms. I will use actions as an example. Actions are personal, real, and mixed (art. 2). Actions are divided into civil and criminal (art. 10). Personal actions arise out of contracts, quasi-contracts, delicts, and quasi-delicts (art. 28). Real actions are

[66] Charles Seruzier, Historical Summary of the French Codes with French and Foreign Bibliographical Annotations concerning the General Principles of the Codes followed by a Dissertation on Codification 66 (French ed. 1845, David A. Combe & Martha Scott Gruning trans. 1979).

petitory (sue the person in possession), possessory (person in possession sues for disturbance of his rights), or hypothecary (mortgage claim) (arts. 43, 46, 62). Proceedings are ordinary, executory, or summary (art. 146). This was obviously a more complex conceptual scheme; it reflected Louisiana's direct connection to the Spanish, French, and Roman law sources of that era.

The French Code was an interesting contrast to the Louisiana Code. While many of the same categories were mentioned in thc French Code, they were mentioned only in passing as if the audience for the work would be familiar with its conceptual scheme. Lawyers and judges in France were university educated in law. The Code contemplated the use of licensed avoués (see part I, book II, titles III, XVII) and discouraged parties from arguing their own case (art. 85). In Louisiana, as in the rest of the United States, there were no university law schools in the European sense. Most lawyers learned their craft by reading law as an apprentice or attending schools that were run as large law offices. Part I of the Louisiana Code, with its extensive classifications and many definitions, thus served an educative purpose useful to the Louisiana bench and bar.

Definitions, the last factor to analyze, tended to follow the pattern just described for scientific categories. The Louisiana Code had the most, the French Code the least, and the New York Code was in the middle. I present some examples from New York. "An action is an ordinary proceeding in a court of justice, by which a party prosecutes another party for the enforcement or protection of a right, the redress or prevention of a wrong, or the punishment of a public offence" (§ 2). Field narrowed this definition in the title on the form of civil actions: "there shall be in this state, hereafter, but one form of action, for the enforcement or protection of private rights and the redress of private wrongs, which shall be denominated a civil action" (§ 69). The Louisiana Code's definition contained a similar idea: "A civil action is one that is brought for private interest ..." (art. 13).

Other definitions were scattered throughout the New York Code. "A judgment is the final determination of the rights of the parties in the action" (§ 245). "An issue of law arises, (1) Upon a demurrer to the complaint, answer or reply ..." (§ 249). "An issue of fact arises, (1) Upon a material allegation in the complaint controverted by the answer; or, (2) Upon new matter in the answer controverted by the reply ..." (§ 250). "A trial is the judicial examination of the issues between the parties, whether they be issues of law or of fact" (§ 252). "Every direction of a court or judge, made or entered in writing, and not included in a judgment, is denominated an order" (§ 400). "An application for an order is a motion ..." (§ 401). The last title concluded with several definitions for real property, personal property, property, district, and clerk (§§ 462-466).

Some of these definitions may have been borrowed from the Louisiana Code. For instance, the New York Code distinguished between a general verdict and a special verdict. "A general verdict, is that by which the jury pronounce generally upon all or any of the issues, either in favor of the plaintiff or defendant. A special verdict is that by which the jury find the facts only leaving the judgment to the court" (§ 260). In Louisiana, the Code defined the two verdicts. "A general verdict is that by which the jury pronounce at the same time on the fact and the law, either in favor of plaintiff or defendant" (art. 520). "A special verdict is that by which the jury find (donne) the facts only, leaving to the court the right of giving judgment on these facts and the law applicable to them" (art. 521).

The most significant definition, nevertheless, for the influence of the Field Code on other American jurisdictions, was the one for "civil action." Its central place in both the New York and Louisiana codes, and its absence in the French Code, invites speculation that Field made use of the Louisiana Code along with other sources in drafting his own rules for New York.

Aggregating all three dimensions for the form of codification, it appears much more likely that the Louisiana Code rather than the French Code influenced David Field in drafting the rules for the New York Code of Civil Procedure.

III. The Substance of Codification

The principal goal of Field's procedure code was "to expedite the predictable enforcement of discretely articulated rights."[67] This task would be facilitated, according to Field's New York experience, by counteracting the potential tyranny of unrestrained, politically appointed, judges. On the one side, legislators, guided by educated commissioners, would create the new procedural law in the form of an intelligible code. On the other side, jurors would be involved more often in trials as a way to reduce judicial determination of factual issues. The Code extended the jury trial right beyond those cases provided for in the state constitution (§ 253).[68] Moreover, a party became automatically entitled to the jury right without previously requesting it, the choice of verdict (general or special) in most cases was up to the jury (§ 261), and there was no provision for a directed verdict.

The Field Code exemplified for procedure the Enlightenment goal of melding democracy, Reason, and natural rights. In France, separation of powers theory greatly reduced the role of the judge in lawmaking and shifted it more fully to the legislature. The French Code of Civil Procedure contained the rules judges were to follow. Field could agree with that idea. In addition, Field's laissez-faire liberalism led him to empower the jury at the expense of the equity judge in ascertaining facts. In post-revolutionary France, after briefly trying the civil jury,

---

[67] *Subrin* 327.

[68] Cf. N. Y. Const., art. I, § 2 ("in all cases in which it has been heretofore used").

the French eliminated it before the enactment of the 1806 Code. Louisiana's Code of Practice, in contrast to the French Code, included a long section on jury trials (arts. 493 - 532). We have seen how the New York and Louisiana definitions on general and special verdicts were similar.[69] New York also followed the Louisiana rule permitting the jury to decide whether to elect a general or special verdict (arts. 521 - 522).

Some of the major reforms in the Field Code — simplified pleading, liberal joinder of parties, and appeals — will be investigated here to determine whether the substance of these reforms can be traced to the French or Louisiana codes.[70]

Pleading reform was at the heart of Field's proposal, since New York still retained ten forms of action for common law cases in 1848. Critics argued that the extreme formalism of common law pleading, often relying on legal fictions, obscured both facts and the applicable law. Defendants frquently pleaded the "general issue," which kept plaintiffs in the dark about what testimony or documents would be used at trial. Equity procedure, on its side, promoted verbosity and delay. The distinction itself between law and equity was sufficiently confusing that it led many litigants to commence their disputes in the wrong court. The New York Code's revolutionary approach to these problems appeared in article 69: "The distinction between actions at law and suits in equity, and the forms of all such actions and suits, heretofore existing, are abolished." Cacophony was replaced with a new civil action, the central concept in both the Louisiana and the New York codes.[71]

In the New York Code, title VI of part II regulated pleadings. Section 142 stated: "The complaint shall contain: 1. [title of the cause, court and county for trial, and parties' names]; 2. A statement of the facts constituting the cause of action, in ordinary and concise language, without repetition, and in such manner as to enable a person of common understanding to know what is intended; 3. [demand for relief]." The Louisiana Code of Practice had a similarly worded article. "A petition is a written document, which the plaintiff addresses to a competent judge, setting forth the cause of action (les motifs de l'action), which he intends to bring against the defendant ... 4. The petition must contain a clear and concise statement of the object of the demand, as well as the nature of the title, or the cause of action (la cause d'action) on which it is founded" (art. 172). The French Code of Civil Procedure contained a similar idea, although it was incorporated into the summons rather than into a complaint or petition.[72]

---

69 See supra text at pt. II.

70 See *Reppy* (supra n. 47) 49 - 51.

71 The Commissioners' Report, citing the 1846 constitutional convention's discussion on the merger of law and equity and the need for one form of practice, pointed out that one form of action prevailed in Europe, Scotland, and Louisiana. First Report (supra n. 7) 72 - 73.

72 "The summons shall contain: 1. [date, the plaintiff's name, profession, domicile, and appointment of his lawyer (avoué)]; ... 3. The object [relief requested] of the

Two features of this similarity are noteworthy. First, the general concept of "cause of action" was used.[73] For the Field Code it became the fundamental litigation unit, around which amendment and the issues of joinder of causes and parties were resolved. Field believed formalistic concepts could reduce judicial discretion and increase certainty. Second, both codes desired to promote clear and concise pleading. Field felt that procedural simplicity meant that the rights of ordinary persons could be vindicated consistently and correctly.[74]

Field intended to reduce the prolixity of pretrial practice by permitting only four types of pleadings — the complaint, answer, reply, and demurrer (§ 156).[75] The Code authorized a reply only when an answer contained new matter (§ 153), therefore most suits in which the defendant raised no affirmative defense could complete the pleading stage in two or maybe three (with a demurrer to make dilatory objections) steps.

The Louisiana Code had even a simpler pleading scheme. The plaintiff's petition (pétition) (art. 172) was followed by either a defendant's answer (réponse) (art. 319) or his dilatory or other special defenses (exceptions et défenses) (arts. 330-331). Article 329 stated that when a defendant in his answer alleged "new facts, these shall be considered as denied by the plaintiff," and no further pleading will be allowed. "The cause is at issue" (art. 357).[76] This is the modern solution adopted in rules 7(a) and 8(d) of the Federal Rules of Civil Procedure, which deemphasize the issue-narrowing function of pleading and require it only to serve the goal of general notice.

The French treatment of pleading used a vocabulary similar to that in Louisiana, but it was premised on a much older civil law tradition that emphasized the mandatory use of university-trained lawyers (avoués) and the more active involvement of judges. The plaintiff began with a summons-complaint (ajournement) that contained the appointment of his avoué and a summary statement of his claim (art. 61). The defendant had eight days to appoint his avoué and to enter his appearance (arts. 72, 75). Under the Code no further pleadings were mandatory at this point. Usually, however, the defendant would answer with his defenses (défenses, exceptions) within 15 days (art. 77), to which the plaintiff had eight

---

demand, and a summary statement of its grounds (l'exposé sommaire des moyens); 4. [court to which the demand is brought and the number of days the defendant has to appear]" (art. 61).

73 The New York Revised Statutes (1830) used a variety of terms: action, proceeding, process, suit, cause, and case. In a few sections, the phrase "cause of action" appeared. Pt. III, chap. VI, tit. 1, § 6; ibid. tit. 3, § 1; ibid. tit. 6, art. 4, § 37; Pt. III, chap. VII, tit. 4, art. 1,§ 2 (2).

74 *Subrin* 329-30. Field argued that "the pleadings in all cases consist of complaint and answer." Field, What Shall Be Done (supra n. 57) 230.

75 The Commissioners referred to the simple pleading structure in Louisiana and Scotland. First Report (supra n. 7) 142-43.

76 The Louisiana Code provided for more complicated lawsuits by allocating most of a chapter to counterclaims (incidental demands) by the defendant (arts. 362-388).

days to reply (réponse) (art. 78). After the defendant had appeared (or failed to appear within the time limit), the plaintiff could take steps to bring the matter to a hearing (poursuivre l'audience) (arts. 79-80). The plaintiff put his case on the calendar by filing a request with the court clerk. The clerk then began a file for the case, including all pleadings (conclusions) exchanged by the parties. The file allowed the judge in charge of the case to stay advised about its status.

The New York Code supporters hoped that the emphasis on facts guided by the concepts "cause of action" and "defence" would lead the parties to learn about the other side's version of the dispute in the pleading stage. This hope was anchored to the requirement of an oath. Once a party verified by affidavit any pleading, "all subsequent pleadings, except demurrers, shall be verified also" (§ 157). Field believed the oath could prevent certain meritless suits and defenses, and would goad litigants to admit undisputed facts.[77] Neither the Louisiana Code nor the French Code used the oath as a mechanism to improve the truthfulness of pleadings. In the Louisiana scheme pleadings did not seem to play as large a role as that envisioned in New York. Nevertheless, parties in Louisiana could attach to a pleading "interrogatories on facts and articles" (art. 347). A party responding to these interrogatories must do so under oath, so that his answers might be used as testimony (art. 348). This type of discovery did not appear in the New York Field Code: pleadings were largely to accomplish the goal of reducing surprise at trial. Stephan Subrin makes the interesting point that after most code pleading states, following the 1938 Federal Rules, eliminated verification of pleadings, the U.S. Supreme Court returned in 1983 to a type of oath backed by sanctions in rule 11 to achive a reduction in frivolous pleadings and motions that "harass or ... cause unnecessary delay or needless increase in the cost of litigation" (rule 11). [78]

The Field Code also facilitated joining in one suit potential parties who had "an interest in the subject of the action" (§§ 117-118). The Louisiana Code of Practice adopted the Spanish concept of cumulation of actions (art. 148), which required a similar community of interest between parties on one side or the other of the lawsuit before they could be joined.[79] The Field Code, however, was more complicated, drawing on earlier liberal equity joinder and more rigid common law practice to yield a tripartite distinction between indispensable, necessary, and proper parties (§§ 117-120, 122).[80]

The concept and treatment of appeals is another area in which the Louisiana Code may have influenced Field Code provisions. The New York Code began part II, title XI: "Writs of error in civil actions, as they have heretofore existed,

---

[77] *Subrin* 330-31.

[78] Id. 331.

[79] See infra text at n. 82.

[80] See First Report (supra n. 7) 124-25.

are abolished, and the only mode of reviewing a judgment, or order, in a civil action, shall be that prescribed by this title" (§ 323). This title on "appeals" terminated the common law writ of error, which was an original writ issued out of chancery at the insistence of a party aggrieved by some error in the proceedings, authorizing the same or a superior court to examine the record upon which judgment was given. The new rule read: "Any party aggrieved may appeal in the cases prescribed in this title" (§ 325). The Louisiana Code likewise envisioned a relatively uncluttered system of appeals. "An appeal is the act by which one of the parties to a suit has recourse to a superior tribunal, in order to have the judgment of an inferior court corrected" (art. 564). "One may appeal from all final judgments . . ." (art. 565). "One may likewise appeal from all interlocutory judgments, when such judgment may cause him an irreparable injury" (art. 566). The Louisiana litigant had a right of appeal from district court in matters exceeding $ 300 to the supreme court (arts. 126, 570, 882). On the other hand, the French Code contemplated a different structure for judicial review. The term appeal (appel) covered only review of a first instance court decision by an intermediate appellate tribunal. It could result, moreover, in examination de novo of both the facts and law from the case (arts. 462-470). Further judicial review, by the French Cour de cassation, occurred under the term "pourvoi" and led solely to reconsideration of legal issues.

For other reforms in the New York Code, I could find no significant substantive link with either the Louisiana or the French Codes. Consider, for example, amendment. The Field Code liberalized a party's ability to amend his complaint or answer and to offer evidence at variance with the pleading (part II, title VI, chap. VI). Neither the Louisiana Code nor the French Code used the scheme adopted in New York of material variance, immaterial variance, and failure of proof, with the distinction between amendment of course versus amendment by leave of court.

The Field Code also liberalized joining in one suit several causes of action (§ 167) or defenses (§ 150). These rules, nevertheless, were still relatively formalistic and owed much to previous common law practice. Causes to be joined all had to fall within one of the following categories: contract; injuries to the person; injuries to property; injuries to character; real property; personal property; or suits against a trustee (§ 167). The Louisiana Code of Practice, by contrast, treated these matters under the Spanish concept of cumulation of actions (art. 148). This was a concept that freely permitted joinder of causes, but required a community of interest between parties on one side or the other of the lawsuit before they could be joined.[81]

---

[81] *McMahon* 52. French civil procedure permits joinder of claims and parties if there are sufficient common issues (connexité) so that it is efficient to try all claims with the joined parties in one action. *Peter Herzog,* Civil Procedure in France 193, 218-19 (1967).

IV. Assessment of the Civil Law Influence

The cumulative impact of the civilian idea of codification, along with numerous similarities in form and substance between the New York Code of Civil Procedure and the Louisiana and French procedural codes, make it likely that David Field directly or indirectly borrowed significant elements from the civil law tradition. Much of the French influence probably made its way to New York via Louisiana. In addition, Louisiana in its 1805 Practice Act and 1825 Code of Practice incorporated substantial Spanish procedural doctrine. Thus, Louisiana was the cultural intermediary between continental Europe and those states that adopted the Field Code of Civil Procedure.

Although the Field Code is one of the watershed events in the history of American civil procedure, its civilian characteristics were gradually eroded by a resurgence of the common law legislative style and by the power of a non-university trained bench and bar that clung to traditional modes of thought, suspicious of the civilian values of simplicity, order, and predictability in legal rules.[82]

Thus, when the New York Commissioners on Practice and Procedure came back to the legislature in 1850 with provisions on evidence and criminal procedure to complete the Code of Procedure, the legislature balked. Common law practitioners by then had struggled through two years of code pleading. Lawyers and judges both felt uncomfortable relying on a small number of principles systematically arranged in a code. Their education, based on Blackstone, emphasized the essential validity of the common law and predisposed them to view reform through the prism of history. As the years passed the bar attempted to return to the familiar routine before 1848 by amending the code to make it more detailed and specific. By the time the code was repealed in 1877 it contained over 3,000 articles.[83]

The inclusion of a civil law style and content in the Field Code was significant, nevertheless, because it affected more than just New York. Newer states from Iowa to the west provided fertile ground for an interest in codes.[84] Before the end of the Civil War, 16 states or territories adopted the Field Code. Since these jurisdictions had only recently been populated by settlers and immigrants, there was less vested interest in established property rights or in the intricacies of the common law system. In addition, lawyers in the new states and territories were from various jurisdictions and tended to be young. A codified system of procedure,

---

82 See *Pound* (supra n. 22) 13-14.

83 *Cook* 193. As Field himself later reflected: "we might as soon expect a Mohammedan to take a Christian to his bosom as a case lawyer, no, I might say, a case-hardened lawyer, to take a code to his." Field, A Short Reply (supra n. 3), quoted in id.

84 Of the jurisdictions that adopted the Field Code prior to 1865, only Georgia was among the original 13 states. *Cook* 198.

simple to understand, promising order and certainty, was an attractive alternative to the complex common law system.[85] The Field Code could be enacted, with minor changes as necessary, without straining the local legal talent.[86]

Those American states that did not adopt the Field Code brought what order they could to their procedural law through the proliferation of case report digests and treatises.[87] Once the Field Code, or digests and treatises, brought some uniformity to procedure, lawyers and the general public felt that the crisis of doctrinal chaos and judicial arbitrariness had passed. Thus a small dose of reform immunized the remainder of the common law system of procedure from major change. One might say that Field was born too late. The intense rationalism of the 18th century, represented by the French Codes, Bentham, and Anton Thibaut (1772-1840) in Germany, was replaced by the 1860s with the historical school of jurisprudence and its emphasis on the organic development of law, represented by German legal science, Sir Henry Maine (1822-1888), Friedrich von Savigny (1779-1861), and James Carter (1827-1905).[88] David Field's legacy of procedural reform prevailed, however, enriched by recourse to foreign experience. His legacy was renewed many decades later, when the next major wave of reform arrived with the Federal Rules of Civil Procedure in 1938.

---

85 Early enactment in California and Arizona might have been helped by the local population's prior experience with the civil law tradition under Mexico and Spain.

86 *Cook* 197-98.

87 E. g., *James Gould,* A Treatise on the Principles of Pleading, in Civil Actions (3d ed. 1849); *Joseph Story,* Commentaries on Equity Pleadings, and the Incidents Thereof, according to the practice of the Courts of Equity, of England and America (5th ed. 1852).

88 See *Pound* (supra n. 22) 16.

STEFAN RIESENFELD

The Impact of German Legal Ideas and Institutions on Legal Thought and Institutions in the United States

To the student of comparative law there can be no doubt that the legal systems of the varius nations do not develop in complete independence but that legal ideas, doctrines, techniques and institutions originating in one are studied, adapted and accepted by others. Language, cultural and political differences may bar or delay that process, but viewed from a broad perspective national boundaries do not isolate legal scholarship or institutional innovations.

In 1829 the German law professors Mittermaier und Zachariä established the Kritische Zeitschrift für Rechtswissenschaft und Gesetzgebung des Auslandes which was designed to keep German-speaking legal scholars informed about developments abroad, especially in other European nations. In the exposition of the purpose of the new periodical Zachariä expressed the hope that it would be read also abroad since "the German legal literature seems to gain more and more ground abroad, especially in France."[1]

The board of editors included scholars from many European countries, among them Foelix in Paris, a native of Frankfurt / Main and correspondent with Justice Story.

My paper is designed to show that, how and the extent to which German scholarship and German legal institutions were transmitted and accepted in the United States.

I. The Channels of Transmission

In a famous speech which the late Max Rheinstein delivered at the annual meeting of the German Society of Comparative Law to celebrate its twentieth anniversary he propounded the thesis that throughout history there have been key-figures in the legal professions who — whether as members of the practicing bar, members of the academic profession, members of the bench or counselors of commercial and industrial enterprises — have been the motors of progress.

[1] *Zachariä,* Über den Zweck dieser Zeitschrift, 1 Krit. Ztschr. f. Rechtsw. u. Gesetzgebg., 1 at 42 (1829).

He called them Rechtshonoratioren.[2] More often than not they looked to foreign materials as source or confirmation of their inspiration. To the extent that these reformers were teachers and writers their ideas and proposals came to fruition only after their impact on their students and contemporaries in the legislatures or on the bench.

Without attempt of being exhaustive, the transmission to the United States of foreign legal thought and institutional arrangements, especially in Germany, is tied to names like Francis Lieber, Joseph Story, John Chipman Gray, Oliver W. Holmes, Roscoe Pound, Edwin Patterson, Karl Llewellyn, and John Dawson. It must not be overlooked, however, that some of these notions came to the United States by way of England or France, through the works of Austin, who had studied in Germany, or Frederick Pollock or R. Saleilles.

Perhaps one of the most interesting episodes in this intellectual legal history is the relation between Lieber, Story, Foelix and Mittermaier. Francis Lieber,[3] was a native of Berlin (born on March 18, 1798) who, because of his liberal activities, had become a *persona non grata* in reactionary Prussia, and been forced to study at Jena, the only University open to him, where he received a doctor's diploma (Dr. of Philosophy) only a few months after his matriculation. After participation in the Greek revolt against Turkish domination which exposed him to treachery and mistreatment, he found refuge in the home of Niebuhr, the famous discoverer of a fragment of Gaius, who was serving as Prussian ambassador at Rome. His host arranged for his return to Prussia where, for a while, Lieber engaged in literary activities. Ultimately, however, he was forced to find a new existence abroad and after a one year's stay in England, decided to emigrate to the United States. There he settled at Boston where he conceived the plan of composing an American encyclopedia and found a publisher who appointed him as editor of the new literary venture.

These editorial responsibilities brought him in contact with the most important figures in American law, in particular Joseph Story and Peter Duponceau.[4] Joseph Story agreed to and did write — although anonymously — the law articles of the Encyclopedia Americana. He became a firm friend of Lieber and through him established contacts with Lieber's close German friend, Professor Mittermaier at Heidelberg[5] and the ex-German French advocate-scholar Foelix.

Without listing all the achievements[6] of Lieber, it should be mentioned that he gained international fame as draftsman of the General Orders No. 100, entitled

[2] *M. Rheinstein,* Die Rechtshonoratioren und ihr Einfluß auf Charakter und Funktionen der Rechtsordnungen, 34 Rabels Z. 1 (1970).

[3] *Frank Freidel,* Francis Lieber, Nineteenth-Century Liberal, 1968; *Lewis R. Harley,* Francis Lieber, His Life, Times and Political Philosophy, 1899.

[4] *Freidel,* Francis Lieber, at p. 69.

[5] Story's Commentaries on the Constitution were reviewed by Mohl in Vol. 7 of the Kritische Zeitschrift.

Instructions for the Government of Armies of the United States in the Field, constituting the first code of rules of land warfare. International law became one of his main concerns until his death in 1872. One year later one of his last projects, the founding of the Institute of Internationl Law, became reality.

A generation later, John Chipman Gray and Roscoe Pound (1870 - 1964) imported the fruits of German legal scholarship into American legal thought. Pound himself described his familiarization with German ideas in the Preface to his 5-volume work on Jurisprudence:

> "In 1887 when I was in my junior year in college my father gave me Holland's Elements of Jurisprudence, Amos' Science of Law, and Maine's Ancient Law. In the next two years I read them over and over ... Thus I came to the Harvard Law School in 1889 with very confused ideas of law. Professor Gray in his preliminary lectures on the law of property introduced me to Austin ... What counted more ... he led me to read Sohm's Institutionen des Römischen Rechts (not then translated) and through Sohm I came to read Puchta's Cursus der Institutionen and the general part of Savigny's System des heutigen Römischen Rechts ... Between 1890 and 1900 I began the course of systematic reading of all I could lay hand upon in Roman law, comparative law, jurisprudence and legal history which I have kept up ever since."

Edwin W. Patterson (1889 - 1965) was Cardozo Professor of Jurisprudence at the Columbia University law school from 1945 to 1957, after having been a professor of that law school since 1922.[7] Like Pound, who had been his teacher in 1920, he took an interest in German legal thought and sources. He made use of this knowledge in his *Jurisprudence: Men and Ideas of the Law,* 1953, which had been used in non-printed form as course materials since 1940. Patterson's "former" collaborator,[8] Karl N. Llewellyn (1893 - 1962), was perhaps that scholar in the United Stated who had the most extensive direct insights in and closest contacts with contemporary luminaries of the German legal order.[9] I met him first when, as a visiting professor at Leipzig in 1928/9, he came to the University of Breslau to deliver lectures on American legal education, which he described, in a German pun, as "Schwimm und Schwamm-Methode", because at the start the student was cast into an ocean of cases and at examination time had to release his learning like a sponge. Since I had spent some times with him I visited Lleywellyn in January 1935 the day after my arrival in the United States on my way to Berkeley. During our conversation he counseled me never to identify a proposal as based on foreign law because such a revelation would be "the kiss of death." This attitude perhaps explains why Llewellyn refrained from references to contemporary German writings and legal theories.

---

[6] One of his outstanding accomplishments was his book 'On Civil Liberty and Self-Government', 1853.

[7] About Patterson, see *H. W. Jones,* Edwin Wilhite Patterson: Man and Ideas, 57 Col. L. Rev. 607 (1957).

[8] Id. at 610.

[9] See, *Jones,* at 612.

II. Basic Notions and Methods of German origin finding acceptance in the United States

The German legal notions which influences developments in the United States, as elsewhere, to an unexplored extent were the basic legal concepts expounded by F. C. von Savigny and his disciples, in particular the concepts of legal transaction (Rechtsgeschäft) or declaration of will (Willenserklärung), contract (Vertrag), and disposition (Verfügung). Savigny discussed these subjects in the third volume of his celebrated System des heutigen Römischen Rechts (1840 - 1849), in particular in § 104 (3) and § 140. Savigny distinguished between unilateral (einseitige) und plurilateral (mehrseitige) legal transactions, called contracts, and distinguished between obligatory (obligatorische Verträge) and dispositive contracts (Veräußerungen). The term actually denotes "alienation." The German expression Verfügung (disposition) was not used either by von Savigny or Windscheid. It appeared in the German Civil Code (e. g. §§ 135 (1) and 185) and was propagated by Sohm.[10]

Savigny's terms and notions were adopted both by English and U. S. authors and today are commonly utilized in unnumerable judicial decisions and legal writings. The expression "legal transaction" was popularized by Roscoe Pound. In his discussion of Acts,[11] he wrote: "Since 1904[12] I have used the term "legal transaction" getting the hint from the New York Code of Civil Procedure.[13] ... [L]egal transaction seems to give a term as near as may be to *Rechtsgeschäft.*"[14] Incidentally, Willenserklärung or Rechtsgeschäft were not coined by Savigny but seemed to have come into use somewhat before the publications of the System des heutigen Römischen Rechts. Use of the term Rechtsgeschäft is ascribed[15] to Hugo, Savigny's teacher at Göttingen. Due to Savigny is also the distinction between obligatory and dispositive contracts although its acceptance in the United States was much delayed. Its essence is the recognition that the transfer of rights from the owner to the successor also requires an agreement between the parties, but that its effect may be conditioned on other occurrences, like registration, transfer of possession etc. It may be of interest that the Civil Code of California since its enactment in 1872 provided in §§ 1039, 1040:

---

10 *Sohm,* Institutionen (8th and 9th ed.), 201 (1899). The English edition by *Ledlie* (2d ed. 1901) correctly translated Verfügung with disposition (p. 216).

11 *Pound,* Jurisprudence, Vol. IV (1959), Ch. 26. Ch. 26 constitutes section of Part 7 with the title Analysis of General Juristic Conceptions.

12 Readings in the History and System of the Common Law (1904).

13 N. Y. Code of Civil Procedure (1849), § 167.

14 *Pound,* Jurisprudence, Vol. IV, p. 422.

15 *Brinz,* Lehrbuch der Pandekten, 2d ed. Vol. 2 (1879), § 522, p. 4; *Pernice,* Rechtsgeschäft und Rechtsordnung, VII Grünhuts Zeitschr. (1880) 465, at 468. Willenserklärung was already used in the General Law for the Prussian States.

1039 Transfer, is an act of the parties, or of the law, by which the title to property is conveyed from one living person to another.

1040 A voluntary transfer is an executed contract, subject to all rules of law concerning contracts in general; except that a consideration is not necessary to its validity.

Obviously, this corresponds to the teaching of the pandectists and prompts the assumption that D. D. Field, the drafter of the Code, was familiar with these doctrines.

In California both assignments of choses-in-action and conveyances of real property by deed are considered as non-obligatory contracts. Deeds are not operative unless accepted by the grantee. Although as late as in 1918, H. T. Tiffany, the author of a much esteemed treatise on Real Property, contradicted the view that a conveyance required acceptance as distinguished from delivery and denied the need for an acceptance and the contractual nature of a conveyance, most jurisdictions' view a conveyance as a bilateral dipositive act. Tiffany's objections are caused by his restriction of the concept of contract to an obligatoy transaction. The same metamorphosis accurred with respect to assignment, i. e. the transfer of contractual rights.[16] Today it is settled that an assignment does not require consideration.[17]

The mechanism of the conclusion of a contract by means of an offer by one party and acceptance by the offeree is likewise a doctrine which seems to have been originated by the German pandectists, subsequent to Savigny and Windscheid. I dealt with evolution of the general law of contracts in my address to the conference on Modern Perspectives of Roman-Dutch Law, held in Lesotho in 1985, entitled "The Impact of Roman Law on the Common Law System."[18] Grotius was the founder of the doctrine that a contract was formed by a promise (promissio) and its acceptance (acceptatio). In this form it was generally repeated by the civilians and we still find it presented in that form in Puchta's Cursus der Institutionen (3d ed. 1854).[19] The transition from promise to proposal or offer (Antrag) occurred in the second half of the 19th century. Offer and acceptance became the components of contracting in the German Commercial Code of 1861.[20] This analysis was adopted and much discussed by Brinz and other writers in the second half of the 19th century.[21] Sir Frederick Pollock used the terms in the first edition of his Principles of Contract (1876).[22]

---

16 *Tiffany,* Delivery and Acceptance of Deeds, 17 Mich. L. Rev. 104 (1918), 103, at 122; but contrast *Savigny,* System, Vol. III, p. 312.

17 Restatement of the Law Second, Contracts 2d., §§ 317 (1), and 327 (1) and (2); § 332.

18 1 Lesotho L. J., 267 (1985).

19 *G. Puchta,* Cursus der Institutionen, 3d. ed. Vol. 2 (1854), p. 39.

20 Allgemeines Deutsches Handelsgesetzbuch, 1861 which included rules on Antrag (offer) und Annahme (acceptance), §§ 317-322.

21 See, *Brinz,* Lehrbuch der Pandekten, Vol. IV (2d. ed.), p. 247 (1892).

There is no question that the German ideas of manifestation of intent, consensus and even "hidden dissent" (versteckter Dissens) found a home on the other side of the Atlantic.[23]

Another German heritage is found in the U. S. law of agency, where the German distinction, worked out by Laband, between the obligatory relation between the principal and agent and the agent's power of representation was consciously adopted by thc authors of the Restatement.[24]

III. Methods of Resolving Conflicts: Jurisprudence of Interests

A further undeniable impact of German ideas on legal thought in the U. S. is the "Jurisprudence of Interests" (Interessenjurisprudenz), a German school which became predominant in the second decade of the 20th century[25] and quickly took hold in the United States. *Balancing of interests*, the counterpart of the German "Interessenabwägung", was readily embraced by the prominent authorities on the bench.[26] Today balancing of interests is considered a necessary ingredient of the judicial process in the U. S. and Felix Frankfurter elevated the "accommodation of conflicting interests" to the main task in constitutional adjudication.

Of course, some of the classical conflicts of interests were discerned and attempted to be resolved since the Middle Ages. Perhaps the best-known of them was the power of a non-owner to vest a bona fide purchaser with good title, thus accomplishing a destruction or transfer of the true owner's title without his consent. Whereas Roman law adhered to the maxim "nemo plus iuris transferre potest quam ipse habet," Germanic and medieval laws developed the principle

---

22 *F. Pollock*, Principles of Contract (1876), pp. 1-8, referred expressly to Savigny's analysis in § 140 of his System and distinguished between agreements and other contracts. He also referred to the German terms Antrag und Annahme as apt technical terms for the elements of a contract. His reference to the 7th edition of Vangerow, § 603 could not be verified.

23 *Farnsworth*, Contracts (1982), p. 487: "Nor would there be a contract in any of the many cases in which in spite of apparent assent, ambiguity or vagueness masks *hidden dissent.*" Unfortunately, no authority is cited for the assertion. The statement is found in the discussion of the new idea of "misunderstanding" (Mißverständnis).

24 Restatement of the Law Second, Agency 2d., §§ 1, 6-8 (1958).

25 The leading exponents of this school were Philipp Heck (1858 - 1943) and Heinrich Stoll (1891 - 1937). Heck's three essays, Das Problem der Rechtsgewinnung (1912), Gesetzesauslegung und Interessenjurisprudenz (1914), and Begriffsbildung und Interessenjurisprudenz (1932) were reprinted in Theorie und Praxis in der Rechtswissenschaft (Dubischar ed., 1968). Stoll's 'Begriff und Konstruktion in der Lehre der Interessenjurisprudenz' appeared in Archiv für civilistische Praxis, Vol. 133 Beilage H., p. 60 (1931). The third essay by Heck and the essay by Stoll were translated into English by M. Schoch and are published under the title 'The Jurisprudence of Interests' (20th Century Legal Philosophy Series, Vol. II, 1948).

26 *Patterson*, Jurisprudence: Men and Ideas of the Law (1953), p. 463.

of "Hand-wahre-Hand."[27] The modern codifications in France, Austria, Germany, Switzerland and Italy adopt, as is well known, a wide variety of solutions which are further complicated by additional differences in the rules governing prescription.

In 1904 the German scholar Victor Ehrenberg published a pioneering article entitled Rechtssicherheit und Verkehrssicherheit, mit besonderer Rücksicht auf das Handelsregister.[28] In this article Ehrenberg showed that the great principles of "security of rights" and "security of transactions" could come into conflict and that the resolution of it required balancing which confronted the legislator or courts with intricate tasks and the need of creating special instruments like public registers. Although there is no evidence available that Ehrenberg's insights were known to scholars in the U. S., it is surprising that the antinomy between the security of rights (or security of acquisitions) and the security of transactions was clearly enunciated by Pound[29] without reference to the German writers on the subject. Through Pound, the ideas of security of rights and security of transactions became an established ingredient of legal analysis in the United States. Consultation of Westlaw has revealed a large number of decisions which rely on one or the other of these principles for their holding, frequently with direct reference to Pound. It is true that U. C. C. § 2-403 (2)-(4) which deals with the acquisition of title to goods from a non-owner does not justify its provision with he need for security of transactions or justifiable reliance on legal appearance. Nevertheless, the Restatement Second on Contracts, dealing with the subject of inconsistent assignments, states in comment (e) to § 342: "In modern times the doctrine of bona fide purchaser has been extended in the interest of security of the transactions." Professor Farnworth cites this comment in support of his corresponding views.[30]

The best example of a clear, though unacknowledged, borrowing from German developments is U. C. C. § 2-615. This section bears the caption:

> "Excuse by Failure of Presupposed Conditions"

and provides for an excuse:

> "if performance as agreed has been made impracticable by the occurrence of a contingency the non-occurrence of which was a basic assumption on which the contract was made."

Anybody familiar with the German doctrine of Geschäftsgrundlage as developed by Oertmann in 1921,[31] its history and adoption by the German Supreme

---

[27] See, *E. Anners,* Hand Wahre Hand, Studien zur Geschichte der Germanischen Fahrnisverfolgung (1952).

[28] 47 Jherings Jahrb. für die Dogmatik des bürg. Rechts, 273 (1904).

[29] *Pound,* Jurisprudence, Vol. I, pp. 423 and 424, Vol. III, pp. 292 and 293.

[30] *Farnsworth,* Contracts, 1982, p. 792, text prior to call to ftn. 19.

[31] *Oertmann,* Die Geschäftsgrundlage. Ein neuer Rechtsbegriff (1921).

Court culminating in its judgment of Nov. 4, 1925,[32] cannot doubt that Llewellyn, who was a visiting Professor in Germany not long thereafter, had plenty of opportunity to become familiar with that dovelopment and patterned his draft after this model. Oertmann's thesis which he called a new legal concept constituted a modification of Windscheid's theory of Voraussetzung (Presupposition)[33] which had been rejected by the drafters of the German Civil Code. Oertmann's teaching rested on Windscheid's ideas and recognized that a non-existence or failure of the basic assumptions of the parties on which their dealing was based (Wegfall der Geschäftsgrundlage) called for a judicial adjustment of their reciprocal obligations. Llewellyn's wording "presupposition" in the title and the phrase "occurrence of the contingency the non-occurrence of which was a basic assumption on which the contract was made" are too close to Oertmann's formulation to render independence in conception a plausible explanation. That the comments make no reference to the apparent source is sufficiently explained by the fact that Llewellyn felt that such reference would be "a kiss of death" and most of all that the Official Comment was not the work of Llewellyn but originally that of Professor Bunn. Professor Farnsworth, apparently, was unaware of the German doctrine.

IV. Acceptance of German Legal Institutions

In addition to Professor Buxbaum's example of adoption in the U. S. of a German legal institution I would like to call attention to the study by U. S. legislatures of the German system governing workers' compensation for industrial accidents[34] and other schemes of social insurance[35] and the impact of the German law and practice relative to cooperatives. Actually, the comparative study of legislation relating to cooperatives is an important and neglected aspect of compararative law.

Although the history of cooperative associations can be traced to the first days of recorded history[36] the impetus for the modern evolution and world-wide spread of cooperatives in various types of enterprises is usually attributed to the cooperative venture, organized by the Equitable Pioneers' Society in Rochdale, Lancashire, England in 1844.[37] The cooperative movement, a by-product of the industri-

---

32 RGZ 111, 320.

33 1 *Windscheid-Kipp*, Lehrbuch des Pandektenrechts (1906), §§ 97-100; *Windscheid*, Die Lehre des röm. Rechts von der Voraussetzung (1850).

34 *Riesenfeld* (with *Maxwell*), Modern Social Legislation (1950), 127-136.

35 *Riesenfeld*, 8-15.

36 *Roy*, Cooperatives: Today and Tomorrow (1964).

37 See, e. g. the entries Cooperatives in 3 International Encyclopedia of the Social Sciences (1968), 390 (authored by P. S. Florence), and 7 Encyclopedia Americana, 746 (authored by H. H. Bakkan); *H. Faust*, Geschichte der Genossenschaftsbewegung (1965).

al revolution, was joined by local artisans and farmers in many countries in Europe and North America, stimulated by ardent promoters and leaders who established personal contacts among themselves. In Germany the principal advocate of the cooperative movement as well the crafter of the legislation governing them was Hermann Schulze-Delitzsch.[38] The cradle of the German cooperative movement was the town of Eilenburg and it is well established that the cooperative movement among the German immigrants in the U. S. A. and that in their native land maintained close personal contacts.[39] It is therefore more than likely that the German legislation on cooperatives of 1867[40] and the drafters of analogous legislation in the United States[41] were aware of their counterparts.

Conclusion

The foregoing exposition should demonstrate that the Atlantic even before the advent of modern communications never barred the crossing of legal ideas and that legal traditions in the U. S. never foreclosed the impact of important legal developments elsewhere, especially in Germany. In a thoughtful essay entitled ‚Die Rezeption U. S.-amerikanischen Rechts in der Bundesrepublik Deutschland,'[42] Professor Stürner reflects on the question whether German law has received more from the law in the United States than *vice versa*. With due respect, I fear that the author underestimates the reception and adaptation of German legal phenomena (Rechtsphänomene) from the middle of the last century to the middle of the present one. The counter-reception movement (from the author's perception) may have declined in recent years; nevertheless, a long-range balance seems to show a substantial reciprocal exchange.

---

38 See, *O. Ruhmer* (with the cooperation of *R. Schlosser*), Entstehungsgeschichte des deutschen Genossenschaftswesens (1937); *Theodor Heuss*, Schulze-Delitzsch, Leistung und Vermächtnis (1956).

39 Id. at p. 77-79, 113.

40 Gesetzessammlung der Preussischen Staaten, 1867, p. 501. In 1868 the law became the law of the Norddeutsche Bund, Bundesgesetzblatt des Norddeutschen Bundes, 1868, p. 415.

41 Mich. Laws 1865, P. A. 288 (an act to authorize the formation of mechanics' and laboring men's cooperative associations); Mass. Acts and Resolves 1866, Ch. 290 (act in relation to the formation of cooperative associations); N. Y. Laws 1867, Ch. 971 (act for the incorporation of cooperative and industrial unions).

42 Festschrift für Kurt Rebmann (1989), 839-860.

RICHARD M. BUXBAUM*

The Provenance of No-Par Stock: A Comparative History

Introduction

Some years ago, while preparing a short paper on the corporation law changes occasioned by the finance-driven merger wave of the 1890s,[1] I came across the casual comment of a contemporaneous proponent thereof that the concept of no-par stock, desirable as a means to prevent naive obsession with par value as a measure of actual value, was a feature of civilian law.[2] It therefore struck me as paradoxical that the well-known German debate of the 1920s, a debate about the reform of company law needed to undo the consequences of the hyperinflation, considered and rejected the American notion of no-par stock.[3] That same debate now has resurfaced as a part of the overall discussion about the modernization of German company law in the context of improving the capability of firms to tap modern capital markets.[4] Thus, it seems interesting and worthwhile to explore this roundtrip path, whose roundtrip character also is confirmed by another

* I thank *Dr. Christian Hammerl*, LL.M., *Mr. Michel Nussbaumer*, LL.M. and *Ms. Monika Flessner*, LL.M., for their substantial research assistance.

[1] *Buxbaum*, The Relation of the Large Corporation's Structure to the Role of Shareholders and Directors: Some American Historical Perspectives, in N. Horn & J. Kocka, eds., Recht und Entwicklung der Großunternehmen im 19. und frühen 20. Jahrhundert — Law and the Formation of the Big Enterprises in the 19th and Early 20th Centuries, 243 (1979).

[2] *Remsen*, Improvement of Corporation Laws, in Proceedings of the NY State Bar Ass'n, Fifteenth Annual Meeting, 135, 138 (1892).

[3] See especially *Lehmann*, Gutachten über die Frage: Soll bei einer zukünftigen Reform des Aktienrechts eine Annäherung an das englisch-amerikanische Recht in grundlegenden Fragen stattfinden?, in I Verhandlungen des Vierunddreißigsten Deutschen Juristentags, 258 (1926) and the discussion and decision at II, 611 (1927). The debate of the 1920s is briefly reviewed in *H. Coing* and *H. Kronstein*, Die nennwertlose Aktie als Rechtsproblem, 14 f. (2d ed. 1962), in the context of their important contribution to the reopening of the issue in the 1950s.

[4] See *Kübler*, Kapitalmarktgerechte Aktien?, 44, Wertpapier Mitteilungen 1853 (1990); *Claussen*, 25 Jahre deutsches Aktiengesetz von 1965 (II), 36, Die Aktiengesellschaft, 10 (1991). See also the slightly earlier discussion of the utility of the concept for Swiss law in *P. Plattner*, Die nennwertlose Aktie de lege ferenda (1964), and the already mentioned German discussion of the 1950s and early 1960s, preceding the Aktiengesetz reform of 1965 (supra note 3).

"coincidence" concerning our approach to this kind of subject matter: While we think of the phenomenon of "the competition of legal regimes" in connection with the Chicago School of Economics, it was already explicitly noted by the German debaters during the Twenties![5] If nothing else results from the trip, it has confirmed once again Klein's point that company law "ist ein unausgesetztes von einander Lernen und Entlehnen."[6]

My aim, in increasing order of generality, is three-fold: first, to discover the actual strands of this transmission of knowledge (or at least of information); second, to test the hypothesis that the borrowing was for domestic purposes, which were not necessarily those of the society in which the borrowed instrument originated — in other words, another case of the pouring of new wine into old bottles; and third, to demonstrate the banal point that the transmission of those elements of law that, in Habermas' terms, are a medium of the systemic world of power and money is more readily accomplished than is the transmission of those elements of law that are an institution culturally embedded in the *Lebenswelt.*[7] One can also examine this last point as an "intra-institutional" issue; that is, at the level of the culture, if it deserves that label, of the business world itself. In that sense, this essay can be seen as an effort to distinguish three types of borrowings: the instrumental and relatively unreflective borrowing of new transactions or behavior patterns by business-world actors; the borrowing of legal institutions in a positive-law sense by legislatures or courts; and, at the level of discourse, the more or less conscious borrowing of legal concepts for their rhetorical value in a new context.

I.

The motives that led to the introduction of no-par stock in the United States are mixed and controversial.[8] I discuss them first, before turning to the first

---

[5] See *Flechtheim,* Vom Aktienwesen in den Vereinigten Staaten, 3 RabelsZ 101 (1929) at 102:

"Diese [große Freiheit und Beweglichkeit des Aktienrechts] wird aber zweifellos auch gefördert durch die Zersplitterung des Rechts und die dadurch hervorgerufene Konkurrenz. Denn die einzelnen Staaten bemühen sich nach Möglichkeit, neue Gesellschaften an sich zu ziehen. Das ist weitgehend möglich, weil zur Inkorporation in einem Staat in der Regel nur ein formeller Sitz erforderlich ist . . .".

[6] *F. Klein,* Die neueren Entwicklungen in Verfassung und Recht der Aktiengesellschaft, 10 (1904). See also *Flechtheim,* note 5, above.

[7] See especially II *J. Habermas,* The Theory of Communicative Action, 356 ff. (T. McCarthy, transl., 1989).

[8] By the time German reformers seriously concerned themselves with the American no-par concept, after the period of hyperinflation, these doubts about the role of no-par stock in aiding stock watering through the transfer of property at inflated valuations for stock had been more or less laid to rest, as the following excerpt from *Flechtheim,* note

comparative component of this paper; namely, the rationalization of those motives.

In 1892, Remsen first mentioned the provenance of no-par stock.[9] By the time of its first adoption, in New York in 1912, the debate about its legitimacy had barely begun; by the early 1920s it was in full flower. To understand this debate, a technical digression is necessary.

The American experience of the last quarter of the 19th Century with the promotion of new enterprises reveals two aspects useful to our inquiry. There was much promoter's fraud, especially in the mining sector.[10] Fraudulently over-

---

5, above, at 109 n. 3 demonstrates (whether convincingly, or whether intentionally unconvincing, the reader will have to judge):

"Früher ist man, besonders bei spekulativen Neugründungen, vielfach so verfahren, daß Aktien gegen überbewertete Sacheinlagen abgegeben wurden. Dann übertrug der Erwerber einen Teil dieser Aktien unentgeltlich an die Gesellschaft ... zurück. Diese Aktien (treasury stock) konnten dann von der Gesellschaft als voll bezahlt zu beliebigem Preise weiterverkauft werden ... Aber man ist doch froh, bei dem System der Aktie ohne Nennwert nicht mehr genötigt zu sein, sich solcher, zwar von den Gerichten nicht mißbilligten ..., aber doch nicht gerade erfreulichen Methoden zu bedienen. Nach Ansicht seiner Verteidiger bedeutet also das System der nennwertlosen Aktie geradezu eine Verbesserung der Aktienrechtsmoral."

Compare *F. Schmey,* Aktie und Aktionär im Recht der Vereinigten Staaten, 243 (1930):

"Das Institut des non par value stock soll von Hause aus dem Zweck der Bekämpfung der Auswüchse des watered stock zu dienen bestimmt gewesen sein; die Praxis hat es aber verstanden, die non par value shares dem Zweck der Kapitalverwässerung in mehr als ausreichendem Maße dienstbar zu machen."

For a brief but broader comparative survey of the institution, see *W. Hallstein,* Die Aktienrechte der Gegenwart, 88 ff. (1931).

[9] "Such an amendment, though somewhat radical, is not altogether novel. It embodies a principle adopted in corporation laws in Germany." *Remsen,* note 2, above. Incidentally, Remsen credits Victor Morawetz, then the leading financial-transaction partner of the famous firm, with suggesting the idea to him in the first place. Ibid. Given Morawetz's familiarity with Continental legal regimes, both from his early study and from his practice — see I *R. Swaine,* The Cravath Firm and Its Predecessors, 381 ff., 461 ff. (1946) — this suggests a further linkage. I cannot find an explicit one in his publications, however; the only reference in *V. Morawetz,* Treatise on the Law of Private Corporations (1882) to no-par stock is to the old turnpike corporation cases stemming from the beginning of that century and discussed below, text at n. 49, id. at 269; nor does his second, 1886, edition, go any further. See also the citations provided in note 15.

[10] See the unwittingly amusing description in *J. Buell,* Suggestions Relating to the Organization of Gold and Silver Mining Corporations (1879). According to II *V. Morawetz,* Treatise on the Law of Private Corporations, 802 (2d ed. 1886), the practice of issuing a mining company's stock as fully paid on the basis of the flimsiest property transfer "is to universal and so notorious, that a person who contracts with an ordinary mining company may usually be presumed to have contracted with a view only to such security as the property transferred to the company may furnish, irrespective of the capital indicated by its charter." He cites California cases of the era which take an even more robust view of the matter.

Another way to view this, however, one particularly relevant to the role of the Kux — see its discussion in Part III below — is to appreciate the peculiarly contingent relation between the value of a discovered ore body and the amount of capital foreseeably

valued properties were sold to new corporations at inflated values and the promoters of these ventures, who had received "watered stock" for those transfers, would profit either from the resale of their stockholdings to the public or from the additional issuance of new stock by the corporation directly to the public under the illusion of the overvaluation.[11] The second aspect concerns the finance-driven mergers of competing industrial enterprises into more powerful structures; exemplary here is the merger of steel companies that led to the formation of United States Steel, arranged by the House of Morgan.[12] These new aggregations often were valued, in asset-and-liability terms, at a far higher amount than that revealed on the balance sheets of their separate predecessors, with the difference posted as goodwill.[13]

To battle the former situation courts had developed a so-called "statutory theory," a theory that made contributors of property automatically liable for the full amount of the par value ostensibly but not in fact represented by the property contribution.[14] This cause of action was available to innocent stockholders and to creditors alike, and did not require separate proof of reliance on the fraud. It rested, however, on the then-prevalent, indeed exclusive, use of high-par stock; i. e., on the issuance of stock at a par value that actually represented the purchase or transfer price.[15]

This doctrine stood in the way of the mentioned merger transactions, which, while not fraudulent, did require a valuation of the contributed assets that was above their earlier stated levels. The obvious solution was the enactment of statutory provisions to make the judgment of the directors in valuing property contributed to their company in exchange for stock conclusive in the absence

---

required to exploit a mine. As a contemporaneous student piece, *Note,* Liability for Stock Issued for Overvalued Property, 19 Harvard L. Rev., 366 (1906), put it:

"[T]he uncertainties of mining have led the courts to sanction the purchase of mining properties at purely speculative valuation, though these rulings have been discredited by recent decisions."

11 These alternatives are the basis of the paradigm cases on recovery found in most American teaching materials: *Old Dominion Copper Mining & Smelting Co. v. Bigelow,* 199 Mass. 488, 86 N. E. 660 (1907); *Old Dominion Copper Mining & Smelting Co. v. Lewisohn,* 210 U. S. 206 (1908); *Old Dominion Copper Mining & Smelting Co. v. Bigelow,* 203 Mass. 159, 89 N. E. 193 (1909).

12 See the discussion of this transaction in *United States v. United States Steel Corporation,* 223 F. 55, 167 (D. N. J. 1915), affirmed, 251 U. S. 417 (1920); and, for secondary review with full primary citations, *F. Allen,* The Great Pierpont Morgan (1956).

13 See generally *W. Ripley,* Main Street and Wall Street (1927).

14 See the leading case of *Du Pont v. Ball,* 11 Del. Ch. 430, 106 Atl. 39 (1918), recapitulating the history of this development.

15 The actual par value might be low; e. g., mining companies often issued "penny stock" — see, e. g., *Buck v. Jones,* 18 Colo. App. 250, 70 Pac. 951 (1902) ($ 1 par) — but so long as the consideration paid for the stock equalled that per-share amount the situation is like that of high-par stock. True low-par stock, whose par value was well below the price paid for it, was a later phenomenon; see the discussion at text between n. 30 and n. 31 below.

of actual (not merely constructive!) fraud.[16] That, indeed, was one of the major accomplishments of James Dill, the Standard Oil Company attorney who drafted and persuaded the New Jersey Legislature to adopt the first fully facilitative corporation law statute in 1888[17] and who was rewarded with a position on New Jersey's highest court, the Court of Errors and Appeals, as a result.[18]

But this was not enough. Courts were restive with the statute's transactionally awkward limitation of their review function to cases of "actual fraud" and often stretched its boundaries[19] — to the displeasure of leading members of the new corporate bar.[20] Even more significantly, they quickly pulled its teeth by ruling it inapplicable to cases in which the board of directors suffered under a conflict of interests, a not-uncommon situation in these financial-house merger situations.[21] In short, the risk of automatic liability for overvaluations could not be automatically dismissed, even if no actual fraud was involved, since a finding of an "unfair" valuation by an even partly interested board of directors, in those days of more or less automatic avoidability of self-interested transactions,[22] remained a possibility.

Something else was needed, and no-par stock was the answer. In my opinion, the very reason used to support it — namely, that the belief in the equivalence of par value with market value was an illusion — discloses its basis in this fear that the concept of par value, if objectively not provided in a merger and revaluation transaction, indeed could lead disappointed creditors and fellow stockholders to this argument and to its automatic vindication by means of the "statutory theory."[23] Thus it is ironic but hardly surprising that the complaints of a major opponent of no-par stock on this very point[24] should be quoted by a court that

---

[16] That was achieved with the introduction of § 49 into the first facilitative code, the Corporation Act of New Jersey, at the time of the 1896 revision. For the significance of this provision, see the comments of its architect, *J. Dill,* New Jersey Corporations, 73 ff. (4th ed. 1910).

[17] New Jersey already had become the leading "modern" company law jurisdiction with its famous 1875 codification. Among its accomplishments was the first provision expressly authorizing the issue of stock against property. See *Keasbey,* New Jersey and the Great Corporations I, 13 Harvard L. Rev. 198, 206 (1899).

[18] See the description of Dill in *L. Steffens,* The Autobiography of Lincoln Steffens 192 ff. (1931).

[19] See especially *Donald v. American Smelting Co.,* 62 N. J. Eq. 729, 48 Atl. 771 (1898) and *Easton National Bank v. American Brick & Tile Co.,* 70 N. J. Eq. 722, 64 Atl. 1095 (1906).

[20] See especially *[G.] Wickersham,* The Capital of a Corporation, 22 Harvard L. Rev. 319 (1909).

[21] See especially *Enright v. Heckscher,* 240 Fed. 863 (CCA 2 1917); but already the cases cited in note 19, above, made this clear.

[22] See *Marsh,* Are Directors Trustees? — Conflicts of Interest and Corporate Morality, 22 Business Lawyer 35, 36 (1966).

[23] See the later realization of this danger in *Livingston v. Adams,* 226 Mo. App. 824, 43 S. W. 2d 836 (1931).

dismissed an action that had been brought against shareholders who had not paid full value for an issue of no-par stock.[25]

Later another benefit was discovered and discussed. If an existing corporation needed more capital, but its stock's market value had fallen below the level of its original issuance price, which itself was the same as its statement of (high, typically $ 100) par, then a further issue of similar stock would have to be placed at a discount from par. The legitimacy of this transaction was debated, and in any event depended heavily on the specific wording of the applicable statute, especially its version of the mentioned "statutory theory."[26] This problem of *Unterpariemission* could be solved flexibly by the use of no-par stock, since its per-share par-equivalent value was derived from its sales price.[27] This special issue, of course, was more a problem of technique than of valuation and can be put aside.

The reasons for not extending the "statutory theory" to the general case of property valuation differ and are not of equal legitimacy. First, without the referent of par value some par-equivalent reference point had to be used to book the incoming capital contribution. This was the concept of "stated capital." Since there was by definition no preestablished par-equivalent value, there was no mechanical way to apply the "statutory theory," given that it referred specifically to the water level of "par."[28] This removal of the easy linkage was strengthened by an inherent attribute of this ascription procedure; namely, the fact that the board of directors had the right to wait to determine the actual value to be ascribed to this no-par stock until actual receipt of that consideration for such stock's issuance, a right only relevant, of course, in the case of no-cash consideration. Of course, "watered stock," i. e., fraudulent overvaluation, still could occur, but only stockholders and creditors who had relied on this "talking fraud" could then complain of it. The second reason rests on the mechanics by means of which the price received for no-par stock was represented in the capital structure of the issuing corporation. Originally, the earliest no-par authorization statutes either stated or implied that the entire amount of the consideration received for the stock would be shown on the balance sheet of the corporation as "capital,"

---

24 *Cook,* Stock Without Par Value, 7 Am. Bar Ass'n Journal 534 (1921):
"The whole theory of stock without par value is 'Let the buyer beware' and 'let the creditor beware.'"

25 *Johnson v. Louisville* Trust Co., 293 Fed. 857 (CCA 4 1923).

26 Thus, compare the leading case of *Handley v. Stutz,* 139 U. S. 417, 430 (1891) with *Enright v. Heckscher,* note 21, above, and *Harman v. Himes,* 77 F. 2d 375 (D. C. Cir. 1935).

27 See *Randle v. Winona Coal Co.,* 206 Ala. 254, 89 So. 790, 795 (1921). It was this market fluctuation problem that "in a large measure, accounted for the substitution of 'nonpar' stock ..., and this changes has tended to relieve the confusion or deception, the ... embarrassment of explanation of discrepancy ...".

28 See *Randle,* note 27, above.

just as full par-equivalent consideration had always been shown.[29] Later, however, it somehow became acceptable, at the time of issuance, to make a separate determination of the proportion of the subscription price that should be booked as "capital" and that which could be shown simply as "contributed surplus" or "paid-in surplus." Whether this result is the consequence of an inadvertent or purposeful loophole in the no-par authorization statute is difficult to reconstruct.[30]

The whole purpose of this flexibility, of course, was exactly the problem of property valuation: The lower the component booked to capital, the less likely that the value of the contributed property lay below that amount and the less likely that a shareholder or creditor could use an "automatic liability" theory to annul the oversubscription or demand further payment by the use of the market price as the measuring rod for the difference.

Within a few years the arguments over the legitimacy of the combined device of no-par stock and flexible attribution between capital and surplus faded from sight. The bar generalized the no-par stock lesson that there was nothing sacrosanct about high-par stock in the sense of the equivalence of par value and subscription price. From that new-found perspective, it was a short step to another concept, that of low-par stock, which quickly became established by custom though never specifically authorized by statute.

In short, our perspective on the original reasons for the introduction of the concept of no-par stock is enriched by considering its and its cousins' subsequent history. From that perspective, it seems clear that property valuation, though not necessarily its flagrantly fraudulent version, was the key issue.[31] The "par illusion" of shareholders, which it behooved the new bar to destroy, indeed may have been an illusion, but not in the sense painted by its detractors. Their version

---

[29] These distinctions are carefully reviewed in *C. Wickersham* [son of G.], A Treatise on Stock Without Par Value of Ordinary Business Corporations (1927).

[30] *C. Wickersham,* note 29, above, at 94 ff. (97) expresses considerably uneasiness at this result but accepts it as available under this type of statute.

[31] The following excerpts from Dill's introduction to his commentary on New Jersey law help make this clear:

"The liability of officers and directors is clearly defined and can result only from the making of a statement known to them to be false at the time it was made.

The law of the State of New Jersey is singularly free from pitfalls and ambiguities[,] leading to personal liberty of stockholders, officers and directors, and stockholders and officers obtain in the fullest sense limited liability.

With respect to the issuance of stock for property purchased, New Jersey has avoided the danger which the laws of many other states have created for holders of such stock. It has eliminated the question of the value of property for which stock is issued, standing by itself, and with the single exception of cases in which there is absolute fraud on the part of the directors there is no liability upon the holders of stock issued for property purchases."

J. Dill, The Statutory and Case Law Applicable to Private Companies Under the General Corporation Act of New Jersey and Corporation Precedents vii f. (3rd ed. 1901) (the quotation is from the Preface to the First Edition, 1898.

made sense for the special case when a corporation, after its initial capitalization, had to issue more stock and could not get the $ 100 (par) share price for it. It did not make sense for the general case of initial capitalization and initial contribution of property as capital.

With this background, it is time to turn to the introduction of the concept itself and to its possible borrowing from Continental antecedents.

II.

As already mentioned, the concept seems to have been first mentioned by Remsen, in 1892. Fifteen years later Shepard, a leading member of the then just-developed commercial and corporate sector of the New York Bar,[32] and the invited pricipal speaker at the Illinois State Bar annual convention in 1907, added some further, sparse remarks about this novel concept:[33]

> Besides precedents or analogies in old companies or associations, ... [t]he general mining law of Prussia enacted in 1865 provides for companies without denominations of shares. Such has, I believe, been the practice in Mexico and other countries, the laws of which it has not been convenient for me to examine.

Of course, he was familiar with the practice of "shares", in the literal sense, used for investment in mines and vessels, and the cited Prussian law is no more than an example of the former. Nonetheless, and not only because it is pleasant to trumpet new-won knowledge with the zeal of a convert, I believe a look at the exact relationship between the capitalization of mines and ship voyages and that of the emerging large corporation of the 19th Century, as this bears on the emergence of the concept of no-par stock, will be instructive.

An authority writing in 1856, roughly at the time that the paths of the *Aktiengesellschaft* and the *Bergbaugewerkschaft* began to diverge, posed the general challenge to the legislator of that day:[34]

> "Ich habe ... behauptet, daß es als ein bedauerlicher Stillstand der Bergrechtswissenschaft bezeichnet werden müsse, daß die ... Berggesetzgebung den Kux, welcher zweifelsohne der Kindheit der industriellen Association angehöre, festgehalten habe, während demselben der mannhafte, thatkräftige Aktienbegriff ringsum längst schon über das Haupt gewachsen sei."

In fact, and partly in consequence of similar complaints about this inadequate legal construct, the earlier Prussian *Aktiengesetz* of 1843 had by the next decade been used for a fair number of new incorporations of mineral-exploitation enter-

---

32 See *Shepard*, Edward Morse, in 17 Dictionary of American Biography 72 (1943).

33 *Shepard*, Corporate Capitalization and Public Morals, in Illinois State Bar Association, Proceedings Part II, 1907, 29, at 56.

34 *G. E. Otto*, Studie auf dem Gebiete des Bergrechtes, 57 (1856).

prises.[35] Indeed, as a further result of complaints about this inadequacy, the Prussian recodification of 1865 gave the promoters of mining companies the choice of moving over to the other entity forms, including that of the *Aktiengesellschaft;* though, because of the parallel inadequacies of the then-extant version of the *Aktiengesellschaft* form for mining enterprises,[36] it left the *Gewerkschaft* available as an option with all its only partly remedied faults.[37] Not until the turn of the century and the new general codifications did this "transfer" of legal form become more common.[38]

What was it about the *Kux,* if inadequate as an engine of capital formation in Germany in 1856, that made it so attractive as an engine of capital formation in the United States in 1892? It was not its inherent merits; it was the fact that, as an old bottle, it could more readily be sold as suitable for new wine than could a new one. Its lack of merit for the modern era can be quickly demonstrated.

III.

The *Kux,*[39] translated so awkwardly as "account-book share" that the original is preferable, derives from the particularities of mining in Europe. Its origins lie in the form in which the mining concession holder, the *Muther,* received the concession patent from the sovereign; namely, already divided into four parts

---

35 See the discussion in *T. Baums,* ed., Gesetz Über Die Aktiengesellschaften Für Die Königlichen Preussischen Staaten vom 9. November 1843 — Text und Materialien 26 (1981) and sources cited there.

36 See the Motive zum Entwurf eines Allgemeinen Berggesetzes für die Preussischen Staaten, in 6 ZBergR, 146 (1865).

37 See generally *von Hingenau,* Beiträge zur Reform des deutschen Bergrechts [Part III], Vol. 4, ZBergR, 426, 436 ff. (1863).

38 See generally *Bitta,* Einfluß der neuen Gesetzgebung auf die bestehenden Aktiengesellschaften und Gewerkschaften, 41 ZBergR, 188 (1900).

39 On its questionable etymology, compare *Ehrenzweig,* Das Wort 'Kux', Vol. 62, ZBergR, 191 (1921) with *Zycha,* Das Wort 'Kux', 62 id. 407 (1921). Both authors accept as probable its derivation from *kokkos,* diminutive *kokkion,* probably as a weight derived from the division into weight or portion of units of St. John's Bread. The *kokkion,* as well as St. John's Bread's rind, the *keration,* came into usage in pharmacy but also, via the Arabic, as the division of units of ships for voyage participations. If this is indeed so, then kernel, carat, and Kux have a common ancestry.

Zycha dispenses with one wonderful error. Ehrenzweig had based an early division of mining shares into sixteenth on a passage in a Bohemian deed of 1327, speaking of sixteenths *(sedecima pars)* "quam in nona parte fabrili in orto humili nobiscum in Kuccis habere dinoscuntur." That is how the original had been transcribed, but Zycha went back to the original deed and found it had been mistranscribed and actually read, in the original, "in *Kuttis*"; i. e., in Kuttenberg. There went one path between St. John's Bread and the mining share. Luckily, this did not bear on the legitimacy of the derivation as such, since it shows up, but in the more traditional division of fourths, thirty-seconds, and one hundred twenty-eighths, in records of the Fifteenth Century.

(Schichten), the better to satisfy the demands of those with property or labor claims on or participations in the discovery. Early on, these parts themselves were divided into two halves each, so that from their origin around 1475 these reified concessions had a total of eight portions. In time, and for obvious reasons of increasing size, complexity, and capitalization requirements, each founding part was doubled several times, from four *Schichten* to 32 *Stämme,* and, already by the end of the 17th Century, to 128 shares or *Kuxen.*[40] In the mid-century, some laws froze it there; others, especially the important *Allgemeines Berggesetz für die Preussischen Staaten* of 1865, increased the statutory number of *Anteile* (shares) to 100 and permitted the Statut or articles of incorporation to set that number as high as 1 000.[41]

The *Kux* was separately interesting — and complicated — because as an original and integral division of the actual concession itself it was a species of real property, and had to be separately (individually!) hypothecated if the tangible property was used as security for loans. These complications led to revisions of the relevant statutes, and to a totally new conception of the Kux, as a species of property, in the *Allgemeines Berggesetz* but not to the abolition of the concept of the *Kux* itself.[42]

It is interesting for our purposes to note the treatment of possible fraudulent promotion of mining ventures in these codifications. According to § 21 of the *Allgemeines Berggesetz,* if the public solicitation of capital was desired, the *Gewerkschaft* had to procure the authorization of the *Oberbergamt.* Often it was refused, on the ground that the public interest would not be served if that many units of potential ownership were available for a venture with a low net worth.[43] The argument was that the issuance of a great number of shares with low intrinsic value would mislead the public into believing that the property was of more value than was the case, and would lead to speculation.[44]

Several attributes of the *Kux* as a share were important in Germany and, I suspect, to its American admirers. It was an open-ended share, the subscription to which carried an ongoing obligation to pay further installments upon the call of the management; and since as a result it could not be measured by a fixed or "par" amount, it was an ideal instrument to issue against promotional services, tangible or intangible property, and underlying neofeudal demands of local lord, church, and manor. Further, all 128 *Kuxen* were authorized at the outset, at the time the concession was granted and as an integral element of that concession.[45]

---

40 See 2 *R. Klostermann,* Lehrbuch des Preussischen Bergrechtes, 215 (1871).

41 Ibid.

42 See generally 1 *H. Achenbach,* Das gemeine deutsche Bergrecht, 290 ff. (1871).

43 See particularly Mitteilungen aus der Praxis der Verwaltungsbehörden, in 27 ZBergR, 243, 257 ff. (1886).

44 Mitteilungen aus der Praxis der Verwaltungsbehörden — Beiträge aus der Anwendung des Allgemeinen Preussischen Berggesetzes, 27 ZBergR, 258 (1886).

In other words, like the later American practice, and unlike the later and still prevalent Continental practice, the corporation came into being before any real shares were issued and any real capital raised.

The open-ended nature of the *Kux* subscription dictated its "no-par" character.[46] It originally was based on the notion that the uncertainties of discovery and exploitation of mineral resources required this ongoing and therefore "uncapped" share participation.[47] Indeed, opponents of the 1865 revision specifically argued that as a result of the new conception of the *Kux,* it would become an object of secondary market trading like the *Aktie,* and thus lose its specific character of catering to the special needs of an enterprise that needed initially uncertain long-term investment more than a specific and single monetary involvement. It was specifically the no-par character of the *Kux* that distinguished it from the *Aktie* in this particular.[48]

In this characteristic was hidden an analogy that the American proponent of the Prussian concept either did not know or had forgotten: At the turn of the 19th Century, shortly after the American Revolution, an early precedent for this version of no-par stock existed in the turnpike corporations, organized to build roads on private subscription. For essentially similar reasons; namely, the uncertain need for capital as a function of the uncertain number of subscribers and of road extensions, these Massachusetts (and other) corporations were uncapped as to maximum subscription, provided no statement of par, and if in default on an installment call were subject to forfeiture via forced sale by operation of law.[49]

Finally, there is a relationship of member to venture in the turnpike company and the mining venture that may be closer than the share-intermediated one of shareholder to modern firm: the possibility of personal liability for enterprise debts above and beyond the sunk capital investment. This additional liability, whether by operation of law or by separate contract implied in fact, was asserted as to both forms of ventures, though in increasingly debatable fashion, for some years after their respective heyday.[50] It is therefore separately interesting, and

---

45 See generally 2 *R. Klostermann,* note 40, above, at 252 ff.

46 Much of the following discussion is well articulated and anticipated in the Motive zum Entwurf eines Allgemeinen Berggesetzes für die Deutschen Staaten, in 5 ZBergR, 55, 145 ff. (1865).

47 This is stressed by the Motive:

"Ein bestimmtes Grundkapital ... entspricht nämlich in der überwiegenden Mehrzahl der Fälle den Verhältnissen des Bergbaues nicht ... Der Bergbau ist vielmehr darauf hingewiesen, laufende Zuschüsse zu nehmen ...".

Motive, note 46 above, at 146. And this is why the new stock corporation law structures was deemed an inadequate vehicle for mining ventures.

48 *Klostermann,* note 40, above, at 279 f.

49 See the brief reference in *Cook,* Stock Without Par Value, 7 ABA Journal, 534, 537 (1921).

50 Cook's statement, note 49, above, at 537, that owners of these shares also were personally and unlimitedly liable for the unpaid debts of the corporation, however,

separately demonstrative of my thesis that new wine was being poured into an old bottle, that this feature simply was not at issue when the no-par stock concept was brought into American corporation-law statutes after the turn of the 20th Century.

In any event, according to one German critic, by mid-century the individual installment obligations were being kept extremely low, so that distant investors might be motivated to continue honoring their open-ended obligation, especially as this was then being rationalized as a way of keeping poor mountain folk off the dole![51] If this explanation is correct, it of course confirms the further assertion that trivial albeit ongoing trickles of capital flowing along no more than 128 rivulets made serious mineral exploitation in this form of firm structure unlikely.

On the other hand, some of these installment obligations must have been of significant amount, since other writers complain that the planned forfeiture of existing shares following excessive calls for further installments had reached the level of serious overreaching if not fraud.[52] In addition, there also developed the further abuse of issuing unregistered shares, both real ones out of the 128 and, what was worse, fictitious ones. The latter's owners, the *"Hockenträger,"* blind or unregistered shareholders, were tapped for original and subsequent installments without the proceeds ever reaching the enterprise.[53]

In short, an originally rational and functional system of capital formation before the days of organized original-issue capital markets deteriorated during the course of the 19th Century into an inefficient and increasingly corrupt one.[54] What was left of it had made the transition to the United States. After World War I, in an interesting reverse flow of concepts, it reappeared in Germany.

---

cannot be confirmed from the case he cites, *Middlesex Turnpike Co. v. Swan,* 10 Mass. 384 (1813). While it is correct that at that date unlimited liability was the norm, the case itself speaks of the separate contract of the subscriber to the promoters of the corporation to pay all calls, a promise on which a direct action of the firm's creditors could be based. See, more explicitly to this point, *Worcester Turnpike Corporation v. Willard,* 5 Mass. 80 (1809).

The distinction is important in comparative terms because the additional liability of the *Kuxschein* holder, following a further call for capital, beyond the surrender of the certificate, was an important and much disputed issue under the German system. See *R. Klostermann,* Übersicht der Bergrechtlichen Entscheidungen, 91 f. (1864), and the relatively late Reichsgericht decision of May 31, 1919, denying that liability, in 60 ZBergR, 425 (1919).

51 *Otto,* note 34, above, at 67 f.

52 Cf. *Löwenstein,* Der Zubußeanspruch der Gewerkschaft, 45 ZBergR 61 (1904).

53 See *Otto,* note 34, above, at 61.

54 The development of industrial-strength mineral exploitation firms and the concomitant gradual disappearance of "one-shot" wasting asset exploitation ventures were one major objective cause, a development also noted in the United States. See generally II *H. Marsh,* Marsh's California Corporation Law 125 f. (1983).

IV.

Its continued and perhaps continuingly questionable role makes a comparative study of the *Kux* in its reincarnation as no-par stock, and of the effort to reintroduce it in Germany for new reasons, separately interesting. It was, after all, the questionable aspects of the American role of no-par stock during the *Gründerjahre* of the United States that both fascinated and frightened Continental academics and practitioners when they debated the value of the concept's introduction into their own legal systems. Thus, a brief look at the German debate, both at the two *Juristentage* of 1924 and 1926 respectively, and in separate commentary from the same era,[55] followed by a recapitulation of the use of comparative materials in these dabates, should be useful.[56]

Two earlier episodes, however, are separately interesting. The German codification of the *Aktiengesetz* in 1884 considered the possibility of using a no-par stock concept, borrowed not from American turnpike company concepts but from the *Kux*, and apparently rejected it.[57] This rejection, "aus wohlerwogenen Gründen," was recalled during the 1926 *Juristentag* debate and used as a separate ground for not reviving the argument, this time an argument indeed based on American sources, again.[58] In fact, the 1884 debate only concerned the *Quotenaktie*, which identifies the percentage of ownership interest on the face of the certificate, not the true no-par share.[59] Nevertheless, the argument at that early date, that par value was necessary to identify profits and losses against a prior frame of reference, was applicable against the no-par concept as well, even though the argument is comprehensible only because at that time the entire subscription amount was attributed to "capital" and not split between it and "contributed surplus," as later became the case.

A second early episode is doubly instructive because doubly comparative. Before World War I the Austrian and German associations met together,[60] and

---

55 See *Flechtheim*, note 5, above.

56 The importance of company law to the emerging industrialization and commercialization of the era is obvious. I count nine times, between 1869 and 1926, that company law issues were the subject of discussion at the *Juristentag*.

57 See the 'Entwurf eines Gesetzes betreffend die Kommanditgesellschaften auf Aktien und die Aktiengesellschaften', reprinted in Hundert Jahre modernes Aktienrecht, 417 ff. (1985).

58 See the comments of Justizrat *Pinner*, in II Verhandlungen, note 3, above, at 635.

59 See *Flechtheim*, note 5, above, at 106 f.; for fuller detail on this distinction, see *Plattner*, note 4, above, at 12 (1964), primarily on Swiss law but on this point of comparative interest.

60 See *Conrad*, Der Deutsche Juristentag 1860-1960, in I Hundert Jahre Deutsches Rechtsleben — Festschrift zum hundertjährigen Bestehen des Deutschen Juristentages 1860-1960, 1, 7 ff. (E. V. Caemmerer, E. Friesenhahn, & R. Lange, eds., 1960). See also *Klein*, Der Deutsche Juristentag und die anderen juristischen Vereinigungen, in Festgabe der Deutschen Juristen Zeitung zum 31. Deutschen Juristentag in Wien, 6 (1912).

in 1906 the issue was on the table in connection with the planned codification of the Austrian company laws. The principal opinion was given by Lehmann.[61] He discussed a variant of no-par stock, though not the then-pending debate in the United States. He recommended rejection of the concept, and did so, interestingly, on grounds the mirror image of those then being used by its American proponents: It confused the public (i. e., investors), which still trusted the par-value concept as a measure at least of contributed capital if not necessarily of actual enterprise value.[62]

The discussion two decades later, after the period of hyperinflation, understandably focused on ways to improve German firms' access to capital. The discussion of no-par stock was introduced by Flechtheim at the 33rd *Juristentag* of 1924.[63] He addressed not only the problem of raising additional capital by means of normal, high-par stock at a time when the market valuation of prior issues of the same stock lay under par, but also the problem that the par-value structure created for a market whose participants measured the health of a company by the relation its dividends bore to the original "par" emission price — an illusion that persists to this day. Discussing the *Quotenaktie,* he mentioned the use of the American no-par stock concept by its proponents, and, I presume unwittingly, completed the circle the concept had traveled:[64]

> "Die einzelne Aktie gibt einen quotenmäßigen Anteil am gesamten Gesellschaftsvermögen, also ähnlich unserem Kux."

Flechtheim thought it would be a useful technical improvement, but rejected it in part because it would require a substantial and systematic revision of large parts of the German company law, in larger part because it was not a feasible way to help German firms out of the straitjacket of "below-par" dividends and "below-par" emissions of new stock for further working capital.[65] Half a decade later Flechtheim ambivalently admired the concept for the flexibility it brought to the valuation of property contributed for capital;[66] but for now it was the systemic problems that led to his, and the meeting's, rejection of the concept.

The issues of capital shortages did not go away, however, and the very next *Juristentag* not only recurred to the problem of forms that would facilitate the

61 Welche Grundsätze des deutschen Aktienrechts werden bei einer Kodifizierung des österreichischen Aktienrechts zu berücksichtigen sein?, in I Verhandlungen des Einunddreissigsten Deutschen Juristentags, 502 (1912).

62 Id. at 527.

63 Verhandlungen des Dreiunddreissigsten Deutschen Juristentags [1924], 386 (1925).

64 Id. at 402.

65 Ibid. See also the companion opinion of *Hachenburg,* who rejected the concept solely on the basis of its easy misuse to the detriment of creditors and emphasized the desirable tendency of the German law to be more protective in this regard than was the freebooting American and English law. Id. at 407, 412.

66 See *Flechtheim,* note 5, above.

influx of foreign capital, but posed the question in comparative terms: "Soll bei einer zukünftigen Reform des Aktienrechts eine Annäherung an das englisch-amerikanische Recht in grundlegenden Fragen stattfinden?"[67] This time it was Lehmann, who already in 1912 had discussed similar issues in his opinion concerning the role of German law in the pending Austrian codification,[68] who reviewed this issue again, and again spoke to the possibility of introducing no-par stock. In a superb comparative essay that rewards reading 65 years later, he focused a major part of his opinion on the role of no-par stock in facilitating new issues of additional capital under the mentioned circumstances.

His main arguments pro and con were taken from a major English enquête held a few years earlier[69] and concerned with the role of below-par emissions and of no-par stock, the former being the British, the latter the American practice. There is no need to recapitulate the substantive issues Lehmann took from this secondary source, since they reflect in the main the arguments long discussed in the United States and already reviewed above. He did sweep aside one misconception about American law that had been bruited at the preceding *Juristentag;* namely, that the capital contributions would not be booked as capital but as surplus, and pointed out (not quite accurately) that the sum received would be entered as capital just as would the contribution for high-par stock.[70] That aside, however, Lehmann still rejected the introduction of the concept into German law, though this time on a different and still technical point: It was a useful concept for new enterprise formations, especially given the frequency with which property, rather than cash, would be contributed by their promoters, property which could be more flexibly valued via a no-par issuance than a high-par one — but Germany was no longer in its *Gründerzeit* and needed new capital for existing firms, not for new firms![71]

The sense of history may be debatable, but the sense that the real problem of the day was the need to raise additional capital for existing but capital-starved enterprises is not. It is revealing that not only the German discussants, but also their English forerunners, discussed the introduction of no-par stock primarily from this perspective.[72] The problem of the post-World War I era lay in the straitjacket that par concepts imposed on the emission of later stock when the earlier stock issue traded below its original (high par) emission price. No-par

---

67 Note 3, above.

68 Note 61, above.

69 I have not located an original publication of the *Wrenbury* Committee Report of 1918, but it is heavily quoted and paraphrased in the 1926 Greene Report, Company Law Amendment Committee Report, Cmd. 2657 (HMSO 1926).

70 Id. at 282. In fact, the contribution would be so ascribed only if the directors took no contrary action. They were, however, free to book so much of the contribution to "stated capital" as they wished, and the rest to "contributed surplus."

71 Id. at 283.

72 See *Greene,* Committee Report, note 47, above, at 9 f., 13.

stock was tempting for that reason, but its benefits were accompanied by detriments that were in part systemic in part contingent. The contingent one was the American experience with property overvaluation, and the fear that the no-par concept would of necessity bring this danger to the German scene. The systemic one was the fact that a number of other legal norms, norms surrounding the par regime, would have to be unraveled and reconstructed before no-par stock could play its desired role of permitting ongoing emissions of stock to be at market rather than at earlier issuance prices. This systemic objection dominated the English and both German debates, and was determinative of the rejection of the American solution.

With that, the German discussion of a reform that would introduce this legal regime was at an end, though the literature wistfully recurred to it for a while longer[73].

Conclusion

To the American proponents and opponents, both before and after its introduction into United States laws in 1912 via New York, the story of no-par stock was the story of property valuation and, underlying that, of enterprise valuation. Its proponents described it as an improvement in corporation law because it would forcibly eliminate the misleading notion that a share was "worth" its par value. Getting rid of this illusion would lead the shareholder to the door of reality. Its opponents described it as achieving an undesirable relaxation of the standards of property valuation and thus as an aid to the deception of fellow subscribers and of creditors.

If the *Kux* was in its twilight at the time of the first American references to its utility, was it its Prussian past or its potential American future — was it its utility for "rolling" subscription calls or its insulating power against judicial second-guessing of property valuations — that intrigued its American sponsors? We can make one assertion with some assurance: The benefit claimed for it in the American literature; namely, its aid in lifting the veil of the illusory equation of par-value ascription from the eyes of American investors, can be found neither in the conceptual nor in the practical descriptions of the role of the *Kux*. That role it had not played in Prussia. If any preliminary conclusion may be ventured, therefore, it would be to suggest that the reference resulted from a rationalization, not a motivation, of the American experiment launched with the no-par stock concept.

---

73 See the sources cited in note 3, above.

MICHELE GRAZIADEI*

Changing Images of the Law in XIX Century English Legal Thought (The Continental Impulse)

I. Introduction

What ideas about the roots of the English legal tradition were current in nineteenth century England? Such a vague question will probably never receive a conclusive answer. Yet, to look for continental influences in nineteenth century English law may involve something different from tracing the continental origins of rules that are now contained in the law reports or in the statute book.

The bare statement of a legal rule makes up only the skeleton of the law. Quite often what is found around it — the reasons given for it or its grounds — is far more important and more interesting than the rule itself.

These opening remarks are directed to draw attention to the changes that some parts of the law in the common law world experienced during the last century. These changes transformed the perception of the historical background of the law and eventually produced a new awareness of the distinctive character of the common law tradition.

Two examples suggest the features and the dynamic of this process. The first is the reaction to the publication in 1869 of a new edition by Finlason of John Reeve's *History of the English Law*[1]. Finlason's contribution to the edition of

* This study was completed with the help of many people. I am greatly indebted to Jim Gordley and Bernard Rudden for their unfailing support and stimulating encouragement. I wish to thank Peter Birks for his comments on my project when it was still at an early stage. I owe to these scholars some valuable observations on the first draft of this essay. Knut Nörr, Mathias Reimann, and Jim Whitman, also made precious comments on it. Paul Jackson kindly read a more advanced version of the typescript. I am also indebted to Judith Mellins and Mary Pearson of the Special Collections, Harvard Law School Library, to Dr. Zutshi of the Cambridge University Library, to Dr. Jutta Weber of the Staatsbibliothek Preussischer Kulturbesitz, Berlin and to Rebecca Margulies for their friendly and efficient help. Finally, I would like to thank my colleagues Gian Maria Ajani, Mauro Bussani, Silvia Ferreri, Ugo Mattei, with whom I first discussed some of the ideas presented in this text. Responsibility for any error is mine.

[1] *J. Reeves,* History of the English Law from the Time of the Romans to the End of the Reign of Elisabeth. A New Edition by *W. F. Finlason,* London, 1869.

this classic work consisted of a long *Introductory Essay* that finds Roman origins for almost every conceivable aspect of the English law — including trial by jury — and of cumbersome footnotes added to the original work in order to "correct" Reeve's opinions. This edition received favourable reviews in England[2]. Trenchant criticism came instead from unexpected quarters. One of the leading figures of the Germanistic school — Heinrich Brunner — published a devastating review of this edition in the *Kritische Vierteljahresschrift für Gesetzgebung und Rechtswissenschaft*[3]. Brunner attacked Finlason for having neglected to make use of the publications of the English Record Commission, as well as for his failure to take notice of the German studies on the subject. Together with the poor rearrangement of the chapters, these flaws showed that Finlason's edition of Reeve's book was not a scholarly one. However, Finlason's *Introductory Essay* and notes to Reeve's text must have really astonished Brunner:

> "Gratifying as it is to see in England, at the present time, a growing appreciation of Roman law, it seems as if the reaction from the indifference formerly felt for this system were running into the opposite extreme. Instead of saying, we admit that our English law is not the only excellent law, but that the Roman law too has its great merits, the English jurist argues in this way: the Roman law is a most exquisite law, consequently our English law is in great part based upon the Roman law. Finlason's "Introduction" is a warning example of the perversities and errors to which such a preconception may lead"[4].

The attempt to link the English law to the Roman law: ". . . is not referred to a 'reception' in the Middle Ages, but it is attributed to the transplanting of Roman life and Roman law into the individual provinces of the Roman Empire, to which of course Britain belonged"[5]. The result is an account of the influence of the Roman law in Britain that Brunner could not share. According to Brunner, rather than proving the points that Finlason strove to make, the constant reference to the Mirror of Justices in the footnotes to the text showed a total lack of critical judgment. To make sure that the message was brought home at least on the other

---

[2] (1869) 27 Law Mag. & L. Rev. 23, esp. 25 ff. The author of this anonymous book review upheld Finlason's opinions about the importance of the Roman component in the history of the English law: "A history of the law in this country ought properly to commence with the Roman period. There can be not doubt that the Roman law formed the basis of our own legal system, whatever additions and modifications the latter may have received from other sources". Praise is poured on the editor of Reeve's work for having taken advantaged of "the labours of Savigny and Guizot", though "he may occasionally have pushed matters a little too far in favour of his own views". This eulogy Finlason's edition is however balanced by some pertinent critical remarks in the book review published in (1869), 4 L. J. 36 (but see also p. 228, 532). They were probably inspired by a reading of the scholarly work of *W. Forsyth,* History of Trial by Jury, Cambridge, 1852.

[3] 13 Krit. Viert. 228 (1871).

[4] 13 Krit. Viert. 228 (1871) at 231; English tr. in 8 Am. L. Rev. 138 (1873) at 139-140.

[5] 13 Krit. Viert. 228 (1871) at 232; 8 Am. L. Rev. 138 (1873) at 140.

side of the ocean, James Barr Ames asked Brunner permission to publish his book-review in English, which was done by the *American Law Review* of 1873[6].

Just a few years after this episode, the judgment of the Common Pleas Division of the High Court delivered by Brett J. in *Nugent v. Smith*[7] revealed that at least some members of the judiciary were inclined to share similar thoughts. On the matter of the liability of common carriers, Lord Holt in *Coggs v. Bernard*[8] had established a rule that "rests as for authority solely on Bracton"[9]. But it "is clear that Bracton, or English judges before him, adopted into the English the Roman law"[10]. Working from this premise, the Court held that every ship-owner or master who carried goods on his vessel for hire incurred liability as an insurer of the good received on board, even if he did not qualify as common carrier. This time criticism came promptly from the bench. The Court of Appeal reversed the decision of the Court below[11]; Cockburn C. J. held that the English rule on the liability of common carriers could not have had Roman origins "as a matter of legal history" since it was first established with reference to carriers by land, upon whom the Roman law imposed no exceptional liability[12]. Neither view of the origins of the rule satisfied O. W. Holmes, however, who published an article in the *American Law Review* to demonstrate that this rule was of "pure Teutonic origin"[13].

According to Holmes, the liability of carriers was a relic of the older and stricter rule on the liability of bailees, rather than an innovation introduced to put carriers on a different footing from other bailees. In England, Holmes' thesis was echoed by T. E. Scrutton, in *The Influence of the Roman Law on the Law of England*[14].

---

6 See Brunner's reply to Ames, 28. 9. 1872, J. B. Ames Papers, Harvard Law School Library, Box 1, f. 4: "Es wird mir selbstverständlich ein großes Vergnügen sein, wenn Sie meine Anzeige von Finlasons Ausgabe des Reeves in einer amerikanischen Zeitschrift publicieren. So scharf meine Besprechung auch gehalten ist, glaube ich gegen Finlason doch nicht ungerecht gewesen zu sein". Professor Hellmut Brunner kindly informs me that no letter from Ames, Holmes or Maitland survives among the papers of Heinrich Brunner in possession of the family.

7 (1875) L. R. 1 C. P. D. 19.

8 (1703) 2 Ld. Raym. 909.

9 (1875) L. R. 1 C. P. D. 19, at 28; also at 30-31 of the report. To support these views Brett J. cited the writings of Sir William Jones and Joseph Story on bailments considered below, par. 2.3; 2.4.

10 (1875) L. R. 1 C. P. D. 19, at 29.

11 (1875) L. R. 1 C. P. D. 423 (C. A.).

12 (1875) L. R. 1 C. P. D. 423 (C. A.), at 430, per Cockburn C. J. — At pp. 428-429, the Chief Justice takes pains to explain that when the ship-owner is not a common carrier the English law is in accord with the Roman law as well as with "... the existing law of all nations that have adopted the Roman law — France, Spain, Italy, Germany, Holland, and to come nearer home, Scotland".

13 *O. W. Holmes*, Common Carriers and the Common Law, 13 Am. L. Rev. 609 (1870), at 610. See below, par. 4.

Eventually the reference to the Teutonic element came under attack and was dismissed without much regret. Looking back on the whole dispute, C. H. S. Fifoot remarked: "The hypothesis of an original reservoir of Teutonic law, presumably of exceptional purity, intrigued the nineteenth-century jurists, but seems to be wholly romantic."[15].

The nineteenth century is gone, but its shadow reaches our epoch. Brunner's metaphor about the prophylactic effect that the early exposure of the English law to the Roman element supposedly had is still lurking in the pages of one of the best introductions to English legal history[16]. This reference to Brunner should at least remind us that an important chapter of what can now be considered as part of nineteenth century intellectual history was written to disprove earlier beliefs about the relation between the English law and the various historical components of the Western legal tradition[17]. It should also help us to keep in mind that the role played in this field by continental suggestions was substantial and by no means confined to the growth of legal history as a specialized subject.

This article explores the impact of continental ideas on the process of doctrinal change that, in the Victorian age, led to a new understanding of the relationship between English law and the continental legal traditions. As this process modified and shaped deeply held convictions, rather than altered existing legal rules, the title of my contribution speaks of a change in the image of the law. Though it would be foolish to imply that in the period covered by this article a common approach to the law dominated on both sides of the Atlantic, nevertheless, to portray the English scene realistically, it is better to consider as part of the picture at least some of those American contributions to legal scholarship that commanded attention in England[18].

---

14 *T. E. Scrutton,* The Influence of the Roman Law on the Law of England, Cambridge, 1885, 187 ff.

15 *C. H. S. Fifoot,* History and Sources of the Common Law. Tort and Contract. London, 1949, at 158, note 28.

16 *J. H. Baker,* An Introduction to English Legal History, 3rd ed., London, 1990, at 33. The paragraph to which the citation refers bears the title: "The isolation of English Law".

17 I use this expression in the sense set forth by *H. Berman,* Law and Revolution. The Formation of the Western Legal Tradition, Cambridge, Mass., 1983.

18 Certainly throughout the nineteenth century one can find common perspectives on the law, as well as a significant trade in ideas, among the English and the American legal cultures. *B. Rudden,* A Code Too Soon: the 1826 Property Code of James Humphreys, in Essays in Memory of F. H. Lawson, London, 1986, p. 101 f., highlights one important instance of such exchanges. Yet it is possible to elaborate on an "Anglo-American legal community" (cp. *R. A. Cosgrove,* "Our Lady the Common Law": An Anglo-American Legal Community 1870 - 1930, New York and London, 1987) only by taking a highly selective approach to such argument. *R. C. Stevens,* Some Unexplored Avenues in Comparative Anglo-American Legal History, 48 Tulane L. Rev. 1086 (1974); Id., Basic Concepts and Current Differences in English and American Law, (1985) 6 Journal of Legal History 337, points out the dangers implicit in this choice.

To tackle the issues raised in this introduction it is necessary to concentrate on a specific set of English materials, which will be chosen among topics such as trusts, contracts, and bailments, that traditionally fall in the domain of what is known as "lawyers' law"[19]. It should be clear, therefore, that this work offers a narrow section, rather than a broad survey, of the period covered. Yet, this section is not chosen at random, because it allows to catch a glimpse of some intellectual innovations that shaped the nineteenth century legal mind. It is obvious, however, that the materials considered below do not necessarily fit into or represent a general and uniform overall pattern. Indeed, the opposite might be true. The label "continental ideas" applies to a variety of influences that over the years were put to very different uses[20]. To delve deeper into these waters, and to get a more complete picture of the influence of continental legal thought in England, it would be necessary to deal with other aspects of the nineteenth century legal world, different from those considered below, and just as important. One should take into account, *inter alia,* the nineteenth century developments in jurisprudence[21]; the debates on law reform and codification[22]; and the state

---

19 This article will not deal with a fascinating problem raised by professor Riesenfeld during the Conference held in Lancaster at beginning of January 1991: i. e. whether and how notions or rules developed in cases argued before those "eccentric jurisdictions" (as Blackstone calls them), like the Admiralty, whose practitioners and judges were knowledgeable of the civil law, passed into the wider corpus of the law. With regard to the nineteenth century law of contract, a good case study of this phenomenon would be the emergence of novation as a distinct legal concept. Cp., e. g., Novation of Contract, (1870-71) 30 Law Magazine & Law Rev. 96. Recent studies provide analysis of the same problem in other fields of the law: see *S. J. Whittaker,* An Historical Perspective to the 'Special Equitable Action' in *Re Diplock,* (1983) 4 Journal Leg. Hist. 3; *A. Chianale,* Osservazioni sulla donazione mortis causa, Riv. dir. civ., 1990, II, 91.

20 For an overall view of nineteenth century juristic writing in England see *P. Stein,* Legal Science During the Last Century: England, in M. Rotondi (ed.), La science du droit au course du dernier siècle, Padova, 1976, p. 21 ff.; *A. W. B. Simpson,* The Rise and Fall of the Legal Treatise: Legal Principles and the Forms of Legal Literature, 48 Univ. of Chicago L. Rev. 632 (1981), at 660 ff., repr. in Id., Legal Theory and Legal History, London and Ronceverte, 1987, at 273 ff. (citations in the following notes are from this reprint). A number of important contributions (to which I am obviously indebted) deal generally with the use of continental ideas in nineteenth century English law: *P. Stein,* Continental Influences on English legal thought 1600-1900 (1977), reprinted in Id., The Character and Influence of the Roman Law, London, 1988; Id., Legal Evolution, Cambridge, 1983, highlights also some of the most crucial aspects of nineteenth century legal theory; *C. H. S. Fifoot,* Law and History in the Nineteenth Century (Selden Society Lecture), London, 1956; Id., Judge and Jurist in the Reign of Victoria, London, 1959; *F. H. Lawson,* Doctrinal Writing: A Foreign Element in English Law?, in Festschrift für Max Rheinstein zum 70. Geburtstag, I, Tübingen, 1969, p. 191 ff.; *G. Gorla,* Il diritto comparato in Italia e nel "mondo occidentale" ed una introduzione al "dialogo civil law-common law", Milano, 1983; *G. Gorla, L. Moccia,* A "Revisiting" of the Comparison between "Continental Law" and "English Law" (16th to 19th Century), (1981) 2 Journal of Leg. History 143; *L. Moccia,* English Law Attitudes to the "Civil Law", ibid.; *C. A. Cannata* and *A. Gambaro,* Lineamenti di storia della giurisprudenza europea, II, 4th ed., Torino, 1990, at 124 ff.

21 In such a broader context, John Austin and his contribution to jurisprudence would occupy a very important place. On this topic there are several in depth studies. See

of legal education[23]; the organization and role of the legal professions[24]; as well as the condition of the judiciary[25]; and the relation of all these matters to the various factors that bear upon legal change[26]. The author of this study is indebted towards those who have dared to cast light upon the larger picture.

The next section of this study (2.1 to 2.4) describes how, in the first half of the nineteenth century, the topics mentioned above presented aspects which were related to the civil law tradition. They were so related either because it seemed possible to trace the origins of certain English institutions back to the Roman law, or because a rational approach to the law fostered the idea that, notwithstanding their (occasional) differences, harmony (if not agreement) between the legal tradition descending from Rome and the common law could be found. A reaction against these ideas gathered strenght in the latter half of the century, and sections 3 and 4 of this article examine how a better knowledge of the Roman law cast doubts on the scholarly achievements of the preceding generation. Of course, in the last decades of the century it was still possible to use civil law materials as

especially *M. Lobban,* The Common Law and English Jurisprudence 1760-1850, Oxford, 1991, p. 223 ff. (with abundant references to the previous literature on the subject).

22 For a general appraisal see *A. H. Manchester,* Modern Legal History of England and Wales 1750-1950, London, 1980, at 38 ff.; *W. R. Cornish, G. de N. Clarck,* Law and Society in England, London, 1989. See also the literature cited below, note 92.

23 There is now a wealth of studies on this topic: cp. *H. G. Hanbury,* The Vinerian Chair and Legal Education, Oxford, 1958; *E. Campbell,* German Influences in English Legal Education and Jurisprudence in the 19th Century, (1959) 4 University of Western Australia Law Rev. 357; *F. H. Lawson,* The Oxford Law School, Oxford, 1968; *P. Stein,* Legal Theory and the Reform of Legal Education in Mid-nineteenth Century England (1979), repr. in Id., The Character and Influence of the Roman Civil Law, (supra note 20), at 251 ff.; *D. Sugarman,* Legal Theory, the Common Law Mind and the Making of the Textbook Tradition, in D. Sugarman, W. Twining (eds.), Legal Theory and the Common Law, London, 1986, at 26 ff.; *M. H. Hoeflich,* The Americanization of British Legal Education in the Nineteenth Century, (1987) 8 Journal of Leg. Hist. 244.

24 On this topic see *D. Sugarman, G. R. Rubin,* Towards A New History of Law and Material Society in England 1750-1914, in G. R. Rubin and D. Sugarman (eds.), Law, Economy an Society, 1750-1914: Essays in the History of English Law, Abingdon, 1984, 1 ff. at 84 ff. (this essay deals also with the other points mentioned in the text above); *D. Sugarman,* Lawyers and Business in England, 1750-1950 (forthcoming); Id., A Hatred of Disorder: Legal Science, Liberalism and Imperialism, in P. Fitzpatrick (ed.), Dangerous Supplements, Resistance and Renewal in Jurisprudence, London, 1991; *R. Cocks,* Foundations of the Modern Bar, London, 1983; *D. Duman,* The English and Colonial Bars in the Nineteenth Century, London, 1983; *B. Abel-Smith, R. Stevens,* Lawyers and the Courts: A Sociological Study of the English Legal System, 1750-1965, London, 1967.

25 *D. Duman,* The Judicial Bench in England, London, 1982.

26 On the relationship between legal change and its historical context see the work of *R. Sacco,* Legal Formants: A Dynamic Approach to Comparative Law, 39 Am. J. Comp. Law 1; 343 (1991), and of *A. Watson,* Legal Transplants, Charlottesville-Edinburgh, 1974. On the role of legal doctrine as a factor of change see *P. G. Monateri,* "Legal Doctrine" as a Source of Law: An Historical Paradox and a Transnational Factor, in Italian Reports to the XII International Congress of Comparative Law (Sidney 1986), Milano, 1986, at 19 ff.

sources of rational models[27]. Yet another and a more damaging challenge to the use of the Roman and civil law, which had been fashionable in the earlier part of the century, came from those scholars who argued that the common law tradition rested on Germanic foundations.

In the last quarter of the nineteenth century, the attempt to bridge the gulf between the civil law and the common law which had been carried out by personalities like W. Jones, J. Kent, and J. Story was held to be misconceived simply because it appeared that, in the end, the one had really nothing to do with the other. The core of the Anglo-American legal heritage came to be perceived as "Teutonic". The glamorous sediments of the civil law laid on its surface through the centuries suddenly became spurious additions to the genuine fabric of the law.

From a doctrinal point of view, the obvious lure of Germanism was that it promised to deliver common law from the doubtful historical and jurisprudential assumption entertained in the first half of the century by eminent judges and jurists alike. The price for this promise was the acceptance of another variety of anachronism which joined true discoveries with *ad hoc* interpretations of the sources.

Even the great English legal historian F. W. Maitland shared the predispositions of his epoch to a certain extent. Yet, one of the most important (and less recognized) accomplishments of this unrivalled master of English legal history was his investigations of the factors that made Enlish legal history — and English law — specifically English, rather than generically "Teutonic". The last section of this study briefly concentrates on Maitland's work in this area.

At first glance, the cosmopolitan attitude displayed by some members of the legal community up to the middle of the nineteenth century seems to be diametrically opposed to the outlook on the relationship between the civil law and the common law which was predominant in the last thirty years of it. But the story told in the following pages does not relate the improbable loss of an imaginary state of grace. No such thing took place.

Even when in the last quarter of the century, several English and American jurists strove to minimize the influence of the legal tradition descending from Rome on the common law, they had to resort to continental scholarship to make the point. On this basis one can safely argue that the latter part of the nineteenth century did not end the intellectual links between English jurists and their continental colleagues.

---

27 Writers on jurisprudence who were influenced by the ideas of John Austin — like Markby and Holland — provide perhaps the most important examples of this use.

II. Civil Law Dresses for the Common Law

1. Trusts and the Roman Law

It is worth taking a closer look at the historiographical error that Finlason was so eager to embrace. It is true that of this error he was one of the boldest advocates, but he was certainly not the only one. There were more learned and more consummate pleaders than the editor of Reeve's *History* to set up the case for a Romanized version of the law after the end of the Roman presence in Britain, up until the Norman conquest and beyond.

If we look for an account of the origins of trusts in the first volume of *The Equitable Jurisdiction of the Court of Chancery* by George Spence[28] we find a description of the origins of uses and trusts based upon the idea that these institutions were off-springs of the Roman *fideicommissa*. Blackstone[29] and Cruise[30], among others, had already mentioned the possible connection between trusts and *fideicommissa*[31]. Spence went further than these writers because he derived the origins of trusts from the Roman law applicable in Roman Britain, which supposedly had survived after the fall of the Roman rule[32].

The first steps in a lifelong intellectual adventure that ended tragically are interesting in themselves[33]. Spence's first printed work was *An Essay on the Origin of the English Laws and Institutions*[34]. This was followed by a translation

---

28 *G. Spence,* The Equitable Jurisdiction of the Court of Chancery, I, London, 1846. The second volume of this massive work was published in 1848.

29 *W. Blackstone,* Commentaries on the Laws of England, II, Oxford, 1766, at 327-329.

30 *W. Cruise,* A Digest of the Laws of England Respecting Real Property, I, 2nd ed., London, 1818, at 331.

31 To my knowledge, F. Bacon, Reading upon the Statute of Uses (read in 1600, first published in 1642), was the first to suggest this hypothesis. See on this point *D. Johnston,* The Roman Law of Trusts, Oxford, 1988, at 283 ff.

32 *G. Spence,* The Equitable Jurisdiction of the Court of Chancery, I, (supra note 28) at 20-21. See also at 439 f. There were difficulties in maintaining this position, which considered entails as the equivalent of *fideicommissa.* Compare on this point *F. W. Sanders,* An Essay on Uses and Trusts, I, 4th ed., London, 1824, p. 7 ff.

33 Standard reference works give the following biographical data. Born in 1787, Spence was the second son of a London surgeon. After taking a M. A. at the University of Glasgow in 1805, he was admitted in 1806 to the Inner Temple, where he was called to the bar on 28 June 1811, elected bencher in 1835, reader in 1845, and treasurer in 1846. After taking silk in 1834, his extensive practice in Chancery matters almost vanished. Member of Parliament (Tory) for Reading in 1826, he was unseated on petition in 1827, but then obtained the Ripon seat and returned to Parliament in 1829 until December 1832. Both in and out of Parliament, Spence spoke in favour of Chancery reform, and voted against his party on the reform bill. He also sustained the cause of legal education, and was one of the original members of the Society for Promoting the Amendment of the Law founded in 1844. He died on 12 December 1850, of wounds he had inflicted himself in a fit of insanity.

of the French Civil Code published anonymously in 1824[35]. Apparently, the study of the French Code to prepare this translation, strenghtened Spence's convictions about the possibility of an intimate relationship between the Roman law and the common law, as he states in the preface to his following book: *An Inquiry into the Origin of the Laws and Political Institutions of Modern Europe, Particularly of those of England*[36]. In these works we already find an outline of the argument later developed in the historical chapters of *The Equitable Jurisdiction of the Court of Chancery:*

> "On the whole, it appears, that whether we contemplate the various revolutions which have taken place in the dominion of this island, and thence draw inferences as to the changes which must have taken place in its judicial institutions; or whether we consider the institutions themselves, and compare them with what existed among the Romans, we shall be led to conclude that the foundation is wholly Roman. In rearing the superstructure, our ancestors, not idly attached to the institutions of antiquity, yet averse to overwhelming innovation, have varied the design as expediency dictated.
>
> Were we to trace our laws concerning property, and the civil relations of individuals, we should be led to a similar conclusion (a); . . . There are undoubtly many of our institutions and laws which cannot be *precisely* traced to any recorded Roman institutions, but it will in general be found that they were not brought "from the forests of the north", thus compurgation, from which trial by peers has been deduced, was originally suggested by the decisory oath of the Romans"[37].

According to one reviewer, Spence's *Inquiry into the Origin of the Laws and Political Institutions of Modern Europe* compared unfavourably with the scholarly *Geschichte des Römischen Rechts im Mittelalter* by Savigny[38].

Far from pursuing a Romanistic sport of his own, Spence was in tune with some of the foremost English historians of his time. In those years the historians John Allen[39] and Francis Palgrave[40] had just begun to develop "a new dialectic

---

[34] *G. Spence,* An Essay on the Origin of the English Laws and Institutions. Read to the Society of Clifford's Inn, in Hilary Term, 1812, London, 1812.

[35] The Code Napoleon; or the French Civil Code, Literally Translated from the Original and Official Edition Published at Paris, in 1804 — by a barrister of the Inner Temple, London, 1824.

[36] Published in London, 1826. It was dedicated to Lord Eldon.

[37] *G. Spence,* An Essay on the Origin of the English Laws and Institutions (supra note 34), p. 24. The second half of the passage quoted above is from the note (a) to Spence's text.

[38] The Roman Law in the Middle Ages, (1827) 1 The Jurist or Quarterly Journal of Jurisprudence, 202, at 208 - 213. However, this anonymous reviewer considered Spence's *Origins:* "extremely valuable, as an indication of the prevalence of more enlightened feelings among the class to which the author belongs, and as an earnest for future exertions".

[39] *J. Allen,* An Inquiry into the Rise and Growth of the Royal Prerogative in England, London, 1830.

between Roman and Germanic components of history"[41] which stressed the importance of the Roman element over the Germanic one. The desire to corroborate this research with the findings of an acclaimed master of Roman law like Savigny led to the appropriation of his name in this doubtful undertaking.

With his *Geschichte des Römischen Rechts im Mittelalter*[42], Savigny had exploded the error according to which Roman law had disappeared in the dark centuries of the Middle Ages. This broad interpretation of his great work was supposed to hold true for England as well. The first volume of the *Geschichte* was translated into English by Elias Cathcart and published in 1829[43]. In a long note appended to Savigny's introductory bibliographic essay, Cathcart argued that the Anglo-Saxon invaders could not have entirely destroyed the Roman municipal institutions: "... there is something apparently incredible in asserting that they were utterly annihilated in Britain by a comparative handful of invaders — too few, even to overawe a people, long accustomed to submission."[44] The character of the invasion, the rudimentary nature of the first laws enacted by the new rulers, the fact that from the earliest times the cities seem to have had their own jurisdictions, all these elements according to Cathcart meant that: "... numerous doctrines of the Roman law appeared to have existed in several cities of Britain, during the early part of the middle ages, along with portions of the old Roman civic system"[45].

In Germany this train of thought received sympathetic treatment in the pages of the cosmopolitan *Kritische Zeitschrift für Rechtswissenschaft und Gesetzgebung des Auslandes* edited at Heidelberg by K. A. J. Mittermaier and K. S. Zachariae[46]. Savigny himself praised the translator's work[47], but with characteris-

---

40 *F. Palgrave,* The History of England, vol. I, Anglo-Saxon Period, London, 1831; Id., The Rise and Progress of the English Commonwealth: Anglo-Saxon Period, London, 1832.

41 *J. G. A. Pocock,* The Ancient Constitution and the Feudal Law. A Study in English Historical Thought in the Seventeenth Century. A Reissue with a Retrospect, Cambridge, 1987, at 384-385. On these authors see also *P. Vinogradoff,* Villeinage in England, Oxford, 1892, at 11 ff.; *P. B. M. Blaas,* Continuity and Anachronism: Parliamentary and Constitutional Development in Whig Historiography and in the Antiwhig Reaction Between 1890 and 1930, The Hague, 1978, at 72 ff.; *J. W. Burrow,* A Liberal Descent: Victorian Historians and the English Past, Cambridge, 1981; *R. J. Smith,* The Gothic Bequest. Medieval Institutions in British Thought, 1688-1863, Cambridge, 1987, 158 ff.

42 Vols. I-VII, Heidelberg, 1815-1831.

43 The History of the Roman Law During the Middle Ages. Translated from the Original German of C. von Savigny by E. Cathcart, vol. I, Edinburgh, 1829. Cathcart was a graduate of the University of Edinburgh. The only work under his name in the British Library Catalogue is a Dissertatio Juridica ad Tit. V, lib. XXXIII Digest. De Optione etc., pp. 18, Edinburgh, 1817.

44 Preface. Note by Translator, XLVIII ff., at LIII.

45 Id., at LXIV.

46 Part of Cathcart's note was reproduced by Mittermaier in an article entitled Fortdauer römischer Municipal — Verfassung in England, Krit. Zeitschrift f. Rechtswissenschaft

tic love for accuracy, he also felt obliged to state that Cathcart's note did not in truth bear upon the survival of the Roman law in England after the retreat of the Roman legions[48]. Despite this warning, the stage was ready in England for further developments.

David Irving's *Introduction to the Study of the Civil Law*[49] did not venture to suggest openly that the English law rested upon Roman foundations, but nevertheless sharply criticized Blackstone for maintaining that the Roman law had fallen into oblivion during the Middle Ages, until the rediscovery of the Pandects at Amalfi[50]. After Savigny's *History of the Roman Law in the Middle Ages* it was possible to query from a new standpoint how much Roman law had found its way into the common law. Irving's book left the answer to this question to "several competent judges"[51], i. e. to an interesting collection of apt quotations from Lord Holt[52], Wood[53] and Cowell[54].

---

u. Gesetzgebung d. Auslandes, 1831, 136 ff. He praised Cathcart: "... als einen mit dem römischen Rechte selbst innig vertrauten wissenschaftlich gebildeten Jurist". The *Inquiry into the Origins*, etc. by Spence (supra note 36), was mentioned by Mittermaier in the same article as a book "voll kühner Hypothesen", written by an author to whom "eine gründliche Kenntnis des römischen Rechts fehlt". The list of the correspondents of the Review included Cathcart as well as other British and American lawyers.

47 *F. C. Savigny,* Geschichte des Römischen Rechts im Mittelalter, 2nd ed., vol. I, Heidelberg, 1834, p. 20.

48 Id., 2nd ed., vol. II, Heidelberg, 1834, p. 167, note (a): "Die am Schluß der Vorrede des ersten Bandes erwähnte Abhandlung von Cathcart betrifft leider nur die Fordauer der Städte Verfassungen, nicht die des Privatrechts."

49 *D. Irving,* An Introduction to the Study of the Civil Law, 4th ed., London, 1837. The third edition of this book had been published in 1823 in Edinburgh with the title: Observations on the Study of the Civil Law. See the book review: Study of the Civil law, (1829) 2 Law Magazine or Quarterly Review of Jurisprudence 480. Irving also published unsigned articles on the Roman law in the widely read Foreign Quarterly Review: Greek texts of Roman Law, (1831) 7 F. Q. R. 374-397; Civil Law: Barkow, Böcking, Blume and Hänel, 17 F. Q. R. 263-276. He wrote the following entries in the Encyclopaedia Britannica, 7th ed.: Canon Law, Civil Law, Feudal Law. Jurisprudence. On Irving's main work and on his connection with the Historical School see *M. Hoeflich,* Savigny and his Anglo-American Disciples, 37 Am. J. Comp. L. 18 (1989), at 21.

50 *D. Irving,* An Introduction to the Study of the Civil Law (supra note 49), at 83-84.

51 Id., at 95.

52 *Lane v. Cotton* (1702) 12 Mod. 472, at 483 per Holt C. J.: "... inasmuch the laws of all nations are doubtless raised out of the ruins of the civil law, as all Governments are sprung out of the Roman Empire, it must be owned that the principles of our law are borrowed from the civil law, therefore grounded upon the same reason in many things." Irving did omit the first line of this quotation, i. e.: "And this is the reason of the civil law in this case, which tough I am loth to quote, yet inasmuch ... etc. ..."

53 *T. Wood,* Institute of the Civil Law, 3rd ed. London, 1721, p. XI: Upon a review, I think it may be maintained, that a great part of the Civil Law is part of the Law of England, and interwoven with it throughout.

54 *J. Cowell,* Institutiones Juris Anglicani ad methodum et seriem Institutionum Imperialium compositae et digestae, epist. ded., Cant., 1605. Cf. p. A-2: "legem nostram communem (quam dicimus) nihil aliud esse quam Romani & feudalis mistionem".

Contrary to the views generally held a few decades earlier, it was clear that the Roman law had been kept alive in some parts of Europe even after the fall of the Roman empire. In this context, did Europe include Britain? The evidence was scarce, but the historical literature of the time was available to warrant an affirmative answer. In his major work, Spence fought his way through the sources[55], and with the help of Palgrave, Allen, Savigny, and a host of other references[56], he produces an insular version of an old story: 'captive Greece which captivates her rude conquerors'[57].

There were those who remained unconvinced. Austin, for example, did not follow Palgrave in his effort to establish *emphyteusis* at the inception of the feudal system[58]. And one could still read in Hargrave and Butler's edition of *Coke upon Littleton*[59], or in other works which represented the older historiographical tradition, a quite different account of the rise of tenures and of the origins of trusts[60]. Abroad, Spence's *Equitable Jurisdiction of the Court of*

---

55 For a recent appreciation of Spence's work see *D. E. C. Yale,* entry G. Spence in *A. W. B. Simpson,* Biographical Dictionary of the Common Law, London, 1984.

56 Spence could not read German. He read Savigny in the English translation by Cathcart, or in the French translation by Guenoux (incomplete as well). With the help of some friends he also consulted Savigny's *Geschichte* in German (cp. The Equitable Jurisdiction of the Court of Chancery, I, p. 131, additional note 2 to Ch. III). He read French, and the writings of the French historians Guizot and A. Thierry are cited in the footnotes of the *Equitable Jurisdiction of the Court of Chancery.* Nevertheless, just as in the case of Cathcart, the reader of this work cannot avoid the impression that the ideas expounded in Spence's writings took shape before he read the most recent foreign literature which was relevant to his thesis.

57 Id., The Equitable Jurisdiction, etc., I, at 1-298, spec. ch. XII, at 277 ff., at 281-282: "... The Anglo-Saxons Codes ... contain so few ordinances relating to the private rights of individuals in civil business, that other regulations must have existed in the cities, and wherever commercial intercourse had awakened or kept alive the faintest sparks of civilization". In the note (a) to this passage, Spence referred the reader to Cathcart's work cited above, note (43) "which Mr. Savigny, in the last edition of his history, has almost adopted as his own, as far as it goes". It is all too easy now to comment unfavourably on this part of Spence's work. When Spence wrote there were no scholarly studies on Bracton's text, which was by itself an endless source of perplexity, nor works on the west Roman vulgar law, which became available only much later.

58 Cp. *J. Austin,* Lectures on Jurisprudence or the Philosophy of Positive Law, 3rd ed. by R. Campbell, II, London, 1869, Lecture LII, p. 880.

59 Coke upon Littleton, by F. Hargrave and C. Butler, I, 19th London, 1832, note 1 at 64; II, at 191 a § VI, 11.

60 See, e. g., *W. Cruise,* A Digest of the Laws of England Respecting Real Property, I, 2nd ed., London, 1818, p. 386; *F. W. Sanders,* An Essay on Uses and Trusts, (supra note 32), 1824, p. 10-13; *J. Parkes,* A History of the Court of Chancery, London, 1828, p. 15; *G. Crabb,* A History of English Law, London, 1829; the book that throughout successive editions became the standard practitioner's reference omitted altogether a discussion of this point: *T. Lewin,* A Practical Treatise on the Law of Trusts and Trustees, London, 1837. The historiographical tradition to which I am referring in the text is well represented by A. Duck, De Usu & Authoritate Juris Civilis Romanorum, Londini, 1689, b. II, ch. VIII, pars III, p. 320 ff., according to whom no continuity could be established

Chancery impressed Mittermaier with the wealth of the materials collected by the author, rather than with the soundness of Spence's critical choices[61]. In the United States, though, the notes to Chancellor Kent's *Commentaries on American Law* reflected a much more favourable appreciation of Spence's work[62].

Indeed, Spence's arguments were at least intriguing and, for many of his contemporaries, persuasive. Lecturing to the students of the Middle Temple, the classicist George Long proclaimed "an idle imagination" the idea that "the Roman Law was ever forgotten or out of use in Europe"[63]. He conceded that: "The history of the Roman law in Britain is the strangest part of its history"[64], but after dropping this remark he nevertheless shared Spence's opinion on the matter[65]. Three articles published in legal periodicals[66] summed up to results of Spence's investigations and accepted the substance of his argument concerning the vital importance of the Roman contribution to the early history of the English law. The prose of Samuel Warren rendered similar arguments accessible to a larger audience[67].

---

between the Roman law and the English law, despite the fact that the Roman law had been administered in Britain under the Roman rule.

61 *K. J. A. Mittermaier,* Englische Rechtsgeschichte, (1847) 19 Kritische Z. f. Rechtswissenschaft u. Gesetzgebung d. Auslandes 137. This article shows an interest for Spence's work because it offered: "die kostbarsten Materialien für die richtige Auffassung germanischer Institute". Not surprisingly, then, Mittermaier was unable to concur with Spence's views about the origins of entails: "bei denen, wie wir glauben, mit Unrecht der Verfasser zuviel den Einfluß der römischen Fideicommisse annimmt, während wir das Einwirken der Idee des germanischen Stammgutsystems darin erkennen." (at 139).

62 *J. Kent,* Commentaries on American Law, I, 6th ed., New York, 1848, p. 546, note a, where Kent adopts Spence's conclusions as presented by an article published in a legal periodical on the origins of the common law (cited below, note 66) (Unless otherwise stated, all the references to Kent's *Commentaries* in this article are to the edition cited in this note).

63 *G. Long,* Two discourses delivered in the Middle Temple. With an outline of the Course, London, 1847, at 84. These lectures persuaded the young Nathaniel Lindley (later Lord Lindley) to attend law courses in Germany. See Lindley's Autobiography, at 28 (manuscript, cited by *M. Dockray,* Savigny and the Squatter, (1985) 6 Journal of Leg. Hist. 109, at 110).

64 Id., at 86.

65 Id., 87 f.

66 The Equitable Jurisdiction of the Court of Chancery, (1846) 5 (N. S.) Law Magazine or Quarterly Review of Jurisprudence 112; The Origins of the Common Law, (1847) L. Rev. 98; Spence's Jurisdiction of the Court of Chancery, (1849-50) 11 Law Rev. 314. The author of this article was aware of Mittermaier's book review (see note 1 at 317).

67 Samuel Warren (1807-1877) studied medicine in Edinburgh in 1826-7. After being admitted to the Middle Temple, he practiced as a special pleader until his call to the bar in 1837. He was made a Q. C. in 1851. Warren's fame rests more on his literary achievements than on his legal works. His novel "Ten Thousand a Year", which touched a number of legal problems and excelled in the farcical description of the lower edge of the legal world, had an enormous success and was translated into French, German and Russian.

After setting before the eyes of his readers a telling portrait of the "actual practitioner's" misery, Warren's *Popular and Practical Introduction to Law Studies*[68] invited the "intelligent practitioner" to avail himself of historical studies[69]. "Il faut éclarircir *(sic)* l'histoire par les lois and les lois par l'histoire", but having (mis) quoted Montesquieu, Warren then referred his readers to "the profound researches of Savigny", or rather to Cathcart, Allen, Palgrave and Spence's *Origin*[70]. Warren's voracious and eclectic *Introduction* put the Contributions of these authers side by side with the more orthodox opinions that found the origins of tenures in the Norman conquest.

The ideas advanced by these authors made significant progress even in higher circles. The inaugural address delivered in 1854 to the Juridical Society by Sir Richard Bethell (later Lord Westbury) leaves no doubts about this: "It is now clear that the Common Law which existed in England at the time of the Norman Invasion, was in great measure derived from the Jurisprudence that had been introduced and administered by the Romans during the 300 years of their dominion in Britain."[71] The fact that of this "lawyers, as a body, appear to have been uninformed from the earliest period down to very recent times"[72] was blamed — without a hint of irony — as one of the causes of the backward state of English legal science and legal practice[73]. Even Sir Henry Maine — one of the great Victorian jurists — found these ideas attractive. He aired them in his early essay on *Roman Law and Legal Education:* "now that the great accumulation of fragments of ante-Justinianean compendia, and the discovery of the Ms. of Gaius, have increased our acquaintance with the Roman law in the only form in which it can have penetrated into Britain, the suspicion of a partial early filiation amounts almost to a certainty."[74] Both in *Ancient Law*[75] and in the *Early*

---

68 The book went through three editions: 1835, 1845, 1863. It did have American editions and imitations such as *J. C. Reed,* American Law Studies; or Self Preparation for Practice in the United States, Boston, 1882. In the following notes references are to the second edition published in 1845. *R. Cocks,* Foundations of the Modern Bar (supra note 24), at 73 ff. describes the changing reactions of the profession towards the subsequent editions of this work, and its significance in the debate over the "old haphazard system of apprenticeship".

69 Id., at 234 ff.

70 Id., 246 ff. Indeed, Warren presented Cathcart's Note to Savigny as an ". . . account of one of the chief results of Savigny's researches". See also at 410, where Lord Holt's *dictum* in *Lane v. Cotton* (supra note 52), and the opinion of Sir W. Jones are quoted to support the idea that a large part of the common law derived from the civil law.

71 (1855-1858) 1 Papers Read Before the Juridical Society 1, at 2.

72 Id., loc. cit.

73 Bethell meant what he said. A first class in classics at Oxford at the age of eighteen, his advice to the pupils in his chambers was: "read the pandects": cp. *T. A. Nash,* The Life of Lord Westbury, I, London, 1888, p. 61; *W. Holdsworth,* A History of English Law, XII, London, 1966, p. 83.

74 *H. S. Maine,* Roman Law and Legal Education, first published in: Cambridge Essays for 1856, reprinted in Id., Village Communities in the East and West, 3d ed. London, 1876, p. 330 f., at 331.

History of Institutions[76] he left the door open to these conjectures. Yet Maine sensed that the argument did not lead too far. Legal orthodoxy was preserved by observing that "every intellectual importation we have received has been instantly coloured by the peculiarities of our national habits and spirit". In the hands of the old English common lawyers, the Roman law "would lose its distinctive character with even greater rapidity than any other set of institutions."[77] The relevance of the Roman law for the English lawyers living in the age of law reform was asserted on other grounds: "It is not because our own jurisprudence and that of Rome were *once* alike that they ought to be studied together — it is because they *will be* alike."[78].

2. *Consideration in Contracts*

The use of foreign concepts to expound indigenous rules is one of the most interesting phenomena for the student of comparative law. It is especially so when the theory imported from abroad does not fit perfectly the facts that it should explain.

The situation which results from the superimposition of the foreign theory on autocthonous materials therefore deserves special attention. Until the foreign theory is set aside it will be part of the law, lingering on as a sort of *obiter dictum* which clouds the operative rules that are actually enforced. Furthermore, this situation will create problems whenever an attempt is made to compare the law which has received the foreign theory, with the law of the country where

---

[75] *H. S. Maine,* Ancient Law Its Connection with the Early History of Society and its Relation to Modern Ideas, 1st ed., London, 1861. My references are to the 10th ed., 1884, with an Introduction and notes by F. Pollock, reprinted with a new preface by R. Firth, Boston, 1963, at 292-293, where Maine considers emphyteusis to be the model: "... whence the Frankish and Lombard Sovereigns got the idea of securing the military service of their followers by granting away portions of their public domain"; The Roman relation between patron and freedman — according to Maine — must have been literally borrowed" in order to fashion: "[t]he duty of respect and gratitude to the feudal superior, the obligations to assist in endowing his daughter and equipping his son, the liability to his guardianship in minority, and many other similar incidents of tenure ...". Maine's debt toward foreign scholarship is a matter for debate. Cp. *J. W. Burrow,* Evolution and Society. A Study in Victorian Social Theory, Cambridge, 1968, at 142 f. Considering how close to Spence's were Maine's views on these topics, one may well think with *R. C. J. Cocks,* Sir Henry Maine. A Study in Victorian Jurisprudence, Cambridge, 1988, at 27 f., that Maine took advantage of the work of his fellow countryman, as well as of more fashionable thinkers.

[76] *H. S. Maine,* Lectures on the Early History of Institutions, 1st ed. London, 1875. (My references are to the 1888 ed., New York, repr. Hein, 1987). In these Lectures, at 295-296, Maine again reminded his readers: "... the curiously strong case which may also be made out for the purely Roman origin of a good many institutions and rules which we are used to consider purely English and Germanic."

[77] *H. S. Maine,* Roman Law and Legal Education (supra note 74), at 331.

[78] Id., at 332.

the theory took shape. If we think of the history ofthe law of contract, the couple *causa* and consideration may well be considered the protagonist of such a story.

In the first half of the nineteenth century English lawyers did not have to look hard to find a close association between *causa* and consideration. It had been established for a long time[79]. Brian Simpson has remarked that the early nineteenth century treatise writers seemed to regard consideration as a local version of the civilian doctrine of *causa promissionis*[80]. In his recent work on the philosophical origins of the law of contract, James Gordley states more precisely that these writers — als Blackstone before them — "... seem to have in mind only the *causa* of an onerous contract, since they all explain that purely gratuitous promises will not be enforced."[81] To this remark one need only to add that, at least since the publication of *A Treatise of Equity with the Addition of Marginal References and Notes* by John Fonblanque[82], the similarity between *causa* and consideration

79 One of most famous examples of this association is provided by the counsel's argument in *Sharington v. Strotton* (1565) Plowden 298, at 302: "For if upon consideration that you are my familiar friend or acquaintance, or my brother, I promise to pay you £ 20, at such a day, you shall not have an action on the case, or an action of debt for it, for it is but a nude and barren contract, *et ex nudo pacto non oritur actio*, and there is no sufficient cause for the payment ...". Earlier cases also relevant on this point are collected and discussed by *J. H. Baker*, The Reports of Sir John Spelman, II, London, 1978, (S. S. volume 94), at 286 ff., spec. 287-292. It is quite another matter, of course, to ascertain the meaning and the importance of this association in the development of the rules on consideration in contracts. One may compare on this last point *A. W. B. Simpson*, A History of the Common Law of Contract, Oxford, 1975 (rep. 1987), at 401-405, 413, with *J. H. Baker*, The Reports of Sir John Spelman, II at 297 ff. A fuller picture of the discussion on this point is given by *J. H. Baker*, On the Origins of the "Doctrine" of Consideration, in M. S. Arnold et al. (eds.), On the Laws and Customs of England: Essays in Honor of Samuel E. Thorne, Chapel Hill, N. C., 1981 at 336-358; *D. J. Ibbetson*, Consideration and the Theory of Contract in Sixteenth Century Common Law, in: J. Barton (ed.), Towards a General Law of Contract, Berlin, 1990, p. 67 ff.

80 *A. W. B. Simpson*, Innovation in Nineteenth Century Contract Law, (1975) 91 L. Q. R. 247., repr. in Id., Legal Theory and Legal History (supra note 20), 171 f., at 186 (citations in the following notes are to this reprint). *P. A. Hamburger*, The Development of the Nineteenth Century Consensus Theory of Contract, 7 Law and Hist. Rev. 241 (1989), throws new light on the early development of the consensus theory of contract, but deals only shortly with consideration, stating that "... the civilian theory was modified in a way that made it compatible with the common law." (at 267). On the development of the consensus theory of contract see as well *J. Oldham*, Reinterpretations of 18th Century English Contract Theory: The View from Lord Mansfield's Trial Notes, 76 Georgetown Law Jo. 1949 (1988).

81 *J. R. Gordley*, Natural Law Origins of the Common Law of Contract, in J. Barton (ed.), Towards a General Law of Contract (supra note 79), 367 ff., at 439; Id., The Philosophical Origins of Modern Contract Doctrine, Oxford, 1991, at 139.

82 This edition, in two volumes, was published in London, 1793-1794. The author of the *Treatise of Equity*, which was first published anonymously in 1737, was probably Henry Ballow. See on this point *A. W. B. Simpson*, The Rise and Fall of The Legal Treatise: Legal Principles and the Forms of Legal Literature (supra note 20), at 288, note 91. According to *J. H. Baker*, An Introduction to English Legal History (supra note 16), p. 398, n. 109, this book contained: "The first coherent English treatise on contract

must have appeared very dubious. Fonblanque indeed observed that "... though we have borrowed the phrase nudum pactum from the civil law, and the rule that decides upon the nullity of its effect, yet (...) the common law has not in any degree been influenced by the notions of the civil law, in defining what constitutes nudum pactum"[83]. Noticing that Blackstone had misquoted the Italian jurist Gravina[84] in order to maintain that every contract in the civil law requires "... a reciprocity or exchange, what the Greeks termed *συναλλαγμα*, the civilians, permutatio"[85], Fonblanque analyzed the rule of the civil law on the point. The conclusion was that a *nudum pactum* by the civil law "... appears to have been an undertaking to give or to do some particular thing or act, which neque verbis praescriptis solemnibus vestitum sit, neque facto aut datione rei transiit in contractum innominatum"[86]. Thanks to the *stipulatio*, the civil law recognized: "... the right of a man to bind himself without any consideration, and merely interposing certain forms ...". The common law on the contrary did not possess an equivalent of the *stipulatio* to give binding force to verbal promises. For this reason, according to the English law "... a consideration of some sort or other is absolutely necessary to the legal validity of a verbal agreement ...". On the other hand, the common law enforced agreements that were considered naked pacts by the civil law. The typical examples were wholly executory agreements, which did not qualify as nominate contracts, such as an entirely executory agreement to exchange two goods[87].

This is not the place to consider whether Fonblanque's picture of the "civil law" was wholly accurate. Certainly his point was well taken. His remarks were noticed by the subsequent editors of Blackstone's *Commentaries*. The thirteenth edition of the *Commentaries* by Edward Christian referred to Fonblanque's "very

...". It had four editions before John Fonblanque added citations and notes to it. Between 1793 and 1820, it went through five editions. Fifteen years before the publication of Fonblanque's edition of Ballow's *Treatise* the judgment of Skynner L. C. B. in *Rann v. Hughes* (1778) 7 T. R. 350 n. had made it clear that, whatever the civil law meant by the phrase *ex nudo pacto non oritur actio*, the common law meant that an action on a parol promise laid only if it was supported by consideration.

83 [H. Ballow], A Treatise of Equity (1793), b. I., Ch. 5, Sect. I, note (a) at p. 326.

84 Id., at p. 327. Fonblanque noted that the citation of J. V. Gravina, De Ortu et Progressu Juris Civilis, book 2, ch. 12 in Blackstone's Commentaries, II, at 444, was significantly mutilated. Gravina's text (1st ed. Lipsiae, 1708, I have consulted the edition published in Rome, 1835, vol. II, p. 30-31) did not run: "In omnibus contractibus, sive nominatis, sive innominatis, permutatio continetur", but rather in: "... contractibus fere omnibus sive nominatis, sive innominatis, permutatio continetur." The qualification *(fere)* was material. It was repeated in a following passage "... ut contractus *fere* omnes facile ad una permutationem revocentur ...". It must be conceded, however, that the title of the chapter from which this excerpt is taken is: "De permutatione contractum omnium elemento". As to the context of Gravina's statements, see *A. Watson*, Chancellor Kent's Use of Foreign Law (this collection) text at note 58.

85 [H. Ballow], A Treatise of Equity, at 328.

86 [H. Ballow], A Treatise of Equity, at 332.

87 Id., at 333.

learned dissertation" on the topic: "That learned gentleman [i. e. Fonblanque] abundantly proves that a consideration was not necessary to constitute a binding contract in the civil law . . ."[88]. Twenty-five years later, John Taylor Coleridge's edition of the *Commentaries* was less explicit but nonetheless keen to qualify Blackstone's treatment of the maxim *ex nudo pacto non oritur actio*[89].

The theoretical difficulties posed by the use of civilian phraseology to express common law rules could be resolved in different ways. One possibility was to strip consideration of its civilian garb and to defend the common law rules on their own merits.

In the first half of the nineteenth century Abraham Hayward took this approach. His name is remembered today because he translated into English Savigny's *Vom Beruf unserer Zeit für Gesetzgebung und Rechtswissenschaft*[90]. Though now almost completely forgotten, in his own time Hayward was not a marginal figure: he was in contact with the most distinguished among his contemporaries, both in England and abroad[91]. Together with W. F. Cornish in 1828 he established *The Law Magazine, or Quarterly Review of Jurisprudence,* of which he was to become the sole editor until June 1844. England thus acquired a vigorous defender of the case against codification[92].

---

88 *W. Blackstone,* Commentaries on the Laws of England, II, 13th ed. by E. Christian, London, 1800, p. 414, note 2.

89 Id., Commentaries, etc., II, 16th ed., by *J. T. Coleridge,* London, 1825, p. 445, notes (3) and (4).

90 *F. C. Savigny,* On the Vocation of Our Age for Legislation and Jurisprudence, (A. Hayward trans.), London, 1831. Shortly after the publication of this translation, Hayward visited Göttingen "in the guise of a staid professor learned in the jurisprudence of England". There he was warmly received by Hugo, Bluhme, J. Grimm, and other scholars. The news of these encounters reached Savigny in Berlin, who wrote to Hayward, to tell him how he followed with "attentive pleasure" all efforts by "some few men of proper tone of mind" to break through the Chinese wall which "in jurisprudence alone" divided England from the rest of the world. Both Hayward's short and colourful account of his days in Göttingen and an excerpt of Savigny's letter to him (hitherto ignored by the literature on Savigny) are reproduced in *H. E. Carlisle* (ed.), A Selection from the Correspondence of Abraham Hayward, Q. C. From 1834 to 1884. With an Account of his Early Life, I, London, 1886, p. 11-16.

91 Cp. *H. E. Carlisle* (ed.), A Selection from the Correspondence of Abraham Hayward, passim.

92 The *Magazine* was one of the harshest opponents of James Humphrey's project to codify the law of property. On this project see *J. R. Dinwiddy,* Early Nineteenth Century Reactions to Benthamism, (1984) Trans. Royal Hist. Soc., 5th ser., vol. 34, 47 ff., spec. 56 ff.; *B. Rudden,* A Code Too Soon: The 1826 Property Code of James Humphreys (supra note 18); *M. Lobban,* The Common Law and English Jurisprudence 1760-1850 (supra note 21), 195 ff. See for instance: Codification Controversy, (1829) 1 Law Magazine 631. The opposite stand on the codification issue was taken by the short-lived The Jurist, or Quarterly Journal of Jurisprudence. See, e. g., Certainty of English law, (1827-1828) 1 The Jurist 405; Written and Unwritten Law, (1829) 2 Jurist 181. Despite their differences, the editors of The Jurist shared with the editor of the Law Magazine an admiration for the law reviews published on the Continent. Among these, the French

Armed with his knowledge of civilian doctrine, Hayward wrote for the *Magazine* a number of articles on mercantile law which acquired some reputation[93]. One of these unsigned articles contained a treatment of consideration which demonstrated how to describe the English rules on consideration without abusing civilian sources. Starting from an utilitarian account of promissory liability[94], Hayward came up with a treatment of consideration which linked this notion with that of bargain:

> "Contracts, it has been already said, are founded on a supposed reciprocity of advantage. There may, indeed, be engagements purely gratuitous, proceeding from the impulse of kindly feeling, without an immediate expectation of return. But these, from their very nature, transcend the authority of law, the object of which is not, as we have seen, to enforce obligations merely honorary, but to regulate the intercourse of men in those transactions in which the maintainance of civil society immediately depends. There cannot, of course, be a *bargain* without consideration. It would be, as Lord Loughborough rightly observed, a contradiction in terms. But we go one step further and say that neither can there be a contract without a consideration"[95].

Fonblanque's note on consideration, however, also provided an excellent starting point for attacking consideration as an anomaly of the English law of contract.

---

journal *La Thémis* (studied by *J. Bonnecase,* La Thémis (1819-1831). Son Fondateur Athanase Jourdan, 2nd ed., Paris, 1914, and more recently by *D. R. Kelley,* Historians and the Law in Postrevolutionary France, Princeton, N. J., 1984, 85 ff., *A. Bürge,* Das Französische Privatrecht im 19. Jahrhundert, Frankfurt a. M., 1991, 152 ff.), paid as much attention to the English scene as did Mittermaier and Zachariä's *Zeitschrift.*

93 See, e. g., J. Story's letter to Hayward dated January 4, 1840: "It may not be without some interest for you to know, that the *Law Magazine* is taken by the University in this place [Harvard], and the whole series from the beginning is to be found in our Law Library and is constantly read by our Law Students. I have long thought that the biographical articles, as well as the articles upon Commercial Law, are so valuable and so generally read, that they would well repay the publishing if printed in distinct volumes" (in *H. E. Carlisle* (ed.), A Selection from the Correspondence of Abraham Hayward, supra note 90, at p. 75). Hayward declared to be the author of many of these articles in the Preface to his Juridical Tracts, London, 1856, but this letter from Story shows that their authorship was a public secret long before the publication of this booklet.

94 A source of inspiration for Hayward was *W. Paley,* Principles of Moral and Political Philosophy, London, 1785, which grounded the binding force of promises on the protection of the expectations voluntarily excited by the promisor (Id., at 166, and b. III, p. I, ch. VI, on contracts). Note, however, that Paley did not deal specifically with gratuitous promises;from the moral point of view they were as binding as the onerous ones.

95 Mercantile Law n. IV, (1829) 2 Law Magazine or Quarterly Review of Jurisprudence 236, at 249-250; see also footnote 2 at 250 for the comparison with the civil law, and p. 255 for the notion of bargain. The disagreement with Fonblanque's treatment of consideration in the note to the *Treatise of Equity* (supra note 82 and 83), is explicit. See, e. g., note 5 to the passage reproduced in the text: "Mr. Fonblanque objects to our law that is defective in not enforcing these honorary obligations. To us the objection seems very unphilosophical". Hayward's reference to 2 Ves. Jun. 188 for Lord Loughborough's judgment is wrong. The correct reference is to *Myddleton v. Lord Kenyon* (1794) 2 Ves. Jun. 392, at 408.

An unsigned article *On the doctrine of nudum pactum in the English Law* published in the *Law Review and Quarterly Journal of British and Foreign Jurisprudence* for 1849 chose precisely this approach[96]. Following Fonblanque's steps, the anonymous author of this piece condemned the view of: "... nearly all the English text-writers on contracts who lay it down to their readers that the rules of the Civil and of the English law in requiring a valid consideration are identical."[97] Surely they were not alike, if by the "civil law" one means the early Roman law, because: "even according to the early Roman system, a contract was valid without consideration; and, *vice versâ,* a contract which by English Law would be perfectly binding, was with them *nudum pactum"* [98]. But it was also possible to take the matter further and to question the soundness of the English rule on consideration in the light of their difference from those on *causa* developed on the Continent in modern times. Thus, the anonymous author cited Voet, Pothier, Mühlenbruch and Hugo to demonstrate that Dutch, French and German law all recognized the binding force of agreements seriously willed by the parties. The English law alone refused to adopt this approach. Its stand was not only isolated, but — according to this view — based on unsound assumptions, as the outcome of cases like *Beaumont v. Reeve*[99] showed. This rough and ready treatment of continental law was pressed upon the reader to support the conclusion that it was desiderable to cut down as far as possible the operation of the: "... ill understood cantilena *ex nudo pacto non oritur actio"* that too often was "made an instrument for the dishonests to defeat their solemn engagements."[100]

If, despite these complaints, consideration and *causa* remained strange bedfellows for a while, a link between them was taken for granted no more. By the middle of the nineteenth century, it was clear that they were not the same thing.

The first edition of Pollock's *Principles of Contract* published in 1876 presented the starting point for further elaboration on this subject:

"As regards many if not most of its principles the English law of Contract is founded on or identical with the Roman. But the doctrine of Consideration, at

---

96 On the Origin of Nudum Pactum in the English Law, (1849) 10 Law Rev. & Quarterly Journal of British and Foreign Jurisprudence 56.

97 Id., at 57.

98 Id., at 58.

99 (1846) 8 Q. B. 483. In this case the plaintiff's declaration in assumpsit stated that she had been "greatly injured in her character and reputation, and prejudiced in and deprived of the means of procuring an honest living ..." as a consequence of the fact that the defendant "had seduced and debauched her and induced and procured her to cohabit with him as his mistress for a long time". The action was brought to enforce the defendant's promise (made after the end of the cohabitation) to pay a yearly sum of 60 £ to compensate the plaintiff and to support her.

100 On the Origin of Nudum Pactum in English Law (supra note 96), at 70. Cp. *P. S. Atiyah,* The Rise and Fall of Freedom of Contract, Oxford, 1979, at 452-453, for other signs of discontent with the working of consideration in contracts in the mid-nineteenth century.

least in the generality of form and application in which we now have it, is believed to be peculiar to England" [101].

In the first edition of his book on the law of contract Pollock, however, did not strive to sever consideration from its civilian double by providing it with a history wholly of its own. On the contrary, he contrasted the different approaches of the Roman, the French and the common law on this matter, but remarked that: "... the English consideration may be directly descended from the Roman *causa*" [102]. The missing link was to be sought in the doctrines of Equity [103].

3. Bailments and Degrees of Negligence

After Lord Holt's judgment in *Coggs v. Bernard* [104], and Sir William Jones' *Essay on the Law of Bailments* [105], the early nineteenth century jurists probably considered bailments one of the most promising fields for legal theory. At least Joseph Story took this view of the subject, as the first of his *Commentaries* demonstrates [106]. This is not surprising. Bailments lie at the crossroad of contracts, torts and possession. Apart from this aspect, which holds true to this day, other reasons influenced Jones and Story in the choice of bailments as a subject worthy of their attention. One was the great practical importance of the topic [107]. Another was that the treatment of bailments raised "questions of rational law", in which:

---

[101] *F. Pollock,* Principles of Contract: Being A Treatise on the General Principles Concerning the Validity of Agreements in the Law of England, London, 1876, at 147.

[102] Id., at 149.

[103] Id., at 150.

[104] (1703) 2 Ld. Raym. 909, at 912 ff. This is one of those cases that mean different things to different people. Compare *D. E. C. Yale,* Of No Mean Authority: Some Later Uses of Bracton, in M. S. Arnold et al. (eds.), On the Laws and Customs of England. Essays in Honor of S. E. Thorne (supra note 79), 383 ff., at 389, with *D. R. Coquillette,* The Civilian Writers of Doctors' Commons London, Berlin, 1988, at 274.

[105] *W. Jones,* An Essay on the Law of Bailments, London, 1781. The fourth and last edition of the book, with notes by William Theobald, was published in 1833. Jones' *Essay* had a spectacular success. It was repeatedly cited in Court [see for one of the first citations Shiells and *Thorne v. Blackburne* (1789) 1 Hy. Bl. 158], and was a source of inspiration for many other authors (see, e. g., the preface to Cruise's *Digest,* cited above note 30). In the U. S. Jones' *Essay* was eulogized by Parker C. J. in *Foster v. The Essex Bank,* 17 Mass. Rep. 479 (1821), at 499, and it had seven editions by 1836 [cp. *J. Parrish,* Law Books and Legal Publishing in America, 1760-1840, 72 Law Library Journal 355 (1979)]. On its place in the history of the doctrinal treatment of the law see *A. W. B. Simpson,* Innovation in Nineteenth Century Contract Law (supra note 80), at 252-253; Id., The Rise and Fall of the Legal Treatise (supra note 20), at 292-293, 299-301.

[106] Cp. *J. Story,* Commentaries on the Law of Bailments with Illustrations from the Civil and the Foreign Law, Cambridge, Mass., 1832, Preface, and § 1. An English edition of this work was published in London, 1839 (by J. Richards & Co.), with a preface and notices on the authors cited by Story written by R. Charnock. Unless otherwise stated, in the following notes citations will refer to this edition.

[107] *W. Jones,* An Essay, etc., at 1-2; *J. Story,* Commentaries on the Law of Bailments, § 1, p. 1.

> "no cause can be assigned why we should not shorten our own labour by resorting occasionally to the wisdom of antient jurists, many of whom were the most ingenious and sagacious of men. What is good sense in one age must be good sense, all circumstances remaining, in another; and pure unsophisticated reason is the same in Italy and in England, in the mind of a Papinian and of a Blackstone" [108].

For all these reasons, bailments were an ideal playground for jurisprudential exercises. Here we are concerned only with two of these, namely the (subsequent) history of Lord Holt's attempt to fix for each class of bailments the degree of care due by the bailee [109], and the analysis of grounds to protect the bailee's relation with the goods against wrongful interferences by third parties.

In the hands of Sir William Jones, the distinctions between different degrees of negligence sketched by Holt acquired philosophical roundness. Following Pothier's position [110] taken against Le Brun [111], Jones settled the tripartite distinction between gross, ordinary, and slight negligence [112]. Just like Holt had done before him [113], Jones fixed the standard of care due by the bailee — and, conversely, the degree of negligence which triggered his liability towards the bailor — according to the nature of the transaction. Only Jones, however, was consistent in the treatment of the topic. He declared as clearly as possible, that only the interests of the parties determined the standard of care to be observed by the

---

108 *W. Jones,* An Essay, etc., p. 14; cp. *J. Story,* Commentaries on the Law of Bailments, § 48, at 34-35. To compare Jones' approach to rational law with the prevailing trends in eighteenth century legal theory see *D. Liebermann,* The Province of Legislation Determined, Cambridge, 1989, at 36 ff., and passim, which sheds new light on the importance of natural law thinking in England during the Georgian age. The complex relationship between the structure of the common law procedure and the pattern of the jurisprudential discourse is highlighted by *M. Lobban,* The Common Law and English Jurisprudence 1760-1850 (supra note 21), esp. at 47 ff., 80 ff.; *C. P. Rodgers,* Continental Literature and the Development of the Common Law by the King's Bench: c. 1750-1800, in V. Piergiovanni (ed.), The Courts and the Development of Commercial Law, Berlin, 1987, at 161 ff., shows, with the aid of compelling evidence, how civil law learning played an important role in the development of the law by the King's Bench during the second half of the eighteenth century.

109 *Coggs v. Bernard* (1709) 2 Ld. Raym. 909, at 912 ff.

110 R. J. Pothier defended the traditional doctrine on degrees in *diligentia* and *culpa* first developed by the Glossators in the Appendix to his Traité du Contract du Marriage, II, Paris, 1772, in reply to Le Brun's *Essay* cited in the following note. On the fate of this doctrine up to the time of Pothier see *H. J. Hoffmann,* Die Abstufung der Fahrlässigkeit in der Rechtsgeschichte, Berlin, 1968; *M. Talamanca,* Colpa civile (Storia), Enciclopedia del diritto, VIII, Milano, 1960, 517 ff.

111 *D. Le Brun,* Essai sur la Prestation des Fautes, Paris, 1764. The author was *avocat au parlement de Paris.*

112 *W. Jones,* Essay, at 9-11 (on the distinction between the different degrees of negligence); at 27-32 (on the different opinions of Le Brun and Pothier). Writers on the civil law had already treated degrees of care and negligence: see, e. g., *T. Wood,* Institute of the Civil Law (supra note 53), at 26-28. Jones, however, did not cite this literature.

113 *Coggs v. Bernard* (1709) 2 Ld. Raym. 909, at 912 ff.

bailee. According to Jones, any transaction may satisfy: the interest of the debtor (e. g. *commodatum*), the interest of the creditor (e. g. deposit), or the interests of both (e. g. pledge). In the first case the bailee is held for slight negligence. Whenever the transaction benefits the creditor alone, the debtor is liable for gross negligence or fraud only. Ordinary negligence triggers liability if both parties have an interest in the transaction [114].

Though neither Kent nor Story followed Jones in every detail, they both accepted his basic scheme [115]. Jones' account of the civilian theory of degrees of *culpa* thus paved the way for their treatment of bailments.

Unfortunately, the nice distinctions expounded by these authors were to be handled before juries who knew little about degrees of negligence. In the closing pages of his *Essay*, Jones suddenly adverted to the possible consequences of this fact. There, he took pains to demonstrate the workability of his doctrine where the final decision on the circumstances of every particular case "to our constant honour and happiness" is left to a jury "freely chosen by the parties", rather than to "a *judge* appointed by the sovereign", as was the case on the continent [116]. This late defence of his work was unsuccessful. Thus, the expression "gross negligence" was employed in jury instructions as well as in judgments to convey the meaning of culpable negligence, rather than in accordance with Jones' tripartition of negligence [117]. Baron Rolfe's famous remark about gross negligence being "nothing more than negligence with the addition of a vituperative epithet" reflected just this use [118].

The impulse to override scholarly distinctions which were a source of embarassment was strong. Part of the trouble was that Jones' theory, like those advanced by his civilian sources, was riddled with ambiguities and contradictions. At least, it was so in the eyes of those who wrote after him [119]. Jones had moved towards an objective definition of "ordinary diligence" by describing it as the care: "which *every person of common prudence and capable of governing a family* takes of *his own* concerns" [120]. However, he had then watered down the objective character

---

114 *W. Jones*, Essay, etc., at 10 f.

115 *J. Kent*, Commentaries on American Law, II (supra note 62), Letc. 40, p. 559. *J. Story*, Commentaries (supra note 106), ch. I, pp. 1-31.

116 *W. Jones*, Essay, at 122-123.

117 See, e. g., Justice Patterson's instructions to the jury in *Vaughan v. Menlove* (1837) 3 Bing. N. C. 468, at 471. The very provinces of the judge and of the jury in actions of negligence remained unsettled until the last quarter of the nineteenth century: *Bridges v. The North London Railway Co.* (1874) L. R. 7 H. L. 213; *Metropolitan Railway Co. v. Jackson* (1877) 3 App. Cas. 193 (H. L.).

118 *Wilson v. Brett* (1843) 11 M. & W. 113, at 115-116.

119 Cp. *J. Story*, Commentaries on the Law of Bailments, at § 63, p. 42-43.

120 *W. Jones*, Essay, at 6; see also at 82-83, 88. *D. E. C. Yale*, "Of No Mean Authority" Some Later Uses of Bracton, in M. S. Arnold et al., On the Laws and Customs of England (supra note 79), at 389, note 30, remarks that "... Jones had good claim to

of this standard by suggesting that the gratuituos bailee, whose goods perished together with the goods bailed, should be exempt from liability, no matter how careless he had been, because he had taken as much care for the goods bailed as for his own [121]. Jones apparently failed to state precisely the criterion by which to decide what constituted "ordinary diligence", and consequently by which to determine the pivotal concept of "ordinary negligence" [122].

The ghosts of the civilian doctrines on *diligentia diligentis paterfamilias* and *diligentia quam in suis* thus fostered disagreement over one of the crucial rules involved in the decision of a liability issue. Was the standard of negligence subjective or objective? Both possibilities received some judicial [123] and doctrinal [124] support, though in retrospect it is tempting to consider the objective standard as the winning choice from the start [125].

It is important to remember that these questions were addressed while a tort of negligence *eo nomine* had yet to emerge, and continuity in pleading between relationship and non-relationship negligence was the rule [126]. As we will see,

---

have invented the reasonable man." But Jones (like Holt before him) was simply introducing to his readers the "bonus paterfamilias" of Roman origin. One is led to think that at birth the English "reasonable man" had more Roman blood in his veins that it is usually admitted. See also on this topic, *Note,* Origin of the Modern Standard of Due Care in Negligence, Washington University L. Quart. 447 (1976), at 457 ff.

121 Id., at 122-123.

122 To be fair to Jones, it should be remembered that this uncertainty reflects the conflicting views about *culpa* that are traceable to the Roman sources (on which see *F. H. Lawson, B. S. Markesinis,* Tortious Liability for Unintentional Harm in the Common Law and the Civil Law, I, Cambridge, 1982, at 22-29).

123 The first possibility is explored in *Shiells v. Blackburne* (1787) 1 Hy. Bl. 158 (a case of mandate); *The William* (1806) 6 Ch. Rob. 316 (obiter). See contra *Doorman v. Jenkins* (1834) 2 Ad. & El. 256; *Vaughan v. Menlove* (1837) 3 Bing N. C. 468.

124 *J. Story,* Commentaries (supra note 106), § 64, p. 43, clearly adopted the objective standard: "The measure, abstractly considered, has no reference to the particular character of an individual; but it looks to the general conduct and character of a whole class of persons". See also Story's judgment in *Tracy v. Wood* 3 Mason, 132 (1822). Kent had a different opinion on this. See Id., Commentaries on American Law, II, 4th ed., p. 562 note (a): "This last position [i. e. that defended by Story] has been ably and learnedly reasoned, but, in my judgment, without success;in such cases great stress is and ought to be laid upon the habits, employment, and character of the depositary, and they are to be taken in consideration; and the adjudged cases do not appear to warrant any other conclusion."

125 A strong case for the objective standard was *Doorman v. Jenkins* (1834) 2 Ad. & El. 256, where a coffeehouse keeper had left the plaintiff's money deposited with him, together with a larger sum of his own, in a cash-box in his tap-room, which was open to the public. The whole content of the cash box was stolen. It was left to the jury — who returned a verdict for the plaintiff — to determine whether the defendant had been negligent in keeping the plaintiff's money. For Taunton J. it was "perfectly immaterial" that the defendant's own money had been in the cash box with that of the plaintiff. See also *Vaughan v. Menlove* (1837) 3 Bing. N. C. 468.

126 *Govett v. Radnidge* (1802) 3 East 62, at 70-71, *per* Lord Ellenborough C. J., delivering the opinion of the Court; *Boorman v. Brown* (1842), 3 Q. B. 511; aff'd (1844)

these discussions over the standard of care had broader consequences; they proved troublesome when negligence eventually began to be perceived as a source of liability in its own right.

4. Bailments and Possession

The bailee's actions against wrongdoers who interfered with the goods bailed traditionally were justified on two grounds[127]. The first was that the bailee had a special or qualified property or a possessory interest in the goods entrusted to him. The second rested upon the bailee's responsibility towards the bailor for the custody of the goods bailed. According to this second view, the bailee could sue the wrongdoer because he was liable towards the bailor for the loss of the damage caused to the goods bailed[128]. Each of these two grounds by itself is apparently self-sufficient. Taken together they may seem contradictory, because the first makes the bailee's action independent of his position towards the bailor, while the second is centered on their relationship. Nevertheless, these two explanations went hand in hand for centuries without trouble. It was Sir William Jones who stirred up the still waters of legal theory on this issue.

Jones asserted that "... every bailee has a temporary *qualified* property in the things of which possession is delivered to him by the bailor, and has therefore, a possessory action or an appeal in his own name against any stranger who may damage or purloin them." This "limited property" in the goods entrusted to the bailee was something English. "By the Roman law, indeed, "even the possession of the depositary was holden to be that of the person depositing"; but with us the general bailee has unquestionably a *limited* property in the goods entrusted to his care ..."[129].

---

11 Cl. & Fin. 1 (H. L.). See on this point *M. J. Prichard, Scott v. Shepherd* (1883) and the Emergence of the Tort of Negligence, (Selden Society Lecture), London, 1976, p. 32; *S. F. C. Milsom,* Historical Foundations of the Common Law, 2nd ed., London, 1981, at 268-269; *P. G. Monateri,* Cumulo di responsabilità contrattuale e extra-contrattuale, Padova, 1989, 187 ff. On the development of the tort of negligence in American law cp. *M. J. Horwitz,* The Transformation of American Law 1780-1860, Cambridge, Mass., London, 1977, at 85 ff.; *G. E. White,* Tort Law in America. An Intellectual History, New York, Oxford, 1980, at 8 ff.

127 The purist may object to the sentence in the text above because the generic word "action" is employed to denote distinct remedies, i. e. trespass, trover, conversion, detinue, etc. Yet, this use is attested by authors like Blackstone, Dicey, Holmes. Here it is justified by the fact that the plaintiff's right to immediate possession is sufficient to maintain any of the aforementioned actions. There is a vast body of secondary works that analyse the historical origins of the rules discussed in this paragraph. This literature, however, does not have immediate bearing on the topic treated in this paragraph, i. e. the approach to these rules in the nineteenth century.

128 For a classical statement of the law on these points see *W. Blackstone,* Commentaries on the Laws of England, II, Oxford, 1766, at 453-454; see also at 395-396.

129 *W. Jones,* An Essay on the Law of Bailments, at 80.

Jones wrote to dispute Coke's reasoning in *Southcote's case*[130], but he failed to persuade Kent[131] and Story[132], whose views were respected in England[133]. For both Kent and Story, the safer opinion was to deny this limited or qualified property of the depositary. They thought that the depositary had only the custody and the possession of the goods bailed[134], which was the ground of the bailee's action.

Even in the discussion of such a narrow point of law, Story's contribution ranks as superior. Story raised doubts about the very terms of the controversy. He certainly had an inkling of the fact that the whole issue turned on a mere matter of words[135]. Yet Story himself added a grain of confusion to the hotchpotch. He did not refrain from adumbrating a fundamental agreement between the common law and the civil law on these matters. Story first showed that the civil law coincided "with what is here stated to be the common law on the point"[136] because it also denied the depositary a special property in the goods deposited. To this harmless remark he then added that the common law and the civil law did not materially differ because they both granted possession to this kind of bailee.

This bold step needed more elaboration. It was true that some civil law authorities (like Pothier) did not support such conclusion. Story, however, did not lack the genius to bridge — or rather to mask — the gulf between the common law and the civil law on the point[137]:

> "The possession of the depositary is certainly, for many purposes, deemed the possession of the depositor in our law, both as to his rights and remedies. And it could scarcely have been the intention of the civil law to declare, that possession did not, in fact, pass to the bailee by the delivery of the deposit. It meant only to affirm, that the possession was not exclusive of that of the bailor; but rather in subordination to it."[138]

Such an approach to the sources was considered a sin only in the latter half of the century. For the moment it plausibly paved the way to the spectacular success of von Savigny's *Treatise on Possession* in the jurisprudential arena[139].

---

130 *Southcote v. Bennet* (1601) Cro. Eliz. 815; 1 Inst. 89 a; 4 Rep. 83 b.

131 *J. Kent,* Commentaries on American Law, II, (supra note 62), Lect. 40, p. 559-611.

132 *J. Story,* Commentaries on the Law of Bailments, at § 93, p. 71 f.

133 See, e. g., W. Theobald's notes to Jones' Essay, at 52 ff.

134 *J. Kent,* Commentaries on American Law, II, at 585. *J. Story,* Commentaries on the Law of Bailments, § 93, p. 71; and see also Id., 9th ed. by J. Schouler, § 93 a ff., p. 94 f.

135 *J. Story,* Commentaries on the Law of Bailments, 9th ed. by J. Schouler, at § 93 g, p. 102 f.

136 Id., at § 95, p. 74.

137 On Story's attitude towards the civil law see *M. Hoeflich,* John Austin and Joseph Story: Two Nineteenth Century Perspectives on the Utility of the Civil Law for the Common Lawyer, 29 Am. J. Leg. Hist. 36 (1985), spec. p. 57 ff.

138 Id., at § 95, p. 75.

Indeed the success of Savigny's book in England was both spectacular and skin-deep, if it is judged by the fact that in 1870 Dicey expounded the law on the subject along the lines laid down by Blackstone without even naming Savigny[140]. Yet, when Dicey was only an emerging legal writer, new trends in legal thought were gaining ground.

III. The Emperor Has No Clothes

In the last quarter of the nineteenth century, the common law world began to reconsider its attitude towards the Romanistic legal tradition. To do so, more than a casual acquaintance with foreign legal doctrine was required. Thus, in the latter part of the century, the intellectual ties between the Anglo-American world and the continental legal science did not loosen. Rather, as amateurs gave way to professionals, and the universities strove to match the achievements of foreign institutions[141], these ties became all the more important[142].

---

139 Savigny's Das Recht des Besitzes was first published in 1803. In 1832, John Austin described it as an outstanding achievement. Cp. *J. Austin,* Lectures on Jurisprudence, I, (supra note 58), at 55; George Long gave a short account of the outcome of Savigny's research on this topic in the entry "Possessio", in *W. Smith,* A Dictionary of Greek and Roman Antiquities, London, 1842, at 779-782. Savigny's book was translated into English in the same year by: *E. Perry,* Von Savigny Treatise on Possession or the Jus Possessionis of the Civil Law, London, 1842. It was eulogized by *N. Lindley,* An Introduction to the Study of Jurisprudence; Being a translation of the General Part of Thibaut's System des Pandekten Rechts, With Notes and Illustrations, London, 1855, p. 282, note to § 213. *J. F. Stephen,* A Digest of Criminal Law, London, 1877, esp. note XI to art. 281, adopted Savigny's theory of possession as a starting point for his treatment of possession in the criminal law. Savigny's Possession was quoted by counsel in *Bridges v. Hawkesworth* (1851) 21 L. J. Q. B. 75, at 77, but, according to Patteson J., the reference to Savigny's work "full as it is of subtle distinctions and nice reasonings" was not conclusive on the point at issue (at 78). On the topic of possession in nineteenth century legal theory, see *C. H. S. Fifoot,* Judge and Jurist in the Reign of Victoria (supra note 20), at 85 ff. See also *M. Dockray,* Savigny and the Squatter (supra note 63), for a possible judicial use of Savigny's theory of possession by Lindley.

140 *A. V. Dicey,* A Treatise on the Rules for the Selection of the Parties to an Action, London, 1870, at 352 ff.

141 There are several signs of an early attention to the German academic world, such as the translation of a piece by Savigny "On the Present State of the German Universities", Monthly Register, 1803, p. 3-6 [reprinted by *R. Wellek,* Ein unbekannter Artikel Savignys über die deutschen Universitäten, ZSS, Germ. Abt., 51, 1931, 529] by H. Crabb Robinson, who later took part in the foundation and the administration of University College, London. Cp. *M. M. Bellot,* University College London, 1826-1926, London, 1929, at 290-292. Yet, it is true that, until the mid-19th century, very little was done in England to improve the quality of legal education at the universities. On the reform of legal education see the literature cited supra note 23.

142 This is true of the English professoriate just as it is for its American counterpart, on which see *M. Reimann,* A Career in Itself. The German Professoriate as a Model for American Legal Academia (this collection), and *D. S. Clark,* Tracing the Roots of American Legal Education, Rabels Z. 1987, 313. It is difficult, however, to say how

From this point of view, it is noteworthy that the older generation was criticized not just because it had resorted to foreign materials to give an account of the law. The complaint was rather than it had done too little to understand those sources and their relation to the present conditions of the law[143], or to look in the right direction, i. e., to those inquiries by foreign scholars who had rescued from obscurity entire fields of the law which did not have a Roman background. Some of the best legal minds of the age advanced similar reproaches, and their criticism was grounded upon the nineteenth century continental literature on the Roman law, or the works on Germanic legal antiquities authored by scholars centered in German-speaking universities.

Part of this story is the use of contemporary Roman law scholarship to show that the importation of civilian doctrines in the Anglo-American area had committed the common law to the wrong theory. There was no reason to cling to doctrines which by then had been abandoned or discredited even in the civil law world, or which had been simply misunderstood from the beginning[144]. The

many English-speaking lawyers spent some time as students in foreign Universities. Writing to Holmes, F. Holtzendorff gives a rough estimate of 60 American law students studying at that time in German Universities. Holtzendorff to Holmes, 9. 5. 1871, O. W. Holmes Papers, Harvard Law School Library, Box 53, f. 9. One may compare this number with the statistics provided by *C. Diehl,* Americans and German Scholarship 1770-1870, New Haven and London, 1978, at 155-159, for the years 1810-1860. Little is known about British lawyers studying abroad. For obvious reasons, any estimate of their number should count students from Scotland (like James Bryce) apart.

143 In the United States, even idols of the older generation like Story and Kent were not spared this kind of criticism. For the new generation of lawyers, Story's "scissored latin and sloppy quotations from the civilians" [review of the Commentaries on the Law of Bailments, 9th ed., by *J. Schouler,* 13 Am. L. Rev. 357 (1879), at 358] disfigured rather than adorned his books. His references to the civil law were considered "interesting as illustrating a harmless phase of the learned judge's vanity", but "of little practical use in these days, when an acquaintance with the civil law is much more extensive and general than it was thirty years ago". [review of the Commentaries on the Law of Promissory Notes, 7th ed., by *J. L. Thorndike,* 1878, 13 Am. L. Rev. (1879) 349 at 350]. The content and the tone of F. Pollock's *Introduction* and *Notes* to Maine's *Ancient Law* (supra note 74), show that similar feelings were at home in England as well. The growth of academic Roman law studies and the diffusion of the teachings of the German Pandectists in English by graduates of the German universities (see, e. g., *F. J. Tomkins, H. D. Jenken,* Compendium of the Modern Roman Law, Glasgow, 1870) may be only one of the factors that account for this kind of criticism.

144 This is the main theme of *O. W. Holmes,* Misunderstandings of the Civil Law, 6 Am. L. Rev. 37 (1871). Holmes' writings received favourable comments by W. G. Hammond, "one of the leading comparative lawyers and legal historians of his period" [*M. Hoeflich,* Roman and Civil law in American Legal Education and Research Prior to 1930: A Preliminary Survey, 3 University of Illinois Law Rev. 719 (1984), at 728]. See Hammond to Holmes, 10. 11. 1871, O. W. Holmes Papers, Harvard Law School Library, Box 43, f. 29: "The 'misunderstandings of the civil law' are innumerable, and their influence on the scientific development of our own has been an unfortunate one". On this topic see also Hammond's letters to Holmes dated 22. 2. 1861, and 25. 8. 1879 [same location]. This kind of inquiry still yields discoveries. See, e. g., *P. Birks, G. McLeod,* The Implied Contract Theory of Quasi-Contract: Civilian Opinion Current in the Century Before Blackstone, (1986) 6 Oxford Journal of Legal Studies 46.

theory of the three degrees of negligence thus came under fire. In the United States, it was first openly attacked from the bench by Curtis J. in 1853[145]. The following year one of the American disciples of Savigny — Luther Cushing — took the same stand in his *Introduction to the Study of Roman Law* to argue that a better knowledge of the Roman law would have spared the common law a false start on this point[146]. By 1870 Shearman and Redfield's *Treatise on the Law of Negligence* noted some controversy over the tripartite approach, but nevertheless stated it as good law[147]. Francis Wharton's *Treatise on the Law of Negligence*[148] and an article published in the *American Law Review* of 1874[149]

145 (1853) 16 How. 474. The claimant was a passenger who had been gratuitously taken on board a steamboat traveling from Sacramento to San Francisco. He obtained compensation for the injuries caused to him by the explosion of one of the boilers of the boat. The behaviour of the masters of the boat was held to amount to gross negligence (it appeared that the boat had been racing on the river with another steamer). Curtis J., delivering the opinion of the court, seized the opportunity to question *(obiter)* the theory of the three degrees of negligence. After a survey of the English and American authorities on this doctrine, Curtis stated that "some of the ablest commentators on the Roman Law, and on the civil code of France, have wholly repudiated this theory of the three degrees of diligence, as unfounded in principles of natural justice, useless in practice, and presenting inextricable embarrassments and difficulties. See Toullier's Droit Civil, 6th vol. p. 239, & c.; 11th vol. p. 203, & c. Makeldey *[sic]*, Man. Du Droit Romain, 191, & c." (at 475). Ironically, these remarks came from a former pupil of Story. See *C. B. Swisher*, The Tawney period, in History of the Supreme Court of the United States, V, New York, London, 1974, at 238.

146 *L. S. Cushing*, An Introduction to the Study of the Roman Law, Boston, 1854, spec. at 195 ff. The title of ch. IV, where the theory of degrees of negligence is analyzed and criticized, is: Utility of the Study of the Roman Law.

147 *T. G. Shearman, A. A. Redfield*, A Treatise on the Law of Negligence, 2nd ed., New York, 1870 (1st ed. 1869), ch. II, p. 19-26, spec. at 18-19. See also the unsigned article: Degrees of Negligence, 5 Am. L. Rev. 38 (1870). Shearman and Redfield remarked that most cases cited against the tripartion of negligence turned on the issue of whether a stipulation against liability for "negligence" was operative when gross negligence was alleged. They thought this could be conceded without rejecting the theory of the three degrees of negligence. In a hitherto unnoticed anonymous book review of this work, O. W. Holmes criticized their acceptance of this theory: "the introduction of degrees of negligence from the civil law has been productive of not good but of unqualified harm. The bewildering perplexity which, in this country, surrounds the question of the respective provinces of the court and of the jury in actions for negligence, is, for most part, owing to the confusion produced by this distinction". 4 Am. L. Rev. 350 (1870), at 351. See also Id., The Theory of Torts, 7 Am. L. Rev. 652 (1873), at 658-659 (on fact and law in negligence cases); Id., Trespass and Negligence, 14 Am. L. Rev. 1 (1880), 30 ff. (same topic).

148 *F. Wharton*, A Treatise on the Law of Negligence, Boston, 1874, reviewed by *L. v. Bar*, 4 Zeitschrift f. d. Privat- und öffentl. Recht d. Gegenwart, 21 (1877). See also the preface to the second edition of this work, Philadelphia, 1878. Wharton criticized the distinction between three degrees of negligence, but in full accord with *J. C. Hasse*, Die Culpa des römischen Rechts, 1st ed., Kiel, 1815, he admitted the distinction between negligence and gross negligence. More generally, on Wharton's stand about the utility of civil law studies see Id., A Commentary on the Law of Contracts, 2 vols., Philadelphia, 1882.

149 The Three Degrees of Negligence, 8 Am. L. Rev. 649 (1874). The author of this unsigned article was *Nicholas St. John Green*. Green criticized Jones' *Essay* as well as

struck the next blow to the tripartition of negligence. Both made it clear again, that the best civilian authorities did not endorse the theory of the three degrees of negligence. By 1880 M. M. Bigelow found that this doctrine had retained: "some faint vitality in England and in various parts of the U. S."[150].

English authors were less ready to join the criticism just mentioned. After all, the cases had unsettled the theory supported by Lord Holt and Sir William Jones, but the judges were still paying compliments to its authors[151]. R. Campbell[152], H. Smith[153], and T. Beven[154] went over the cases as if this doctrine still had a bright future ahead. Beven indeed pugnaciously defended it. According to him it would have been an "patient absurdity" to think that the provisions of the Prussian *Landrecht* concerning the degrees of negligence were abrogated in Germany simply because they had become the target of doctrinal criticism. Since the distinction between three degrees of negligence had been "recognized as of binding force in our law", Beven urged, it was not less absurd to maintain: "that English judge-made or customary law should be affected by the most learned historical investigations of jurists engaged in the interpretation of a foreign system."[155] Pollock[156] and Clerk and Lindsell[157] took a wiser course. The first simply adopted the standard of the reasonable man, without saying a word about degrees of negligence. The latter two denied the existence of degrees of negligence

---

Story's *Bailments*. The first was described as an example of the "... powers of the human mind to color everything by the light of preconceived opinion". (at 655). The second was blamed for failure to take notice of: "the recent labors of those European civilians whose studies have thrown light upon some things in the Roman law which had been previously obscured by the works of the Glossators and the Commentators." (at 662). On the relations between Green, Holmes and Wharton see *H. Hovenkamp*, Pragmatic Realism and Proximate Cause in America, (1982) 3 Journal of Leg. Hist. 3, at 16-17.

150 *M. M. Bigelow*, Elements of the Law of Torts, Cambridge, 1880, p. 286. Bigelow's announcement of the decline of this doctrine was perhaps premature. Cp. *S. D. Elliott*, Degrees of Negligence, 6 So. Cal. Law Rev. 92 (1933), at 114 ff.

151 See Lord Chelmsford's judgment in *Giblin v. Mc Mullen* (1868) V. Moore N. S. 434, at 460.

152 *R. Campbell*, The Law of Negligence, London, 1871. The author was a member of the Scottish and of the English bar and one of the editors of John Austin's *Lectures on Jurisprudence*. Campbell's book simply equated negligence with *culpa*. *T. W. Saunders*, Treatise on the Law Applicable to Negligence, London, 1871, also had a paragraph on degrees of negligence (§ 1, p. 3), but just as the earlier and more successful book of *C. G. Addison*, Wrongs and Their Remedies, Being a Treatise on the Law of Torts, London, 1860, it can hardly be considered as something more than a bare collection of cases.

153 *H. Smith*, A Treatise on the Law of Negligence, London, 1880.

154 *T. Beven*, Principles of the Law of Negligence, London, 1889, Ch. III, Degrees of Negligence, p. 16-45.

155 Id., at 19-20. Beven made it clear that the degrees of negligence were to be taken as established *in abstracto* rather than *in concreto*.

156 *F. Pollock*, The Law of Torts, London, 1887, at 355.

157 *J. F. Clerk*, *W. H. B. Lindsell*, The Law of Torts, London, 1889, at 355.

but conceded that "there were undoubtly degrees of care". "These degrees of care, however, it is impossible to classify, for they are infinite in number, each special set of circumstances requiring its own particular degree"[158]. To come to a safe conclusion, the two authors adopted as a standard what "a reasonable and prudent man" should have done under the circumstances"[159]. It was left to the care of a New Zealander to put a tombstone with a proper inscription on the theory of the three degrees of negligence[160].

Reading this literature, one is led to the conclusion that these contributions were inspired by different thoughts. To oversimplify, there were scholars like Cushing and Wharton who maintained that a knowledge of contemporary Roman law scholarship was one of the basis of a theoretically sound approach to the law, and there were those like Holmes, Bigelow and Salmond who were more inclined to consider the civil law a world apart.

This latter starting point it perhaps the most interesting one.

A new wave of historical research had done much to do away with the uncertain historical premises blithely accepted by some of the leading figures of the older generation. The impulse to "clean the house" originated in Germany; American and English scholars eagerly followed suit.

In a sense the English speaking world was repaid with its own money — plus interest, of course — because the German historical and juridical thought had in turn drew inspiration from the British contribution. It is out of place here to explore how this happened. Nevertheless, it should at least be remembered that one of the founding fathers of the Historical School — Gustav Hugo — translated into German the forty-fourth chapter of Edward Gibbon's *Decline and Fall of the Roman Empire* on the Roman law, in order to bring new ideas into the field of Roman law studies[161]. Savigny himself, in his early lectures on *Juristische Methodenlehre,* mentioned to his audience Hugo's translation of Gibbon[162].

---

158 Id., at 355. See, for a similar approach in American law, the opinion of the Court delivered by Justice Bradley in *New York Central Railroad Co. v. Lockwood,* 17 Wall. 357, 84 U. S. 627 (1873), at 641.

159 Id., at 356. The authority cited for this proposition was the classical definition of negligence given by Baron Alderson in *Blyth v. Birmingham Waterworks Company* (1856) 11 Ex. 781, at 784.

160 *J. Salmond,* The Law of Torts. A Treatise on the English Law of Liability for Civil Injuries, London, 1907, p. 25, § 6, "The Standard of Care", note 3: "There are no authorities which compel us to admit that distinctions so vague and impracticable in their nature, so unfounded in principle, and so clearly rooted in historical error as to the rules of Roman Law, form any genuine part of the law of England".

161 Eduard Gibbon's historische Übersicht des Römischen Rechts, aus dem Englischen übersetzt, und mit Anmerkungen begleitet von Professor Hugo in Göttingen, Göttingen, 1789. Gibbon's achievement in the field of Roman Law is investigated by *J. H. Hoeflich,* Edward Gibbon, Roman Lawyer, 39 Am. J. Comp. Law 803 (1991). On the importance of this translation see the entry on G. Hugo in Allgemeine Deutsche Biographie, XIII, Leipzig, 1881, at 323: "Hugo's Vorrede dazu ist sein wissenschaftliches Programm";

These episodes should not be considered as isolated occurrences. From the second half of the eighteenth century onwards, England occupied a very special place in the German culture. Whenever the debate turned upon an issue connected with national identity (and certainly law was one of them), the value of the English experience was stressed. From Justus Möser's discovery that the spirit of the ancient Germanic freedom had been kept alive and thriving in England[163], to Otto von Gierke's refurbishment of the Germanic components of the German legal traditon, a ripple it not a torrent of ink was spilled over the English experience[164].

It was England seen through German eyes. With respect to private law this remark refers to a well known fact. Among the most powerful reasons to further the study of English law in Germany there was the hope of finding across the Channel the evidence needed to disinter entire fields of the law which the reception of the medieval Roman law had buried in continental Europe[165]. Second-

---

P. Stein, Legal Evolution (supra note 20), at 54-56; *P. Cappellini,* Systema Juris, I, Milano, 1984, p. 175 ff.; *J. Q. Whitman,* The Legacy of the Roman Law in the German Romantic Era, Princeton, N. J., 1990, p. 84: "Gibbon's Chapter 44, in turn, inspired the great revival of Roman-law scholarship in Germany that began with Gustav Hugo of Göttingen (who translated Gibbon's chapter) and culminated with Savigny".

162 *F. C. Savigny,* Juristische Methodenlehre (G. Wesenberg, ed.) Stuttgart, 1951, at 35: "Man kann auch die Gesetzgebung als einen Teil der Geschichte eines solchen betrachten. Von dieser Bearbeitung, namentlich des römischen Rechts, existiert ein treffliches Muster von Gibbon in seiner Geschichte des Verfalls des Römischen Reiches, der ihr ein besonderes, das 44. Kapitel widmet (übersetzt von Hugo, Göttingen 1789)".

163 Justus Möser (1720-1794), mostly remembered for his patriotic writings, *Advocatus Patriae* of the Bishoprick of Osnabrück since 1747, had a first hand knowledge of England. *C. Antoni,* La lotta contro la ragione, (1st ed. 1942), Firenze, 1968, p. 87 ff. [German tr. by *W. Goetz,* Der Kampf wider die Vernunft, 1951] points to this knowledge as an important factor in the intellectual formation of Möser. See also on this *C. E. Mc Clelland,* The German Historians and England. A Study in Nineteenth Century Views, Cambridge, 1971, p. 18-19 (and the whole book for a survey of the changing attitudes of nineteenth century German historians and jurists towards England). According to *W. F. Sheldon,* The Intellectual Development of Justus Möser: the Growth of a German Patriot, Osnabrück, 1970, p. 53, Möser's six months in England were enough to develop a more critical view of England than the one he had in his youth. As Möser remarked in a letter to a friend, the best place to lose one's anglophilia was in England. For a well-balanced assessment of Möser's influence on Savigny see *J. Schröder,* Justus Möser als Jurist, Köln, 1986, at 81-86.

164 See, e. g., von Gierke's comments on the different paths of German and English legal history in *O. v. Gierke,* Das deutsche Genossenschaftsrecht, I, Berlin, 1868, p. 819. The sentiments voiced by Gierke turned sour when England and Germany started to compete on the European scene: cp. *C. E. Mc Clelland,* The German Historians and England (supra note 163), at 205.

165 This *Leitmotiv* is quite common in the nineteenth century German literature on English law. See, e. g., Mittermaier's book review of Spence (supra note 61), and Brunner's letter to Holmes, (infra note 188). From an English point of view this perspective yielded odd results whenever the topic dealt with by the foreign researcher had a contemporary edge. See, e. g., F. W. Maitland's remarks on *H. Brunner,* Das Anglo-Normannische Erbfolge System, Leipzig, 1869, contained in the unsigned article: The

ly, this remark means that, if there is such a thing as a German doctrinal style, the writings of the nineteenth century *juristische Germanistik* reveal its features just as the contemporary German scholarship on the Roman law does. Valuable as they were, in several cases the works of the *Germanisten* marked "... einen erneuten Höhepunkt pandektischer Verfremdung rechtshistorischer Interpretation."[166]

Yet, in the Anglo-American area, the knowledge of this literature helped to bring about the demise of the Romanesque hypothesis which had been fashionable in the earlier part of the century.

Both in England and in the United States, the transition to a new understanding of the common law tradition was not accomplished in one day, nor was it the feat of one thinker, however influential. Nevertheless, in retrospect, we can identify the works that marked a turning point in the history of nineteenth century historical and legal scholarship[167]. Among these works, which were published between 1870 and 1880, one finds: W. Stubbs' *Select Charters and other Illustrations of English Constitutional History*, as well as Stubbs' major historical work, *A Constitutional History of England*[168]; K. E. Digby's *Introduction to the History of the Law of Real Property*[169]; the *Essays on Anglo-Saxon Law* written by the Harvard historian Henry Adams and his associates[170]; M. M. Bigelow's two

---

Law of Real Property, published in the Westminster Review of 1869 [reprinted in H. A. L. Fisher (ed.), The Collected Papers of Frederic William Maitland, I, Cambridge, 1911, 162 ff., at 174 ff.; cited hereinafter as C. P.].

166 *F. Wieacker*, Privatrechtsgeschichte der Neuzeit unter besondere Berücksichtigung der deutschen Entwicklung, 2nd ed., Göttingen, 1967, at 454, with reference to Otto v. Gierke's *Deutsches Privatrecht*. For a general evaluation of the achievements of the *Juristische Germanistik* see *G. Dilcher, B. R. Kern*, Die juristische Germanistik des 19. Jahrhunderts und die Fachtradition der Deutschen Rechtsgeschichte, ZSS Germ. Abt., 101, 1984, 1 ff.; *M. Reimann*, Nineteenth Century German Legal Science, 31 Boston College L. Rev. 837 (1990), spec. 858 ff.

167 See in general on this change *P. B. M. Blaas*, Continuity and Anachronism: Parliamentary and Constitutional Development in Whig Historiography and in the Antiwhig Reaction Beween 1890 and 1930, (supra note 41) at 153 ff.; *J. W. Burrow*, A Liberal Descent. Victorian Historians and the English Past (supra note 41), at 119 ff., and also *C. H. S. Fifoot*, Law and History in the Nineteenth Century (supra note 20); *M. Howe*, Justice Oliver Wendell Holmes, II, Cambridge, Mass., 1963, ch. 5, p. 135 ff. It would be wrong to say that German historiography was the only force at work. Close attention was also paid to the works of French historians such as F. Guizot and A. Thierry.

168 *W. Stubbs*, Select Charters and other Illustrations of English Constitutional History Form the Earliest Times to the Reign of Edward the First, Oxford, 1870; Id., The Constitutional History of England, in Its Origin and Development, Oxford, 1874-1878. After the publication of the *Select Charters* "... any medieval study not founded upon original sources was an anachronism" (*C. H. S. Fifoot*, Law and History in the Nineteenth Century, supra note 20, at 5-6). On the work of Stubbs see the literature cited above note 167.

169 *K. E. Digby*, An Introduction to the History of the Law of Real Property, Oxford, 1875. Together with Stubbs' *Select Charters*, this work was widely used as a text book for law students.

volumes: *Placita Anglo-Normannica: Law Cases from William I to Richard preserved in Historical Records*, and the *History of Procedure in England*[171], which hit the market at beginning of the new decade.

The common theme pursued by these contributions was the necessity to go back to the "wide plains of northern Germany"[172], or indeed to any other *Ur*-place, to establish the roots of common law institutions on a steady foundation. Stubbs expressed what was to become a widespread conviction when he proclaimed that: "the first traces ... of our national history must be sought not in Britain but in Germany ..."[173].

---

170 Essays in Anglo-Saxon Law, Boston, 1876. The contributors to this volume, which was dedicated to C. W. Eliot, were: H. Adams, H. Cabot Lodge, E. Young, J. Laurence Laughlin. The *Essays* were reviewed anonymously by Holmes: 11 Am. L. Rev. 327 (1877), to whom Adams left in 1881 many of the books he had used to work with his students (*M. Howe,* Justice O. W. Holmes, II, supra note 167, at 146-147, see also, on the relationship between Holmes and Adams, *S. Novick,* Honorable Justice, Boston, Toronto, 1989, at 124, and passim). On the importance of this collection of essays in the history of American legal historiography see *R. W. Gordon,* Introduction: J. Willard Hurst and the Common Law Tradition in American Legal Historiography, 10 Law and Society 9 (1975), at 14 f. For a recent assessment of the merits of the *Essays* see *P. Wormald,* A List of Anglo-Saxon Law Suits, (1988) 17 Anglo-Saxon England 247. Before the publication of the Essays in Anglo-Saxon Law the North American Review, of which Adams had become editor in 1870, published books reviews of *R. Sohm,* La procedure de la Lex Salica, tr. M. Thevenin, Paris, 1873, 188 North Am. Rev. 416-425 (1874); *H. Brunner,* Die Entstehung der Schwurgerichte, Berlin, 1874; 199 North Am. Rev. 199-223 (1874); *P. Laband,* Die Vermögensrechtlichen Klagen nach den sächsischen Rechtsquellen des Mittelalters, Königsberg; *A. Heusler,* Die Beschränkung der Eigenthumsverfolgung bei Fahrnhabe und ihr Motiv im deutschen Recht (in FS. zu Homeyers fünfzigjährigem Doctorjubilaeum, Basel, 1871) 121 North Am. Rev. 210-216 (1875) [signed with the initials M. T. = Marcel Thevenin?].

171 *M. M. Bigelow,* Placita Anglo-Normannica: Law Cases from William I to Richard I Preserved in Historical Records, London, 1879; Id., History of Procedure in England from the Norman Conquest. The Norman Period (1066-1204), London, 1880. Bigelow was Professor of Law, Boston University, from 1873 to 1921.

172 Essays in Anglo-Saxon Law, p. 1.

173 *W. Stubbs,* Select Charters, etc. (supra note 168), at 3. Quite often, as in the contemporary continental literature, this approach went hand in hand with the use of racial arguments to extol the virtues of national institutions. The growth of this ideology in Victorian England is described by several studies. See *S. Collini, D. Winch, J. Burrow,* That Noble Science of Politics, Cambridge, 1983; *H. A. Mac Dougall,* Racial Myth in English History, Montreal, 1982, at 89 ff., and *A. Briggs,* Saxons, Normans and Victorians, in Id., The Collected Essays of Asa Briggs, II, Brighton, 1985, at 215 ff. See also *J. Herbst,* The German Historical School in American Scholarship. A Study in the Transfer of Culture, Itaca, N. Y., 1965, at 99 ff., 115 ff. Anglo-Saxonism as ideology served many purposes. *R. Cosgrove,* "Our Lady the Common Law": An Anglo-American Legal Community (supra note 18), p. 59 ff., highlights one of them, i. e. its rhetorical use to strengthen the bonds between English and American jurists.

IV. The Return of the Anglo-Saxons

To be sure, many of these pathbreaking contributions to the analysis of the historical background of the common law tradition display some striking examples of naive anachronism. Today's legal historians would not subscribe to assertions such as those contained in M. M. Bigelow's *History of Procedure in England:*

> "the distinction which prevails in English Law between actions of contract and actions of tort is from an historical point of view, as well as internally considered, clearly marked. In the earliest of the Germanic codes, the Salic Law, breaches of contract were attended with a substantive right of distraint, while torts were not, and this distinction, under modifications, has continued throughout the history of the English law."[174]

Paradoxically, this kind of approach to legal history makes it also clear why these arguments were all too important to be left in the hands of the historians or the antiquarians. Legal theory claimed its share in the adventure.

More than anyone else, O. W. Holmes took upon himself the task to dispel any doubt about the immediate relevance of these researches for his contemporaries. It has been rightly observed that *The Common Law* is a polemic book, with a strong bias against the Romanistic tradition as represented by the German legal theory of its time[175]. Nevertheless, to turn against this tradition, and to dismiss any attempt to dress the common law with civilian clothing, Holmes had to look to Germany as well. In his work he drew inspiration from German scholarship no less than others did[176]. The difference between Holmes and some

---

[174] *M. M. Bigelow,* History of Procedure in England from the Norman Conquest. The Norman Period (supra note 171), p. 200; see also pp. 147-148. Brunner reviewed this book as well as Bigelow's Placita Anglo-Normannica in ZSS, Germ. Ab., 2 (1881), 202-214. See now for an appreciation of Bigelow's work *R. C. van Caenegem,* English Law Suits from William I to Richard I, London, 1990 (S. S. vol. 106), pp. XIV-XV.

[175] *M. Reimann,* Holmes' *Common Law* and German Legal Science, in R. W. Gordon, (ed.). The Legacy of Oliver Wendell Holmes, Stanford, Ca., 1992, p. 72 f., unfolds the whole background of Holmes' attitute towards the Romanistic tradition as represented by the German *Pandektenwissenschaft.* Reimann convincingly argues for the possibility that Holmes' attack on German legal science was meant to strike nearer targets as well, that is, formalism in general and Langdell's approach to the law in particular. The similarity between Langdell's methodological assumptions and some the tenets of nineteenth century German legal theory has received attention from other scholars as well: Cp. *U. Mattei,* Tutela inibitoria e tutela risarcitoria, Milano, 1987, at 62-63; *U. Mattei,* Stare Decisis. Il valore del precedente giudiziario negli Stati Uniti d'America, Milano, 1988, p. 121 f., at 133-134. For an appraisal of the American trends in legal theory in the second half of the nineteenth century see *J. E. Herget,* American Jurisprudence, 1870-1970, Houston, Tex., 1990, at 8-53.

[176] *E. N. Little,* The Early Reading of Justice Oliver Wendell Holmes, 8 Harvard Libr. Bull. 163 (1954) lists the books and articles that Holmes read between 1865-1880, according to the entries in his note book (the "black book"). The rest of this list for the years up to Holmes' death is still unpublished. See Holmes' "black book", O. W. Holmes

of his contemporaries was that he treasured the literature on Germanic legal antiquities, and used it to free the common law from Romanesque incrustations[177]. "I shall use the history of our law so far as it is necessary to explain a conception or to interpret a rule, but not further."[178] Yet this much was enough to cut off at the root the supposed link between the common law and the civil law tradition[179].

It is worthwhile to briefly go over Holmes' treatment of the topics considered in the first part of this article to see the outcome of his approach. Holmes tackled the theoretical problems raised by bailments and possession, firstly in his article on *Possession* published in the *American Law Review* for 1878[180], and then in *The Common Law*[181]. To write on this topic Holmes read and took notes on the works of several writers on German law[182].

Papers, Harvard Law School Library, Paige Box 1. This reading list, as well as Holmes' notes taken from the materials he read, gives a fair picture of Holmes' debt to German (and more generally European) legal science.

177 It is obvious that this is by no means the only purpose of this "famously Delphic text" [see *R. W. Gordon,* Holmes' Common Law as Legal and Social Science, 10 Hofstra L. Rev. 719 (1982)]. It is also clear that Holmes used other intellectual tools apart from the incursions into legal history considered below to strengthen his arguments. These aspects of his work will not be considered here. If what is said in the text is true, then there is no need to conclude as R. W. Gordon reluctantly does: "that in his origins-hunting Holmes is simply carrying out the genteel antiquarian lawyer's task of tracing the formal antecedents of modern rules, and showing [. . .] that he could do it with far greater erudition than any Anglo-American writer had yet brought to that task." (at p. 733).

178 *O. W. Holmes,* The Common Law, 1st ed. 1881 (M. De Wolfe Howe, ed.) Boston, Toronto, 1963, p. 6; (all citations to *The Common Law* in the notes below refer to this edition).

179 Holmes did not object to the study of the Roman law as such. See Id., The Path of the Law, 10 Harvard L. Rev. 457 (1897) at 475-476. What he wanted to combat was the use of civilian categories and theories imbued with philosophical assumptions he did not share to build a theory of the common law. The following statement mirrors precisely this concern: Id., The Common Law, at 133: "It is desiderable to prove the native origine of our law of bailment, in order that, when theory comes to be considered, modern German opinion may not be valued at more than its true worth."

180 *O. W. Holmes,* Possession, 12 Am. L. Rev. 688 (1878) [hereinafter cited as Possession]. See also Id., Common Carriers and the Common Law, 13 Am. L. Rev. 609 (1879) at 610.

181 Id., The Common Law, Lecture V, p. 130 ff. (The Bailee at Common Law); Lecture VI, p. 163 ff. (Possession).

182 Holmes' "black book", O. W. Holmes Papers, Harvard Law School Library, Paige Box 1, pp. 18-20, notes from: Savigny on Possession, Perry transl.; p. 21: *R. Schmidt,* Über die Natur des Besitzes, Krit. Viert. XII, p. 63-85 [this article reviewed von *Jhering,* Beiträge zur Lehre des Besitzes, Jena 1868; through it Holmes learned about Jhering's theory of possession, see *Holmes,* Possession, 717, note 7, and his letter to Jhering cited infra note 187]; pp. 52-59: *Bruns,* Das Recht des Besitzes in Mittelalter und der Gegenwart, Tübingen, 1848; p. 60-62: *Windscheid,* Pandekten; p. 63: *Puchta,* Art. Besitz in Weiske, Rechtslexicon, II, Leipzig, 1844, p. 41-73; p. 69: *A. Heusler,* Die Gewere, Weimar, 1877. The footnotes to Holmes' published writings, as well as his reading list

It is one of the pages of his note book (the "black book") that one finds the germ of the idea which was then developed in his articles for the *American Law Review* and in *The Common Law:*

> "The absurdity of making bailee's responsibility over ground to his action vs third persons, shown by giving bailor trespass when bailee's liability is greatest viz, when he is borrower. But it may have been that as in Germany bailor had originally no remedy except against bailee. Heusler Gewere 490-495 but cf. Bracton 62 f. end Cok on Litt. 89 a"[183].

At the end of the first sentence of this note Holmes put the letters "Eka", which make sense only if interpreted as "Eureka". Holmes' article on possession then disposed of Sir William Jones' Essay as "... an attempt to adjust German law to Roman conceptions."[184]. The cases and the other authorities like Bracton (and Beaumanoir) that considered the bailee's responsibility towards the bailor for the custody of the goods bailed as a ground to protect his relationship with the goods were served with the notice that they represented an "inverted explanation" of the true foundation of the bailee's actions against the wrongdoer[185]. Holmes argued that this rested with the fact that originally only the bailee could sue the wrongdoer who interfered with the goods, as he only had possession of the goods bailed. This was why the bailee was strictly responsible to the bailor for any damage suffered by the goods, or for their loss[186]. "... [I]n this as in other respects, the English followed the traditions of their race", while "... it would shake the German theory of possession to its foundation to admit the possibility of such persons being possessors."[187].

(supra note 176), make abundantly clear that these notes summarized only a part of what he read. Undoubtedly some of his knowledge of the literature on the old Germanic folk-laws was obtained second hand, by consulting the literature on these topics in English, such as the book reviews and the Essays in Anglo-Saxon Law cited above, note 170.

183 "Black book", O. W. Holmes Papers, Harvard Law School Library, Paige Box 1, p. 66.

184 Id., Possession, at 693.

185 Id., Possession, at 693-694; Cp. Id., The Common Law, at 132, 134-135.

186 Id., Possession, at 689-690, 697-698; Id., The Common Law, at 132, 191-192. For a recent discussion of these points see *S. Ferreri,* Le azioni reipersecutorie in diritto comparato, Milano, 1988, at 32 ff.

187 Id., Possession, at 697-698; cp. Id., The Common Law, at 138: "... our law of bailment is of pure German descent." Holmes wrote the passage cited in the text when Jhering had just began to attack Savigny's theory of possession. He voiced his sympathy for Jhering's stand on this topic by naming him as a "man of genius" both in his article on possession and in The Common Law. The same feeling was expressed in the letter to Jhering which accompanied a copy of his article on possession. "Unfortunately I was only able to get at reviews of your work, but not to see the original. I have however derived so much pleasure from what I have read of yours that alone would have led me to lay these fragments before your eyes." O. W. Holmes Jr. to R. v. Jhering, 1. 7. 1878, Staatsbibliothek Preussischer Kulturbesitz, Berlin, 2 h 1880 (21).

On receiving a copy of Holmes' article on possession Heinrich Brunner wrote to Holmes: "Was Sie über die Stellung des bailee, insbesondere aus den Yearbooks beibringen, erscheint mir als eine namhafte Förderung der germanistischen Besitzlehre." [188] As an exponent of the Germanist wing of the Historical school, Brunner rejoiced about Holmes' treatment of possession:

> "Um germanistische Rechtsideen gegen die Anschauungen der Romanisten zur Geltung zu bringen, ist das ältere und neuere englische Recht für uns Germanisten ein reichlich gefülltes Arsenal von Waffen, welches in Deutschland bis jetzt nur selten verwertet worden ist. Um so erfreulicher ist es, wenn uns von jenerseits des Oceans ein Bundesgenosse kommt." [189]

The disturbing association between *causa* and consideration in the law of contract was removed by providing the latter with an Anglo-Saxon pedigree. "It has been thought that this rule was borrowed from the Roman Law by the Chancery, and after undergoing some modification there, passed into the common law. But this account of the matter is at least questionable." [190] Though with "great hesitation" and with "... a full appreciation of the objections which might be urged" [191], Holmes argued that the requirement of consideration in contracts was a survival of the formalism employed during the Anglo-Saxon period for every bargain of sale [192].

Undoubtedly Holme's masterpiece in this perspective is the article *Early English Equity,* written, as he says, to lay bare the error that the substantive law developed by the English Chancery was merely the product of its procedure, which had been borrowed from the canon law. Thanks to the distinction between substantive law and procedure, Holmes was able to maintain that: "... the Chancery, in its first establishment at least, did not appear as embodying the superior ethical standards of a comparatively modern state of society correcting the defects of a more archaic system" [193]. This meant that the "greatest contribution to the substantive law which has ever been set down to the credit of the Chancery" [194] — i. e. uses and their offspring, namely trusts — had Teutonic origins.

---

188 Brunner to Holmes, 21. 8. 1878, O. W. Holmes Papers, Harvard Law School Library, Box 38, f. 6.

189 Same letter.

190 Id., The Common Law, at 200. This was a clear departure from the traditional treatment of the topic, which Holmes had not disputed in the article: Common Carriers and the Common Law (supra, note 180), at 613, note 1.

191 Id., at 201.

192 Id., at 201-204. Holmes thought that the presence of "transaction witnesses" was required in the case of sale. According to him, however, the early common law enforced also simple contracts not based upon a *quid pro quo* such as the contract of suretyship, see Id., at 204-205.

193 *O. W. Holmes,* Early English Equity, (1885) 1 Law Q. Rev., 162, at 163. Cp. Id., The Common Law, 268-271.

194 Id., Early English Equity, at 162.

The Germanic *Salman* studied by Beseler and other *Germanisten* was the ancestor of the feoffee to uses[195], or rather "... the latter was the former transplanted."[196].

A cleavage between the Roman sources and the English law — or at least some of its central institutions — was eventually apparent.

What was the aftermath of this effort to draw from legal history the materials which legal theory needed[197]? It is well known how, one after another, the historical interpretations sustained by Holmes came under attack.

A German scholar who taught Roman law at Oxford, Ernest Schuster, noted in the *Law Quarterly Review* that the historical evidence on the Germanic folks-laws did not unequivocally support Holmes' analysis of the bailee's position toward the goods bailed. For Schuster, the old *actio furti* of the Roman law provided a possible alternative model for the actions given to protect the bailee's relationship with the goods bailed[198]. Shortly after the publication of Schuster's article, Ames wrote to Holmes to spell out his discontent about Holmes' reconstruction of the position of the bailee in the early common law:

> "I had hoped to find more satisfactory evidence than I have yet discovered as to bailor's rights against a wrongdoer. But I cannot yet see my way to adopt your view that the bailee's liability was a consequence of his exclusive right of action against the wrongdoer, even if that exclusive right of action was demonstrable. I still incline to believe that Beumanoir and Bracton were right."[199]

An article by J. H. Beale also dealt with Holmes' reconstruction of the bailee's legal position so to show its intrinsic weakness[200]. Pollock was among the few

---

[195] Holmes' interest in this "Paradestück der Germanistik" (see *K. O. Scherner,* Salmannschaft, Servusgeschäft und Venditio Iusta, Wiesbaden, 1971, p. 3; see also on the *Germanisten* contributions to the study of this institution *G. Otten,* Die Entwicklung der Treuhand im 19. Jahrhundert, Göttingen, 1975, esp. p. 54 ff.) was kindled by a "hint from Henry Adams", as he remembered at the age of ninety-one. Holmes to Wigmore, 14. 3. 1932, O. W. Holmes Papers, Harvard Law School Library, box 15, f. 19: "Egotism leads me to protest that I think I preceded Maitland on the derivation of the law of equitable trusts, after a hint from Henry Adams as to Beseler."

[196] *O. W. Holmes,* Early English Equity, at 164.

[197] On this point see *S. Touster,* Holmes a Hundred Years Ago: *The Common Law* and Legal Theory, 10 Hofstra L. Rev. 673 (1982).

[198] *E. Schuster,* Liabilities of Bailees According to German Law (1886), 2 Law Q. Rev. 188, at 191-192, 199-205. See also on this point Brunner's remarks to Holmes in the letter cited supra, note 188. *H. Coing,* Europäisches Privatrecht, I, München, 1985, at 508, remarks that the role of the *actio furti* as *Ersatzklage* in medieval law is still unclear. For a comparison between the Roman and the Germanic notion of theft see *R. Zimmerman,* The Law of Obligations, Cape Town, 1990, 945 ff.

[199] Ames to Holmes, 25. 1. 1888, O. W. Holmes Papers, Harvard Law School Library, Box 37, f. 9.

[200] *J. H. Beale,* The History of the Carrier's Liability, 11 Harvard L. Rev. 158 (1897). Beale did not concur with Holmes in holding that originally all bailees were strictly liable for any loss or damage caused to the things bailed. According to him, Holmes did not explain "... why this doctrine should not have survived in the case even of all

who seized immediately the importance of Holme's treatment of possession, i. e. its break with the continental theories of possession indebted to Savigny's *Das Recht des Besitzes*[201]. Indeed, Pollock wrote to Jhering to state what Jhering's work on possession had meant for both Holmes and himself: "Was die Hauptsache betrifft, wir dürfen mit Ihnen getrost und lustig rufen: Pereat animus domini!"[202].

The history of consideration in contracts advanced by Holmes did not convince Pollock[203] nor Maitland[204]. J. B. Ames became its staunchest critic. He refused to accept Holmes' idea that consideration in contracts "was simply a modified generalization of *quid pro quo* to raise a debt by parol"[205], and denied that the early common law recognized parol contracts not based upon a *quid pro quo*[206]. These reservations about Holmes' historical approach to consideration casted serious doubts about his theory, which found an Anglo-Saxon background for

common occupations, but only in the case of the common carrier of goods; nor does he account for the fact that the carrier is absolutely liable, not merely, like the bailee once, for the loss of the goods but, unlike the bailee, for injury to them" (at 158). He wrote to Holmes to soften a possible reaction to this criticism: Beale to Holmes, 28. 10. 1897, O. W. Holmes Papers, Harvard Law School Library Box 66, f. 15. Nevertheless, when Beale's article was reprinted in Select Essays in Anglo-American Legal History, III, Cambridge, 1909, 148 ff., an editorial note (probably by Pollock) was inserted to reassert Holmes' thesis: "... Mr. Justice Holmes' explanation fits perfectly with the tenor of the primitive law, while the learned Essayist's explanation does not fit at all." (note 4 at 149-150).

201 *F. Pollock, R. S. Wright,* An Essay on Possession in the Common Law, Oxford, 1888, spec. p. 5. Holmes' appreciation of this book tells something about what was for him the lasting meaning of his achievement: *O. W. Holmes,* The Path of the Law, 10 Harvard L. Rev. 457 (1897), at 475.

202 Pollock to Jhering, 30. 7. 1889, Staatsbibliothek Preussischer Kulturbesitz, Berlin, 2 h 1890 (20). See also Pollock to Jhering, 9. 11. 1888, same location, 2 h 1890 (28) (announcing his work on possession and recognizing indebtness to Jhering's work on possession). In the letter dated 30. 7. 1889, Pollock remarked that if Jhering's theory was right: ... denn es würde alsdann, prinzipiell gefaßt, das Römische Besitzrecht mit dem englischen Gemeinrecht ganz gut übereinstimmen. Wir haben hier gar keine Besitztheorie von subjectiver Art, wie Sie solche bekämpfen. Die Detention, wenn sie nur nicht ganz unbewußt ist — d. h. das in irgend einem eigenen Interesse ausgeübte Innenhaben — erzeugt normaler Weise Besitz." When Pollock wrote these words the idea that Jhering's reconstruction of the Roman law of possession effectively narrowed the gap between the common law and the Roman law on possession had already found supporters in England: cp. *J. M. Lightwood,* Possession in the Roman Law, (1887) 3 Law Q. Rev. 3; Id., Book Notice of Jhering, Der Besitzwille, Jena, 1889 (1889) 5 Law Q. Rev. 315 (Pollock sent the page proof of this book notice to Jhering, together with the letter cited above). See also *C. H. S. Fifoot,* Judge and Jurist in the Reign of Victoria (supra note 20), at 89 ff.

203 *F. Pollock,* Principles of the Law of Contracts, 7th ed., 1902, at 174-175, and note t.

204 *F. Pollock* and *F. W. Maitland,* The History of the English Law Before the Time of Edward I, vol. II, 2nd ed., Cambridge, 1898, p. 214, note 2.

205 Cp. *J. B. Ames,* The History of Express Assumpsit, 2 Harvard L. Rev. 1 (1888), espec. at 18.

206 *J. B. Ames,* Parol Contracts Prior to Assumpsit, 8 Harvard L. Rev. 252 (1894).

a central piece of the law of contract such as the doctrine of consideration. Ames disagreed with Holmes also about the early history of trusts. According to Ames, before the first decree in favour of the cestui que uses: "there was and could be no doctrine of uses. One might as well talk of the doctrine of gratuitous parol promises in our law of to-day."[207].

If Holmes' contribution to legal history was controversial, it had however at least one undisputed merit. It spurred English and American jurists to develop a stronger awareness of the position of the common law vis à vis the civil law. From this point of view, the differences between Holmes and most of his contemporaries, including many of those who questioned the soundness of his views on the history of key institutions of the common law, were really of minor importance. Holmes' inclination to find a Germanistic (or "Teutonic") background for the common law was widely shared[208].

The successive editions of Pollock's *Principles of Contract* bear the mark of the change of attitude towards this issue. The statements in the first edition of this book which insisted on the similarity between the English and the Roman conceptions of contract were removed from the text[209], and the continuity of the

---

207 *J. B. Ames,* The Origin of Uses, in Id., Lectures on Legal History, 232 ff., at 237. Ames wrote to Holmes to present his views on this topic. After having read *Heusler,* Institutionen des Deutschen Rechts, II, 652 ff. "... much the best account of the executor and Salman that I have met with", Ames was "... not disposed to attach much importance to this relationship in its bearing upon the English use." Ames to Holmes, 19. 1. 1887, O. W. Holmes Papers, Harvard Law School Library, Box 37, f. 8. See the reply by Holmes, 25. 1. 1887, same location, Box 37, f. 9, and the rejoinder by Ames, 30. 1. 1887, ibid. Ames' criticism of Holmes' theories was followed by a note of protest from Holmes. Cp. on this episode *M. D. Howe,* Justice Oliver Wendell Holmes, II (supra note 167), at 230-231.

208 Just like Bigelow and Pollock, Ames thought that the common law was "essentially of Teutonic origin" (Lectures on Legal History, at 34). Keen as he was to qualify Holmes statements on the origins of uses, Ames indeed conceded that "the feoffee to uses, down to the beginning of the fifteenth century, was the German Salman or Treuhand under another name." (Lectures on Legal History, 235).

209 The recantation can be dated from the third edition of the Principles of Contract, London, 1881, esp. p. XI f., where Pollock discusses Holmes' work on contract, and its "leading idea ... that our procedure, and our legal theory so far as thereon founded or therein involved, are of native Germanic origin, and the resemblances to Roman law, save so far as they consist of features common to all archaic law, may be regarded as superficial." In later editions of this work, Pollock followed Ames instead of Holmes on the history of consideration, but the very letter which he wrote to congratulate Ames for his essay on the history of assumpsit makes clear what was by then his basic conviction on this topic. See Pollock to Ames, 23. 6. 1888, J. B. Ames Papers, Harvard Law School Library, Box 1, f. 8: "I must send you a word of congratulation on the history of Assumpsit. You seem to me to have got at last to the bottom of the puzzle, or at any rate much nearer to it than anyone before. [...] The Romanist spook of causa may now be dismissed, I think, as finally exorcised, played out, and discredited spook. On the whole I believe more and more in the indigenous character of the Common law." In a note to his Principles of Contract, 6th ed. 1894, at 701, he expressed the same point of view. For Pollock the "scarce bear of Romanist elements upon any substantial part

common law from Anglo-Saxon times down to the present became once again seriously tenable[210]. In the pages of the *Columbia Law Review*, H. D. Hazeltine, later a member of the Cambridge Law Faculty, maintained that the history of the formal contract: "began in the far-off misty days of the early Anglo-Saxon custom, and from those days to the year 1910 its history has been unbroken"[211]. The members of the judiciary who failed to keep up with the pace of change became liable to criticism. Pollock went as far as to correct the judge who failed to consider the Germanic rather than the Roman law as the historical precedent of the English law on earnest money[212]. In cases like *The Winkfield*[213], this intellectual climate allowed counsel to join the latest academic tug-of-war over the origins of the rules to be applied by the Court.

Probably Holmes himself felt this was a slippery slope, as he adverted to the danger of blind adherence to time-honoured rules[214]. The sharpest reaction to this tendency came however from Albert Venn Dicey. First in a letter to Holmes[215], then in a book review of *The Common Law*[216], Dicey remarked that the historical

---

of the structure of the common law" was now "a matter of feeling rather than of proof." See also the following notes.

210 *F. Pollock,* The Continuity of the Common Law, 11 Harv. L. Rev. 423 (1898).

211 *H. D. Hazeltine,* The Formal Contract of Early English Law, 10 Col. L. Rev. 609 (1910), at 617.

212 *F. Pollock,* Contracts in Early English Law, 6 Harv. L. Rev. 389 (1892), at 392, note 4, reprinted in *F. Pollock* and *F. W. Maitland,* The History of the English Law Before the Time of Edward I, vol. II (supra note 204), p. 184 ff., at 208, note 2, with reference to the judgment of Sir Edward Fry in *Howe v. Smith* (1884) 27 Ch. Div. 89, at 102.

213 *The Winkfield* [1902] P. 42 (C. A.). This case decided that the Postmaster-General, as bailee of the mail on board the ship sunk by the defendants' vessel, could recover the full value of the mail destroyed in the collision, despite the fact that he was not liable to the bailors (i. e. the senders) for the loss of the mail.

214 *O. W. Holmes,* The Path of the Law (supra note 179), spec. at 469, 474.

215 Dicey to Holmes, 19. 1. 1880, O. W. Holmes Papers, Harvard Law School Library, Box 42, f. 8. Dicey's letters to Holmes tell also something about the professional ideals, the beliefs, and the frustrations of a nineteenth century English law professor: "I am coming more and more to the belief that judge-made law is in quality, almost always better than statute law. Its great defect is that it tends to make exceptions more prominent than rules. (...) The corrective to it seems to me to be not so much legislation as systematic professorial teaching. A Professor's lecture as inevitably gives prominence to principles as a decision gives prominence to exceptions and I am quite convinced that professorial lectures & writing very rapidly tell on the judges. Story, & within the last ten years Savigny, have created the law of England as to the conflicts of laws." Dicey to Holmes, 28. 9. 1881, O. W. Holmes Papers, ibid. In later years Dicey had some afterthoughts on this point: "... I envy you for making law from the judgment seat instead of mistating it as I have probably done in law books or spoiling it as Bryce and every other M. P. certainly does in Parliament." Dicey to Holmes, 19. 4. 1896, ibid.

216 Review of Holmes' The Common Law, The Spectator, Literary Supplement, June 3, 1882, pp. 745-747, reprinted in 10 Hofstra L. Rev. 712 (1982). The authorship of this unsigned review is established by *S. Touster,* Holmes a Hundred years Ago: The Common Law and Legal Theory, ibid., at 673 ff.

materials assembled by Holmes had no bearing upon the theoretical discussion of the doctrines of the law which was the true object of the book. He expressed again the same point of view with even greater force in *An Introduction to the Law of the Constitution,* where he seized the opportunity of dealing with the relationship between law and history which was offered by Edward Augustus Freeman's *Growth of the English Constitution*[217/218].

Though Dicey's protest was justified, it neglected the simple fact that legal rules do not exist in a void. They fit into a wider framework, which is less apparent only when it is too obvious to be questioned. But after all, perhaps, it was this framework that was uncertain.

German fields and forests, no less than the broken capitals of Rome, were not the ideal setting for an English play. To treat English legal history simply as a branch of "die germanische Rechtsgeschichte"[219] meant to underrate those factors that made English law English rather than "Teutonic".

It may seem bold to give all credit for a breakthrough in new directions to one person. Yet it is appropriate to do so, when we consider F. W. Maitland's contribution to the clarification of this crucial issue[220].

---

217 *E. A. Freeman,* The Growth of the English Constitution, London, 1872.

218 *A. V. Dicey,* Introduction to Study of the Law of the Constitution (1st ed. 1885). [the following citation is from the 10th ed., 1939, reprinted with an Introduction by *E. C. S. Wade,* London, 1961, p. 13 f.]. Dicey reproduced part of the table of contents of Freeman's book, which introduced the subject to his readers in the following way: "The Landesgemeinden of Uri and Appenzell; their bearing on English Constitutional History; political elements common to the whole Teutonic race...", and then commented: "All this is interesting, erudite, full of historical importance, and thoroughly in its place in a book concerned solely with the "growth" of the constitution; but in regard to English law and the law of the constitution, the *Landesgemeinden* of Uri ..., and a lot more of fascinating matter are mere antiquarianism [...] Let us eagerly learn all that is know, and still more that is not known, about the Witenagemót. But let us remember that antiquarianism is not law, and that the function of a trained lawyer is not to know what the law of England was yesterday, still less what it was centuries ago, or what it ought to be to-morrow, but to know and be able to state what are the principles of law which actually and at the present day exist in England. For this purpose it boots nothing to know the nature of the *Landesgemeinden* of Uri, or to understand, if it be understandable, the constitution of the Witenagemót. All this is for a lawyer's purposes simple antiquarianism. It throws as much light on the constitution of the United States as upon the constitution of England; that is, it throws from a legal point of view no light upon either the one or the other." See also Id., Law and Public Opinion in England During the Nineteenth Century, 2nd ed., London, 1914, at 457 ff.

219 *F. W. Maitland,* The Laws of the Anglo-Saxons, C. P., III, 447, at 457.

220 *S. F. C. Milsom,* F. W. Maitland, (1982) 66 Proceedings of the British Academy 265, reprinted in Id., Studies in the History of the Common Law, London and Ronceverte, 1985, 261, at 274, asserts that "Maitland had nothing to stand on" to write about English legal history as "There was no legal history worth the name" before him. Considering the work of English historians like Stubbs, and Maitland's debt to continental legal historians, I doubt this can be taken as literally true. Certainly in the case of Maitland this assertion is a convenient rhetorical device.

V. The "Englishry of English Law"[221]

Just like Holmes, Pollock, and the foremost scholars of his age, Maitland had contacts with continental jurists[222]. He fully mastered the foreign literature relevant to his field of studies. Like others, Maitland worked with conceptual tools and shared historical interpretations first tested abroad to an extent that today's English[223] or American[224] historians are unable to accept. His position in the controversy over the "village community" — i. e. the early forms of agricultural and tenurial arrangements — which set aflame the nineteenth century academic world appears to be that of a "moderate germanist"[225]. Maitland's translation into English of a part of Otto v. Gierke's *Das deutsche Genossenschaftsrecht*[226]

---

221 The title of this paragraph reproduces the marginal note to *F. Pollock* and *F. W. Maitland,* The History of English Law Before the Time of Edward I (supra note 204), vol. I, at 188.

222 The importance of Maitland's meeting with the Russian scholar Paul Vinogradoff (a former pupil of Mommsen and Brunner in Berlin) is stressed by many of his biographers. See, e. g., *C. H. S. Fifoot,* Frederick William Maitland. A Life, Cambridge, Mass., 1971, p. 58 ff., 121 - 122. Vinogradoff was only one of the many European scholars with whom Maitland had contacts. Among those who corresponded with him one finds: H. Brunner, O. Gierke, R. Gneist, F. Liebermann, J. Redlich, J. Brissaud. See F. W. Maitland Papers, Cambridge University Library, Add. 7006, 7007, 7008, 8130.

223 With regard to Maitland's researches on seisin, this opinion is clearly expressed by *C. H. S. Fifoot,* Judge and Jurist in the Reign of Victoria (supra note 20), at 109. It is adumbrated in much of what Milsom has written on the topic. See especially his *Introduction* to the reprint of *F. Pollock* and *F. W. Maitland,* The History of English Law Before the Time of Edward I, Cambridge, 1968, at p. XXXVI; and also Id., F. W. Maitland (supra note 220). The observation is not wholly new. In his review of The History of the English Law, H. Brunner noted with a tone of satisfaction that this work made: "Considerable use [. . .] of conceptions peculiar to German law. German legal expressions, such as "thinglike" and "thinglikeness" (dinglich; Dinglichkeit), are introduced into English legal speech", (1896) in: Political Science Quarterly, 534 at 535 (the original was published in ZSS, Germ. Abt., 17, 1896, p. 125).

224 Cp. *S. E. Thorne,* Introduction, to Bracton de Legibus et Consuetudinibus Angliae (ed. G. E. Woodbine), I, Cambridge, Mass., 1968, at XXXII ff.

225 See *J. W. Burrow,* "The Village Community" and the Uses of History in Late Nineteenth-Century England, in N. Mc Kendrick (ed.), Historical Perspectives. Studies in English Thought and Society in Honour of J. H. Plumb, London, 1974, 255, at 275.

226 *O. v. Gierke,* Political Theories of the Middle Ages, Cambridge, 1900 (A Translation of Das Deutsche Genossenschaftsrecht, III, 1881, ch. II, § 11, pp. 502-644). In his correspondence Maitland showed admiration for Gierke's work ("a great book", a "splendid thing"), but also said that its author was "too metaphysical". See *C. H. S. Fifoot,* The Letters of Frederick William Maitland, Cambridge, 1965, p. 86 (see also p. 204, p. 209). A review of *Political Theories of the Middle Ages* was published by R. Hübner in ZSS, Germ. Ab., 22, 1901, at 443-448. For recent analysis of von Gierke's main work see: *O. G. Oexle,* Otto von Gierkes "Rechtsgeschichte der deutschen Genossenschaft", in N. Hammerstein (ed.), Deutsche Geschichtswissenschaft um 1900, Stuttgart, 1988, 193 ff., at 206 f.; A. Black (ed.), Community in Historical Perspective. A Translation of Selections from "Das deutsche Genossenschaftsrecht" by Otto von Gierke, Cambridge, 1990; and more generally on Gierke's and the Germanists positions in the German debate on codification see *M. John,* Politics and the Law in Late Nineteenth Century Germany, Oxford, 1989, reviewed by *M. Reimann,* 39 Am. J. Comp. Law 196 (1991).

associated his name with that of the last great exponent of the Germanistic school[227].

Considering these facts, one could portray Maitland as a later prophet of the same gospel preached by Holmes and Pollock before him. This temptation should be resisted. More than others, Maitland used his knowledge of the European scene to fertilize a crop of home-grown products. When he was writing, the wild speculations about the importance of the Roman component in the early history of the English law which had been current in the first half century were beating a full retreat[228]. At the same time Germanism had been constantly gaining ground. Maitland insisted time and again on the importance of English "peculiarities" like the forms of actions[229], the Inns of Court[230] and the trust, in order to stress the originality of the English legal experience. This was certainly done vis à vis the legal tradition which descended from Rome but also — and perhaps with greater force — against the exorbitant claims of Germanism[231].

Maitland's treatment of the trust is a good example of his ability to advance in this new direction without quarreling with those whose opinions he effectively challenged. Whereas Holmes' dowsing rod pointed to the *Salman* as the first ring of an unbroken chain which stretched to reach the modern English trustee, Maitland highlighted the possible influence of the Roman medieval law on the

---

227 *G. Dilcher,* in G. Dilcher, B. R. Kern, Die juristische Germanistik des 19. Jahrhunderts und die Fachtradition der Deutschen Rechtsgeschichte (supra note 166), p. 1, at 3.

228 They are dismissed as totally unsupported by the sources in *F. Pollock* and *F. W. Maitland,* The History of English Law Before the Time of Edward I, vol. I (supra note 204), p. XXXI-XXXII. See also on this point Maitland to Pollock, 18. 10. 1890, in *C. H. S. Fifoot,* The Letters of Frederick William Maitland (supra note 226), at 84-87. Old ideas were slow to die. In 1930 it was still necessary to repeat that the ancient custom of London which prohibited the citizen who had a wife and children from disposing by his will of more than one-third of his personal estate was not proof of the survival of the Roman Law in the custom of the City. See *W. G. Hart,* Roman Law and the Custom of London, (1930) 46 L. Q. R. 49.

229 See Maitland's note on this topic inserted in *F. Pollock,* The Law of Torts, London, 1887, p. 467 ff.; Id., Why the History of the English Law is not Written (1888), in C. P., I, p. 480 f. at 485, where Maitland caricatures what was probably the typical attitude towards this topic in the last decades of the nineteenth century: "It is easy to persuade us that the early history of Roman law is interesting. To know all about the Roman formulary system, that is juristic science; to know anything about our own formulary system, which we only abolished the other day, that would be barbarian pedantry." See also *F. Pollock* and *F. W. Maitland,* The History of The English Law Before the Time of Edward I, vol. II (supra note 204), p. 558 ff.

230 Maitland's celebration of these institutions was timely. On the Inns of Court at the end of the nineteenth century see *R. Cocks,* Foundations of the Modern Bar (supra note 24), at 223-224.

231 Maitland's half-serious display of concern for the "process of annexation" or the "occupation of a considerable tract" of the history of English law, carried on by foreign scholars, becomes intelligible against this background. Cp. *F. W. Maitland,* Why the History of English Law is Not Written (supra note 229), at 482-483; Id., The Laws of the Anglo-Saxons, C. P., III, 447.

growth of the use[232]. By carefully contrasting the legal position of the trustee with that of the *Treuhänder* described by Alfred Schultze[233], Maitland proved the attempt directed at finding Germanic lineage for this English institution weak[234].

According to Maitland, "The most specifically English of all our legal institutes . . ."[235] — the trust — was also the key to understanding why unincorporated bodies in English law enjoyed an autonomy unknown abroad. A "legal trickery unworthy of exploration"[236] like the trust, which Gierke had found "elusive"[237], had worked in England as an excellent surrogate of legal personality. The role of the trust in English law explained why a subject like group personality, that on the other side of theChannel was overburdened with the social, political and jurisprudential implications brought in the forefront by the last great champion of the *juristische Germanistik,* stirred little interest in England[238].

---

232 See *F. W. Maitland,* The Origin of Uses, 8 Harvard L. Rev. 127 (1894), reprinted in *F. Pollock* and *F. W. Maitland,* The History of English Law Before the Time of Edward I (supra note 204), vol. II, at 228 f., and in Id., C. P., II, 403 ff. In these places Maitland acknowledged the value of Holmes' contribution, but remarked also that the legal condition of the property left to the first Franciscan friars settled in England could have provided a model for the growth of the use. For a discussion of the various theories advanced on this point see *S. W. De Vine,* The Franciscan Friars, the Feoffment to Uses and Canonical Theories of Property Enjoyment before 1535, (1989) 10 Journal of Legal History 1.

233 *A. Schultze,* Die langobardische Treuhand und ihre Umbildung zur Testamentvollstreckung, (Gierke's Untersuchungen), Breslau, 1895, which treated the Salman as "Urtypus des germanischen Treuhänders" (p. 37).

234 Cp. *F. W. Maitland,* Trust and Corporation, C. P., III, 321 ff.; first published in Grünhut's Zeitschrift für das Privat- und Öffentliche Recht, Vol. 32, p. 1 (1905). The article was translated into German by the Austrian jurist Joseph Redlich with whom Maitland corresponded in order to have a clearer picture of the Austrian and the German law on the legal status of unincorporated bodies (See Maitland to Redlich 10. 1. 1904, Cambridge University Library Add. 8130; Redlich to Maitland, 17. 2. 1904, Add. 7007, 275 and Maitland to Redlich 18. 3. 1904, Add. 8130). Maitland's correspondence with Redlich tells also something about the difficulty of writing for the German readers: "You German jurists are such terrible fellows that the more I think of addressing you the less I like it. I hear one saying "Nichts neues!" and another saying that all my notions of jurisprudence are addled and muddled" (Maitland to Redlich, 12. 8. 1903, C. U. L., Add. 8130, 2).

235 *F. W. Maitland,* Moral Personality and Legal Personality, C. P., III, 304, at 317.

236 Id., at 317.

237 *F. W. Maitland,* The Unincorporated Body, C. P., III, 271 at 272: "I do not understand your trust", these words have been seen in a letter written by a very learned German historian familiar with law of all sorts and kinds". See also Id., Lectures on Equity, (A. H. Chaytor, W. J. Whittaker, eds.), Cambridge, 1909, at 23.

238 Id., at 317. See also Id., Trust and Corporation (supra note 234). Indeed, in 1911 Holmes wrote to Pollock that he had "never realised the corporation entity question as a very burning one". See M. Howe (ed.), Holmes-Pollock Letters, Cambridge, Mass., 1961, at 115 (and cp. at 174). *M. J. Horwitz,* Santa Clara Revisited: The Development of Corporate Theory, 88 West Virginia Law Review 173 (1985), at 179, states that Maitland was wrong in thinking that the English were not interested in a subject that

Curiously, Maitland's vindication of the originality of the English legal experience was singularly free from nationalistic tones.

Maitland could not have had a better occasion than the Rede lecture on "English Law and the Renaissance" delivered in 1901 to strike the nationalistic chord[239]. Yet, he refrained from taking this step. "National character, the genius of a people, is a wonder-working spirit which stands at the beck and call of every historian"[240]. However, instead of evoking this spirit, Maitland looked for sensible arguments to explain the fact that the high tide of Roman law mounting in Renaissance Europe had not left a permanent mark on the English legal system. What he found is still worthy of mention, even though one of the key arguments presented in the lecture — i. e. the real possibility of a "reception" of the civil law in the sixteenth century — is now considered unfounded[241].

According to Maitland, the common law withstood the supposed threat to its continuity posed by the civil law because it was learned law, no less than the Roman law taught by the universities[242]. Contrary to the early Germanic laws, which had not been shaped and administered by lawyers and did not possess the qualities which were necessary to compete with the medieval Roman law, the "... English law was and had long been lawyers' law, learned law, taught law, *Juristenrecht*"[243]. English law had lost its innocence long before the Renaissance.

---

was seriously discussed in many other countries. Certainly the intellectual history of the subject — which for Horwitz is "quite clear" — pre-dates 1887, the year that according to Horwitz saw the publication of von Gierke's Das Deutsche Genossenschaftsrecht. The first volume of Gierke's unfinished masterpiece was in fact published in 1868. See on the development of corporatism in America *J. Q. Whitman,* The Individual Ultrascended: Early German Corporatism in America (this collection).

239 *F. W. Maitland,* English Law and the Renaissance, Cambridge, 1901; reprinted in Select Essays in Anglo-American Legal History, I, Boston, 1907, at 168 ff. This lecture should be read together with Maitland's Introduction to *O. v. Gierke,* Political Theories of the Middle Ages (supra note 226). The two essays were written in the same years and in part they deal with the same questions.

240 Id., at 23.

241 See *W. Holdsworth,* A History of the English Law, IV, London, 1924, at 252-93; *S. E. Thorne,* English Law and the Renaissance, in La storia del diritto nel quadro delle scienze giuridiche, Firenze, 1966, p. 437 ff.; *D. Jenkins,* English Law and the Renaissance. Eighty Years on: in Defence of Maitland, (1981) 2 Journal of Leg. History 107 ff., has tried to revive Maitland's argument but this attempt is put to rest by *G. R. Elton,* F. W. Maitland, New Haven and London, 1985, at 84-86 (see also at 79 ff. for a discussion of the historiographical debate provoked by this lecture). *G. Gorla,* Il diritto comparato in Italia e nel "mondo occidentale", etc. (supra note 20), at p. 516 ss.; *J. Baker,* English Law and the Renaissance, (1985) 44 Cambridge Law Jo. 46, esp. at 51 ff.; *K. W. Nörr,* The European Side of English Law: A Few Comments From a Continental Historian, in H. Coing and K. W. Nörr, Englische und kontinentale Rechtsgeschichte: ein Forschungsprojekt, Berlin, 1985, p. 19 ff., shed from different perspectives new light on the nature of the problems addressed by Maitland.

242 *F. W. Maitland,* English Law and the Renaissance (supra note 239), at 25 f.

243 *F. W. Maitland,* Introduction to *O. v. Gierke,* Political Theories of the Middle Ages (supra note 226), at XIII.

Indeed, far from being a mere repository of unvarnished "Teutonic" treasures, it was *Juristenrecht,* just the opposite of the kind of law idealized by the fathers of the Germanistic school. This essential feature of the English law was a key factor to explain why the fate of the common law had been different from that of other bodies of law which on the Continent had been supplanted by the Roman law.

Probably at the root of Maitland's position on this crucial issue there was also the keen appreciation of the fact that the German legal and historical scholarship did not speak with one single voice[244]. Certainly he felt that most of the foreign literature available to elaborate on the early conditions of the common law could not be taken at face-value:

> "Many of the theories of the great Germanists, the jurists who have been reconstructing ancient Teutonic law, raise suspicions in our insular minds. Their authors, while they are striving to minimise the influence of Roman law, and while they are in the very act of protesting that all is *deutsch* as *deutsch* can be, introduce ideas and distinctions which do not come natural to the Englishman, but look to him like Roman ideas and distinctions that are striving to conceal their Romanism"[245].

Considering how Maitland's debt towards foreign scholarship was subtly qualified by his own insights, one may at this point query whether it is really appropriate to speak of this great scholar as "influenced" by the intellectual exchanges he had with his foreign colleagues, or by the foreign literature he read. It is all too easy to deal with this doubt by observing the Maitland himself was always ready to acknowledge his debt to foreign scholarship. To a lesser or greater extent, the problem raised by this query may indeed be restated with respect to any of the figures considered above. Perhaps then, the answer to this thorny question may be sought by applying a test devised by Maitland himself. I hope it will not be found too crude, or disrespectful, only because for once it does not apply to an outlandish savage:

> "The process that is started where barbarism is brought into contact with civilization is not simple. The hitherto naked savage may at once assume some part of the raiment, perhaps the hat, of the white man. When after a while he puts these things

244 Maitland's Introduction to Gierke's Political Theories of the Middle Ages shows full awareness of this fact. The controversies which divided German legal science had an echo in correspondence addressed to Maitland. See Gierke's letter to Maitland dated 18 April 1898, F. W. Maitland Papers, Cambridge University Library, Add. 7006, 66, for Gierke's disappointment about the reaction of Sohm and Heusler to his work on the Genossenschaften.

245 *F. W. Maitland,* Book review of Brunner, Forschungen zur Geschichte des deutschen und französischen Rechtes, (1894) English Historical Review 593, at 594. According to Maitland, Brunner had avoided this mistake. For Brunner's warm appreciation of Maitland's review see Brunner to Maitland, 25 July 1894, F. W. Maitland Papers, Cambridge University Library, Add. 7006, 45.

aside and learns to make for himself clothes suitable to the climate in which he lives and the pursuits in which he is engaged, we see in this an advance, not a relapse; and yet he has abandoned some things that belong to the white man"[246].

[246] *F. W. Maitland,* Domesday Book and Beyond, Three Essays in the Early History of England, Cambridge, 1897, at 225.

MATHIAS REIMANN

A Career in Itself
The German Professiorate as a Model for American Legal Academica

Introduction

In 1928, Karl Llewellyn came to the University of Leipzig as a visiting professor to teach a course on the Case Law System in America[1]. Though a common lawyer among civilian jurists, he was a co-equal, albeit temporary, colleague on the faculty. He was a law professor as the Germans understood the term — a full-time, professional teacher und scholar. He came from a different legal culture, but he belonged to the same, the academic, breed[2].

Had, for example, Joseph Story been invited to Leipzig a century earlier, his position would have been a very different one. The German faculty would have considered him a "special guest" but not really a colleague. Though the holder of an endowed chair at Harvard, Story was not a full-fledged law professor. As a Supreme Court Justice who taught only part time he was not a professional academic. He not only came from a different legal system, but he was also essentially a practitioner[3].

Both Story and Llewellyn were outstanding, but also typical, law teachers of their time. In antebellum America, there were virtually no professional legal academics. The typical law professor taught, like Story, only part-time or after retirement from office. He was distinguished primarily as a member of the bench or bar, not by his scholarship. His function was to train practitioners while he by and large left the development of the law to the judges and, perhaps, the legislators. Furthermore, he ranked as a teacher at a professional school, not a university faculty member because law schools were at best affiliated with, but not fully integrated in, the universities.

---

1 See *K. Llewellyn*, Präjudizienrecht und Rechtsprechung in Amerika (Leipzig 1933).

2 Karl Llewellyn (1893 - 1962) spent two years in commercial practice, began to teach at age 26, and became a full-time academic at age 29; *W. Twining*, Karl Llewellyn and the Realist Movement (London 1973); pp. 100 - 101.

3 Josef Story (1779 - 1845) joined the U. S. Supreme Court at age 32. After 18 years on the bench, he was appointed Nathan Dane Professor at Harvard at age 50, but even then he taught only part-time, *K. Newmyer*, Supreme Court Justice Joseph Story (Chapel Hill 1985), pp. 74 - 76, 248 - 249.

The typical twentieth century American law teacher is a very different being. He or she is a "homo academicus"[4], a professional, full-time academic like Llewellyn. This is so generally taken for granted that a restatement of the basic job criteria sounds almost banal: The modern law professor is qualified mainly by virtue of his scholarship, not primarily because of his practical experience. His function is not only to train future lawyers but also to influence the law through his writing. As a faculty member, he is a member of an academic institution.

Self-evident as this job description may seem, it is of relatively recent vintage. The modern American legal academic is a product of what has been called the age of "classical orthodoxy" in American law[5], the fifty years after the Civil War. During this period the law schools gradually replaced the old generation of part-time teachers with a new breed of career scholars. The change began at Harward where president Eliot integrated the law school into the university and where the appointment of James Barr Ames in 1873 as the first law professor without any experience in practice rang in a new era. From Harvard, the movement spread to other elite institutions and later spread to the majority of American law schools. By the eve of World War I, the trend towards professionalization of legal academics had taken firm root[6].

This process has been described and explained by others in a variety of ways[7]. This paper neither endorses nor disputes their results. It rather supplements them by adding a hitherto neglected perspective. In confining themselves strictly to the domestic context, existing studies do not consider the foreign influence on the rise of the new law professors[8]. This foreign influence, however, contributed

---

4 See *P. Boudieu*, Homo Academicus (transl. by P. Collier, Cambridge UK 1988, French orig. 1984).

5 *T. C. Grey*, Langdell's Orthodoxy, 45 U. Pitt. L. Rev. 1 (1983) (hereafter cited as *Grey*), at p. 2 et passim.

6 Already in 1900, legal academics had founded their own professional organization, the Association of American Law Schools, initially within the American Bar Association; in 1914, they broke away from the umbrella organization altogether. Contemporaries sensed that the times of the part-time teacher in the leading law schools were over, *A. Kales*, Should the Law Teacher Practice Law?, 25 Harv. L. Rev. 253 (1912); *E. Thayer*, Note, 25 Harv. L. Rev. 259.

7 *J. Auerbach*, Unequal Justice (New York 1977) (hereafter cited as *Auerbach*), pp. 74-101; *L. Friedman*, A History of American Law (2nd ed. New York 1989) (hereafter cited as *Friedman*), pp. 606-620; *K. Hall*, The Magic Mirror. Law in American History (New York 1989) (hereafter cited as *Hall*), pp. 218-224; *M. Rheinstein*, Einführung in die Rechtsvergleichung (3. Auflage, München 1987), pp. 179-191; *M. Rheinstein*, Die Rechtshonoratioren und ihr Einfluß auf Charakter und Funktion der Rechtsordnungen, RabelsZ 34, p. 4 (1970); *J. H. Schlegel*, Between the Harvard Founders and American Legal Realism, 35 J. Leg. Ed. 311 (1985) (hereafter cited as *Schlegel*); *R. Stevens*, Law School. Legal Education in America from the 1850s to the 1980s (Chapel Hill 1983) (hereafter cited as *Stevens*), pp. 51-81. For a contemporary perspective see Kales, Law Teacher, at p. 253.

significantly to the shaping of modern American legal academia, and is therefore important for our understanding of its origins and of its impact on the course of the American legal culture.

While American law professors strove to become full-fledged academics they were looking for models which they could emulate. A general model of the academic role existed in their own country, namely in other disciplines with professional academics. Law professors indeed attempted to become "legal scientists" by emulating academics in the humanities (mostly in history and philosophy) as well as in the natural sciences (mostly in chemistry and biology). Others have studied this aspect extensively, and it is not my concern here[9].

However, models from other disciplines were of limited use, because their existence did not prove whether, and if so how, *lawyers* could attain the status full-fledged academics as well — a question much debated in America at the time. After all, law was still widely regarded as a trade learned directly from other lawyers in practice rather than as a scholarly subject taught by academics in a university. If the law teachers wanted models of *legal* academics, scarcity of domestic precedent forced them to look abroad.

The most obvious place to look to was England, since the ties of the common law heritage and the language endured. Yet, the mother country of the common law had never developed an academic legal tradition. In fact, in mid-nineteenth century England there was hardly any university study of law, and academic legal scholarship outside of the Roman law was virtually nonexistent[10].

In contrast, law as an academic subject, and law teachers as full-fledged academics had been flourishing on the European continent for centuries. In the nineteenth century, Germany in particular ranked as the citadel of legal learning. There the law professors were indeed "legal scientists" — they worked as full-time scholars, professionals responsible for the development of law, and vested with pretigious academic positions. These learned men became the role models for many legal scholars in postbellum America and thereby influenced the American jurists' conception of the proper qualifications, role, and status of legal academics.

---

[8] *Stevens* vaguely hints at the influence of "German scientism" on the development of American law schools, pp. 51, 134. The foreign influence on American legal education is the topic of *D. Clark,* Tracing the Roots of American Legal Education, 51 Rabels Zeitschrift 313 (1987) (hereafter cited as *Clark*).

[9] See e. g. *Grey; M. Speciale,* Langdell's Concept of Law as Science: The Beginnings of Anti-Formalism in American Legal Theory, 5 Vt. L. Rev. 1 (1980).

[10] *P. Stein,* Legal Evolution (New York 1980) (hereafter cited as *Stein*), pp. 78-79; *D. Sugarman,* Legal Theory, the Common Law Mind and the Making of the Textbook Tradition, in: W. Twining (ed.), Legal Theory and Common Law (New York 1986) (hereafter cited as *Sugarman*), p. 26, at pp. 28-29.

This papers addresses the German influence on the development of early American legal academia in three major parts. It first distinguishes and describes *The Elements of the Model.* It shows how leading Anglo-American scholars were intrigued by their German colleagues' professional expertise as scholars, their specialized responsibility for the development of the law, and their institutional status in the universities. As a result, the early American academics shaped their self-image in substantial part after the German professoriate.

The second part offers an interpretive view of *The Attraction of the Model* by putting the rise of the new American law professors into the context of broader trends in late nineteenth an early twentieth century Western societies. The emergence of full-time, career academics was part of three interconnected developments: the professionalization of jobs, the specialization of functions, and the institutionalization of learning and science. The German legal and academic culture preceded America at the time in all three areas, which helps to explain why American scholars looked for Germany to guidance.

In conclusion, this paper addresses *The Fate of the Model* after the classical age. On the one hand, the positive image of German legal academics declined rapidly around the time of World War I in America, but on the other hand, the results of the influence of the civil law model persisted. Its effects still manifest themselves in the American law professoriate today, although the model influenced the image of the profession more strongly than it affected the substance of its work. Finally, by helping to shape a new group of actors in the U. S., the European model also affected the American legal culture at large.

At the outset, three clarifications are in order. First, while this paper deals primarily with American law professors, it also considers several leading scholars in Great Britain, where a similar though less pronounced and less rapid professionalization of legal academics took place around the same time[11]. As American and British scholars still considered themselves very much one family, any sharp separation of the two groups would be artificial.

Second, while the paper focuses on the German professoriate as the model, "German" does not denote a nationality but the German speaking legal culture in late nineteenth and early twentieth century central Europe. It encompasses Germany itself as well as Switzerland, Austria, and some regions in Eastern Europe. In this wider sense the teachers at the universities of Berlin, Vienna, Prague, and Zurich were all "German" professors.

Finally, even in this broader sense, the German legal culture represented the civil law tradition as a whole. Limiting this article to the German influence in no way implies that Anglo-American law professors entirely disregarded academ-

---

11 See *Sugarman,* p. 29; generally *A. Engel,* From Clergyman to Don (Oxford 1983), pp. 257-285.

ics in other continental countries. Yet the focus on the German legal culture is appropriate because common law jurists considered it the leader of the civil law tradition at the time.

I. The Elements of the Model: Three Dimensions

Among nineteenth century Anglo-American legal scholars German legal academia commanded widespread admiration and fascination. This does not mean that all, or even most, American law professors considered German law teachers their models. Nor does it imply that those who did uncritically admired and unconditionally emulated German scholars. Yet, many among the leading figures, who set the standards and provided the guidance for the rest, believed that becoming a legal academic meant following the German lead. This belief can be extrapolated from all sorts of evidence, from express acknowledgements to surrounding circumstances. That American legal scholars perceived the German professoriate as a model manifests itselfs especially in three modes: the American admiration of German scholarly expertise (infra 1.), the attempts of American jurists to assume the special responsibility for the development of the law which their German colleagues had long commanded (2.), and the American aspiration to the academic status which the German professors already held (3.).

1. Professional Expertise: "The Learning of a German Professor"

When Christopher Columbus Langdell, the man who had established the new Harvard Law School, celebrated his 25th anniversary as a member of the faculty in 1895, Mr. Justice Gray, speaking before the Harvard Law School Association, lauded the legal scientist as well the common lawyer.

> [H]e looks at the law of our country, as it must necessarily be looked at, in the double aspect of a science to teach principles, and of a practical rule to govern affairs. He has all the learning of a German professor, and all the practical sense of an English and American common lawyer[12].

Law had two sides. As a "practical rule to govern affairs", it depended on the "pratical sense of a common lawyer". As a "science", i. e. a set of "principles", however, the "learning of a German professor" became crucial. For many among Justice Gray's present audience as well as among the later readers of his speech, the "learning of a German professor" was not a mere phrase, but held connotations of specific qualities and rang of famous names. What were these qualities, and who were the people with whom Langdell was ranked?

---

[12] *Mr. Justice Gray,* Speech, Harvard Law School Association Report of the Ninth Annual Meeting (Boston 1895), p. 50.

Nineteenth and early twentieth century Anglo-American legal literature praised two major aspects of German legal academics. It extolled German professors as scholars who had created a true legal science in their historical and systematic works, and it praised their teaching, from which many Anglo-Americans sought to benefit by studying under German professors.

As scholars, the German professor enjoyed an illustrious reputation in the common law world. The most revered was clearly Friedrich Carl von Savigny, the founder of the historical school of law and the mastermind of nineteenth century German jurisprudence. Several of his works had been translated into English[13], and to many leading Anglo-American law teachers Savigny presented the outright prototype of a legal scholar. He commanded tremendous prestige as a Roman law scholar, legal historian, legal scientist and, generally, as an "epoch making man"[14]. Maitland extolled him as "the herald of evolution, the man who substitutes development for manufacture, organism for mechanism, natural laws for Natural law"[15], and Federick Pollock openly attested to Savigny's profound influence on his work[16]. For Justice Gray's and Langdell's American contemporaries, Savigny occupied the rank of the great figure of legal science. His biographer in the volume on the "Great Jurists of the World" called him "the Newton or the Darwin of the science of law"[17]. Josef Beale, himself one of the new professional academics in America, found that "[t]he impulse given to legal study by the work of Savigny and his school has in the last generation spread over the civilized world and profoundly influenced its legal thought" and emphasized Savigny's significance for the "age of scientific scholarship" which had just begun in America[18].

---

13 The most important translations were: *F. C. von Savigny,* Geschichte des römischen Rechts im Mittelalter, vol. I (Heidelberg 1815), transl. by E. Cathcart as History of the Roman Law During the Middle Ages (Edinburgh 1829); *F. C. von Savigny,* Vom Beruf unserer Zeit für Gesetzgebung und Rechtswissenschaft (Heidelberg 1814), transl. by A. Hayward as On the Vocation of Our Age for Legislation and Jurisprudence (London 1831); *F. C. von Savigny,* Das Recht des Besitzes (Giessen 1803), transl. by E. Perry as A Treatise on Possession (London 1848); *F. C. von Savigny,* System des heutigen römischen Rechts, Bd. I (Berlin 1840), transl. by W. Holloway as System of the Modern Roman Law (Madras 1867); *F. C. von Savigny,* System des heutigen römischen Rechts, Bd. VIII (Berlin 1849), transl. by W. Guthrie as Private International Law (Edinburgh 1869); *F. C. von Savigny,* System des heutigen römischen Rechts, Bd. II (Berlin 1840), transl. by W. Rattigan as Jural Relations or the Roman Law of Persons (London 1884). F. W. Maitland began, but never finished, a translation of *F. C. von Savigny,* Geschichte des römischen Rechts im Mittelalter (6 vols. Heidelberg 1815-1831), see *H. A. L. Fisher,* Frederick William Maitland (Cambridge UK 1910), p. 53.

14 *Taylor,* The Science of Jurisprudence, 22 Harv. L. Rev. 241 (1909), p. 243.

15 Quoted after *C. H. S. Fifoot,* Judge and Jurist in the Reign of Victoria (London 1959), p. 9.

16 *F. Pollock,* A First Book of Jurisprudence (5th ed. London 1923), p. VII.

17 *J. Montmorency,* Friedrich Carl von Savigny, in J. MacDonell & E. Manson (eds.), Great Jurists of the World, vol. 2 (Boston 1914), p. 561, at p. 586.

Savigny's Romanist colleagues were hardly less famous among Anglo-American legal scholars and impressed the common lawyers with the clarity and systematic logic of their expositions. Among the earlier generation of Romanists, Thibaut, Mackeldey and Puchta were translated and celebrated[19]. Puchta in particular represented the virtues of systematic German jurisprudence. The work of this "great master"[20], a contemporary academic observer wrote,

> gives a good deal of law, but gives it in such logical shape and in such luminous style that it captivates the reader. It is much to be regretted that there is no similar work in English ... If the reader can imagine Sharswood's Blackstone, Parsons on Contracts, Washburn on Real Property, and Willard's Equity condensed into three volumes, infused with the spirit of modern philosophic inquiry and couched in language as fresh and limpid throughout as that of Chancellor Kent, he will form some idea of Puchta as a jurist[21].

Of the later generation of Romanists, American academics admired most of all Bernhard Windscheid for his contributions to legal doctrine as well as for the systematic order of his magisterial treatise on the Law of Pandects, and Rudolf von Gneist, Carl Georg Bruns, and Rudolf von Jhering were famous names as well[22]. Rudolf Sohm's "Institutes" became a standard text on Roman law[23].

In the newly emerging field of legal history, German professors were the acknowledged leaders, as Pollock's homage to Heinrich Brunner[24] and Maitland's procurement of an honorary doctorate from Cambridge for Felix Liebermann in 1896 illustrate[25]. Anglo-American legal historians revered the German scholars

---

18 *J. Beale*, The Development of Jurisprudence During the Past Century, 18 Harv. L. Rev. 271 (1905), p. 283; see also *M. Hoeflich*, Savigny and his Anglo-American Disciples, 37 Am. J. Comp. L. 17 (1989).

19 *A. F. J. Thibaut*, System des Pandektenrechts (orig. 2 vols. 1803), transl. by W. B. Lindley (later Lord Lindley) as Introduction to the Study of Jurisprudence (London 1855); *F. Mackeldey*, Lehrbuch des heutigen römischen Rechts (orig. 1814), transl. by P. I. Kaufmann as Compendium of Modern Civil Law (London 1845); see also *F. Mackeldey*, Handbook of the Roman Law (M. Dropsie transl. Philadelphia 1883). Translations from the works of Puchta and other German jurists were published by W. Hastie as Outlines of the Science of Jurisprudence (Edinburgh 1887).

20 *W. Hastie*, id., Translator's Preface, p. XXIX.

21 *J. M. Hart*, German Universities (New York 1878) (hereafter cited as Hart), p. 126.

22 *M. Smith*, Four German Jurists (Bruns, Windscheid, Jhering, Gneist), 10 Pol. Sci. Q. 664 (1895); 11 Pol. Sci. Q. 278 (1896); 12 Pol. Sci. Q. 21 (1897); 16 Pol. Sci. Q. 641 (1901) (hereafter cited as *Smith*, vol. / page).

23 *R. Sohm*, Institutionen. Geschichte und System des römischen Privatrechts (Leipzig 1883), transl. by J. C. Ledlie as The Institutes (Oxford 1892).

24 *F. Pollock*, In Memoriam: Frederick William Maitland, 23 L. Q. R. 137 (1907), p. 137.

25 *C. H. S. Fifoot*, Frederick William Maitland — A Life (Cambridge / Mass. 1971), p. 124. Besides Brunner and Liebermann, Maitland particularly admired Otto von Gierke. He translated a section of vol. III of Gierke's Das deutsche Genossenschaftsrecht (Berlin 1881) and published it as Political Theories of the Middle Ages (Cambridge UK 1913).

for having turned legal history into a science. Speaking before a Harvard audience, Oliver Wendell Holmes frowned at "Story's simple philosophizing" but expressed confidence that things were improving now that American scholars followed their German colleagues[26]. He praised the "German exactness in detail"[27], while Maitland emphasized the German "delicacy of touch and . . . subtlety of historical perception"[28].

Even the Harvard Law Review found itself judged by the standards that German scholarship had set. The issue in honor of Langdell, Frederick Pollock opined at the above mentioned celebration for the dean, "need not fear comparison with the festival collection of essays produced at any German university". In other words, it was like a German "Festschrift", and at least for Pollock that was praise enough[29].

Beyond the renown of their scholarship, many German professors also enjoyed an international reputation as outstanding teachers. Arguably the most famous teacher, Karl Adolf von Vangerow presented lectures on the Pandects in Heidelberg which were praised by James Bryce in England[30] and described by one American student, himself later a university teacher, as a brilliant exercise in logical presentation.

> Seated on a small raised platform near the center of the room, the lecturer spoke for an hour and a half in an easy, clear, sustained voice, without any pause, and without break on one of the most complicated points in Roman law. He had no notes, not even a schedule, only a slip of paper . . .; yet the ideas and words came forth as clear and logical and well placed as if the lecturer had such an insight into and such a grasp of his subject that his discourse seemed to be nothing less than the easy, spontaneous process of organic evolution — it seemed to grow itself out of his brain . . . it was a masterly didactic statement of the clear, crystalline truths of the law, introducing nothing superfluous, omitting nothing necessary, and putting everything together in the right place."[31]

Comparison to a lecturer as impressive as von Vangerow was the highest honor Holmes could bestow upon the Harvard law faculty. In 1886, during the rise of the case method, he lauded the lectures of the past generation of the

---

26 *O. W. Holmes,* The Use and Meaning of Law Schools, and their Methods of Instruction, 3 L. Q. R. 118 (1887) (also published in 20 Am. L. Rev. 919, 1886), p. 120.

27 Unsigned review of *H. Adams* et al., Essays in Anglo-Saxon Law, 11 Am. L. Rev. 327 (1887); the review is attributed to Holmes by *M. Howe,* Justice Oliver Wendell Holmes, Jr., vol. II (Cambridge / Mass. 1963), p. 147 fn. 28.

28 Quoted after *C. H. S. Fifoot,* Maitland, p. 158.

29 *F. Pollock,* The Vocation of the Common Law, Harvard Law School Association, Report of the Ninth Annual Meeting (Boston 1895), p. 13.

30 *J. Bryce,* On the Academical Study of the Civil Law (New York), p. 17; *J. Bryce,* The Methods of Legal Science, in J. Bryce, Studies in Histoy and Jurisprudence (New York 1901), p. 605, at p. 633.

31 *Hart,* p. 60-61.

Harvard professors, likening particularly Parker's and Parsons' "enthusiasm of the lecture room" to von Vangerow's[32].

It is no wonder that many Anglo-American jurists sought to learn from such German professors. As a result, there was substantial personal contact between the admirers and the admired, through which the latter influenced the former's conception of legal academia. In most cases, Anglo-Americans travelled to Germany, but in some, German academics also came to America.

It was quite common for late nineteenth century Americans to spend some time at a German university. Since Edward Everett had obtained his Ph. D. from Göttingen in 1817[33], the overall reputation of German academic institutions and teachers had induced thousands of Americans to study in Germany with numbers peaking in the closing decades of the century. Although a comparatively small percentage of them were law students, even their numbers ran into the hundreds[34]. At least in law, no other country's institutions of higher learning at that time drew as many American students. English universities offered virtually no course of legal study, and the reputation of the French law faculties by and large did not match that of their counterparts in Berlin, Leipzig, Heidelberg, or Göttingen.

Foreign students who had listened to celebrated jurists like Savigny or Bluntschli, Puchta or von Vangerow, returned home full of praise for German lecturers. Many among the students from Great Britain or America later followed the academic path of their German teachers. Already early in the century, Americans like David Hoffmann[35], Englishmen like John Austin[36] and J. J. Park[37], and Scots like John Reddie[38] had obtained German law degrees and had taught and published in their home countries. Particularly during the classical age of American law, several of the future leaders of the new generation of professional academics studied under famous German professors.

James Barr Ames was the most prominent of the students. In 1869 and 1870 he attended various German universities and returned to America imbued with

---

32 *O. W. Holmes,* Harvard Celebration Speech, 20 Am. L. Rev. 919 (1886), p. 922.

33 See *C. F. Thwing,* The American and the German University (New York 1828) (hereafter cited as *Thwing*), pp. 25-26.

34 The numbers quoted in the literature vary substantially, see e. g. *Clark,* 320-322; *D. Shumway,* The American Law Students of the University of Göttingen, German American Annals, New Series 1910, pp. 171-185; *J. Herbst,* The German Historical School in American Scholarship (Ithaca / N. Y. 1965) (hereafter cited as *Herbst*), pp. 8-9; *Thwing,* pp. 18, 207-218; *Hart,* pp. 158-160, 394.

35 On Hoffmann see *P. Stein,* The Attraction of the Civil Law in Post-Revolutionary America, 52 Va. L. Rev. 403 (1966), pp. 423-425; *C. Warren,* History of the Harvard Law School, vol. I (New York 1908, reprinted 1970), p. 179.

36 On Austin see *A. B. Schwartz,* John Austin and the German Jurisprudence of His Time, 1 Politica 178 (1934).

37 On Park see *Stein,* p. 72.

38 On Reddie see id., pp. 72-73.

German scholarship[39]. One need only browse through the collection of his "Lectures in Legal History"[40] to find ample evidence of German influence. The references to Germanist scholars like Brunner, Heusler, Sohm and Schröder abound. Ames was also familiar with Romanist scholarship, German doctrinal works, commentaries, and court decisions. Though a common lawyer at heart, he frequently consulted civilian works throughout his life. The first of the new professional legal academics and the later dean of the Harvard Law School, he considered German learning the model for modern, scientific jurisprudence[41].

Studies at the University of Göttingen in 1877-78 under Rudolf von Jhering and others left their mark on Christopher Tiedemann, who went on the become a professor of law first at the University of Missouri, later at New York University. Today largely overlooked, Tiedemann was one of the most prolific writers and most influential teachers of his time. His own preference for treatise writing reflects the influence of the German Pandectist tradition. Tiedemann also penned a variety of short articles in which he demonstrated his familiarity with and admiration for the works of German legal academics[42].

A few years later than Tiedemann, E. Munroe Smith obtained his doctorate in law in Göttingen. He joined the Columbia faculty in 1890 and taught Roman law and comparative jurisprudence. His contributions to the ongoing debates about legal education and codification attest to the influence of his studies in Germany on his ideas[43]. He openly expressed his gratitude to his German teachers and his respect for their learning in a series of articles on Bruns, Windscheid, Jhering, and Gneist[44]. A legal historian as well, Smith wrote the leading book on European legal history[45].

Legal historians were particularly drawn to the German scholars. The leading example was Henry Baxter Adams who was profoundly influenced by his teacher Bluntschli while studying in Germany. After obtaining his doctorate there in 1876, Adams joined the Johns Hopkins faculty. Though not a professor of law, he was one of the leading exponents of the American historical school of law[46].

---

39 *J. B. Ames,* Lectures on Legal History (Cambridge / Mass. 1913) (Memoir), p. 4; see also *E. Patterson,* Historical and Evolutionary Theories of Law, 51 Col. L. Rev. 681 (1951), p. 694.

40 *J. B. Ames,* id., passim.

41 See infra. notes 98-99, and accompanying text.

42 See e. g. *C. Tiedemann,* Methods of Legal Education, 1 Yale L. J. 150, p. 151.

43 See e. g. *M. Smith,* Statute Law and Common Law, 2 Pol. Sci. Q. 105 (1887).

44 *M. Smith,* supra note 22.

45 *M. Smith,* The Development of European Law (New York 1928).

46 *Thwing,* p. 164, see also *E. Samuels,* The Young Henry Adams (Cambridge / Mass. 1948), pp. 53-68; Adams vividly expressed his admiration for German legal historiography in his review of the works of Maine, Nasse, and Sohm in 114 N. Am. Rev. 196 (1876).

Exposure to German thought shaped the ideas of men like Ames, Tiedemann, Smith, Adams and others about professional academics and scholarship. Upon their return to their home countries, they carried these ideas into their own universities, disseminated them among their colleagues and passed them on to their students. Furthermore, images of the German professoriate were also brought to America by German academics themselves.

Many came as emigrants long before the 1930s and 1940s, some even during the antebellum period. Charles Follen, who held a doctorate in law from Giessen (1818) and had taught private law in Jena (1818) and Basel (1821-24), came to the U. S. for political reasons in 1825 and lectured on civil and Roman law at Harvard in 1834[47]. Francis Lieber, likewise a political refugee, purused a long and often troubled career in American higher education and finally taught law at Columbia after the civil war[48]. Both Follen and Lieber were academic generalists rather than specialized law professors, but this strengthened rather than impaired their standing as representatives of the breadth of German erudition.

A later, and perhaps more important case in point, was Ernst Freund who had studied in Berlin and Heidelberg where he obtained his doctorate in law in 1884[49]. Like many of the later emigrants, he started over again after he had come to the U. S. and attended Columbia Law School and the School of Political Science. He began teaching at his alma mater but then spent the rest of his life at Chicago, where he helped to establish the new university. Freund published widely on German law and legal education[50]. His German teachers had awakened his interest in legislation and administrative law, areas which his American colleagues continued to neglect woefully. Freund, like Pound, saw a great need to establish a science of legislation, for which he hoped to lay the foundation[51].

Most German jurists, though, came to the U. S. as visitors only, invited because their American brethren looked for guidance in solving the problems of modern jurisprudence. "The problems", Munroe Smith wrote, "which have engaged the attention of German jurists during this century [are], in large degree, universal problems; and the solutions which they have reached should be of interest to all who care for legal science."[52] The interest in German legal scholarship grew

---

47 On Follen see *G. Frankenberg,* Karl Follen (1796-1840). Unbedingt für Bürgergleichheit, in Kritische Justiz, Streitbare Juristen (Baden-Baden 1988), pp. 33-43; *C. Warren,* History of the Harvard Law School (New York 1908), p. 493.

48 *F. Freidel,* Francis Lieber (Baton Rouge 1947); *S. Riesenfeld,* The Impact of German Legal Ideas and Institutions in the United States, in this volume.

49 *O. Kraines,* The Worlds and Ideas of Ernst Freund (Univ. of Alabama 1974); *A. Smith,* Preface to E. Freund, Standards of American Legislation (2nd ed. Chicago 1965), pp. IX-X.

50 *E. Freund,* The Study of Law in Germany, 1 The Counsellor 131 (1892); *E. Freund,* The Proposed German Civil Code, 24 Am. L. Rev. 237 (1890); *E. Freund,* The New German Civil Code, 13 Harv. L. Rev. 627 (1899).

51 *E. Freund,* Standards of Legislation (Chicago 1917).

particularly strong after the enactment of the German Civil Code in 1900. In 1907-08, Rudolf Leonhard, a professor of law at the universities of Marburg and Breslau, came to Columbia as the Kaiser-Wilhelm Exchange Professor[53], lectured on German jurisprudence and Roman law, and published articles in leading American law journals[54]. Roscoe Pound invited Eugen Ehrlich, the founder of sociological jurisprudence, to give a series of lectures at the Lowell Institute[55].

The superior reputation of the German professoriate is probably most strikingly illustrated by the decision of the Carnegie Foundation in selecting the reporter for its ambitious study of the case method of instruction, one of the most hotly disputed issues in American legal academia in the early twentieth century. The Foundation was looking for an academic with "wide knowledge of the law, a familiarity with its practical application, and, above all, a scholarly and broad-minded view of education and its function in civilization." While there was no lack of candidates from domestic universities, the officers of the Foundation thought "that it would be difficult to obtain from any teacher of law or any practitioner of law in America a thoroughly sound, fair-minded, and scholarly report"[56]. Accordingly, they chose Josef Redlich, a professor of law at the University of Vienna. Redlich was expected to and did bring the perspective of German legal science to the task, constantly comparing American legal education with its German counterpart in his final report[57]. Even the case method, America's most original contribution to modern legal education, thus came under German academic scrutiny, but even the critics of Redlich's report never doubted his credentials as an evaluator[58].

52 *Smith* X / p. 666.

53 His visit at Columbia was part of an exchange program between the University of Berlin on the German side, and Harvard and Columbia on the American side. The program was supported by the two countries' leaders, Emperor Wilhelm II and President Roosevelt, and included professors from all sorts of faculties, not only law. It flourished for about a decade and ceased during World War I; see *B. v. Brocke,* Der deutsch-amerikanische Professorenaustausch, Zeitschrift für Kulturaustausch 1981, 128; *G. Ritter,* Motive und Organisationsformen der internationalen Wissenschaftsbeziehungen und die Anfänge einer auswärtigen Kulturpolitik im deutschen Kaiserreich vor dem Ersten Weltkrieg, in *L. Kettenacker, M. Schlenke, H. Seier,* Studien zur Geschichte Englands und der deutsch-britischen Beziehungen (München 1981), 153, at pp. 160-169.

54 Leonhard's opening lecture, Methods Followed in Germany by the Historical School of Law, appeared in 7 Col. L. Rev. 573 (1907); see also *R. Leonhard,* The Vocation of America for the Science of Roman Law, 26 Harv. L. R. 389 (1912 / 13).

55 *R. Pound,* An Appreciation of Eugen Ehrlich, 36 Harv. L. Rev. 129 (1922).

56 *H. Pritchett,* Preface to J. Redlich, The Common Law and the Case Method in American University Law Schools, Report to the Carnegie Foundation for the Advancement of Teaching, Bulletin 8 (1914), pp. V - VI.

57 *J. Redlich,* The Common Law and the Case Method in American University Law Schools.

58 Redlich later joined the Harvard faculty as the Charles Stebbins Fairchild Professor of Comparative Public Law, *A. E. Sutherland,* The Law at Harvard. A History of Ideas and Men, 1817-1967 (Cambridge / Mass. 1967), p. 293.

The high esteem enjoyed by German legal academics in the Anglo-American culture formed only part of a broader phenomenon. It stood in the context of the general reputation of German scholars in the late nineteenth and early twentieth century to which legal academics not only contributed, but from which they also profited. In 1917, John Henry Wigmore, yet another member of the new academic generation in America, stated that in the last generation "Germany has been generally spoken of in this country as the preeminent home of science and lerning among modern nations[59]." Indeed, Anglo-American scholars considered German scholarship and science leading in fields as diverse as history and theology, archeology and economics, chemistry and physics, biology and human medicine[60]. Thus the "learning of a German professor" evoked images not only of Savigny and Windscheid, but also of the universalist von Humboldt, the historian von Ranke, the theologian Schleiermacher, the chemist Liebig, and the physicists Kirchoff and Bunsen. In some cases, direct links existed between legal scholarship and other fields. Savigny closely cooperated with the Germanist and linguist Jakob Grimm as well as with the historian Niebuhr, just as his fame was connected with the reputation of early nineteenth century German philology[61], and Theodor Mommsen, a formidable Roman lawyer, earned renown as a leader in classical studies.

The erudition of these people symbolized the cultural heritage of the old world. At least from the American perspective, the leading jurists among them were not narrow-minded specialists but scholars broadly educated in the best continental tradition. But the German professors were not only impressive legal scholars and teachers, they also maintained and developed the law and thus functioned as the intellectual leaders of the profession.

2. Specialized Responsibility:
"A Wholesome Influence Upon the Development of the Law"

The vocation of a law professor, James Barr Ames announced in 1901, extended beyond teaching.

> His position gives him an exceptional opportunity to exert a wholesome influence upon the development of the law by his writing. If we turn to the countries in which the vocation of the law-professor has long been recognized, to Germany, for instance, we find a large body of legal literature, of a high quality, the best and greater part of which is the work of professors. The names of Savigny, Windscheid, Jhering and Brunner at once suggest themselves[62].

---

59 *J. H. Wigmore,* A Proposal to Restore the True Status of French Science and Learning in America, 49 Chicago Legal News 243 (1917) (hereafter cited as *Wigmore*).

60 See *Thwing*, pp. 160-187.

61 The discovery of the manuscript of Gaius' Institutes by Niebuhr and Savigny in 1816 boosted the Anglo-American interest in Roman law; see e. g. *L. Cushing,* An Introduction to the Study of the Roman Law (Boston 1854), pp. 142-143 (§ 275).

The law professor as a scholar thus had a responsibility to contribute to the development of the law, and the Germans had shown how that ought to be done. Ames and many of his colleagues had specific ideas of the "legal literature" which the professor should produce, and of the kind of "wholesome influence upon the development of the law" which they should exert. These ideas reflect the jurisprudential need of the classical age to build a principled order in a legal system that threatened to deteriorate into utter disorder. This alarming drift towards chaos had two major reasons.

First, while the common law had never been very systematic and orderly, at least the various forms of action had provided categories in which to organize the material along procedural lines. With the gradual abolishment of these categories and with the introduction of a uniform civil action in the mid and late nineteenth century, such organization vanished. Since other categories were not yet in place, there was not generally accepted way of organizing the law at all[63]. Second, the growing number of states in the U. S. federal system accelerated the slide into chaos. Particularly after the Civil War, hundreds of state and dozens of federal courts poured out a flood of decisions which the emerging National Reporter System stored in ever greater numbers and which threatened to make the system totally unmanageable. The original (English) idea of a common law consisting of a limited number of principal decisions that most lawyers could memorize or at least easily research became completely illusory[64]. In addition, dozens of state legislatures produced more and more statutes regulating private rights and public affairs with little regard to established common law rules. As a result, postbellum American legal literature is replete with signs of anxiety that whatever order there once had been in the legal system was turning into complete disarray. The common lawyers realized that they had never developed a set of principles of substantive law out of which a systematic order could be built[65].

Detecting such principles and buildung such an order became the foremost jurisprudential agenda of the classical age. The methodological tool which was to make that possible was "legal science". According to widespread agreement, a scientific approach to law would reveal the order inherent in the apparent legal

---

62 *J. B. Ames*, The Vocation of the Law Professor, in J. B. Ames, Lectures on Legal History (Cambridge / Mass. 1913), 354 (orig. published in 30 Am. L. Reg. 129, 1900) (hereafter cited as *Ames*), p. 364.

63 *Friedman*, pp. 621-629.

64 For data on the rapidly growing output of the courts, see *Hall*, pp. 227 and 229.

65 See e. g. *C. Platt*, The Proposed Civil Code of New York, 20 Am. L. Rev. 713 (1886), p. 717; *W. Schofield*, Uniformity of Law in the Several States as an American Ideal, 21 Harv. L. Rev. 416, 510, 583 (1908). This situation had a profound impact on the young Holmes' view of the law, see *M. Reimann*, Holmes' "Common Law" and German Legal Science, in R. Gordon (ed.), The Legacy of Oliver Wendell Holmes, Jr. (Stanford 1992), 72, pp. 76-78.

chaos, just as the natural sciences were revealing the natural order underlying the apparent chaos of nature. The external manifestation of that legal science was to be the scholarly literature. Through this scientific, scholarly literature, then, legal academics could save the common law system from conceptual anarchy and present it as a logical arrangement[66].

For many Anglo-American jurists in the postbellum period, the role model of the legal scientist as savior of the legal system was the German law professor. Leading common law teachers knew that their German colleagues had already done what they themselves were still trying to accomplish. Out of a chaos comparable to the postbellum American situation, German legal academics had, apparently through legal science, built a systematic legal order[67]. Their work had two major components. Through thorough historical analysis, i. e., scientific legal historiography, they had first reached an understanding of the fundamental principles of their law. Then they had connected these principles to form a comprehensive system through logical construction[68]. Ames had exactly these two kinds of scholarship in mind when he elaborated on the "Vocation of the Law Professor" — the works of the German jurists he named represented both historical study and system building. Ames and many of his colleagues then sought to emulate German academics in both regards — as legal historians as well as systematizers[69].

The American "historical school" at Harvard and elsewhere in the postbellum period explored the history of the common law in order to find the true underlying principles of its historical evolution[70]. In this endeavor, the German legal historians acted as important guides, and their influence is well documented in the footnotes of writers like Holmes, Ames, Gray, Pound, and others. Of course, the German professors were not the only guides. As scientists, American scholars wanted also to become evolutionists like Darwin, and as legal historians, they also followed Maine and Maitland. But the detection of the fundamental legal

---

66 See *G. Gilmore*, The Ages of American Law (New Haven 1977), pp. 58-60; *R. Pound*, Taught Law, 37 Rep. Am. Bar Assn. 975 (1912), pp. 998-991; *Stevens*, p. 131; for England see *Sugarman*, p. 29.

67 *A. Kocourek*, Translator's Preface to A. Gareis, Introduction to the Science of Law (Boston 1911), p. XIII fn. 2. This legal order was enshrined in the German Civil Code (Bürgerliches Gesetzbuch) of 1900 which was much admired in the common law world for its logical arrangement, see e. g. *F. Maitland*, The Making of the German Civil Code, in F. Maitland, 3 Collected Papers 474 (Cambridge 1911), p. 484; *E. Borchard*, Jurisprudence in Germany, 12 Col. L. Rev. 301 (1912), p. 304.

68 See *M. Reimann*, Nineteenth Century German Legal Science, 31 Boston Coll. L. Rev. 837 (1990), pp. 858-874.

69 See *H. Taylor*, The Science of Jurisprudence, 22 Harv. L. Rev. 241 (1909), p. 249, calling for a combination of historical research and logical systematization.

70 A good example is *J. C. Gray*, The Rule Against Perpetuities (1886); see *S. Siegel*, John Chipman Gray, Legal Formalism, and the Transformation of Perpetuities Law, 36 U. Miami L. Rev. 439 (1982).

principles through tracing the law's historical development had its origins in Savigny's works and was, as Anglo-Americans openly recognized, the fundamental credo of the German historical school[71]. Holmes acknowledged the model provided by German legal historiography[72] and was later himself extolled by Pollock who likened Holmes' work in the common law to what Savigny had done for the Roman law[73]. The American historical school produced such an impressive amount of historical scholarship that Josef Redlich wrote in 1914 that "what Savigny and his pupils and the entire legal-historical school of Germany accomplished for the common law of Germany has been performed in no less admirable fashion in the last half century for the English common law by such men as Thayer, Langdell, Ames and Bigelow in America."[74]

When it came to the law professors' responsibility for systematizing the law, German legal academics were the unrivalled leaders at the time. The conceptualization and systematization of the Roman law as the common law of continental Europe under Savigny and his disciples made such a strong impression in the common law world that many leading Anglo-American academics openly urged the common lawyers to follow the same path[75]. Here the ancient reputation of the Roman law as the archetype of a refined jurisprudence and the modern reputation of systematic German scholarship blended to form a highly attractive model[76].

Americans like Ames and his generation at Harvard sought to follow the German scholars, particularly as treatise writers who presented huge areas of law, as the German Pandectists had done, in form of a clearly structured, comprehensive order[77]. To be sure, the legal treatise as such was not a German invention. A treatise tradition existed in the common law as well[78], but its products could

---

71 See e. g. *E. Freund,* Historical Jurisprudence in Germany, 5 Pol. Sci. Q. 468 (1890); *Rose,* Controversies of Modern Continental Jurists, 2 South. L. Rev. 551 (1876); *Anon,* The German Historical School of Jurisprudence, 14 Am. Jurist 43 (1835).

72 See supra note 27.

73 *F. Pollock,* Ad Multos Annos, 31 Col. R. Rev. 349 (1931).

74 *J. Redlich,* The Common Law and the Case Method, supra note 57, p. 43.

75 Probably the earliest believer was John Austin who opined that turning from English common to Roman law (as organized by the German scholars) meant to "escape from the empire of chaos and darkness to . . . the region of order and light", *J. Austin,* Lectures on Jurisprudence, vol. I (5th ed. London 1885), p. 58.

76 See *J. Bryce,* On the Academical Study of the Civil Law (New York 1871); A Rejoiner by the Lord Chief Justice of England, in O. W. Holmes, Collected Legal Papers (New York 1920), p. 160.

77 For the U. S., see *G. E. White,* Tort Law in America. An Intellectual History (New York 1980), p. 34; *W. Schofield,* The Relation of the Law Schools to the Courts, Meeting of the AALS 1908, 2 Am. L. Sch. Rev. 194, 204 (1908), p. 205; for England, see *Sugarman,* passim; *E. Campbell,* German Influences on English Legal Education and Jurisprudence in the 19th Century, 4 U. W. Australia L. Rev. 357 (1957-59).

78 *A. W. B. Simpson,* The Rise and Fall of the Legal Treatise, 48 U. Chi. L. Rev. 632 (1981).

not satisfy the late nineteenth century's need for "scientific" legal scholarship. The works of Blackstone, Kent, and Story lacked both a sound basis in scientific legal history and a rigorously systematic order. "As a class", Ames opined, "our treatises are distinctly poor." They were simply not the works of true legal scientists, and in the "absence of a large professorial class" better work could hardly be expected. Germany, however, had such a class, and it produced truly scientific treatises from which Anglo-American jurists had "much to learn" if they wanted to produce "a high order of treatises on all the important branches of the law, exhibiting the historical development of the subject and containing sound conclusions based upon scientific analysis." Ames' wishes soon came true as Anglo-American jurists produced major systematic treatises on common law subjects from the 1870s on, books that "would rank with the best in any country."[79] The extent to which the German model directly influenced Anglo-American treatise writers varied, but the idea that it was the "proper sphere of professorial activity ... to reduce the mass of legal rules to an orderly series of principles" clearly came from the continental legal tradition which was at the time represented specifically by German legal academia[80].

The role and function of a German legal scientist were highly attractive to the rising legal academics in the U. S. because they implied a claim to leadership in the profession. If law professors were the finders of the law's basic principles, and the keepers of its systematic coherence, they bore the ultimate responsibility for its well-being. They would become, as their German counterparts already were, "the lights of the legal profession"[81], and they would even stand, as their German colleagues already did, above both judges and legislators[82].

The judges would have to listen to them because the scholars would be the ultimate authorities on law as a science. The professors would in fact be the ones "to correct ... the principal defect in the generally admirable work of the judges", namely to work out the principles and the system of the law[83]. This job required scientific investigation and scholarly conceptualization, a job to which only academics brought enough time and a sufficiently detached perspective. Their treatises would "render invaluable service to the judge and ... [would] exercise a great influence on the further development of our law.[84]" As a result,

---

79 *Ames*, pp. 365-366.

80 *A. V. Dicey*, Can English Law be Taught at the Universities? (1883), p. 18; Dicey agreed with Ames on the proper responsibilities of legal academics and names, among others, Savigny, Vangerow, and Bluntschli as leading examples, id. p. 27.

81 *Ames*, p. 364.

82 This leadership was evinced, as an American observer notes, by the professors' dominance in the largest German professional organization for lawyers, the Deutscher Juristentag, see *C. McClelland*, Professionalization and Higher Education in Germany, in *K. Jarausch*, The Transformation of Higher Learning 1860-1930 (Chicago 1983), p. 306, at p. 319.

83 *Ames*, p. 366.

84 Id., p. 367.

the scholars' importance would achieve levels as high as in Germany where "the influence of their opinions in the courts is as great or even greater than that of judicial precedents.[85]"

The legislators were equally well advised to listen to the new academics. With regard to codification, still a much debated issue in the "classical age", the German experience was direct evidence that a code required extensive scholarly preparation. Many, if not most, Anglo-American jurists knew that the Germans had heeded Savigny's early admonition and had avoided the mistake of premature codification. They had first relied upon their scholars to systematize their law and only thereafter had gone about codifying it in a scientific manner[86]. American scholars argued that if codification were to be performed at all, the academics at least had to lay the groundwork first, using German scientific jurisprudence as their guide[87]. The professors were also to have "a wholesome influence ... as an expert counselor" on legislation in general. This influence could be exercised in one of two ways — "either by staying or guiding the hand of the legislator"[88]. Here turn-of-the-century American legal academics divided. Some continued the common lawyers' traditional hostility towards statutory law; scholars like Ames as well as practitioners like Carter protested against legislation tearing apart the delicate fabric of the common law. For them, the job of the legal scholar was to make legislation unnecessary by developing the law through legal science alone[89]. In support of that agenda, they drew on Savigny's conception of legal science as a superior alternative to legislation.[90] Others supported legal and social reform through statutory lawmaking. Led particularly by Pound and Freund, they called for statutes based on sound legal principles. For them, the job of the legal academic was to assist the legislators in drafting sensible and clear statutes. They often also invoked German ideas of legal science, but they had the later nineteenth century jurisprudence in mind which served as a basis for, rather than as an alternative to, statutory law[91]. Significantly, both adversaries and advocates of reform legislation agreed that the scholar must guide the legislator. They just disagreed on whether the guide should prevent or promote his followers' activities.

In the search for their roles and function in the legal process, the new American professional legal academics thus saw the German professors demonstrate the

---

85 Id., p. 364; see also *R. Posner,* The Decline of Law as an Autonomous Discipline, 100 Harv. L. Rev. 261 (1987), p. 262.

86 See *M. Reimann,* The Historical School Against Codification: Savigny, Carter, and the Defeat of the New York Civil Code, 37 Am. J. Comp. L. 95 (1989).

87 *Ames,* p. 368; *A. Kocourek,* Translator's Preface to K. Garais, supra note 67.

88 *Ames,* p. 367.

89 Id., pp. 367-368; *J. C. Carter,* On the Proposed Codification of Our Common Law (New York 1884), p. 75.

90 See *M. Reimann,* The Historical School Against Codification, supra note 86, pp. 101-107.

91 *R. Pound,* Mechanical Jurisprudence, 8 Col. L. Rev. 605 (1908), pp. 612, 622.

legal scientists' responsibility and supreme importance. For Ames and his colleagues, emulating Savigny or Windscheid promised to make them as imortant in the profession as these scholars had been. Whether this promise has been fulfilled for American legal academics is open to debate but it is clear that the ambition to become the profession's leaders has influenced the American professors' self-definition and boosted their self-esteem.

3. Institutional Status: "They Have Always Been University Men"

In 1874, James Morgan Hart, a Princeton graduate and later a professor at Cornell, published a description of the German universities based on his personal experience as a student in Berlin and Göttingen[92]. Hart observed that German academics differed from their American colleagues because they were

> men who started life as theoreticians and never made the effort to become practitioners. To them the university was not a mere preparatory school, where they might remain long enough to get their theoretical training, and then turn their backs on it forever. On the contrary, it was an end, a career in itself. They have always been university men, and never expected to become anything else."[93]

German university teachers were professional, career academics, while American professors were (generally speaking) not. Hart was characterizing the German professoriate in general but having obtained a doctorate in law, his description reflected most of all his experience with legal academics.

In the classical period, law faculties in the U. S. began to change, first at the elite institutions, then elsewhere. Their ambition was twofold. Personally, American law professors sought to transform themselves from mere lawyers teaching practical skills into career academics teaching an intellectual discipline. Institutionally, this striving for the status of professional scholars entailed the claim to integrate the law schools into the universities as co-equals of other departments, and thus to recognize the law teachers as full members of the university faculties. The main argument advanced by American law professors to persuade themselves that they were really scholars, and the university that they really belonged in it, lay in their ubiquitous claim that law constituted a science. If law was a science, its development belonged in the hands of scientists, i. e. academics as full-time researchers and teachers. And if law was a science, it could "scarcely be disputed that it [was] one of the greatest and most difficult of sciences, and that it need[ed] all the light that a most enlightened seat of learning can throw upon it.[94]"

---

[92] Hart received his J. U. D. from the University of Göttingen in 1864 and became a professor of English at the University of Cincinnati and at Cornell.

[93] *Hart,* p. 252.

[94] *C. C. Langdell,* Harvard Celebration Speech, 3 L. Q. R. 118 (1887).

The universities on the European continent, and at the time particularly the culture of German legal academia as the incarnation of legal science, provided a ready model for American jurists. German law professors possessed the dual status that American law teachers coveted: they were career scholars, and they were integrated members of highly regarded universities. In nineteenth century Germany, teaching law meant a full-time, full-fledged career. Legal scholars chose the academic path immediately after obtaining their doctorate. In order to qualify as law professors, they pursued extensive postdoctoral studies, published substantial scholarly work reviewed by their faculty, and were thereupon awarded the *venia legendi,* the official license to teach at a university. They then taught for several years as private docents, i. e. without a permanent position, while they applied for vacant professorships. A professorship was awarded on the basis of scholarly merit and promise[95]. Once appointed, a German professor "never expected to be anything else" but a professor[96]. He was a lifetime academic who devoted virtually all his time and energy to teaching, research, and writing, and who had "but one aim in life: scholarly renown."[97]

The first career legal academic of this sort in America was James Barr Ames. Appointed at Harvard solely because he showed great potential as a teacher and scholar, he was truly and exclusively a "university man". Harvard's president Eliot, who had pushed for the appointment, fully realized that the selection of Ames was setting the trend for the future.

> In due course . . . there will be produced in this country a body of men learned in the law who have never been on the bench or at the bar, but who nevertheless hold positions of great weight and influence as teachers of law, as expounders, systematizers, and historians. This, I venture to predict, is one of the most far-reaching changes in the organization of the profession that has ever been made in our country."[98]

The European, and specifically German, model behind this change is manifest. Eliot's own words hinted at it. Nowhere did legal academics have more "weight and influence as teachers of law" than in Germany, and the tripartite characterization of their function as "expounders, systematizers and historians" accurately described the various dimensions of the German historical school of law that dominated the nineteenth century. Eliot knew this perfectly well. Having travelled to Germany some years before in order to study its university system, he had learned to admire its professionalized academia. When he revolutionized Harvard University, he followed in part the German model[99].

---

95 *Hart,* pp. 252-254.

96 Id., p. 252.

97 Id., p. 261.

98 Quoted after The Centennial History of the Harvard Law School (Boston 1918), p. 31; see also *Stevens,* p. 38.

99 See *Clark,* pp. 319, 326-327; Eliot, however, did not slavishly copy the German university system; in fact, he considered some of its features unfit for American purposes, and with respect to some faculties, particularly human medicine, also followed the

Ames himself evinced the German element in the evolution of the new legal scientists. As a former student in Germany and a lifelong admirer of German legal and historian scholarship, he subscribed to the notion of law as a science and saw German jurisprudence as its most impressive realization. It is no wonder that he urged his academic colleagues to follow the German path [100]. As a scholar and teacher, Ames was so successful that young professors who were career scholars and who "never expected to be anything else" ruled the field in the American law schools within less than a generation. John Henry Wigmore, Samuel Williston, Joseph Beale, James Parker Hall, Austin Wakeman Scott, Wesley Hohfeld, and many other leading figures all came to teaching in their late twenties or early thirties after at most a short time in practice [101].

The rise of the new academic jurists was part and parcel of the transformation of the law schools from trade schools into integral parts of the universities. For the law professors, this meant advancement from mere law teachers to university faculty. This process of integration and advancement benefitted, again, from the German model. Eliot's reforms at Harvard resulted from the observations he had made on the continent where the law faculties were not only parts of the universities but had actually laid the groundwork for the modern university culture. As Joseph Beale noted, "[t]he creation of professional schools as real and integral parts of our own universities" could "be traced directly to the European practice" [102].

This does not mean that the integration of the Harvard law faculty into the University at large resulted simply and solely from Eliot's enthusiasm about European universities. There were other reasons as well. Most importantly, Langdell had managed to persuade Eliot that law was a science and thus belonged in a university [103]. Yet, even this reason was connected with the German influence in a subtle way. When Landell advanced, and Eliot finally listened to, the legal science argument, both men knew perfectly well that on the Continent, and especially in Germany, law had long been regarded as a science and had therefore long been a full-fledged university subject. In other words, they knew that in Germany and other European countries, law already had the prestige and position that Langdell claimed it should now enjoy at Harvard as well. Langdell openly admitted that he wanted to place the law school "in the position occupied by

---

French model, see *J. James*, Charles Eliot, vol. I (London 1930), pp. 135-138; *A. Chase*, The Birth of Modern Law School, 23 Am. J. Leg. Hist. 329 (1979), pp. 334, 340, 343-346. But for a professionalized corps of law teachers, German provided by far the best model.

100 See supra notes 81, 83-85 and accompanying text.

101 For biographical information see *Schlegel*, pp. 311-312, fns. 3-12.

102 *J. Beale*, The Place of Professional Education in the Universities, 9 (Chicago) Univ. Rec. 42 (1904), p. 43.

103 See *Sutherland*, The Law at Harvard, note 58, p. 159.

the law faculties in the universities of continental Europe"[104], and Eliot regarded Germany as a model country in academic matters. Thus, German legal science and German universities provided Langdell with the best available live specimen for his plan, and Eliot with powerful practical evidence that the plan made sense.

From the perspective of the law teachers themselves, these changes towards the European model promised a dramatically improved status. Looking to Europe revealed that the position of legal academics was more powerful and prestigious in Germany than anywhere else at the time. Law professors were not only firmly established but also traditionally one of the most numerous and influential groups in the universities. They not only enjoyed the status of civil servants which meant life-tenure and a guaranteed pension but they also worked under conditions, as scholars as well as teachers, that looked enviable to their American colleagues.

As scholars, law professors, like all German academics, pursued law as a science, i. e. worked in an investigative spirit. Thus, they enjoyed the freedom of scientists. They could engage in virtually any research they fancied and could rely on an extensive support staff, consisting of research and teaching assistants with law degrees, often already with doctorates. Law professors, particularly those at the head of a research institute, formed an elite group recruited from the best legal minds in the country[105].

As teachers, German professors seemed equally blessed. As Americans realized, the Germans' privilege of *Lehrfreiheit* (freedom of teaching) meant that they could not be told by any superior what to teach. The faculty worked the necessary, basic curriculum out for itself. Beyond that they were completely free to offer whatever they wished and to teach in any style they pleased. Moreover, unlike their American colleagues, they taught students who came to the university with a strong educational background. All German university students had attended the *Gymnasium,* passed a rigorous exam in the humanities as well as in the sciences in order to gain admission to the universities, and were expected to be intellectually and personally mature. English readers learned from Savigny that "teacher and learner have a reciprocal effect on each other; the one feels himself compelled to foresight and correctness, the other learns to esteem himself, and thus each gives to the other what he receives from him.[106]" A professor, an American observer noted two generations later, did not have to waste his time drilling mindless listeners. "His relation to his hearers is that of one gentleman speaking to another . . . He addresses his pupils as men who know perfectly well what they are about and whom he must seek to enlighten or convince"[107]. In

---

104 *Langdell,* Harvard Celebration Speech, note 94, p. 124.

105 This was aptly described for an American audience by *Hart,* pp. 249-264.

106 *F. C. von Savigny,* On the Present State of the German Universities, orig. published in 3 The Monthly Register 3 (1803); republished by *R. Wellek,* Ein unbekannter Artikel Savignys über die deutschen Universitäten, SZG (germ. Abt.) 51, 529, p. 535.

107 *Hart,* p. 268.

short, even as a teacher, a German law professor was a legal scientist who purported to train not lawyers, but jurists[108]. In essence this meant that German university instruction benefitted from already having serious admission standards at a time when American law schools just began to introduce them. Stanford's President Jordan hoped "to see the time when Harvard, and Yale, and Columbia, and Cornell, and Stanford, and the rest will see fit to devot[e] themselves, as the universities in Germany do, to professional work — law being a part of it."[109]

Moreover, German law professors had almost complete control over the reproduction of the academic corps. In contrast to the traditional American, lateral recruitment of law teachers on the basis of practical experience, the German career structure focused on scholarly merit and thus entailed professorial control over access to academic positions. In other words, German law professors trained their own successors[110]. This looked attractive not only because it ensured the continuity of academic knowledge (and thus, allegedly, the progress of science) but also because it implied power over the transmission of academic authority. It was clear that if American legal academics could acquire such power, they would have their own system of reproduction. Langdell's promotion of Ames as his own anointed successor was the first manifestation of this new system which is now in place everywhere in American legal academia.

These conditions seemed as wonderful to many late nineteenth century American scholars as they had to Austin when he wished he was "a German professor"[111]. Last but not least, a German academic enjoyed a social prestige of which his American colleagues could only dream. In the university town, an American law student observed, "nobody ... can outrank him"[112]. Scholars, rather than judges, had always ranked as the great men in the continental legal tradition but in nineteenth century Germany their social status reached its high water mark. The epitome, for German as well as many foreign observers, was, again, Savigny. Of old nobility and independent wealth, he had chosen an academic career, to the considerable amazement of his contemporaries but to the immense benefit of the standing of legal (and other) scholars. A scholar of formidable erudition and impeccable style, Savigny was not only a close friend of the Prussian king, he also wielded tremendous influence on the reorganization of the German university system as a whole, and great political power as a cabinet member[113].

---

108 Id., p. 252.

109 *D. S. Jordan*, The Law School and the University, Address, 2 Am. Law School Rev. 194, 198 (1908), p. 200.

110 See *Hart*, pp. 257-258.

111 Quoted after *C. H. S. Fifoot*, Judge and Jury in the Reign of Victoria, p. 86.

112 *Hart*, p. 267. American academics were fascinated not only with the status of German legal academics but with the position of other kinds of scholars as well, see *R. Veysey*, The Emergence of the American University (Chicago 1965), p. 128.

113 See *F. Wieacker*, Gründer und Bewahrer (Göttingen 1959), p. 119; *F. Wieacker*, Privatrechtsgeschichte der Neuzeit (2nd ed. Göttingen 1967), p. 383.

In the wake of his prestige, the leading German legal academics advanced to members of the cultural and social elite of their times.

II. The Attraction of the Model: Three Contexts

The new American legal academics were intrigued by the German professoriate because they wanted to become "legal scientists", and Germany provided the best available model for that. The German professoriate's model function is best understook in the context of three more general phenomena in nineteenth and early twentieth century Western culture: the increasing professionalization of jobs in modern civilization (1.), the growing specialization of functions in society (2.), and the institutionalization of science in the universities (3.).

1. The Professionalization of Jobs

The emergence of the new career academics was essentially a professionalization process. For Story's generation, law teaching and scholarship had meant a part-time job, but beginning in the 1870s it gradually turned into a full-time profession. Becoming a legal academic now entailed a separate career track with its own entry requirements (potential as a scholar and teacher), recruitment rituals (the law school hiring procedures), levels of advancement (from assistant to associate to full professor), and professional ethos (to treat law as a science, and an academic career as an end in itself)[114]. When the Association of American Law Schools was founded around the turn of the century, legal academics even had their own professional organization which was independent and distinct from the bar associations[115].

To some extent the professionalization of legal academics was simply part of the general professionalization of jobs that began to affect many occupations at the time, but it was also intimately connected with the professionalization of legal practice in particular. When admission requirements for the bar were gradually raised, the self-taught lawyer of the Lincoln variety gave way to the professionally trained and examined attorney. It was only a question of time before legal practice virtually required a law degree, first to gain access to the higher strata of the profession, then to be admitted to the bar at all[116]. Such a degree, however, had to come from a school that provided a professional educa-

---

114 About the professionalization of academic activity see generally *B. Barnes,* About Science (New York 1985), pp. 9 - 10; *S. Rothblatt,* The Diversification of Higher Learning in England, in *K. Jarausch,* The Transformation of Higher Learning, 131, at p. 134; and see *M. Larson,* The Rise of Professionalism (Berkeley 1977).

115 See note 6.

116 *Friedman,* pp. 652 - 654; in 1870, only about one quarter of those admitted to the bar had a law school degree, but in 1910 already about two thirds had, *Auerbach,* p. 94.

tion. Professional training, in turn, required professional trainers. The new law teachers themselves never tired of proclaiming that their services were indispensable if the bar wanted as its members lawyers with a thorough understanding of the law. This, the professors argued, only legal academics could ensure[117]. The explosion of numbers of law schools and law students in the postbellum decades proves that the legal profession believed them. The modern, full-time American law professor was thus a by-product of, as well as a prerequisite for, the professionalization of the bar.

Becoming professional teachers also made it possible for the new law professors to become professional scholars. The reasons were largely economic. Only then did teaching pay enough money to live on without legal practice and to concentrate on academic work[118]. Instead of practicing, the professors now had to teach their classes to earn a living, but producing scholarship was much more easily reconciled with teaching than with the demands of practice. Thus, teaching law and writing became the typical combination of activities only when professional legal academics had emerged.

Scholarship and teaching were exactly the two qualities that Anglo-American jurists admired in their German colleagues. The major reason for the impressive "learning of a German professor" and his "enthusiasm of the lecture room" was precisely that a German law teacher was a fully professional academic who did virtually nothing else but teach and write. For people like Savigny, Puchta, Windscheid or Jhering it was economically unnecessary and professionally inconceivable to practice law on the side. They received a professorial salary that allowed them a comfortable life because their services were higly valued[119]. Since in their legal culture becoming a lawyer had for centuries invariably required studying law at a university, academic law teachers had long been indispensable[120]. They had always considered teaching and writing a natural combination. As professional academics, they cultivated "legal science" in their scholarship and then disseminated it in the lecture hall and seminar room.

---

117 *A. V. Dicey,* Can English Law Be Taught in the Universities, supra note (80), p. 10. For a provocative interpretation see these professorial aspirations in terms of market control, see *Schlegel,* pp. 320-322.

118 See *Rothblatt,* The Diversification of Higher Education in England, id.

119 The economic situation and the working conditions of German legal academics were dramatically improved during the 19th century, see *R. Kawakami,* Die Begründung des "neuen" gelehrten Rechts durch Savigny, SZG (rom. Abt.) 98, 308, pp. 307-311; *H. Kantorowicz,* Savigny and the Historical School of Law, 53 L. Q. R. 326 (1937), pp. 329-323.

120 Their importance was enhanced by the virtual monopoly they enjoyed in training future state bureaucrats. In 1817, the study of law became a requirement for entry into the Prussian state bureaucracy; the southern German states followed suit in the next few decades, see *W. Bleek,* Von der Kameralausbildung zum Juristenprivileg (Berlin 1972), pp. 104, 262-285.

Thus, the Anglo-American admiration for German professors was in a sense the admiration of full-fledged professionalism by colleagues who were just making the transition from amateurs to professionals themselves. Common law jurists realized that their German colleagues were ahead of them on a road they, and many other groups in society at the time, were currently taking.

2. The Specialization of Functions

Professionalization went hand in hand with growing specialization of functions in society. Contemporaries were very much aware of the increasing division of labor, whether they considered it the social equivalent of the functional diversification in the evolution of biological organisms or, as with Durkheim, a necessary and desirable development in modern society[121].

The rise of professional legal academics was a dual instance of this differentiation. It was, first and foremost, a diversification of the legal profession. Within the group of lawyers as a whole, a sub-group (scholars) developed by focusing exclusively on a particular kind of legal work[122]. Even within the new sub-group itself, legal scholars gradually specialized, but the generalist common law tradition and the relatively small size of the faculties at the time slowed this process down. Second, the emergence of the new law professors meant, at the same time, the birth of a new sub-group of academics. There was then a group of academics that dealt exclusively with law. The new law professors were thus both lawyers specializing in academic work, and academics specializing in the law. The term "legal scientist" nicely captures both these dimensions.

Their new roles as specialists in "legal science" lay at the root of the law professors' claim to intellectual leadership within the legal profession[123]. If law was, as they claimed, essentially a science, then they, as specialists in this regard, understood it better than anyone else. Their specialized function put them in a superior position, at least in their own view, to understand, systematize, and develop the law for several distinct reasons. First, they could fully concentrate on these tasks free from the distraction by the daily trifles of legal practice. Second, they could view the law from a higher vantage point because they could afford to focus on its grand outlines and developments. Finally, they could consider it from an entirely neutral position since they did not have to represent

---

121 *G. Simmel,* Über sociale Differenzierung, Staats- und socialwissenschaftliche Forschungen, vol. X, 1 (Leipzig 1890); *E. Durkheim,* The Division of Labor in Society (G. Simpson transl. New York 1933, French orig. 1893); *R. Mayntz, B. Rosewitz, U. Schimanek, R. Stichweh,* Differenzierung und Verselbständigung. Zur Entwicklung gesellschaftlicher Teilsysteme (Frankfurt 1988).

122 See *W. C. Robinson,* A Study of Legal Education, Its Purposes and Methods, reprinted from the Catholic University Bulletin, April 1895 (Washington 1895), p. 22.

123 See generally *E. Purcell,* The Crisis of Democratic Theory (Lexington 1973), pp. 77-78.

clients (like attorneys), decise real cases (like judges), or worry about the next election (like legislators). Attorneys, judges, and legislators were thus well-advised, the new legal academics thought, to heed their advice.

It was in part the German professors' very function as "legal scientists" and their resulting position as the recognized intellectual leaders of the profession that Anglo-American jurists found to attractive. The major reason behind the German academics' distinguished role and enviable position, however, was their complete specialization in academic work. The differentiation of functions among lawyers was more firmly established and more highly developed in Germany than in the common law world. In the civil law culture, some lawyers had specialized in teaching and scholarship since the middle ages. In nineteenth century Germany, being a legal academic was thus a traditional and clearly defined role in its own right[124]. Furthermore, the specialization even among legal academics was more advanced than in the common law world. German law teachers were not just professors of law in general but rather professors of a particular field, like Roman or German law, commercial law or legal history. The size of their faculties allowed them to focus all their attention on their area of specialty and thus to develop a high degree of expertise within its limits[125]. As highly specialized "legal scientists", they were undistracted, aloof, and neutral students of the law's deepest historical roots and broadest systematic coherence. Therefore these scholars were undoubtedly the intellectual leaders of the profession as a whole.

When Anglo-American law teachers were intrigued by the German "legal scientists" and by their leading role within the profession they were, in a sense, intrigued by advanced specialization and by the power and prestige that it bestowed. German law professors were specialized (both as a group, vis-a-vis

---

[124] See *R. Stichweh*, Der frühmoderne Staat und die europäische Universität. Zur Interaktion von Politik und Erziehungssystem im Prozeß ihrer Ausdifferenzierung, Rechtshistorisches Journal 5, 135 (1987).

[125] James Bryce clearly recognized that the superiority of German universities resulted in part simply from the greater number of professors which entailed greater division of labor and thus greater specialization, see *J. Bryce*, Preface to I. Conrad, The German Universities in the Last Fifty Years (Glasgow 1885). In 1870, the Harvard law faculty consisted of three professors, see *J. B. Ames*, Professor Langdell — His Services to Legal Education, 20 Harv. L. Rev. 12 (1906). At the same time, there were about five times as many law professors at the University of Berlin, not counting about half a dozen private docents. I could not obtain any exact numbers for 1870, but in 1893 there were nineteen professors and eight private docents. In 1870, the numbers were probably marginally lower (the average German law faculty was about 15 % smaller in 1870 than in 1893); for the German data see *W. Lexis*, Die deutschen Universitäten, vol. I (Berlin 1893), pp. 146, 411-419; see also *E. Heymann*, Hundert Jahre Berliner Juristenfakultät. Deutsche Juristenzeitung 1910, 1103, pp. 1187-1188. When Langdell became dean, the Harvard Law School offered less than one dozen lectures per week, *Ames*, id. The University of Berlin listed about three dozen lectures, not counting seminars and so-called "exercises", see *Lexis*, id.; *Hart*, pp. 108-110.

practitioners, and with that group, vis-a-vis each other) and thus influential to a degree of which their common law colleagues could, at least for the time being, only dream. It is no wonder, then, that the former were an attractive model for the latter.

3. The Institutionalization of Science

The beginning specialization of a group of American lawyers in academic work and their professionalization as full-time law professor took place within the context of the transformation of the American university. The old, mostly small, and often clerically dominated institutions whose concept of higher education was teaching established dogma, gradually gave way to the modern, large scale, completely secularized universities which emphasized scientific research and training. Science (in the sense of methodical search for verifiable knowledge), for centuries mostly the private affair of individual sages, acquired a home in the modern institutions of higher learning [126].

Recognition of their professionalism and specialization as legal scientists required the new American law professors' membership in the new institutions of science [127]. A university could establish a full career track for legal academics which greatly facilitated both their professionalization an specialization. As university faculty members, law professors could work in a truly investigative spirit for which there was little or no space in a trade school. Within the university, they worked according to academic criteria — they could introduce academic admission requirements and thus teach better students, and they could recruit faculty according to scholarly promise and thus find more congenial colleagues. All this amounted to a life in unfettered academic freedom. And it was an honorable life; university faculty status was also a matter of prestige. While Americans have not consistently ranked academics above practitioners, being a law professor at a university with a learned faculty and selected students was a dignified position and certainly superior to that of a mere law teacher at some private trade school with no academics pretensions.

This kind of university faculty status with its implications of academic freedom and social prestige impressed American observers when they looked at the German "university men". This enviable position of the German professors was ultimately a result of the rapid and thoroughgoing institutionalization of learning and science in nineteenth century Germany. German law teachers had always been university faculty members, but they acquired most of their academic freedom and social prestige only with the unprecedented rise of the German institutions of higher learning [128]. This rise took place half a century earlier than

---

126 See *Stevens*, p. 20.
127 *Schlegel*, p. 321.

in the common law world. From their relatively modest state and parochial character, the German universities had since the foundation of the University of Berlin in 1810[129] grown into highly diverse and powerful academic institutions, which in the eyes of most American observers were second to none. State-run, well-funded and divided into several distinct faculties, they had no equals on American soil in terms of size, sophistication and resources at the time. Together with the military and the new industries, they were the pride of Germany and held an "impregnable position"[130]. They provided an ideal institutional framework for the rapid professionalization of, and specialization within, science at a time when American universities were just beginning to overcome their amateurish and provincial nature.

The lead of the German law professoriate over their American colleagues was thus also a result of the general German lead over America in the institutionalization of science and learning in the modern universities in the nineteenth century. Behind the model of the "German professor" stood the model of he German university, of which he was not only a member but in the creation of which he had actually been instrumental. The model function of the German university was, of course, not limited to law; it affected the humanities and sciences to an even larger degree[131]. However, in order to show that their discipline was a science and that they were therefore entitled to university membership with all its privileges and benefits, the law professors needed the German model more than most other academics.

Thus the admiration of the new American law teachers for their German colleagues reflected the German lead in broader social trends at the time. The German legal and academic culture was ahead of its American counterpart with respect to the professionalization of lawyers in general and of law teachers in particular, the specialization of academics, and the institutionalization of learning and science in modern universities. American law professors hardly saw it in these terms, but when they admired the "learning" of a German professor",

---

128 *F. Schnabel,* Deutsche Geschichte im 19. Jahrhundert, vol. 5: Die Erfahrungswissenschaften (Freiburg 1965), pp. 46-47, 158-160.

129 Its new scientific spirit is captured by *W. v. Humboldt,* Antrag auf Errichtung der Universität Berlin (1809), in W. v. Humboldt, Werke in fünf Bänden, vol. IV (Berlin 1864), p. 113, and by *F. C. v. Savigny,* Rezension von F. Schleiermacher, Gelegentliche Gedanken über Universitäten im deutschen Sinn (1808), in F. C. v. Savigny, Vermischte Schriften, vol. IV (Berlin 1850), p. 251.

130 *Hart,* p. 261.

131 The literature on the influence of the German university model on American institutions of higher learning is vast, see e. g. *Herbst,* pp. 1-4; *Thwing,* passim; *L. O'Boyle,* Learning for Its Own Sake: The German Universities as a Nineteenth Century Model, 25 Comp. Studies in Soc. & Hist. 3 (1985); *F. Thilly,* Preface to F. Paulsen, The German Universities (transl. by F. Thilly and W. Elwang, New York 1906, German orig. 1902), pp. V-VIII; *A. A. Pochmann,* German Culture in America 1600-1900 (Westport / Conn. 1978), pp. 304-328.

envied his "wholesome influence on the development of the law", and coveted his position as a "university man", they addressed essentially these three aspects.

III. The Fate of the Model: Three Developments

Today, German legal academia can hardly be considered a model for American law teachers. In fact, the opposite has perhaps become true in some respects. What, then, happened to the model function of the German professoriate? The answer seems paradoxical at first glance. The image of a "German professor" declined rapidly around the time of World War I, but the effects of its influence persisted and can be felt even today. They are most clearly visible in American legal academia itself. But they are also noticeable in the legal at large.

1. The Decline of the Image

In 1918, the Michigan Law Review published a lenghty article by John M. Zane on "German Legal Philosophy"[132]. A contemporary reader, used to the almost ubiquitous praise lavished upon German legal scholarship in the past fifty years, probably expected yet another homage to German learning. He was in for a surprise. For page after page, Zane polemicized against the "Prussian professiorial mental hypocrisy"[133] and the "abnormal self-conceit ..., the blindness and incapacity for self-examination that come from self-conceit" and that made "German legal philosophy of law utterly worthless."[134] Zane's relentless hostility (and the fact that a major law review published his essay), was not typical for the new attitude towards German legal academia, but it was symptomatic.

For two generations, the German law professoriate had served as a lodestar for many of the new American legal academics, but in the second decade of the twentieth century, the model lost its appeal. Before 1914, praise of German legal scholars abounded in the American literature; by 1918, it had by and large disappeared. The changed attitute towards German learning is illustrated by John Henry Wigmore's call for an academic reorientation away from Germany and towards France in 1917[135]. Within a few years, and in an uncompromising manner that Llewellyn deemed typical of the common lawyers' attitude towards the civilian legal culture[136], American academics had lost interest in their German colleagues.

---

[132] *J. M. Zane,* German Legal Philosophy, 16 Mich. L. Rev. 287 (1918).

[133] Id., p. 339.

[134] Id., p. 374.

[135] *J. H. Wigmore,* A Proposal to Restore the True Status of French Science and Learning in America, 49 Chicago Legal News 343 (1917).

[136] *K. Llewellyn,* The Case Law System in America (transl. by M. Ansaldi, Chicago 1989, German orig. 1933), p. 111 fn. 2.

There were various reasons for this change, some obvious, others subtle. Their individual contributions cannot be clearly separated because they all worked in concert. Still, one can distinguish three major causes — the war, a change in intellectual climate, and — perhaps ironically — the development of American universities in part after the German model.

The war affected the German model function on a practical, ideological, and cultural level. As a practical matter, it made the continuation of contacts between Anglo-American and German scholars difficult because communication and travel were interrupted. In 1907, it had been easy for Rudolf Leonhard to come to Columbia, but seven years later Eugen Ehrlich could not travel to the Lowell Institute to meet Pound anymore[137]. For years to come, personal contacts between legal scholars on both sides of the Atlantic almost ceased.

On an ideological level, the war and Germany's role in it quickly tarnished the image of all things German, including academic institutions and teachers. The growing American hostility towards German scholars was not a sudden reaction but had a history. From an American (and English) perspective, German scholarship had long presented a dilemma because it was academically admirable yet politically suspect. After all, it represented the intellectual side of an undemocratic and increasingly aggressive Empire. When the war broke out, the American unease with the resulting tension became intolerable. Even for those Americans who tried to separate German scholarly accomplishment from German militarism, enthusiasm for German learning was made exceedingly difficult when German academics openly endorsed the German military efforts and goals[138]. Americans were less and less ready to admire German scholars supporting a Kaiser whose U-boats sunk the "Lusitania"[139].

As a result of war and defeat, Germany lost most of its former appeal as a culture. From 1871 to 1914, it had been a rising power, its military, economy and, as a result, its self-confidence matching England's and surpassing France's. Its ascendancy and energy had fascinated American intellectuals and added to the lustre of its academics. After 1918, Germany was on the verge of collapse,

---

137 *R. Pound,* An Appreciation of Eugen Ehrlich, 36 Harv. L. Rev. 129 (1922).

138 In their 1914 Declaration, German academic teachers identified with the German war efforts and angrily rejected the foreign attempts "to make a difference, professedly in our favor, between the spirit of German science and of what they call 'Prussian militarism'", quoted after *Herbst,* p. 166. Otto von Gierke, much admired as a scholar by his Anglo-American colleagues, expressed his enthusiasm about the German war goals tactlessly in an October 1914 to Oliver Wendell Holmes, see *S. Novick,* Honorable Justice (Boston 1989), pp. 312-313. For American reactions, see *Herbst,* p. 169, fn. 6 with further references; *Wigmore,* note 135, pp. 344-345.

139 The British passenger-ship "Lusitania" was sunk by a German U-Boat on May 7, 1915. Roughly 1 200 passengers died, among them about 100 Americans. The incident triggered sharp protest by the U. S. government and greatly fuelled the anti-German sentiment in America.

its military, economy, and its self-confidence shattered. It evoked, at best, sympathy, but no longer admiration.

A second reason for the decline of the German model lay in the profound change in the American intellectual climate around the turn of the century. The rise of pragmatism made the much admired nineteenth century German legal science, and with it its leading representatives, look outdated[140]. This did not happen nearly as suddenly as it may appear at first glance. Doubts about German jurisprudence had existed throughout the "classical age". American legal academics were fascinated by "legal science", and particularly by its German version, but they were also common lawyers. After all, Justice Gray had praised Langdell not only because his learning compared to that of a German professor, but also because he had the "practical sense of a common lawyer"[141]. German professors, however, often lacked this practical sense in the eyes of many Americans. Nineteenth century German legal science, particularly the "Pandektenwissenschaft" as its man branch, was broadly conceptual and highly formalistic. Thus, even admirers of German law professors condemned their "tendency to excessive generalization" that "easily lead to useless abstraction"[142]. As Rudolf Leonhard self-consciously admitted at Columbia, German legal academics were regarded not only as symbols of erudition but frequently also of formalism and abstractness[143].

With the increasing "revolt against formalism"[144] in America, the conceptual and abstract jurisprudence that had dominated the "classical age" gradually fell into discredit. From Holmes' Darwinist approach to Pound's "sociological jurisprudence" to American Legal Realism, the trend in American legal thought was away from a conceptual and abstract and towards a sociological and pragmatist view of law. As a result, the German professors of the "Pandektenwissenschaft" from Puchta to Windscheid looked more and more like vestiges from a by-gone jurisprudential age. Their image lost its attraction because they were identified with the "mechanical jurisprudence" now openly under attack and slowly abandoned[145].

---

140 *T. Veblen,* Imperial Germany (New York 1964, orig. ed. 1915), pp. 226-229. Also, the intellectual reputation of the German universities in the U. S. began to suffer after 1900, see *Veysey,* supra note 112, pp. 130; *Herbst,* pp. 5, 217-218.

141 See note 12. Many contemporaries considered this "practical sense" essential for a legal academic as well, see *A. Kales,* Should the Law Teacher Practice Law?, 25 Harv. L. Rev. 253 (1912), p. 258; *H. Stone,* The Importance of Actual Experience at the Bar as a Preparation for Teaching Law, 3 Am. L. School Rev. 199, 205 (1912); *J. C. Carter,* Law, Its Origin, Growth and Function (New York 1907), p. 275.

142 *Smith X,* p. 682; see also *Hart,* p. 272.

143 *R. Leonhard,* note 54, p. 678. Leonhard assured his audience that he did "not forget that our science must be a practical one", id.

144 *M. White,* Social Thought in America. The Revolt Against Formalism (New York 1949).

145 *R. Pound,* Mechanical Jurisprudence, 8 Col. L.Rev. 605 (1908), pp. 608-611.

This does not mean that German ideas lost all their influence on American legal thought during this change of paradigms. When the view of law as a social science replaced the conceptual and historical jurisprudence, German ideas actually played a major role. Pound for one, drew heavily on Jhering and Ehrlich[146] and even saw the new German Civil Code, mistakenly, as a manifestation of sociological jurisprudence[147]. Yet, Ames' veneration of Windscheid, and Pound's respect for Jhering were very different matters. Ames and his generation admired the learned German professors themselves, i. e. their erudition, influence, and status. Pound and other reformers, like Cardozo[148], were interested only in their insights. In other words, Windscheid was important to Ames as a symbol of classical legal science but Jhering mattered to Pound only as a source of ideas.

This difference in focus was in large part due to the third major reason behind the decline of the German model. In Pound's times, the need for such a model had virtually disappeared. The first generation of American career academics had looked for a model abroad because it could find none at home, but the second generation, which began to enter the law faculties around the time of World War I, found its role models in the first and did not need to look any further. The professionalization, specialization, and academic integration of law professors had already made enormous progress[149]. American law teachers were now career scholars and university faculty in institutions that had come a long way since 1870. The Harvard Ames joined in 1873 simply did not compare to a German law faculty. The Harvard of Pound after World War I, however, did. Like American higher education generally, it had become so institutionally refined and intellectually sophisticated that the need to look overseas for guidance was much diminished.

In short, the war made the German model unacceptable, the new intellectual climate made it look old-fashioned, and the first generation of professional scholars in America made it unnecessary. Once American law professors had followed their German colleagues by becoming professional legal academics themselves, the German model lost most of its utility.

---

146 *R. Pound,* The Scope and Purpose of Sociological Jurisprudence, 25 Harv. L. Rev. 140 (1912), pp. 140-147; see also *J. Herget, S. Wallace,* The German Free Law Movement as the Source of American Legal Realism, 73 Va. L. Rev. 399 (1987), and *J. Herget,* The Influence of German Thought on American Jurisprudence, 1880-1918, in this volume.

147 See *Pound,* note 145, p. 613.

148 Cardozo also drew heavily on modern German legal thought, see the footnotes of *B. Cardozo,* The Nature of the Judicial Process (New Haven, Conn. 1921).

149 *Schlegel,* p. 311-312.

2. *The Effects on Legal Academia*

The attraction of the German model waned but the results of its influence persisted. While few present-day law professors are aware of that continental heritage, American legal academia still displays features once modelled after the continental prototype. This does not mean that modern American legal scholars are mere copies of their nineteenth century German colleagues. Other factors contributed to the definition of their profession as well. Therefore, the civilian influence must be seen as one, albeit essential, element among many. American legal academics developed as a hybrid breed, similar to their European colleagues in important ways, but not in all respects. This holds true with regard to both their perceptions of the academic role and the substance of their work, albeit to varying degrees.

With regard to their perception of the academic role, modern American law professors closely resemble their continental counterparts as an analysis of its basic features — qualification, responsibility, and status — at once shows. Of course, even in shaping the job description of a legal academic, American professors did not adopt all aspects of the German model. Substantial differences remain concerning the recruitment and promotion of law teachers [150], the internal organization of the faculties [151], and the professors' position within the universities [152]. Their comparatively strong interest in legal education and their professional and geographic mobility also distinguish American law teachers from the majority of their continental colleagues. These differences reflect the influence of the English college, the idiosyncrasies of the American university system, and the preferences and values prevailing in American society at large. Still, the paradigm of a legal academic as a professional, specialized, and academically integrated jurist whose only job is to teach law students and to produce legal scholarship has virtually no roots in any of these other elements. Its model is the civil law professor, represented in the nineteenth century by the German university scholar.

---

150 The American model combines recruitment on the basis of scholarly promise (rather than accomplishment) with the tenure process, while the German model combines recruitment on the basis of scholarly accomplishment with immediate permanent appointment. For a vivid description of the French system, which is highly similar to its German counterpart, see *Bourdieu,* note 4, pp. 84-105.

151 American law faculties are less compartmentalized than German ones. They particularly lack the German division into "Institutes" each of which consists of an "Ordinarius", i. e. a full professor at its head, and a support team or researchers, teaching assistants (with law degrees), and clerical staff.

152 American law teachers are employed by and thus dependent on their universities (or law schools), but they have virtually nothing to do with the state. German legal academics are civil servants of the state, thus their dependency on the university is small, while the state bureaucracy in the respective ministeries wields substantial power over them.

Yet, influence on the self-definition of a profession is not the same as influence on a professions' perception of its field. While American and European law professors are rather similar with regard to the former, they differ substantially with respect to the latter. An in-depth exploration of the differences in the perceptions of continental and American legal academics, and of the interplay between the image of a profession and its predispositions towards its work, would require a full-fledged study in its own right and is not the goal of this essay. Suffice is to point to two particularly salient features that set American academics apart from continental scholars.

First, American professors have essentially remained case lawyers. Despite the interest in the conceptualization and categorization of law, so prominent during the classical age, they continue to see law much more in individual disputes than in general, abstract concepts. This is true in their teaching, where the case method triumphed over the alternative, civilian styles urged by many contemporaries around the turn of the century[153], and in their writing which focuses mostly on concrete disputes rather than on abstract principles. All this reflects the continuing influence of the case law heritage of their culture. Even in their role as quasi-civilian academic jurists, American legal academics have remained common lawyers at heart.

Second, American law teachers are imbued with the spirit of law reform to a degree that from a European perspective borders on obsession. They are far less engaged than their civilian colleagues in analyzing and systematizing existing law, and much more interested in challenging and changing it. Innovation is more important to them than continuity, originality more valuable than order, argument for a position more essential than exposition of knowledge. This is so because they are products not only of the classical age of American law but also of the progressive era of American politics, of pragmatism in American philosophy, and of a marriage between law and social sciences[154]. Even as inhabitants of the academic ivory tower, they feel responsible for improving society.

This descrepancy between quasi-European role and Anglo-American predispositions in their work makes it tempting to characterize modern American law professors as Anglo-American minds in a continental body. There is a lot of truth in such a characterization but still misses an essential point — even the substance of the American legal academics' work has been substantially influenced by the European model in an important respect.

When American law teachers turned full-fledged academics, that entailed not only a change of their professional role but also a change in the nature of their discourse. The traditional, English common law process served the goal of finding

---

153 See e. g. *W. Keener,* Methods of Legal Education, 1 Yale L. J. 143 (1892), p. 145 (quoting J. Bleecker Miller); *Hart,* p. 55, see also *Clark,* p. 332.

154 *Auerbach,* p. 74-93, *Rheinstein,* note 7, pp. 66, 185-186.

individual justice through law. Since the nineteenth century, American legal reformism added to this process the goal to enhance *social justice through law.* Both of these goals reflect, albeit in different ways, the decidedly instrumental view of law which has been one of the hallmarks of the Anglo-American legal tradition.

The new American law professors, however, have added a very different perspective on law. They have institutionalized a discourse the goal of which is to find *truth about law.* To them, law is no longer only an instrument of practical (individual or social) justice, it is also an object of scientific study regardless of immediate practical utility [155]. This perspective was by and large foreign to traditional common lawyers; it reflects a scholarly view of law which has been one of the hallmarks of the civilian jurist. Thus where the modern American law professor seeks to find truth about law rather than justice through law, she is the heir to the academically oriented continental, not to the practically minded Anglo-American, tradition.

Karl Llewellyn's persona and work nicely illustrate the result of all these mixed influences on American legal academia. With regard to his professional position and role, he could easily have passed for a German professor. Yet, much of his work, case law-based and reform-orientied, differed markedly in style and substance from the more abstract and conservative endeavors of his colleagues in Leipzig. At the same time, he shared with them, in his jurisprudential efforts, the search for insights into the structure and nature of law and thus the academic perspective in the continental sense. In all these respects, he continues to exemplify the modern American law professor.

3. The Impact on the Legal Culture

The influence of the German model went beyond modern American legal academia. By contributing to the formation of a new group of legal actors, it also affected the American legal culture at large, albeit in an indirect fashion. The rise of the new professoriate modelled after the European image meant that the American legal culture as a whole has moved much closer than before to the continental tradition. This happened in two particular ways. The emergence of a group of professional scholars with an academic perspective on law brought the American legal culture closer to the civilian approach. And the existence of professional legal scholars in the U. S. greatly facilitated the building of bridges for communication across the Atlantic, furthering the mutual assimilation of the two legal worlds.

The rise of legal scholars fashioned after old world ideas changed the American culture, because it amounted to the large-scale import of academic perspectives

155 Indeed, the search for knowledge about law for knowledge's sake is what makes its study academic rather than practical.

on law into a legal tradition hitherto largely devoid and often openly contemptuous of them. As a result, American law is no longer an almost exclusively practical, but has become a partially academic affair. This is true not only in legal theory but also in practice. The key factor here is the academic monopoly in legal education. In stark contrast to the situation in a century ago, but very much like the longstanding tradition in Europe, virtually every American practitioner today receives his legal training from law professors in academic institutions. Academics have thus become the gatekeepers of the profession; their approval (to wit, according to academic standards) is an indispensable entry requirement. The first role models for most future lawyers are academics, not practitioners. Their first impression of law is the academic view, not the practical side[156].

Academic perspectives have entered legal practice directly as well because law professors have frequently undertaken practical jobs. They draft legislation and advise litigants and courts. As masterminds behind many twentieth century law reforms, they influence the rapid development of modern American law to a degree which approximates and in some areas surpasses that of legislatures and courts. In many instances, their academic reputation even helps them onto the bench. After all, Story became a law professor because he was an eminent judge, but Frankfurter, himself a student of Ames, became a judge because he was an eminent law professor.

Through their work as teachers, scholars, law reformers, and sometimes judges, American law professors have thus injected academic matter into most areas of law and legal work. As a result, the modern American legal culture is almost unthinkable without its academic elements. To be sure, the practical and pragmatic aspects still dominate, but they are tempered and modified by academic perspectives to a degree unheard of in any common law country prior to this century. Civil and common lawyers still hold different views about the academic nature of law, but the difference is no longer near absolute, it is merely one of degree.

The corps of American academic lawyers shaped after the European model has also been the single most important factor in building bridges between the legal worlds of Europe and America. Since the closing decades of the last century, most of the communication across the Atlantic (and across the Channel for that matter) took place not between legal practitioners but between academics. Since the 1930s, the emigrant jurists coming from Europe to the U. S. provided vital links, but they found a new home in the American universities only because

---

[156] While American law professors continue to claim that they teach students "to think like a lawyer", they mostly teach students to think like legal academics. A lawyer must think about law from the point of view of an advisor, businessman, litigant, or judge, i. e. from a practical, inside perspective. It is highly fashionable in leading American law schools today, however, to think about law from a political, social, historical, anthropological or philosophical, i. e. from a theoretical, outside perspective. That may be very interesting, but it is hardly the perspective of a practicing lawyer.

they entered roughly familiar terrain[157]. They found law professors as they understood the term because these professors had been fashioned after the European scholars under which the emigrants had studied and with whom they had worked[158]. European academics like Max Rheinstein could continue their work because they recognized colleagues in Beale, Williston, Wigmore and others whose work and methods resembled those of the legal scholars in Europe[159]. Due in large part to these emigrants, the increasing communication between the American and continental legal cultures after World War II again occurred primarily on the academic level. Particularly in the first decades, professors were virtually the only members of the legal profession to become temporary guest workers in the respective other system. While the improvement of travel and communication technology play an important role, exchange of law teaching, transmission of ideas through scholarship, opportunities for graduate studies abroad all depend ultimately on the existence of roughly comparable academic cultures in both the old and the new worlds. In this manner, the transatlantic similarities among legal academics, largely a result of the European influence in the U. S., have been important catalysts in the process of approximation and assimilation of the legal systems.

Legal systems have always borrowed from each other. They have imported rules, copied techniques, and adopted styles of reasoning. The shaping of American legal academia after the civilian, especially the German model is an instance of yet another kind of borrowing — the emulation of professional roles and perspectives. For the American legal culture, the rise of professional legal scholars emulating their European colleagues, and the concomitant influence of academic perspectives on law, essentially entailed a step away from the practical orientation of the common law and towards the academic predilections of the civil law. The American legal culture is no longer shaped only by the lawyer representing the common law heritage, the judge like Joseph Story, but also by the jurist epitomizing the civil law tradition, the academic like Karl Llewellyn.

---

157 The majority, however, found mostly immense difficulties. The story of the German emigrant jurists is now told by *E. Stiefel, F. Mecklenburg,* Deutsche Juristen im amerikanischen Exil (1933-1950) (Tübingen 1991).

158 This assessment was confirmed by two emigrant scholars with firsthand experience, Stefan Riesenfeld and Eric Stein, in talks with the author.

159 *Max Rheinstein,* Karl Nickerson Llewellyn, 27 RabelsZ 601 (1962), p. 602.

JAMES E. HERGET*

The Influence of German Thought on American Jurisprudence, 1880-1918

In the late nineteenth century the philosophy of law in the United States was generally an imitation and continuation of developments in England modified through some influence from the works of Friedrich Carl von Savigny.[1] The Austinian school was predominant, and the historical school, following either Sir Henry Sumner Maine or Savigny, had some disciples as well. The natural law school had even fewer adherents. At the turn of the century, however, this situation began to change significantly. Several American scholars fluent in German began to read the works of German and Austrian writers who were on the leading edge of jurisprudential developments in their respective countries. Four scholars in particular can be identified as having absorbed ideas from German language materials and transmitted them to an English speaking audience through their own works: Arthur F. Bentley, political theorist; John Chipman Gray, legal scholar; Albion W. Small, sociologist; and Roscoe Pound, legal scholar.[2]

Arthur F. Bentley (1870-1957) was educated at York College, the University of Denver, and Johns Hopkins University where he received his bachelor's degree in 1892. He studied for a year in Germany and returned to Johns Hopkins, earning his Ph. D. in 1895. After serving as an instructor in sociology at the University of Chicago in 1895-96, he became a reporter for Chicago newspapers for the next fourteen years. He published *The Process of Government,* his only contribution to jurisprudence, in 1908. In 1910 Bentley went to live in rural Indiana where he continued a life of research and writing. His work in this period

---

* Professor of Law, University of Houston.

1 For further explanation of this situation see *J. Herget,* American Jurisprudence, 1870-1970 at 31-62 (1990). Note that German ideas also influenced American thinking indirectly through the British writers who drew upon German sources, expecially Thomas E. Holland.

2 Oliver Wendell Holmes, Jr., the best known American legal philosopher of this period, did not read German well in his early formative years. However, he did read Rudolf von Jhering's 'Geist des Römischen Rechts' in a French translation, and Jhering's 'Der Kampf um die Rechtswissenschaft' was translated into English in 1879. Nevertheless, Holmes attributes practically none of his ideas to German sources. Whether this is in fact true or not is another question which cannot be answered within the compass of this article.

centered primarily around linguistics, and he cooperated on several papers with philosopher John Dewey whom he had met at the University of Chicago.

John Chipman Gray (1839 - 1915) was educated at Harvard College and the Harvard Law School. After serving in the Civil War he returned to Boston and founded the law firm of Ropes and Gray with a former law school friend. He lectured at the Harvard Law School and later became a chaired professor at that institution, although he kept his hand in the practice of law until his death. Gray became known as one of the greatest scholars in the field of property law. He gave a series of lectures at Columbia University in 1908, and these were published in the following year as *The Nature and Sources of the Law*. This work was one of the first jurisprudential treatises published in America.

Albion W. Small (1854 - 1926) received a bachelor's degree from Colby College in 1876, briefly attended a theological seminary, spent two years studying in Germany in 1879 - 81, and earned a Ph. D. from Johns Hopkins in 1889, where he studied under Richard Ely, the "Vienna School" economist. Small taught history and political economy at Colby College from 1881 to 1888 and was its president from 1889 - 91. He became head of the department of sociology at the University of Chicago in 1892, the first department of its kind and possibly the most outstanding in America for the next twenty years. Small founded and edited for many years the American Journal of sociology, the original academic journal for the subject in America. Its volumes contain many works by German Sociologists. Small's best known work is *General Sociology: An Exposition of the Main Development in Sociological Theory from Spencer to Ratzenhofer* (1905).

Roscoe Pound (1870 - 1964) received bachelor's and doctoral degrees in Botany from the University of Nebraska. He attended the Harvard Law School for one year in 1889 - 90 where he became friends with John Chipman Gray. Pound taught law at Nebraska (1895 - 1906), Northwestern University (1906 - 1909), the University of Chicago (1909 - 1910), and Harvard (1910 - 1947) where he was dean of the law faculty from 1916 to 1936. He was the most prolific writer on jurisprudential subjects in the United States and the founder of the school of sociological jurisprudence. Pound was fluent in German and kept abreast of legal developments in Europe.

The authors who most frequently attracted the Americans' attention were legal scholar Rudolf von Jhering, sociologists Ludwig Gumplowicz, Georg Simmel and Gustav Ratzenhofer, and "free law" advocates Eugen Ehrlich and Hermann Kantorowicz. Other German authors also were cited frequently by the Americans. These authors represented a new direction in jurisprudential thought, a movement toward conceiving law in terms of conflicting social interests and finding its sources in the moral, political and economic phenomena of society. This diffuse movement in Germany eventually became differentiated into the free law movement (also called sociological jurisprudence), the jurisprudence of interests, and the sociology of law. In the United States it first crystallized into the sociological jurisprudence of Roscoe Pound; it was later modified into legal realism and the social science of law.[3] Although legal realism has been called the only true American contribution to the philosohy of law, the following discussion should demonstrate that legal realism was anticipated by the free law movement over a quarter of a century earlier, and the influence of the German theorists has not been adequately understood in the United States.

The flow of ideas from the German theorists to American legal literature was not a simple straight transmission. For example, Jhering's work directly influenced American thinking; yet Jhering's work also stimulated developments in the German free law movement and in the jurisprudence of interests, which in turn influenced American thinking. French theorist Francois Gény also had some impact directly on the Americans and at the same time on the free law movement. Thus, rather than simply restating the ideas of the new movement, the Americans drew from various sources and, in a sense, participated in the extension of the new ideas. Their work, for the most part, does not appear to have been known to the Germans, and it cannot be said that there was any influence in the other direction. Some of the free law scholars did think that the Anglo-American style of judicial lawmaking, as illustrated by reported judicial decisions, approximated what they conceived to be the method of "free law finding;" however, they apparently were not aware of any theoretical work being done by the Americans.

The plan of this paper will be: (1) to describe the most influential ideas of the German authors; (2) to demonstrate how those ideas were seized upon by the Americans and used in their own works; (3) to repeat this process with other authors or groups of authors; (4) to summarize the resulting jurisprudential theory in America; and (5) to indicate briefly the significance of those theories for American jurisprudence in later years.

Jhering

Our starting point must be with the work of Jhering (1818-1892). He was the earliest of the German scholars to turn to the new way of thinking, and, indeed, can be regarded as the initiator; he was clearly the most influential individual scholar among all of those considered herein. The four principal works cited by American scholars were: *Der Geist des römischen Rechts auf den verschiedenen Stufen seiner Entwicklung* [The Spirit of Roman Law at the Various Stages of Its Development] (4 vols. 1852-65); *Der Kampf um's Recht* [The Struggle for Law] (1872); *Der Zweck im Recht* [Purpose in the Law] (2 vols. 1877-83); and *Scherz und Ernst in der Jurisprudenz* [Levity and Seriousness in Jurisprudence] (1885).

[3] *Herget,* note 1, at 147-227.

Although originally an adherent and propounder of the traditional German legal science, Jhering changed directions in mid-career and initiated an approach in which the relationship between law and other aspects of society became important. An able writer, Jhering humorously criticized the prevailing conceptual jurisprudence. He created satirical parodies of the trappings of *Begriffsjurisprudenz* such as the hair-splitting machine, the hydraulic interpretation press, the dialectic drill, and the like in a "heaven of legal concepts." In this he was the first respected scholar to attempt to undermine prevailing orthodoxy.

Jhering's efforts were not limited to negative criticism, however. He described the generation of law, the official coercive rules of the state embodied in authoritative materials, as the result of a struggle between conflicting individuals and groups. In this struggle certain social interests are advanced by the parties. These social interests can be viewed subjectively as the aims or desires of the group or the individuals in it, or objectively in terms of their social usefulness. He maintains that people should strive to assert their rights at all times because by doing so their interests can be compromised or adjusted with competing interests to become public policy for the benefit of all. Failure to assert one's interests results in a failure of the system to reach an accomodation that is socially most useful. Jhering very much admired what he conceived to be the character of Englishmen who always stood up for their rights.[4]

Perhaps what is most significant about Jhering's work is his attempt to analyze the meaning of law in terms of its interaction with other facets of society. To this end he used the concept of purpose *(Zweck)*. Individuals and groups act egotistically to achieve and secure their own interests. In doing so, they achieve at the same time the purposes of all of society. The analysis of interest and purpose expounded by Jhering bears a resemblance to the classical economic theory of Adam Smith in which each individual, acting in his own economic interest, puts into motion the entire scheme of distribution of goods and services that serves society as a whole (serves the social "purpose" of economic wellbeing). The operation of law must be viewed in the same light, i. e., related to the economic and social functions (purposes) that it performs. Thus, a true explanatory exposition of law must go beyond analysis of the self-contained system of legal rules and concepts; it must account for the social needs of the people and explain how those needs are reconciled through law and legal institutions.[5]

For Jhering an adequate theory of law should define and explain both law and justice. In his view law (in the collective sense) is the formal institution that provides the security of the conditions of social life. The conditions of social

---

[4] See *R. Jhering,* The Struggle for Law, 61 - 63 (trans. Lalor 1879).

[5] As an example Jhering explains how the concept of equality, as an abstract ideal, is of no value in understanding the law. Rather, particular claims of equality must be evaluated in terms of the purposes that such claims would serve. See *R. Jhering,* Law as a Means to an End, 276 - 77 (Husik trans. 1914).

life include the possibility of attaining many of the valued things in life in addition to survival. Since these things vary from society to society and vary over time, the purpose of law is always relative to a particular culture. Nevertheless, just laws and legal institutions, in an objective sense, are those that most fully accomplish the purposes predominant in a particular society. The ultimate criterion of justice in thus overall utility.

Jhering's Influence on the Americans

While sociologist Albion Small seems not to have been influenced by Jhering, political scientist Arthur Bentley was very impressed with the work of the German scholar. In his only jurisprudential work, *The Process of Government,* he said of Jhering:

> If there is any man who has set out with equal ability, equal equipment, and equal scientific determination to face without flinching every difficulty in this field, I have not come across his work. *Der Zweck im Recht* must be reckoned with, page for page, by everyone who seeks to understand the process of government and the function of law in social life.[6]

Bentley devotes a subchapter of 35 pages to a discussion of Jhering's work. While recognizing Jhering's contribution to the advancement of thinking about law as a social institution, he nevertheless criticizes Jhering for attempting to include too many diverse phenomena under the concept of *Zweck,* for failure to explain the relationship between interests *(Interesse)* and purposes *(Zwecke),* and for similar methodological confusions. Being one of the first behaviorists, Bentley attacks Jhering's use of psychic states as causes of phenomena, and he finds the psychology implicit in Jhering's work quite unsatisfactory.

It is clear that Jhering's attempt to deal with the relationship between social life and law, and his rejection of the formal legal science of his time, had a great impact on Bentley. Bentley says:

> He [Jhering] broke away from "pure reason" as a principle of interpretation ... He brought moral phenomena into a systematic working relation to legal phenomena, and studied both in connection with economic phenomena. He strove to make all his interpretations in social terms, explaining in this way the individual's psychic life, both in its egoistic and altruistic phases. His point of approach in this attempt was, I feel safe in saying, far superior to that of Spencer's for he did not merely project a biological man into an unreal and hazy social world, but studied a (comparatively speaking) very real and social man directly. His special studies of laws, of morals, and of institutions showed a very rich insight into social meanings and values, and were indeed epoch-making.[7]

---

6 *A. Bentley,* The Process of Government, 56-57 (1908).

7 Id., 83.

The influence of Jhering on Bentley can best be seen in the theory that Bentley himself advanced. He emphasized process, maintaining that the legal process was a part of the larger governmental process and that this process consists of a constant assertion of interests by various groups. In Bentley's view government (including decisionmaking by courts) becomes understandable only in terms of competing interest groups, their exercise of influence on officials, and the officials' mediation between different groups. The notion of group struggle, following Jhering, is the conceptual key to Bentley's analysis. He elaborated the conflict-of-interests idea; he played down the importance of substantive law and written doctrine; he directed attention to the actual behavior of courts; and he used the notion of function in describing particular activities.

John Chipman Gray was also familiar with several of Jhering's works. He was favorably impressed with Jhering's distinction between two kinds of legal fictions (historic and dogmatic) and the different functioning of each, a distinction Gray thought was "one of the many services which [Jhering] has rendered to the science of Jurisprudence."[8] Although one criticizes a writer of Jhering's ability "with diffidence," Gray nevertheless was critical of Jhering on several points, including whether there could be rights without a "subject," and whether judges or jurists (legal scholars) were more impartial. Gray endorses the German scholar's analysis of "legislative intent" and his view that law is formed through conscious struggle rather than passive acceptance of social change.[9]

Gray's own views on law reflect some indebtedness to Jhering "who is always worth listening to."[10] The latter's skepticism of the mechanical operation of logic and legal concepts to determine decisions is shared by Gray. And, on a broader plane, Gray sees the "sources" of law, his main concern, as including a broad social dimension (custom, economic factors, morality) as well as the formal sources of legislation and judicial precedent.

Roscoe Pound, the most important American theorist of this time, also felt the impact of Jhering's thinking and reflected some of the German master's ideas in his own writings. Jhering, "a jurist by the grace of God," is cited in almost every one of Pound's jurisprudential articles through 1916. In his major presentation of sociological jurisprudence, Pound summarizes the various schools of jurisprudential thought and classifies Jhering as a "social utilitarian;" Pound observes:

> Prior to Jhering the theory of law had been individualist. The purpose of law was held to be harmonizing of individual wills in such a way as to leave to each the greatest possible scope for free action. Such was the view both of philosophical and of historical jurists. Jhering's, on the other hand, is a social theory of law. The

---

8 *J. Gray,* The Nature and Sources of the Law, 30 ff. (1909).

9 Id., at 281.

10 Id., at 59.

> eighteenth century conceived of law as something which the individual invoked against society, an idea which is behind our American bills of rights. Jhering taught that it was something created by society through which the individual found a means of securing his interests, so far as society recognized them. Although much ingenious philosophical criticism has been directed against this theory, it has not affected the central point. The conception of law as a securing of interests or protecting of relations has all but universally superseded the individualist theory.[11]

Pound finds that Jhering has influenced legal thinking in several important ways, although the philosophical side of his position was open to criticism. Nevertheless, Pound concludes:

> Jhering's work is of enduring value for sociological jurisprudence . . . The conception of law as a means toward social ends, the doctrine that law exists to secure interests, social, public and private, requires the jurist to keep in touch with life.[12]

The European Sociologists

The European sociologists, Ludwig Gumplowicz, Gustav Ratzenhofer, and Georg Simmel, contributed to American theory in the field of sociology and also demonstrated the relationship of sociology to law. While one would perhaps not expect the work of sociologists to have much of an impact on another discipline such as legal theory, the ideas of these German pioneers worked their way into the jurisprudence of Roscoe Pound and, through Pound, into the thinking of the American legal realists in the 1930s. The new tendency to view law from the standpoint of conflicting interests suggested that the ultimate "sources" of law lay in society itself. This meant that a method of studying society became important for the understanding of law.

The new science of sociology, given birth by Compte and Spencer in the mid 1800s, began reexamining its premises at the turn of the century. Rejecting earlier crude mechanical and biological approaches to the new science, sociologists on both sides of the Atlantic sought new methods and strategies for studying society. Several ideas had moved to the forefront in discussion of the theoretical basis of sociology. These were: that social behavior should be viewed as a process; that the process consisted of a conflict or struggle between competing interest groups; and that the scientist must concentrate not on psychic forces or ideas, but rather on explanatory concepts that are functions of the actual behavior of people in society (behaviorism). Although these ideas were elaborated and critiqued in both Europe and America, the original influence, particularly of the first two, seems to have been from Europe (Germany and Austria) to America.

---

11 *Pound,* The Scope and Purpose of Sociological Jurisprudence (pts. 1 - 3), 24 Harv. L. Rev. 591 (1911), 25 Harv. L. Rev. 140, 489 (1912).

12 25 Harv. L. Rev. 140, 146 (1912).

Gumplowicz

The Europeans who led this movement in the 1890s were Gumplowicz, Ratzenhofer, and Simmel.[13] Ludwig Gumplowicz (1838-1909) was professor of law in the University of Graz, Austria. He published several books on sociology and on the application of his sociological ideas to law.[14] His *Grundriss der Sociologie* [Outlines of Sociology] (1885) was translated to English in 1899.[15] The thinking of Gumplowicz that proved to be influential can be summarized as follows. Following Compte, Spencer, and Darwin, he believed that social phenomena are governed by universal laws analogous to the scientific laws that govern the inanimate universe. These laws are causal in nature; hence, like physics and chemistry, sociology must study what is, not what ought to be; it must be a value-free science. To understand social phenomena the scientist must view human activity as a struggle between various groups in which the stronger subjugate the weaker. As a result of this struggle social institutions evolve over time according to natural laws of development. The desire for material gain — self interest — is the motivating engine that creates group conflict and drives socal processes. Human beings cannot control this course of social evolution, but can learn how the process works.

Gumplowicz' Influence on the Americans

Arthur Bentley's thinking was strongly influenced by Gumplowicz, and he expressly acknowledged his personal intellectual debt to the Austrian.[16] In the penultimate chapter of his book Bentley briefly describes the "development of group interpretation" which preceded his own work. He points to Marx, Gumplowicz, Simmel, and Ratzenhofer as the seminal thinkers. Gumplowicz, in Bentley's view, "has taken the most important step toward bringing out clearly the nature of the group process." He is critical of Gumplowicz in two respects, however. He thinks that the Austrian scholar interprets "the social process directly in terms

---

13 The work of Karl Marx had considerable influence in Europe, but much less impact in America. See the discussion of Marx and American Marxist thinking in Bentley, note 6. Also, in the latter part of the first decade of the twentieth century the ideas of Gabriel Tarde, the French sociologist, were widely discussed among Americans, including Roscoe Pound.

14 *L. Gumplowicz,* Allgemeines Staatsrecht (1877); Rechtsstaat und Socialismus (1881); Verwaltungslehre mit besonderer Berücksichtigung des österreichischen Verwaltungsrechts (1882); Grundriß der Soziologie (1885); Die sociologische Staatsidee (1892); Geschichte der Staatstheorien (1905).

15 *L. Gumplowicz,* Outlines of Sociology (Moore trans. 1899). He also published an article in English in the American Journal of Sociology (edited by Small): *Gumplowicz,* An Austrian Appreciation of Lester F. Ward, 10 Am. J. Soc. 643 (1905).

16 See *Bentley,* note 6, at 479.

of [exclusive social classes, but does] not make the further analysis into the underlying specific interest groups which they represent;" and also that Gumplowicz has "left the 'psycho-social' phenomena in a awkwardly nondescript position." By this Bentley means that Gumplowicz has failed to reduce ideas or social abstractions to functions of behavior in his theory.[17]

Albion Small also saw Gumplowicz' work to be of importance for the advancement of sociology, but he regarded the latter's theory as having been improved upon and superseded by that of Ratzenhofer. Small rejected the Social Darwinism of Gumplowicz and criticised his complete discarding of the individual in favor of the group as a basic conceptual unit of sociological inquiry.[18]

Roscoe Pound's work reflects a familiarity with the writings of Gumplowicz (15 citations in four articles). Pound classifies the Austrian's early work as being in the mechanical stage of sociological jurisprudence.[19] However, his later work is cited as an example of the unification (final) stage of this development.[20] These "stages" are borrowed from the work of Albion Small.

Simmel

Georg Simmel (1858-1918), philosopher and sociologist, spent most of his professional life associated with the University of Berlin, although he never held a chair there.[21] He was a prolific writer, and his work included a number of articles in English in the American Journal of Sociology.[22] Simmel did not work

---

[17] "A special illustration of the way in which Gumplowicz allows a very marked non-groupal factor, in the form of an idea not broken down into its representative characteristics, to intrude into his interpretations, is his assertion that the 'neu aufgetauchte Idee' of the 'Rechtsstaat' had a very powerful influence upon the German and Austrian law-making and administration in the middle of last century. The fact which he indicates in this manner is, of course, not to be denied, that there was activity in transforming legislation and administration, and that the 'Rechtsstaat' was prominently mentioned as present. We may allow to Gumplowicz the implied belief that the 'Rechtsstaat' idea itself can be explained as a psycho-social product of group factors. But much more than that is necessary. The 'Rechtsstaat' must be functioned in its representative value in group terms of the very hour and place of its alleged working in order to find its value. When Gumplowicz gives the 'idea' itself such potency as he does, he merely indicates one spot at which his theory is not adequately elaborated." Id., at 471.

[18] See *A. Small,* General Sociology, 86-87, 499, 600 (1905).

[19] *Pound,* The Scope and Purpose of Sociological Jurisprudence, 25 Harv. L. Rev. 489, 491 (1912). As a reformer Pound is critical of Gumplowicz' determinism.

[20] Id., at 509, citing Geschichte der Staatstheorien, sec. 122 (1905).

[21] In the last four years of his life he held a chair at the University of Straßburg.

[22] *Simmel,* Superiority and Subordination as Subject Matter of Sociology, 2 Am. J. Soc. 167 (1896); The Persistence of Social Groups, (3 pts.) 4 Am. J. Soc. 662, 829 (1898), 4 Am. J. Soc. 35 (1899); A Chapter in Philosophy of Value, 5 Am. J. Soc. 577 (1900); The Number of Members as Determining the Sociological Form of the Group,

out a systematic theory of sociology, but provided keen insights and subtle substantive analyses. Two of Simmel's ideas that found favor with American readers can be mentioned. First, like Gumplowicz, he analyzed social phenomena in terms of group interaction; but in a complex society individuals become associated with different groups on different bases. For Simmel this association with different groups and the interests they represent defines the individual. Second (owing something here to Spencer), Simmel believed that social forms develop through social processes and persist or decay according to their usefulness, a type of functionalism. Simmel did not share the view (held by Compte, Spencer, and Gumplowicz, among others) that sociology was a science of laws on the analogy to the physical sciences. He denied the existence of laws of social development or of history in general. Rather than causal explanations, Simmel favored psychological explanation.

Simmel's Influence on the Americans

Simmel's work was highly respected by both Small and Bentley. Bentley viewed him as brilliant and important, but primarily because his writings served as an antidote or corrective to the shortcomings of Gumplowicz. For Bentley the spade work had been done by the Austrian, but had been extended and corrected by Simmel.[23] Bentley was nevertheless critical of Simmel, primarily for failing to bring a thoroughly behavioristic method to his work.[24] Small also thought Simmel was "one of the keenest thinkers in Europe," and admired his insights.[25] However, Small preferred the more systematic approach of Ratzenhofer.

Ratzenhofer

Gustav Ratzenhofer (1842-1904) published six books relating to sociology and political science after retiring from a career in the Austrian army.[26] The

8 Am. J. Soc. 1 (1902); The Sociology of Conflict, (3 pts.) 9 Am. J. Soc. 490, 672, 798 (1903); Contribution to Sociology of Relations, 11 Am. J. Soc. 359 (1905); Sociology of Secrecy and Secret Societies, 11 Am. J. Soc. 441 (1906); How is Society Possible, 16 Am. J. Soc. 372 (1910). The more prominent of Simmel's sociological writings in the original German include: *G. Simmel,* Über soziale Differenzierung: Soziologische und psychologische Untersuchungen [On social Differentiation: Sociological and Psychological Investigations] (1890), and Soziologie: Untersuchungen über die Formen der Vergesellschaftung [Investigations into the Forms of Socialization] (1908). Parts of the latter work were published much earlier.

23 *Bentley,* note 6, at 472.

24 Id., at 473-476.

25 For example, Small favorably describes Simmel's notion of the "form" of the group as an abstraction from the concrete individuals comprising the group. *A. Small,* note 18, at 498. This notion closely resembles Plato's concept of "forms."

works most cited by Americans were his first, *Wesen und Zweck der Politik* [The Essence and Purpose of Politics] (1893) and *Die sociologische Erkenntnis* [Sociological Cognition] (1898); he also published in the American Journal of Sociology.[27] While much of Ratzenhofer's works was couched in the abstractions of German metaphysics, his restatement and interpretation by Albion Small eliminated much of this unwanted baggage for American readers. More than any of the other European sociologists discussed herein, he was strongly influenced by Jhering, and his theory is built around the conflict of group interests. To some extent he also followed his countryman, Gumplowicz.

Ratzenhofer maintained that social phenomena are rooted in biological drives, primarily for food and sex, so that human beings naturally exist in a state of hostility. The advantages of cooperation lead people to form groups to advance their interest, and the size and complexity of these groups grows with time. The conflict between groups at all levels produces social structure and culture; cultural sanctions, including law, come to replace the sanction of physical force. Ultimately "civilization" develops in which primitive conquest and exploitation are eliminated, and individuals share equitably in the goods of life.

Ratzenhofer's Influence on the Americans

Bentley recognized Ratzenhofer's contribution to social theory as a major one, although he critized it for failing to become completely behavioral and for confusing his thinking through the use of murky and unnecessary metaphysics.[28] Bentley recognizes that the Austrian "provided us much excellent description of the practical processes of politics from a groupal point of view," and that Small has translated and edited this work "not only sympathically, but in a manner that is frequently a decided inmprovement on Ratzenhofer himself."[29]

It is Small, as suggested, who was most impressed by Ratzenhofer and who adopted much of the latter's theory as his own. Parts IV and V (211 pages) of Small's major work, *General Sociology*, are, as he acknowledges, essentially a modified restatement of the position of Ratzenhofer.[30] This includes Ratzenho-

26 *G. Ratzenhofer,* Wesen und Zweck der Politik (3 vol. 1893); Die sociologische Erkenntnis (1898); Der positive Monismus und das einheitliche Princip aller Erscheinungen (1899); Positive Ethik (1901); Die Kritik des Intellekts (1902); Soziologie: Positive Lehre von den menschlichen Wechselbeziehungen (1907) (published posthumously).

27 *Ratzenhofer,* Problems of Sociology, 10 Am. J. Soc. 177 (1904). See also *Small,* Ratzenhofer's Sociology, 13 Am. J. Soc. 433 (1908); *Bentley,* Simmel, Durkheim, and Ratzenhofer, 32 Am. J. Soc. 256 (1926).

28 *Bentley,* note 6, at 476-479.

29 Id., at 476.

30 Small also often referred to the work of Albert E. Schäffle, another German sociologist.

fer's idea of the function of law in civilization. Law is viewed as an intermediate in the transition from struggle to complete cooperation. It emerges as a product of the "undetected logic" of association.[31] Small says:

> Now, what has law to do with this process [of becoming civilized]? We spoke of law above as restraint. From our present outlook, law is rather record, registration, proclamation of the secured logical result. While law is primarily and immediately restraint of the individual, it is essentially a rationalizing of the association. It is thus an induction of all the individuals into larger liberty. It induces them to act together in a way that widens the scope and enriches the content of life for each.
>
> For instance, the logic of association discovers the unreason, the uneconomy, of murder; and consequently the law, speaking for social reasons and social utility, says: "Thou shalt not kill." The logic of association discover that theft is social fallacy; and consequently the law decrees; "Thou shalt not steal . . ."
>
> Whatever has demonstrated itself, in the logic of association, as true, is properly expressed by society in the imperative mood, to command the action of individuals. In this sense, law is the social schoolmaster.[32]

In another passage Small discusses Ratzenhofer's view of constitutional law. He sees the function of such law as serving as the basis on which interests may be secured. It provides "legal mediation between interests, including the governmental interest." The potential conflict between government and people "disappears in proportion as all interests are admitted to legal participation in the struggle for existence." Constitutional law is "an implied equilibrium of interests."[33]

From Sociology to Jurisprudence

While the influence of European sociologists on American sociologists is clear, we may now ask how the sociological theory of Bentley and Small translated into legal theory? The answer here is the strong influence of Small on legal scholar Roscoe Pound and the lesser influence of Bentley on Pound and others.[34]

The influence of Bentley on Pound is somewhat problematic. At some point Pound read Bentley's book, and it is cited in his articles. However, it seems likely that Bentley's insistence on a pure form of behaviorism would not have

---

31 This principle of logic is stated as follows: "Act for reasons, and always for more reasons, and in proportion as the reasons establish rank and precedence among themselves as reasons, until action is finally in harmony with all the reasons, correlated according to their intrinsic value." *Small,* note 18, at 358.

32 Id.

33 Id., at 295-296.

34 It is possible that Bentley inspired Joseph W. Bingham to do his remarkable bit of jurisprudence. See *Herget,* note 1, at 154-155. However, I have found no evidence to support this connection.

appealed to Pound. Bentley did, however, have significant influence on other legal theorists.[35]

In contrast, Small's influence on Pound is clear. Pound was a close colleague of Edward A. Ross, another pioneer of American sociology, during their years at Nebraska.[36] Ross awakened Pound's interest in sociology and its value in understanding law.[37] When Pound went to Chicago in 1907 he became acquainted with Albion Small and served on the faculty of the University of Chicago with Small in 1909 - 10. Small's brand of sociology was especially congenial to Pound's way of thinking. It was not deterministic; it contained elements of pragmatism, yet retained notions of organicism tracing back to Spencer and Darwin. It placed as central to understanding and explaining society the idea of conflict of interests, an idea already accepted by Pound in more general form from Jhering. It viewed the legal process as a civilized type of struggle between interests and the law itself as the securing of such interests. Small's General Sociology (1905) and his later work, The Meaning of Social Science (1910), are cited and quoted throughout many of Pound's articles, and there can be no doubt that Small played a large part in furnishing the sociological knowledge and viewpoint that Pound needed to create his sociological jurisprudence.

The Free Law Thinkers

This brings us to the most important German influence on American jurisprudence: the works of the free law movement. This movement began as a reaction to the excesses of German legal science *(Rechtswissenschaft)*, the activity that engaged most of the legal scholars during the nineteenth century.[38] Itself a reaction to earlier natural law thinking, German legal science sought to develop the traditional sources of law, both Germanic and Roman, through scientific elaboration. It was assumed that inherent within the law was a system or order

---

35 See, for example, *Llewellyn*, The Constitution as an Institution, 34 Colum. L. Rev. 1 (1934). Llewellyn says, "I am indebted to Bentley's magnificent study ... Why so profound and incisive a book has found so little echo, I cannot make out. Morris Cohen led me to it. I feel like entitling this paper *A Rediscovery of Bentley.*"

36 Biographical information on Pound is taken from *D. Wigdor*, Roscoe Pound: Philosopher of Law (1974), and *P. Sayre*, The Life of Roscoe Pound (1948).

37 Ross had also studied in Germany in the course of his education. He moved on to the University of Wisconsin from Nebraska, and Pound went to Northwestern University in the City of Chicago. But the two stayed in contact for many years. Pound admired Ross' work, particularly his book, Social Control (1901), which dealt with law in sociological terms. Ross was also an avid reformer and probably, influenced Pound in that direction as well. Another, slightly older, American sociologist who had an impact on Pound as well as on Ross and Small was Lester F. Ward. See *Wigdor* and *Sayre*, id.

38 For an excellent explanation of German legal science, see *Reimann*, Nineteenth Century German Legal Science, 31 Boston Coll. L. Rev. 837 (1990).

that gradually evolved over time. The materials of study were the historical laws, but the object was to bring out the natural system implied in the fragmentary and historically contingent specific laws. Legal scientists, using logical deduction and inference, abstracted the principles and order out of the specifics, creating grand concepts and doctrines. As this activity proceeded, the work of the scholars became more and more formal and abstract *(Begriffsjurisprudenz)*. Needless to say, this kind of scholarship did not lend itself to practical legal reform; indeed, implicit in its assumptions was the notion that mere politicians could not change the law; it would evolve naturally.

At the same time that the abstract doctrinal elaboration of the law (especially the Roman) was taking place, codification was proceeding as well. A code of civil procedure was enacted in 1877, and, after several drafts greatly influenced by the scholars, the German civil code was enacted in 1896, to take effect in 1900. In comparison with the Napoleonic code of nearly a century earlier, the German code was more systematic and abstract. Its language reflected much of the conceptual landscape created by the legal scientists.

One of the doctrines worked out by the scholars was *die logische Geschlossenheit des Rechts*, or the logical closure of the law. From the point of view of this conceptual jurisprudence the law had to be internally consistent, self-sufficient, autonomous, and all-inclusive. There could be no gaps. Proper logical elaboration would extend the principles of the law to every conceivable situation by the operation of logic.

It is primarily in reaction to this idea that the free law movement began.[39] Lawyers and judges knew that there were indeed gaps in the law. Both before and after the advent of the magnificent scientific civil code, cases regularly arose in which the application of the provisions of written law was ambiguous. Certain scholars began to point out that the king had no clothes. This raised the question: How should the courts decide these cases? What sources should the judge turn to when the authoritative ones were of no help?

The critique started as early as 1872.[40] One widely cited piece by von Bülow was written in 1885.[41] In the following year the great legal anthropologist, Josef

---

39 For general discussion of the free law movement, see *K. Muscheler*, Relativismus und Freirecht: Ein Versuch über Hermann Kantorowicz (1984); *K. Muscheler*, Hermann Ulrich Kantorowicz: Eine Biographie (1984); *K. Riebschläger*, Die Freirechtsbewegung (1968); *J. Schmidt*, Das Prinzipielle in der Freirechts-Bewegung (1968); *F. Gény*, Method of Interpretation and Sources of Private Positive Law, 519-563 (1919, trans. Mayda 1954); *Foulkes*, On the German Free Law School, Archiv für Rechts- und Sozialphilosophie 367 (1969). For compilations of free law writings, see *A. Foulkes* and *A. Kaufmann*, Gerechtigkeitswissenschaft: Ausgewählte Schriften zur Freirechtslehre von Ernst Fuchs (1965); *T. Würtenberger*, Rechtswissenschaft und Soziologie: Ausgewählte Schriften zur Wissenschaftslehre von Hermann Kantorowicz (1962).

40 *F. Adickes*, Zur Lehre von den Rechtsquellen (1872).

41 *O. Bülow*, Gesetz und Richteramt [Statutory Law and Judicial Office] (1885). Bülow, professor of civil procedure at Heidelberg, Gießen, Tübingen, and Leipzig, was

Kohler, lent his authority to this line of development.[42] Kohler was an intellectual giant whose main works were in the areas of legal history and ethnology.[43] Others followed the examples of Bülow and Kohler.[44] At the same time the French scholar Francois Gény published his masterpiece, *Méthode d'interprétation et sources en droit privé positif* [Method of interpretation and sources of private positive law] (1899), which discussed the problem of "gaps" and the non-authoritative sources of law used by the French courts to fill them. Gény was familiar with the German writings in this area, and, in turn, the German scholars read Gény's work. Indeed, Gény became world-renown.[45] His influence on the free law thinkers was so great that Hermann Kantorowicz, a leader of that movement, has been quoted as saying, "I would give everything I have done, and more, to have written Gény's *Méthode.*"[46]

The movement widened its critique as it became more popular. In the first decade of the twentieth century the *Freirechtler* came to criticize *Begriffsjurisprudenz* itself and the use of false logic to justify court decisions. The whole of

---

a leader in the movement to make the law of procedure an independent branch of public law. He was an acknowledged authority on the German code of civil procedure of 1877. Most of his scholarly work was in the area of civil procedure; however, he wrote three somewhat jurisprudential pieces at the turn of the century: Heitere und ernste Betrachtungen über die Rechtswissenschaft (1901); Klage und Urteil, 21 Zeitschrift für das Zivilprozessrecht 265 (1903); Über das Verhältnis der Rechtsprechung zum Gesetzesrecht, 10 Das Recht 769 (1906).

42 *Kohler,* Über die Interpretation der Gesetze, 13 Zeit. für das Privat- und Öffentliche Recht 1 (1886); see also Die schöpferische Kraft der Jurisprudenz, 25 Jahrb. für die Dogmatik des heut. röm. und deutschen Privatrechts 262 (1887).

43 Kohler was professor of law in Würzburg (1878) and Berlin (1888). In addition to his ethnological and historical studies, he was also known for his work in patents, copyright, and trademark law, and for his modified Hegelian legal philosophy. He also wrote poetry, novels, and a history of art. Two of his more than 500 works are: Einführung in die Rechtswissenschaft (1902), and Lehrbuch der Rechtsphilosophie (1909). The latter was translated into English as a part of the Modern Legal Philosophy Series: *J. Kohler,* Philosophy of Law (trans. Albrecht 1914). In 1912 Roscoe Pound called Kohler "the first of living jurists." *Pound,* The Scope and Purpose of Sociological Jurisprudence, 25 Harv. L. Rev. 140, 155 (1912).

44 *Ehrlich,* Über Lücken im Rechte, 17 Juristische Blätter 447 (1888); *Heck,* Book Review, 37 Zeitschrift für das gesamte Handelsrecht 277 (1890); *M. Rümelin,* Werturtheile und Willensentscheidungen im Civilrecht (1891); *Stampe,* Die Lehre von der Abretung der Vindication, 80 Archiv für die Civilistische Praxis 305 (1893); *H. Dernburg,* Die Phantasie im Recht (1894); *Steinbach,* Die "guten Sitten" im Recht, 4 Deutsche Juristen-Zeitung 47 (1899); *E. Zitelman,* Lücken im Recht (1903); *O. Meyer,* Rechtsnormen und Kulturnormen (1903); *E. Ehrlich,* Freie Rechtsfindung und Freie Rechtswissenschaft (1903). *K. Wurzel,* Das juristische Denken (1904).

45 Gény was successively professor of law in Algiers (1885), Dijon (1889), and Nancy (1901-31). In addition to numerous articles and monographs Gény wrote two substantial works: The Méthode, mentioned in the text above and published in an expanded two-volume edition in 1919, and Science et technique en droit privé positif: nouvelle contribution à la critique de la méthode juridique (4 vol. 1914-1924). These and other works have been translated into several languages.

46 *K. Llewellyn,* The Common Law Tradition 422 n. 46 (1960).

traditional German legal science came under fire. The dramatic call went out for a revolution in jurisprudence.[47]

Two authors in particular stand out both for their centricity to the movement and for their influence in America: Eugen Ehrlich and Hermann Kantorowicz.[48] In later years Ehrlich pursued an empirical sociology of law of his own making, an outgrowth of the free law insights. Kantorowicz, always a legal historian, later became more famous for his historical work, and indeed, drew back from some of his earlier free law positions.[49] Ernst Fuchs, a Karlsruhe practitioner, was the foremost polemicist of the movement. Another early free law thinker, Philipp Heck, parted company with the *Freirechtler* at an early date and began to form his own school of thought, the *Interessenjurisprudenz*.[50] Heck's approach, deriving directly from Jhering, replaced the analysis of law in terms of traditional concepts with an analysis based upon the conflicting interests represented in legislation.[51]

Led by Kantorowicz, Ehrlich, and Fuchs, there was an outpouring of writing pro and con the new movement.[52] Even more conventional scholars were moved

---

47 The battle cry was sounded in Hermann Kantorowicz 'Der Kampf um die Rechtswissenschaft' (1906).

48 Their principal works were: *E. Ehrlich,* Freie Rechtsfindung und freie Rechtswissenschaft [Free Law Finding and Free Law Theory] (1903); Soziologie und Jurisprudenz [Sociology and Jurisprudence] (1906); *H. Kantorowicz,* Der Kampf um die Rechtswissenschaft [The Battle over Legal Science] (1906); Rechtswissenschaft und Soziologie [Legal Science and Sociology] (1911). Of equal importance to the movement in Germany was Ernst Fuchs. However, Fuchs was hardly cited in America. His most prominent works were: *E. Fuchs,* Schreibjustiz und Richterkönigtum (1907); Recht und Wahrheit in unserer heutigen Justiz (1908).

49 See *Muscheler,* Relativismus, note 39.

50 See *M. Schoch,* ed., The Jurisprudence of Interests (1948).

51 Philipp Heck, successively professor of law in Greifswald (1891), Halle (1892), and Tübingen (1901-28), taught admiralty, commercial law, obligations, property, and German legal history. He is regarded as the founder of the jurisprudential school of Interessenjurisprudenz in Germany. Others associated with that school were Max Rümelin, Heinrich Stoll, and Rudolf Müller-Erzbach. Heck's principal works include Das Problem der Rechtsgewinnung [The Problem of Ascertaining the Law] (1912, 2d ed. 1932); Gesetzesauslegung und Interessenjurisprudenz [Statutory Interpretation and the Jurisprudence of Interests] (1914); Grundriss des Schuldrechts [Outlines of the Law of Obligations] (1929, 2d ed. 1958); Grundriss des Sachenrechts [Outline of Property Law] (1930); Rechtserneuerung und juristische Methodenlehre [Legal Renewal and Juristic Methodology] (1936).

52 Some of the other significant scholarly works in this period would include: *A. Bozi,* Die Fortbildung des Rechts durch die Rechtsprechung, 10 Das Recht 206 (1906); Die Weltanschauung der Jurisprudenz (1907); *L. Brütt,* Die Kunst der Rechtsanwendung (1907); *J. Gmelin,* Quousque? Beiträge zur soziologischen Rechtsfindung (1910); *M. Rumpf,* Zum jetzigen Stande der Lehre von der adaequaten Verursachung im Zivilrecht, 49 Jherings Jahrb. 395 (1905); Gesetz und Richter: Versuch einer Methodik der Rechtsanwendung (1906); *E.Stampe,* Unsere Rechts- und Begriffsbildung (1907); *E. Zitelmann,* Die Gefahren des B.G.B. für die Rechtswissenschaft (1896). For a more expansive bibliography of free law literature, see the appendix in *Muscheler,* Relativismus, note 39.

to modify their views, and the free law thinking crept into standard textbooks and treatises.[53] Although the thinking of these writers was not uniform and they differed among themselves on many points, their message can be generalized in two directions.

Much of the free law movement consisted of negative criticism of the *Begriffsjurisprudenz* (also often called constructive jurisprudence). This negative critique can be summarized into four categories: (1) traditional legal science with its reliance on formal and conceptual methods of interpretation is fundamentally erroneous, a remnant of scholasticism, and judicial decisions that are justified by argument confined to the "autonomous" legal system are suspect; (2) certainty in law is illusory when based upon syllogistic arguments that are often manufactured *ad hoc* to conceal the real (social, informal) basis of decision; (3) the doctrine of separation of powers that separates law making and law applying into the legislative and judicial functions is not reflective of reality; the judge does and must participate in the formation of law; (4) the formal law is not a comprehensive closed system, but contains large gaps that give no guidance for particular cases.

From a positive point of view the free law movement advocated what may loosely be called a new "method," although some scholars have questioned whether such a method was ever really worked out.[54] It can roughly be described as follows: the judge's primary function is to do justice in the individual case in the light of the principles and policies set out in the official state law. But, since the official law is admittedly insufficient or ambiguous in many cases, the judge must be creative and draw upon other sources for the basis of his decision. Judges have always done this, but sometimes they have disguised their use of other sources by pretending to deduce conclusions logically from official norms and concepts so as to appear not to be making law. They should be frank and open about this activity, and they should explain clearly why they have chosen to apply the unofficial sources. In some cases the official law may dictate results that are so completely at odds with accepted ideas of justice that the judge must reject the formal law and apply the unofficial sources. The function of the legal scholar in this view is to elaborate what the law should be in various situations by bringing to bear the informal sources that weigh upon judicial decision. The scholar must assist the judge. In doing so he must become a kind of legal sociologist.

Obviously, these "informal sources" become an extremely important part of the method of the free law thinkers. They are, of course, the free law; or, perhaps

---

[53] See, e. g., *H. Dernburg,* Das Bürgerliche Recht des deutschen Reichs und Preussens (3rd ed. 1906); Pandekten (1892); *J. Kohler,* Einführung in die Rechtswissenschaft (2ed. 1905); Moderne Rechtsprobleme (1907); Lehrbuch der Rechtsphilosophie (1909).

[54] See *Riebschläger,* note 39, at 107 - 109; *Schmidt,* note 39, at 79 - 90.

more accurately, the law is freely found and fashioned (or should be) by judges from a variety of sources. There was much disagreement among the free law thinkers over how to characterize these sources. However, it can be said that the *Freirechtler* did not limit their sources of law to statute and custom as the traditional jurisprudence did; they insisted upon looking toward, among other possibilities, the social consciousness of the people, economic realities, factual (sociological) data, social utility, the sense of justice *(Rechtsgefühl)* of the specific case (equity), and the policies or purposes that underly the statutory law. For some free law thinkers a hierarchy of priority of such sources was suggested in order to avoid judicial subjectivity; for others no such ranking was possible, and free law finding was regarded essentially as an art.

The views of the free law school on the education of judges and lawyers is of some interest. They advocated a well rounded education in the social sciences and humanities with emphasis on sociology and psychology. Study of pure legal rules apart from context was discouraged. Knowledge of history and of the cultural characteristics of society was regarded as important. It was argued that the research and writing of legal history in particular must be revised to demonstrate the development of the law in the context of other social phenomena; legal history as pure doctrinal change was rejected as too narrow and misleading.

From a political point of view the *Freirechtler* were generally left-liberal or socialist under a regime that was very conservative. Their criticism of cases decided by the German courts reflected a sympathy for the underdog, although they did not view things in terms of class struggle. Their advocacy of greater freedom for judges generally coincided with an advocacy of results that would liberalize the conservative policies of the legislature. When the Weimar Republic was established after World War I as a liberal government, and while the judges remained conservative (sometimes hostile to the new constitution), the political tables were turned. Favoring greater judicial discretion in the new context meant allowing the judges to undermine, through interpretation, the liberal policies of the new government. Kantorowicz and others narrowed or abandoned their free law doctrine as it came to be applied by reactionary judges.[55]

These ideas, while somewhat amorphous and expounded against the background of German legal science and the new code, nevertheless expressed a deeper desire to obtain a wider understanding of law and especially the judicial process. The latter had never before been a particularly significant concern in German legal theory, although it was central to post-Holmesian jurisprudence in America.[56] The new view also offered reformers of the law a sympathetic

---

[55] See *Muscheler*, Relativism, note 39, at 161 - 174; *Muscheler*, Biography, note 39, at 42 - 58; *Riebschläger*, note 39, at 75 - 90.

[56] Holmes directed jurisprudential attention to the judicial process. See *Herget*, note 1, at 46. There is the possibility, to date undocumented, that Holmes' thinking was

orientation, and it made relevant the work of the newly emergent social sciences, particularly sociology and economics. As a jurisprudential commodity, free law had a certain attractiveness.

Influence of Free Law Thinking on the Americans

John Chipman Gray certainly cannot be regarded as a free law thinker; his work clearly belongs to the analytical school. But he departed from most exponents of that school in a very important way. Gray shifted the perspective on law from viewing it as the product of an authoritative legislator to viewing it as the rules and principles that courts draw upon and employ in making their decisions. While courts do draw upon legislation and judicial precedent for their rules of decision, for Gray those sources are insufficient to explain adequately how judges decide cases. He maintains that the sources courts actually use include custom, the opinion of legal scholars, common morality, and the judge's own personal morality.[57] It might be thought that Gray borrowed this idea from Oliver Wendell Holmes, Jr., whose famous statement of it was given in 1897.[58] However, an earlier article published in 1892 by Gray shows that he had already adopted this viewpoint.[59] Gray may have arrived at this perspective on his own, but it is also possible that he got the germ of it from an early free law thinker, Oskar von Bülow. In his 1909 treatise, explaining how courts have the final word on what statutes apply to a case and what they mean, Gray relies on the German's work, quoting therefrom:

> A judicial decree is as much as a statute the act of the law-making power of the State ... The power of Law is stronger than the power of Legislation, a legal judgment maintains itself even if it contradicts a statute. Not by its legislative, but by its judicial determinations, the law-regulating power of the State speaks its last word.[60]

The viewpoint implied in this statement is, of course, the essential thesis that Gray presents in his treatise. It is an idea that opens up the inquiry about "sources" of law to social and moral phenomena as well as the formally legal.

When Roscoe Pound began teaching jurisprudence at the University of Nebraska in 1903, he prepared "Outlines of Jurisprudence" which he revised and

---

strongly influenced by Jhering. See *Kelley,* A Critical Analysis of Holmes' Tort Law, 61 Wash. U. L. Q. 681 (1981); *Frank,* A Conflict with Oblivion, 9 Rutgers L. Rev. 425 (1954).

57 *J. Gray,* note 8, at 551, 598, 642.

58 See *Holmes,* The Path of the Law, 10 Harv. L. Rev. 457 (1897).

59 *Gray,* Some Definitions and Questions in Jurisprudence, 6 Harv. L. Rev. 21 (1892). However, see *Holmes,* The Law Magazine and Review, 6 Am. L. Rev. 593 (1872), reprinted in 44 Harv. L. Rev. 788, 789-90 (1931).

60 *Gray,* note 8, at 164, quoting from *O. Bülow,* Gesetz und Richteramt (1885).

greatly expanded from time to time as he taught the course in subsequent years.[61] The original outline primarily set forth an analytical jurisprudence of the British type, based upon the seminal work of Austin; in fact, it was subtitled "Chiefly from the Analytical Standpoint."[62] As we have noted, at this time Austinian analysis was the only thing that passed for jurisprudence in England, and it was the dominant school in America.[63] However, Pound's learning was broad enough that the Outlines also briefly mentioned what Pound then called the metaphysical school, the historical school, and the "critical school." The latter apparently referred to some early free law thinking.

In 1904 Pound published a short article in which he attempted to sort out the various contemporary schools of thought. He says:

> Hitherto it has been possible to divide jurists into three principal groups, according to their views of the nature of law and of the standpoint from which jurisprudence should be approached. We may call these groups the Philosophical School, the Historical School, and the Analytical School. On closer analysis, the Philosophical School falls into two: the Eighteenth Century Law of Nature School, still represented by a Rousseauist school in France, and a Later Philosophical School, of which there are numerous varieties [citing Lorimer and Ahrens]. The historical jurists may be distinguished into the German Historical School, whose method is philosophical and historical, and the English Historical School, whose method is comparative and historical.[64]

Pound also advances the thesis that a new school is emerging from the old ones, a school he calls the sociological.[65] He acknowledges Jhering as the leader of this movement, and he cites works of Kohler and Post as examples. He also refers to Ehrlich's *Freie Rechtsfindung und freie Rechtswissenschaft* [Free Law

---

61 The fifth edition of this compilation was published in 1943. *R. Pound,* Outlines of Lectures on Jurisprudence (5th ed. 1943).

62 See *Wigdor,* note 36, at 110. In 1912 a two-part book entitled 'Introduction to the Study of Law' by *Roscoe Pound* and 'Law Books and How to Use Them' by *John C. Townes* was published by the American School of Correspondence. Pound's part of this publication sets out a typical Austinian analysis of the law with no hint of his sociological jurisprudence or other points of view. This is quite anachronistic, considering Pound's rapid change in thinking between 1903 and 1912, and leads to the conclusion that he must have based the text primarily on the original Outlines.

63 See *Herget,* note 1.

64 *Pound,* A New School of Jurists, 4 Univ. Neb. Studies 1 (1904).

65 "We should naturally expect a new school to emerge from this breakdown of the older schools and there are many signs that such an event is in progress. Jurists are coming together upon a new ground from many different starting points. Some of them profess to find this new ground, potentially at least, in the schools from which they set out. But here is much to indicate that, instead of a further variation of one of the old creeds, an entirely new creed is to be looked for. The rising and still formative school, to which we must look henceforth for advance in juristic thought, may be styled the Sociological School." Id., at 2. This theme is repeated with revisions in Pound's most important work on sociological jurisprudence, *Pound,* note 11.

Finding and Free Legal Science] (1903). Pound is optimistic about the future of the new movement, concluding:

> A school which studies [law] as a social mechanism will do no little service if it but deliver us from the condition of dry rot which juristic thought has hitherto contracted in periods of enactment and codification, and preserve or restore the juristic ideals of reason and justice, which, for a time, we seem fated to lose or to forget.[66]

From 1904 to 1912 Pound published several articles in which he discussed the thinking of the "new school."[67] He managed to keep abreast of the German literature even though his career took him to positions at three new universities during this period. Pound pointed out the necessity for judges to make law and to draw upon morality in the process. Although he did not use the term "gaps", he clearly saw the many situations in which the formal law did not provide a rule for decison.[68] An adequate jurisprudence would have to take into account social and moral factors presently considered irrelevant to legal discourse. Pound urged that the "traditional legal pseudo-science" be vastly broadened. "The modern teacher of law should be a student of sociology, ecnonomics, and politics as well."[69] In addition, proper funding for sociological research in law should

---

66 Id., at 18.

67 In these articles Pound cites the following free law works: *A. Bozi,* Die Weltanschauung der Jurisprudenz (1907); *L. Brütt,* Die Kunst der Rechtsanwendung (1907); *H. Dernburg,* Das bürgerliche Recht des deutschen Reichs und Preußens (3d ed. 1906), Pandekten (1892), Lehrbuch des Preußischen Privatrechts (3 vol. 1875-80); *E. Ehrlich,* Freie Rechtsfindung und freie Rechtswissenschaft (1903), Soziologie und Jurisprudenz (1906), Die Erforschung des lebenden Rechts, 34 Schmollers Jahrb. 129 (1911), Die Rechtsfähigkeit (1909); *E. Fuchs,* Schreibjustiz und Richterkönigtum (1907), Recht und Wahrheit in unserer heutigen Justiz (1908); *J. Gmelin,* Quousque? Beiträge zur soziologischen Rechtsfindung (1910); *H. Kantorowicz,* Der Kampf um die Rechtswissenschaft (1906); Rechtswissenschaft und Soziologie (1911), Zur Lehre vom richtigen Recht (1909); *J. Kohler,* Rechtsphilosophie und Universalrechtsgeschichte, in Holtzendorff, Enzyklopädie der Rechtswissenschaft (7th ed. 1913-15), Einführung in die Rechtswissenschaft (1902), Moderne Rechtsprobleme (1907), Lehrbuch der Rechtsphilosophie (1909); *M. Rumpf,* Zum jetzigen Stande der Lehre von der adäquaten Verursachung im Zivilrecht, 49 Jherings Jahrb. 395 (1905), Versuch einer Methodik der Rechtsanwendung (1906); *E Stampe,* Rechtsfindung durch Konstruktion, 10 Deutsche Juristen-Zeitung 417 (1915); *W. Wurzel,* Das Juristische Denken (1904); *E. Zitelmann,* Lücken im Recht (1903), Die Gefahren des B.G.B. für die Rechtswissenschaft (1896).

68 "The points of contact between law and morals, the points at which the individual reason and judgment of the judge, reflecting the desires of the dominant element of society, come into play, are three: discretion, judicial law-making, and interpretation." *Pound,* Spurious Interpretation, 7 Colum. L. Rev. 379, 380 (1907).

69 *Pound,* The Need of a Sociological Jurisprudence, 19 Green Bag 607, 611 (1907). He goes on to say: "He should know not only what the courts decide and the principles by which they decide, but quite as much the circumstances and conditions, social and economic, to which these principles are to be applied; he should know the state of popular thought and feeling which makes the environment in which the principles must operate in practice. Legal monks who pass their lives in an atmosphere of pure law,

be forthcoming from the same sources that fund research in the physical and medical sciences.[70]

Pound found Kantorowicz' characterization of the traditional theory of the mechanical application of law, the "green table" metaphor, so enlightening that he translated and quoted it in three separate articles.[71] Approving of the work of the new school, "whose cry is for *freie Rechtsfindung,*" Pound says:

> To this school, the essential point is a reasonable and just solution of the individual case. It conceives of the legislative rule as a general guide to the judge, leading him toward the just result; but it insists that within wide limits he should be free to deal with the individual case so as to meet the demands of justice between the parties and accord with the reason and moral sense of ordinary men. It insists that application of law is not purely mechanical process ... "Whoever deals with juristic questions," says a contributor to this controversy, "must always at the same time be a bit legislator;" that is, to a certain extent he must make law for the case in hand.[72]

Pound argued that the new school in Germany had brought out into the open the use of social and moral precepts in the application of the law, something that traditional jurisprudential approaches had swept under the rug. It had demonstrated that courts did indeed resort to these "non-legal" sources, although often denying it, and that they were often compelled to do so. How this process operates should be the focus of study. Americans denied its operation, too, but "We have a great deal of *freie Rechtsfindung* in America, while disclaiming it in theory."[73]

---

from which every wordly and human element is excluded, cannot shape practical principles to be applied to a restless world of flesh and blood." Id.

70 Id., at 608.

71 "A superior magistrate with academic training, sits in his cell armed only with a thinking-machine, although one of the finest type. His sole furniture is a green table upon which there lies before him the official statute-book. One may hand him any case you please, actual or moot, and, performing his duty, he is prepared by the aid of pure logical operations and a secret technique intelligible only to himself, to indicate with absolute exactness the decision already determined by the law-maker in the statute-book." *Pound,* The German Movement for Reform in Legal Administration and Procedure, 1 Bull. Comp. L. 31, 32 (1908); *Pound,* Enforcement of Law, 20 Green Bag 401, 404 (1908). *Pound,* note 11, at 596. The passage is taken from *H. Kantorowicz,* Der Kampf um die Rechtswissenschaft 7 (1906).

72 *Pound,* The German Movement, Id., at 32-33. Pound is quoting from *Zitelmann,* Die Gefahren des B.G.B. für die Rechtswissenschaft 19 (1896).

73 *Pound,* Enforcement of Law, note 71, at 407. Pound also says: "To a large and apparently growing extent the practice of our application of the law is, after all, that jurors or courts, as the case may be, take the rules of law as a general guide, determine what the equities of the cause demand, and contrive to find a verdict or render a judgment accordingly, wrenching the law no more than is necessary. Many courts today are suspected of ascertaining what the equities of a controversy require, and then raking up adjudicated cases to justify the result desired. Occasionally we find a judge avowing frankly that he looks chiefly at the ethical situation *inter partes* and does not allow the law to interfere therewith beyond what is inevitable. This is essentially what the German equitable school contends for ..." Id., at 405-406.

Pound advocates that students of the law in America should maintain an awareness of contemporary legal consciousness.[74]

In these articles Pound also suggests a concept of justice that is close to that stated by some of the free law thinkers.[75] He says that justice, from a modern sociological perspective, amounts to nothing more than the satisfaction of wants or a coordination of such satisfactions.[76] One of the serious problems of the new century is the failure of courts to recognize the wants and needs of the times. It is instructive to compare Pound's political position with that of the *Freirechtler*. Although a Republican, Pound was a progressive reformer. Many state legislatures, and occasionally Congress, were enacting social legislation that attempted to combat the evils of industrialization. The courts, and the Supreme Court in particular, were hostile to such legislation and often invalidated it on dubious constitutional grounds. Pound opposed these decisons, characterizing them as conceptual jurisprudence, and he pleaded for a more informed type of decision-making in which the courts would take into account social realities.[77]

As an example, Pound refers to several reactionary decisions of the U. S. Supreme Court in the following way:

> The manner in which the Fourteenth Amendment is applied affords a striking instance of the workings today of a jurisprudence of conceptions. Starting with the conception that it was intended to incorporate Spencer's Social Statics in the fundamental law of the United States, rules have been deduced that obstruct the way of social progress. The conception of liberty of contract, in particular, has given rise to rules and decisions which tested by their practical operations, defeat liberty.[78]

In his three-part article entitled *The Scope and Purpose of Sociological Jurisprudence* Pound attempted to restate his thinking on the subject. He revived the thesis that the traditional schools of jurisprudence were gradually coming, each from its own direction, to a sociological perspective. Historical jurisprudence, according to Pound, had moved to ethnological and anthropological studies with emphasis on descriptions of legal culture. The philosophical school had moved

---

74 *Pound,* note 69, at 615.

75 Although there is the embryo of an ethical theory in Pound's early works, as stated in the text, the full development of the normative side of his philosophy came somewhat later. See *Pound,* A Theory of Social Interests, 15 Proc. Am. Sociol. Soc. 16 (1921). See also, *R. Pound,* Introduction to American Law (1919); *R. Pound,* The Spirit of the Common Law (1921); *Pound,* Legislation as a Social function, 18 Am. J. Sociol. 755 (1913); *Pound,* Justice According to Law, (pts. 1-3), 13 Colum. L. Rev. 696 (1913), 14 Colum. L. Rev. 1, 103 (1914).

76 *Pound,* Enforcement of Law, note 71, at 403.

77 The U. S. Supreme Court remained much more conservative than the legislatures until 1936. It did not become liberally activist until the mid 1950s (the "Warren Court").

78 *Pound,* Mechanical Jurisprudence, 8 Colum. L. Rev. 605, 616 (1908). Pound refers to the infamous Lochner case familiar to students of American constitutional law: *Lochner v. New York,* 198 U. S. 45 (1905). Cases of this type are further discussed in *Pound,* Do We Need a Philosophy of Law?, 5 Colum. L. Rev. 330 (1905).

to neo-Kantianism as exemplified by Stammler and neo-Hegelianism as exemplified by Kohler. Both came to draw upon social ideals and social fact. The analysts have increasingly used historical method and accordingly have turned toward factual study.[79]

Pound then tells us that sociological jurisprudence has gone through four stages, a classification that Pound credits to Small, although in actuality Small was talking about stages of sociology itself.[80] These stages are: (1) the mechanical (or deterministic) stage, exemplified by the writings of Marxists like Brooks Adams of the early works of Gumplowicz; (2) the biological stage represented by the works of Post, Vaccaro, and Menger; (3) the psychological stage, illustrated by Gierke, Ward, and Tarde; (4) the stage of unification, or contemporary stage, in which the useful aspects of the preceding approaches are combined. Pound, himself, was representative of this stage.

What are the characteristics of the sociological jurisprudence that Pound was advancing? He suggests a six part program for the legal scholars of the new age. (1) Study the actual social effects of legal institutions and doctrines. (2) Use sociological study in preparation for legislation. (3) Study the means of making legal rules effective. (4) Develop a new legal history in which the relationship between social change and legal change is chronicled. (5) Urge the equitable application of the law in which legal rules are guides to the judge, leading him toward the just result, but allowing him to be free to meet the demands of justice in the context of the case. (6) Reform the law so that it more effectively implements society's values [does justice].[81]

In describing and explaining the latest stage of sociological jurisprudence Pound relies upon and quotes from the writings of the free law scholars as well as the work of Albion Small. Included as authorities are Bozi, Ehrlich, Fuchs, Gmelin, Kantorowicz, Kohler, and Wurzel. Ehrlich's *Freie Rechtsfindung und freie Rechtswissenschaft* and Kantorowics' *Der Kampf um die Rechtswissenschaft* and *Rechtswissenschaft und Soziologie* are Pound's favorite sources, and he quotes extensively from the latter. Pound himself largely (and fairly) attributes his new jurisprudence to the free law thinkers and to Jhering and Kohler. In

---

79 The reader may note that there is ambiguity in the use of the word "jurisprudence" by Pound. It may mean "philosophy of law" or "legal method" or "legal science" or something else. This ambiguity runs throughout his work.

80 *Pound,* note 11, at 491.

81 At the end of this article Pound shows five ways in which the sociological jurists are distinguished from other schools: "1. They look more to the working of the law than to its abstract content. 2. They regard law as a social institution which may be improved by intelligent human effort, and hold it their duty to discover the best means of furthering and directing such effort. 3. They lay stress upon the social purposes which law subserves rather than upon sanction. 4. They urge that legal precepts are to be regarded more as guides to results which are socially just and less as inflexible molds. 5. Their philosophical views are very diverse." Id., at 516.

fifteen articles on jurisprudential themes written between 1904 and 1917, Pound cited 132 German authors a total of 493 times, often quoting from their works using his own translation.

Other Americans also transmitted the free law concepts to an American audience, although most of this comes later than the pioneering work of Pound. Among these scholars were Morris R. Cohen,[82] Charles Grove Haines,[83] Edwin M. Borchard,[84], William H. Page,[85] and Benjamin N. Cardozo.[86] In addition, the Science of Legal Method, a volume of the Modern Legal Philsophy Series, published under the sponsorship of the Association of American Law Schools in 1917, contains a good sampling of free law thinking translated into English.[87]

The "New" American Legal Theory

The rest of the story is easy to tell. Pound's work, which included many more articles and several books after 1918, became the most authoritative jurisprudence in America. It was altered and extended in the 1920s and 1930s by many scholars under the banner of legal realism, the best known jurisprudential development in American history.[88] A few of the legal realists acknowledged some German influence,[89] but most of them thought their thinking was original or was derived

---

82 *Cohen,* Recent Philosophical-Legal Literature in French, German and Italian (1912-1914), 26 Int. J. Ethics 528 (1916). See also *Cohen,* A Critical Sketch of Legal Philosphy in America, in 2 Law: A Century of Progress 266 (1937). Although Cohen was a philosopher and not a lawyer, he was an influential figure in American jurisprudence for almost half a century.

83 *Haines,* General Observations on the Effects of Personal, Political, and Economic Influences in the Decisions of Judges, 17 Ill. L. Rev. 96 (1922). Haines was a political scientist who relied heavily on free law thinkers in this seminal article.

84 *Borchard,* Jurisprudence in Germany, 12 Colum. L. Rev. 301 (1912). Borchard was one of a handful of highly respected American law professors who had a command of German.

85 *Page,* Professor Ehrlich's Czernowitz Seminar of Living Law, 14 Proc. Assoc. Am. L. Schools 46 (1914). Ehrlich had been scheduled to addresss the annual meeting of the Association of American Law Schools in 1914, but the outbreak of World War I prevented him from attending. Professor Page presented his paper.

86 *B. Cardozo,* The Nature of the Judicial Process (1921). Next to Holmes, Cardozo was probably America's most prominent judge. In this book he relies on several free law thinkers.

87 Association of American Law Schools, The Science of Legal Method (1917). This volume contains works by Ehrlich, Gény, Wurzel, and Gmelin (stating Fuch's views). Roscoe Pound had a hand in selecting these works.

88 See *Herget,* note 1, at 171-193.

89 For example, *Jerome Frank* in his rebellious book, Law and the Modern Mind (1930), says at page 229, "An acquaintance with [free law thinker Karl Georg] Wurzel is indispensable to an understanding of the unfortunate consequences of the certainty illusion in law. No other single writer has as carefully observed the relation between the search for a legal Absolute and the peculiarities of juridical thinking."

from Pound. One of the leaders of realism, Karl Llewellyn, acknowledged Bentley as an intellectual parent as well.[90] The dominance of the old British jurisprudential ideas had been broken. Analytic jurisprudence in the style of Austin, Holland, and Salmond was old hat.

The "new" American jurisprudence, which I have elsewhere called the "Poundian Paradigm,"[91] directly reflected the ideas of the German thinkers discussed above. The negative critique of conceptual jurisprudence was essentially the same as that of the free law school; the targets, however, were the "Restatement of the Law" being formulated by the American Law Institute, certain conceptual legal treatises, and many court decisions. On the positive side, the "method" to be followed by judges and scholars was to investigate the "real" reasons or causes of judicial decisions, and to expose phony decisionmaking. Scholars would elaborate the relevant "social policy" that courts should follow, and judges would give opinions in which the policy (non-formal sources) upon which their decisions were really based would be fully articulated and discussed: Legal scholars would undertake empirical studies to determine relevant social facts, and legal historians would write the history of law in its actual context, not as the internal unfolding of logical doctrine.

The writings of Jhering, Kohler, Gény, and the free law scholars all plowed new jurisprudential ground. They delivered telling criticism against conceptual jurisprudence. They promoted a view of law that acknowledged and accepted judicial creativity, and they opened the question of "sources" to be consulted by the judges in exercising their creativity. This opened inquiry into how these sources, located "in society," were to be systematically investigated. The German sociologists had created sociological strategies relevant to this inquiry, and these were accepted by the American social scientists and transmitted to legal scholars. The new German thinking offered a jurisprudence that gave room to law reform. Roscoe Pound was the recipient directly and indirectly of all of these influences. The citations and quotations in his writings demonstrate beyond any doubt his great intellectual indebtedness to these thinkers. As Pound's "sociological jurisprudence" became modified and extended to become American "legal realism," the life of the original continental ideas was further extended. Building upon this base, the "Law, Science and Policy" of Lasswell and McDougal, the "social science of law," and even "law and economics" became possible.[92] The influence of German thought was indeed great.

---

90 See note 35.

91 See *Herget,* note 1, chap. 6 and 7.

92 For these developments see *Herget,* note 1.

JAMES Q. WHITMAN

Early German Corporatism in America: Limits of the "Social" in the Land of Economics

Among the welter of ideas and movements of the last century, corporatism stands out, not only as one of the strangest, but also as one of the most influential. Indeed, it has been suggested that the twentieth century has been, not the century of socialism, nor the century of free market liberalism, but the "The Century of Corporatism."[1] That may overstate the importance of the movement. But there can be little doubt that corporatism has been potent and widespread. In particular, much of the twentieth century western world has displayed, in some measure, what could be called "cartel corporatism." This peculiarly modern variety of corporatism mixes political and economic power: Firms, in a cartel corporatist system, are organized into politically powerful cartels. Workers, for their part, are organized into politically powerful corporative labour unions. And cartels and labor unions together call many of the shots in society.[2]

The theoretical roots of this cartel corporatism lie in the German Second Reich, in the work of social theorists like Albert Schäffle and Adolph Wagner, as well as in the governmental innovations of Otto von Bismarck. From the Germany of these men, the theory of cartel corporatism radiated throughout most of the industrial world in the decades after 1870 or so. But cartel corporatism has radiated only throughout *most* of the industrial world. Neither the practice nor the theory of corporatism has ever had much success in penetrating the United States. Only the N.R.A. experiment of 1933-35 brought corporatism of any scale to America, and that experiment failed abjectly[3] — so abjectly, indeed, that more than one scholar has been moved to ask, "Why is there no Corporatism in the United States"?[4]

---

[1] *P. Schmitter,* Still the Century of Corporatism?, in F. Pike and T. Stritch, eds., The New Corporatism: Social-Political Structures in the Iberian World (Notre Dame, 1974).

[2] For corporatism in contemporary Western Europe, see, e. g., the systems surveyed in G. Lehmbruch and P. Schmitter, eds., Patterns of Corporatist Policy-Making (Beverly Hills, 1982).

[3] Most recently discussed in *D. Brand,* Corporatism and the Rule of Law: A Study of the National Recovery Administration (Ithaca, 1988); see also *J. Whitman,* Of Corporatism, Fascism and the First New Deal, in American Journal of Comparative Law 39 (1991): 747 - 778.

[4] *G. Wilson,* Why is there no Corporatism in the United States?, in G. Lehmbruch and P. Schmitter, eds., Patterns of Corporatist Policy-Making; *R. Salisbury,* Why not

Yet if it is true that corporatism has failed in the United States, it is also true that German social thought was highly influential in the United States during the 1870s and 1880s[5] — precisely the period when modern corporatist theory was first taking shape in Germany. Why, then, did this powerful German influence of the 1870s and 1880s not become a corporatist influence? In this contribution, I will try to identify some of the obstacles to German corporatist influence in America. The nature of those obstacles reveals, I will suggest, something about the differences between German and American societies in the later nineteenth century. It reveals, as well, something more generally about why the United States has proven resistant to some of the most important elements of European sociolegal thought.

I.

The term "corporatism" is far from easy to define. A number of rather dry and abstract political science definitions have been offered.[6] None of these is quite capable of capturing the emotions stirred in corporatist thinkers by the corporatist vision. The corporatist vision is of a society in which individual identity has been transcended. In the corporatist society, individuals have been assembled into guild-like corporate bodies. In its pre-modern form, corporatist theory had a distinctly anti-commercial tinge.[7] But modern corporatism has

---

Corporatism in America?, in P. Schmitter and G. Lehmbruch, eds., Trends Toward Corporatist Intermediation (Beverly Hills, 1979).

5 See *J. Herbst,* The German Historical School in American Scholarship: A Study in the Transfer of Culture, (Ithaca, 1965); *J. Dorfman,* The Role of the German Historical School in American Economic Thought, in American Economic Review: Papers and Proceedings, 45 (May, 1955): 17; *H. Hovenkamp,* The Antitrust Movement and the Rise of Industrial Organization, in Texas Law Review 68 (1989): 112; *H. W. Farnam,* Deutsch-Amerikanische Beziehungen in der Volkswirtschaftslehre, in Die Entwicklung der deutschen Volkswirtschaftslehre im neunzehnten Jahrhundert. FS Gustav Schmoller (Leipzig, 1908); *N. Balabkins,* Not by Theory Alone . . . The Economics of Gustav von Schmoller and its Legacy to America (Berlin, 1988).

6 P. Schmitter's somewhat cryptic definition of corporatism runs: "A system of interest representation in which the constituent units are organized into a limited number of singular, compulsory, non-competitive, hierarchically-ordered, and functionally differentiated categories, recognized or licensed (if not created) by the state." *Schmitter,* Still the Century of Corporatism?, 93. J. T. Winkler's definition: "an economic system in which the state directs and controls predominantly privately-owned business according to four principles: unity, order, nationalism and success." *Winkler,* Corporatism, in Archives Européennes de Sociologie 1 (1976): 103. The term, as Charles Maier points out, has been used to characterize almost any "linkage of public institutions and organized interests." *Maier,* 'Fictitious bonds . . . of wealth and law': On the Theory and Practice of Interest Representation, in *Maier,* In Search of Stability: Explorations in Historical Political Economy (Cambridge, 1987), 228 n. 3.

7 See esp. the description of Charles Loyseau's vision of a society of orders in *R. Mousnier,* Les Institutions de la France sous la Monarchie Absolue, 2d ed., 2 vols. (Paris, 1990), 1: 14-23.

proven rather different. Modern corporatists have tended to prescribe a society in which the basic representative units — the modern guilds — are labor unions and cartelized trade associations, well-integrated into the commercial order.[8]

Corporatism is, however, more than just a theory of economic organization. It is also a theory of politics. For corporatists argue that economic identity should be the basis of political representation. Thus corporatists have typically preached "berufsständische Vertretung," or "political representation by occupational status."[9] Modern corporatists have pressed this notion to the limit, typically favoring some form of a Nation Economic Council as a replacement for a purely political parliament. In the classic design for an industrial corporatist government — that of the Stato Corporativo of Mussolini — society was thus to be organized into Fascist industrial associations and Fascist unions, which served as the political representatives of economic society before the supreme state power.[10]

These basic elements — favoring, or even mandating, membership in a corporative association; and favoring the replacement of a parliamentary order with some type of "representation by occupation" — both had their modern origin in post-1848 Germany.[11] To be sure, modern German corporatist theory should be traced back, to a large extent, to Romantic idealizations of an imagined Middle Ages.[12] But the advocacy of a specifically *industrial* corporatism — that is to say, a corporatism whose "occupational status representation" is through labor unions and cartels — was a product of the period after 1848.[13] Nor is this surprising. It was only after 1848 that German unions and cartels developed.

---

[8] Co-operatives have also appealed to the corporatist impulse, though I will not discuss them in this paper. See the discussion below note 111 and accompanying text.

[9] See esp. *H. Herrfahrdt,* Das Problem der berufsständischen Vertretung von der französischen Revolution bis zur Gegenwart (Stuttgart / Berlin, 1921).

[10] Fully described in *A. Aquarone,* L'Organizzazione dello Stato Totalitario (Torino, 1965).

[11] For the preeminence of Germany's corporatist tradition, see *U. Nocken,* Korporatistische Theorien und Strukturen in der deutschen Geschichte des 19. und frühen 20. Jahrhunderts, in U. v. Aleman, ed., Neokorporatismus (Frankfurt a. M., 1981): 23-24.

[12] *Nocken,* Korporatistische Theorien, 24-25. The French tradition was also of first importance in the earlier nineteenth-century. See *M. Elbow,* French Corporatist Theory, 1789-1948 (1953); *M. Bouvier,* L'État sans politique: Tradition et modernité (Paris, 1986).

[13] There is some dispute among scholars about whether the beginnings of German industrial corporatism should be dated to the years around 1850 or the years around 1880. In an important article of 1978, U. Nocken traced the beginnings of twentieth-century German corporatism to the period 1850-1914, during which he saw a "mixed system of state corporatism and pluralism" at work. *Nocken,* Corporatism and Pluralism in Modern German History, in D. Stegmann, et al., eds., Industrielle Gesellschaft und politisches System (Bonn, 1978): 37-56. By contrast with Nocken, W. Abelshauser identifies 1879 as the birthdate of modern German Corporatism in Germany, in European History Quarterly 14 (1984): 285-318. Both discussed in *V. R. Berghahn,* Corporatism in Germany in historical perspective, in A. Cox and N. O'Sullivan, The Corporate State:

German corporatist theory cannot, indeed, be understood without a background glance at the rise of German unions and cartels. I will begin with unions. The history of the misery that accompanied German industrialization, and of the accompanying rise of the German labor movement, is familiar. That experience of industrial misery and labor organzation stimulated a significant volume of incipient labor corporatism after 1848: A number of figures advocated corporative workers' groups as a means of alleviating industrial suffering. Advocacy of such workers' groups first appeared in the most poorly integrated of North German social groups: the Catholics of the Rhineland[14]; in particular, it came from the Bishop of Mainz, Baron von Ketteler, who began a lifework of pious meliorism amid the misery of the new industrial workers of the Rhineland in the years after 1848. In the 1850s, Ketteler began to argue that Germans should work to ease the lot of industrial workers by reviving, in new form, medieval guild society: workers should unite in corporative associations.[15] Catholic labor theory flourished in subsequent years, reaching its intellectual height with Franz Hitze's *Kapital und Arbeit,* published in 1880.[16] From the 1850s onward, moreover, theorizing about some sort of revival of guild society, as an antidote to the labor problem, began to appear outside the Catholic camp as well. Of works that showed some measure of Ketteler's influence, two in particular deserve mention. It was in 1868 that Otto von Gierke's *Deutsches Genossenschaftsrecht* began appearing. Also of prime importance among those with Catholic roots was Lujo Brentano, the later *Kathedersozialist,* who wrote a highly influential 1871 book praising English trade unions.[17]

Corporatism and State Tradition in Western Europe (Hants, 1988): 106-108. H.-U. Wehler places the beginnings of "organisierter Kapitalismus" around the same time that Abelshauser places the beginnings of corporatism. See *Nocken,* Korporatistische Theorien, 20 (contrasting later dating of Winkler to 1896).

In practice these are differences only of emphasis. If one considers the fostering of unions critical, 1848 marks the watershed date; if one considers the fostering of industrial cartels critical, the watershed date is closer to 1879.

14 For the importance of the Catholics, see *H.-J. Teuteberg,* Geschichte der industriellen Mitbestimmung in Deutschland (1961); *U. Hientzsch,* Arbeitsrechtslehren im Dritten Reich und ihre historische Vorbereitung, 2 ff. (1970). For labor law theory in this light, see also *Teuteberg,* Die Doktrin des ökonomischen Liberalismus und ihre Gegner, in H. Coing and W. Wilhelm, eds., Wissenschaft und Kodifiktion des Privatrechts im 19. Jahrhundert Frankfurt a. M., 1977) 2: 47-73. Ketteler's main work was 'Die Arbeiterfrage und das Christenthum' (1864).

15 I cannot discuss here the important French influence on Ketteler, on which see *Hientzsch,* Arbeitsrechtslehren, 22.

16 See generally the discussion in *R. Bowen,* German Theories of the Corporative State, with Special Reference to the Period 1870-1919 (New York, 1947), 96 ff. See also *Hientzsch,* Arbeitsrechtslehren, 25.

17 *L. Brentano,* Die Arbeitergilden der Gegenwart, 2 vols. (1871-72). Discussed in *Teuteberg,* Industrielle Mitbestimmung, 284-285. For Brentano's importance, see also *J. Ewerling,* Vom Einigungsamt zum Treuhänder der Arbeit, 3 (1935). See generally *J. Sheehan,* The Career of Lujo Brentano: A Study of Liberalism and Social Reform in

All of this work displayed a characteristically German belief that "social" organizations should somehow supplant the individual as the basis of a sound social order. Much of this work, including that of Ketteler himself,[18] also showed signs of an anti-parliamentarism that would characterize continental corporatist thought for the succeeding eighty years. This was characteristic of the time. A variety of anti-parliamentary writings appeared in the period 1848 - 1870.[19] These included the work of the Prussian conservative E. L. von Gerlach, who declared that "only a corporatively organized people *[ständisch-gegliedertes Volk]* is capable of self-government"[20]; but a liberal figure like Robert von Mohl could also express anti-parliamentary views during this period.[21]

Two of the critical themes of later industrial corporatism — emphasis on the "sociale" or "genossenschaftlich," and anti-parliamentarism — were thus already present before 1870. The same themes continued to characterize German thought during the rise of the wide-spread cartelization that characterized the Second Reich. The German economy became heavily cartelized in the last decades of the nineteenth century.[22] After an initial phase from the 1830s to the 1850s, German cartelization began, as it were, to "take off," particularly, as elsewhere,[23] after the onset of the "Great Depression" in 1873.[24] By the late nineteenth century

---

Imperial Germany, (1966), and esp. 6 - 45 for Brentano's youthful Rhenish Catholicism and his English experience.

18 See the discussion of *H. Heffter,* Die Deutsche Selbstverwaltung im 19. Jahrhundert: Geschichte der Ideen und Institutionen (Stuttgart, 1950), 570. That Ketteler, and the German Catholic political leaders who absorbed his influence in the 1870s, should have been anti-parliamentary, is not, of course, surprising. The 1870s were the years of the *Kulturkampf* — years when Catholics suffered serious persecution in Germany at the hands of Bismarck and the parliamentary majority, years when the Catholic Center Party was the only party in the German *Reichstag* that openly represented a single group interest.

19 See the discussion in *Bowen,* German Theories of the Corporative State, 63.

20 Quoted in *Bowen,* German Theories of the Corporative State, 61.

21 *P. Paur,* The Corporatist Character of Bismarck's Social Policy, European Studies Review 11 (1981): 434 - 35.

22 On German cartelization, see generally *E. Maschke,* Outline of the History of German Cartels from 1873 to 1914, in F. Crouzet, W. Chaloner, W. Stern, eds., Essays in European Economy History, 1789 - 1914 (1969), 226. But see also *V. Hentschel,* Wirtschaft und Wirtschaftspolitik im Wilhelminischen Deutschland. Organisierter Kapitalismus und Interventionsstaat? (Stuttgart, 1978), 103.

23 E. g., *C. Freedeman,* Cartels and the Law in France before 1914, French Historical Studies 15 (1988), 462.

24 See generally *H. Pohl,* Die Entwicklung der Kartelle in Deutschland und die Diskussion im Verein für Socialpolitik, in H. Coing and W. Wilhelm, eds., Wissenschaft und Kodifikation des Privatrechts im 19. Jahrhundert (Frankfurt a. M., 1979) 4: 208 - 9. The 1850s saw the establisment of a number of trade associations, a process that continued, particularly in the period 1870 - 73, when heavy industry pressed for tariff protection. Noteworthy products of the 1870s were the so-called Langnamverein, the Verein zur Wahrung der gemeinsamen Interessen in Rheinland-Westfalen, founded in 1871, in the potent Centralverband deutscher Industrieller, founded in 1875. *Paur,* Bismarck's Social Policy, 433 - 34.

cartels, often formalized into syndicates, exercised control not only over prices but also over output and product quality,[25] and the last two decades before the outbreak of World War I saw an intensification of cartelization in Germany, encouraged by favorable decisions of the Reichsgericht.[26]

Just as trade unions did, these cartels tended to attract the interest and support of German social and economic theorists, eager so find "social" alternatives to the individualism of "Manchester liberalism and laissez-faire thinking."[27] The first pro-cartelist salvos along these lines were fired by the Austrian Friedrich Kleinwächter in 1833. Kleinwächter's book quickly attracted the attention of leading German scholars. Albert Schäffle took note of Kleinwächter's arguments in favorable 1883 review.[28] Lujo Brentano, long the champion of organized labor, added his voice in papers of 1888 and 1889 to the chorus of admiration for organized capital. Brentano saw in cartels, as he saw in unions, "social organizations."[29]

By the mid-1890s, these new "social organizations" had begun to attract the support of numerous others of the circle of the *Verein für Socialpolitik,* the organization of prominent academics known as *Kathedersozialisten,* or "tenured Socialists." The 1894 meeting of the Verein was devoted to the cartel question, and it produced a large volume of favorable theorizing.[30] The leading national economist Gustav Schmoller provided a résumé of the proceedings highly favorable to cartels.[31] Cartels grew, he said, from the "soil of free contract and free

---

25 *Pohl,* Entwicklung der Kartelle in Deutschland, 212.

26 *Pohl,* Entwicklung der Kartelle in Deutschland, 215 ff.

27 *Pohl,* Entwicklung der Kartelle in Deutschland, 224.

28 Zeitschrift für die Gesamte Staatswissenschaft 1 (1883). Schäffle observed what Kleinwächter had not observed: that cartels were characterized by their monopolistic tendency. But Schäffle nevertheless praised the power of cartels to stabilize production, and to foster social solidarity. Schäffle was also the author of an influential 1898 study, the importance of which is discussed in *F. Blaich,* Kartell- und Monopolpolitik im kaiserlichen Deutschland: Das Problem der Marktmacht im deutschen Reichstag zwischen 1879 und 1914 (Düsseldorf, 1973), 241.

29 *Pohl,* Entwicklung der Kartelle in Deutschland, 225. The similarity of Brentano's and Schmoller's skepticism about laissez-faire is noted in *Balabkins,* Not by Theory Alone, 30.

30 *Pohl,* Entwicklung der Kartelle in Deutschland, 225-27. This theorizing was notable in particular for its influence on the Reichsgericht. The Reichsgericht's definitive 1897 decision, in the famous case of the Saxon wood pulp cartel, cited the proceedings of the 1894 conference of the Verein für Socialpolitik, Kleinwächter, Brentano and others. Entscheidungen des Reichsgerichts in Civilsachen 38 (1897), 156-7. It should be noted that this decision only affected the law under the Gewerbeordnung. When, three years later, however, the Bürgerliches Gesetzbuch came into effect, it included two provisions on "gute Sitten," articles 138 and 826, which could potentially have been invoked against cartels, just as comparable provisions had been invoked in France. See *F. Walker,* The Law Concerning Monopolistic Combinations in Continental Europe, in Political Science Quarterly 20 (1905): 20-21.

31 Schmoller called cartels "eine naturgesetzliche, eine nicht zu hindernde, auf Ersparung an Produktionskosten und technische Verbesserungen der Produktion gerichtete

right of association and union"; from the same soil in which "modern social forces generally come together and crystallize."[32] The same favorable tone marked the 1905 proceedings of the Verein, on the subject "Cartels and the State." Important in particular for the contributions of Alfred Weber and, once again, of Schmoller, the 1905 proceedings again ended by endorsing cartelization as a beneficent social force.[33]

And strikingly, the proceedings endorsed cartelization as a force preferable to American-style trusts.[34] Indeed, the great German campaign in the following decade was against the Trust, widely denounced as a mischievous American threat to the healthy German economy.[35] This German hostility to American forms is highly relevant to my subject, and it deserves some attention. Robert Liefmann's classic discussion of the differences between trusts and cartels reveals something of the German understanding of what set their cartelized society apart from American society. Like Schmoller, Liefmann emphasized the free formation of cartels as associations:

> The term 'Cartels' we take to mean *voluntary agreements between* — or as we have called them, *associations of* — *independent enterprises of a similar type to secure a monopoly of the market* ... The cartels ... do not go so far as to take away completely the independence of the individual firm, and are therefore to be distinguished from mergers — in which one firm is completely absorbed in another and the former owner loses his proprietary rights altogether. They differ in this respect from the *monopolistic amalgamations*, in which *all* or nearly all the forms in a particular branch of trade are brought into one concern, thus abolishing completely the economic independence of former individual undertakings. The special form of amalgamation known in America as the trust has precisely the same effect ...[36]

When Germans looked at their cartelized society, they saw freely formed associations: saw, as it were, *social* concentration. Germany was the land of cartels, of independent firms voluntarily cooperating, of associations. America, in German eyes, lacked these social values. Rather than cooperation, American had consolidation. Rather than association among independent firms, America had the "abolition of independence."

Entwicklung." Quoted in *Pohl*, Entwicklung der Kartelle in Deutschland, 229-30. For a longer list of Schmoller's ideas about "die günstigen Folgen" of the cartel movement, see *G. Weippert*, Die wirtschaftstheoretische und wirtschaftspolitische Bedeutung der Kartelldebatte auf der Tagung des Vereins für Socialpolitik im Jahre 1905, in Jahrbuch für Sozialwissenschaft 11 (1960): 135.

32 Cartels, he added, in the course of a natural evolution, had developed "einen *halböffentlichen* Charakter." Both quoted in *Weippert*, Kartelldebatte, 135.

33 See *Weippert*, Kartelldebatte, 135-36.

34 For Schmoller's views, see *Weippert*, Kartelldebatte, 135-36.

35 See generally *F. Blaich*, Der Trustkampf (1901-1915) (Berlin, 1975).

36 *R. Liefmann*, Cartels, Concerns and Trusts, trans. anon. (London, 1932), 7, 10-11.

II.

By the 1880s, German social thinkers had thus developed a substantial body of theory favorable to the formation of two kinds of "social organization," unions and industrial cartels. This theory provided the background for the first efflorescence of modern German corporatist theory, with its characteristic organicist fervor.

The social theory of corporatism was developed by a number of prominent figures, among them Franz Hitze, Franz Baader, Karl Marlo, and the unsavory anti-Semite Adolph Stoecker.[37] A full discussion of German corporatism would have to include all these men, and perhaps others.[38] But, in order to keep within the limits of an essay, I will focus on three figures: two scholars linked with the *Kathedersozialisten,*[39] Albert Schäffle and Adolph Wagner, and one great statesman, Otto von Bismarck. Schäffle was the most thoroughgoing visionary corporatist of the period. Wagner, whose thinking was in some ways (though only in some ways) quite close to Schäffle's,[40] was the German theorist most influential in America. And Bismarck lent an international prestige to corporatism only he was capable of lending.

Schäffle's career followed one of the standard trajectories of the mid-nineteenth century: like, for example, Richard Wagner and Bachofen, he was a young '48 liberal who turned, in the 1850s, to the politics of disillusionment with liberalism. Intimations of his mature corporatism appeared in an 1856 article entitled "Abbruch und Neubau der Zunft" ("The Guild: Its Collapse and its Resurrection").[41] He spent the subsequent twenty years mixing unsuccessful political activity with his academic career. A truly happy match of political influence and scholarly activity came for him only after 1878, when Bismarck abondoned the National

---

37 Discussed, e. g., in *Nocken,* Korporatistische Theorien, 26 ff.; see generally, *Bowen,* German Theories of the Corporative State. Also useful is *P. Becher,* Vergleich und Kritik der sozialpolitischen Auffassungen bei Lujo Brentano, Adolph Wagner, Georg von Hertling und Franz Hitze, diss. München, 1965.

38 Perhaps even such a less deeply corporatist figure as Gustav Schmoller. On Schmoller as corporatist, see *Bowen,* German Theories of the Corporative State, 124.

39 For the association of Schäffle and Wagner, in part indirect, with the *Kathedersozialisten,* see, e. g., *A. Müssiggang,* Die soziale Frage in der historischen Schule der deutschen Nationalökonomie (Tübingen, 1968), 130 n. 22; *Bowen,* German Theories of the Corporative State, 122. It should be noted that Wagner himself expressed resentment at being associated with the *Kathedersozialisten.* See *H. Rubner,* Geleitwort, in Rubner, ed., Adolph Wagner. Briefe, Dokumente, Augenzeugenberichte, 1851 - 1971 (Berlin, 1978), v.

40 Both Schäffle and Wagner advocated an organicist vision of a modern industrial society characterized by "a highly selective program of state intervention designed to preserve a 'balance of forces' in economic life." *Bowen,* German theories of the Corporative State, 123. Nevertheless, it is notoriously the case that Wagner was far more statist in his inclinations than was Schäffle. See the discussion below.

41 Reprinted in Gesammelte Aufsätze (Tübingen, 1885) 1: 37 - 45.

Liberals and began to take an interest in corporatist policies.[42] At home in the mature Bismarckian Reich, Schäffle went to work advocating a system of political economy based on the organicism he espoused in works such as his *Bau und Leben des sozialen Körpers (Structure and Life of the Social Organism)* (1st ed. 1875-78). In this and other works[43] Schäffle embarked on the immensely influential corporatist project: the project of founding a new corporative society on trade unions, cartels and trade associations.[44] Schäffle's main concern was industrial peace. In the new order that he envisaged, the basis interests of society would be sorted out through negotiation between the great collective representative organizations of labor and capital, officially recognized and nurtured by a state that would provide "firm, authoritative guidance."[45] True to the corporatist tradition, and to his own history of doubts about liberalism, Schäffle saw his corporative order as incompatible with purely parliamentary government. Fearing that pure parliamentarism would lead to revolution in the end, Schäffle wanted to see "Economic Chambers," based on occupational associations, added to existing representative institutions.[46]

A more statist style of thinking came from Schäffle's fellow editor of the *Zeitschrift für die gesamte Staatswissenschaft,* Adolph Wagner.[47] Despite a quarrelsome personality,[48] Wagner was widely respected as the leading advocate of a state socialism that would mesh with nationalist aspirations, and he gave both prestige and rhetorical force to an organicist variety of political economy akin to that of Schäffle. Like Schäffle, Wagner looked fondly back on guild society, believing that new corporative organizations such as unions could restore the "Standesehre," the sense of status-based honor, of an earlier age.[49] As he put it in 1877, borrowing the language of Germanic law upon which Gierke had placed

---

42 *Bowen,* German Theories of the Corporative State, 125 ff.

43 In particular his Die Aussichtslosigkeit der Sozialdemokratie (1885). See *Bowen,* German Theories of the Corporative State, 132; *Nocken,* Korporatistische Theorien, 28; and the discussion in *Grebe,* Die Arbeiterfrage bei Lange, Ketteler, Jörg, Schäffle, Historische Studien, pp. 91, 105 ff.

44 *Bowen,* German Theories of the Corporative State, 132; *Nocken,* Korporatistische Theorien, 28; and the discussion in *P. Grebe,* Die Arbeiterfrage bei Lange, Ketteler, Jörg, Schäffle, Historische Studien, 283 (repr. Vaduz, 1965), pp. 91, 105 ff.

45 Quoted in *Bowen,* German Theories of the Corporative State, 133; for Schäffle's idea of "staatliche Planwirtschaft," see also *H. Winkel,* Die deutsche Nationalökonomie im 19. Jahrhundert, Erträge der Forschung, 74 (Darmstadt, 1977), 129.

46 *Bowen,* German Theories of the Corporative State, 136. Schäffle's fears and plans are sensitively discussed in *Grebe,* Die Arbeiterfrage, 113-14.

47 Like Schäffle's, Wagner's thought really took firm shape in the late 1870s, at the time of Bismarck's political divorce from the liberals. *E. Clark,* Adolf Wagner: From National Economist to National Socialist, Political Science Quarterly 55 (1940): 394. Clark's article, relied upon by Bowen, is, as its title suggests, a largely polemical piece to be used with caution.

48 See generally *Rubner,* ed., Wagner.

49 *Becher,* Vergleich und Kritik, 112.

his stamp, he desired that production should be "directed from above, but carried out communally *[genossenschaftlich]*." [50] This entailed state sponsorship of the workers' and employers' associations that were appearing on the German scene.[51] It also entailed vigilance against the depredations of laissez-faire liberalism and democracy.[52] Political evolution had forced upon society the recognition of the necessity of quasi-public bodies: "In the period of constitutional development characterized by the general extension of full citizenship, theorists have at last begun to recognize the organic relation between the state and the smaller corporative bodies. We have now begun to recognize the so-called 'self-governing corporative bodies' *[Selbstverwaltungskörper]*, though to be sure such bodies have only begun to organize in the late stages of the current age."[53] To be sure, Wagner differed, from Schäffle and many other contemporaries, in the great strength of his statism. In particular, he frowned on the free private formation of cartels; what was called for was compulsory cartelization, monopolization, and state seizure ("Verstaatlichung") of a wide range of industries and institutions. Prime candidates for "Verstaatlichung" included "Common carriers (railroads!), banks, insurance companies, certain plants (illumination and gasworks) . . . etc., as well as traditionally public or communal domains, forests, mines"; also candidates for "Verstaatlichung" were monopolies which earned monopoly profits.[54] This process of "Verstaatlichung" would not, however, produce a wholly statist result. Rather, what would arise would be something more corporatist: a society in which the people were represented both by the state and by intermediate corporative bodies: society would be "the community, as it is represented in the economic realm on behalf of both the greatest and the lesser circles of the populations: through state, local community *[Gemeinde]*, and similar bodies."[55] Statist though it might be, this was incipient corporatism, a philosophy of "self-governing corporative bodies."

Contemporaneously with the rise of the social theory of Schäffle and Wagner came political scheming from an enthusiast of Schäffle, the Prince von Bismarck. In Bismarck, the anti-parliamentary aspect of corporatism came to the fore. Bismarck had a "life-long preference" for Estates-type representation.[56] But it was only in the late 1870s, as he abandoned his alliance with the National

---

50 Wagner, letter to Der Staatsozialist, 20 Dec. 1877, in *Rubner*, ed., Wagner, 158. For Wagner's enthusiasm for German as opposed to Roman law, see *Wagner,* Grundlegung der politischen Ökonomie (Leipzig, 1893) 1: 23.

51 *Becher,* Vergleich und Kritik, 84 (pointing out, however, that Wagner retreated from these ideas in the 1890s); *Clark,* Adolf Wagner, 397.

52 *Clark,* Adolf Wagner, 396.

53 *A. Wagner,* Finanzwissenschaft und Staatssozialismus, in Zeitschrift für die gesamte Staatswissenschaft 43 (1887): 94.

54 *Wagner,* Grundlegung, 1: 746.

55 *Wagner,* Grundlegung, 1: 747.

56 *Paur,* Bismarck's Social Policy, 429.

Liberals, and as a variety of new industrial pressure groups formed,[57] that Bismarck yielded to his increasing distaste for the *Reichstag*[58] and embarked on a course of corporatist experimentation. In 1878, his adviser Bleichröder proposed to Bismarck a new economic-political order: a Reich economic council, superimposed on a variety of Reich commissions, representing various economic interests, was to be established in an effort to sap the power of the Reichstag in economic matterns. This plan eventually formed the basis of Bismarck's most elaborate corporatist experiment: the Prussian Economic Council, composed of seventy-five representatives of commerce, industry and agriculture, was established in 1881 to deliver economically informed views on all legislation. The intent was to weaken the Reichstag,[59] and eventually to establish a Reich Economic Council.[60] The scheme was not a success in practice,[61] and Bismarck's corporatist scheming abated after 1884.[62] Out of office after 1890, however, Bismarck resumed his corporatist theme, and his influence on later German corporatism was strong.[63]

Indeed, despite moments of uncertainty and failure among these men, by the later years of the Second Reich, German corporatism was well on the road toward its twentieth-century development — toward the preaching of indissoluble union of state and industrial corporative bodies as it would be preached during World War I, and then again in Weimar and in the first years of the Third Reich. To be sure, full-bodies corporatist theory had yet to appear. But when it did appear — in the thought of Schäffle's student Othmar Spann,[64] of Wagner's follower Wichard von Moellendorff,[65] or of the state-heavy avowed corporatism of the Nazis[66] — it continued to carry the traces of Second Reich hopes for a marriage of "the greatest and the lesser circles", of state and cartelized industry and labor.

---

[57] For the appearance of industrial professure groups as background to Bismarck's corporatist activity, see *H. Böhme,* Big Business Pressure Groups and Bismarck's Turn to Protectionism, 1873-79, Historical Journal 2 (1967): 218-36; *Berghahn,* Corporatism in Germany, 110-11.

[58] *Paur,* Bismarck's Social Policy, 427 ff.

[59] *Paur,* Bismarck's Social Policy, 438-39.

[60] *Paur,* Bismarck's Social Policy, 440 ff. But contrast *Berghahn,* Corporatism in Germany, 111: "On closer inspection, the anti-parliamentary thrust of Bismarckian corporatism is inseparable from its anti-Socialist design."

[61] *Paur,* Bismarck's Social Policy, 440.

[62] *Paur,* Bismarck's Social Policy, 453 ff.

[63] *Paur,* Bismarck's Social Policy, 455.

[64] See *J. Pichler,* ed., Othmar Spann, oder Die Welt als Ganzes (Wien, 1988).

[65] *K. Braun,* Konservatismus und Gemeinwirtschaft, Duisburger Hochschulbeiträge 11 (Duisburg, 1978).

[66] *A. Barkai,* Das Wirtschaftssystem des Nationalsozialismus: Der Historische und ideologische Hintergrund, 1933-1936, Bibliothek Wissenschaft und Politik, 18 (Köln, 1977), 70.

III.

The fascination that Second Reich scholarship had for foreigners in general,[67] and Americans in particular, is familiar. Numerous Americans, destined to become the first minds of the country, went to Germany to study with the figures whose activities I have catalogued. German influence on American scholarship reached well back into the early nineteenth-, and indeed the late eighteenth-centuries.[68] Nevertheless, it was only during and after the 1870s that American studies of German social science began in earnest.[69] Once those studies began, however, German influence was strongly felt; indeed, the German historical approach "dominated industrial organization theory for several decades,"[70] as American thought experienced a period of substantial Germanization.[71] An extended series of American intellectual pilgrimages to Germany — to learn from a professoriate whose "degree of perfection," as F. W. Taussig put it, "astonished the world"[72] — began in 1873, when J. B. Clark, later Professor at Columbia, went to study with Knies and Roscher. Clark was followed by many, including, among the most promiment, H. W. Farnam, Simon Patten, R. T. Ely, A. T. Hadley,[73] E. R. A. Seligman, Albion Small, Taussig, and more. By 1908, twenty active American professors boasted German doctorates.[74] The largest number had studied with Gustav Schmoller, Johannes Conrad, and in particular with Wagner.[75] Numerous intellectual events marked the spread of German learning in America through the agency of these men.[76]

---

67 For the French case, see the famous study of *C. Digeon,* La Crise Allemande de la Pensée Française (1870-1914) (Paris, 1959).

68 During the first generations, the learning Americans brought back from Germany was largely philological. *C. Diehl,* Americans and German Scholarship, 1770-1870 (New Haven, 1978). Nevertheless there were other contacts. Friedrich List himself was an exile in Pennsylvania, and he published, in 1827, an Outlines of American Political Economy, which he later incorporated into his 1840 textbook. *Farnam,* Deutsch-Amerikanische Beziehungen, 6; *Balabkins,* Not by Theory Alone, 90-91. Samuel B. Ruggles took an interest in German statistical methods as early as 1863 (cf. *Dorfman,* German Historical School, 18), and Henry C. Carey paid homage to German scholarship in his 1867 Principles of Social Science. Carey was, however, more noticed in Germany than in America. *Farnam,* Deutsch-Amerikanische Beziehungen, 6-7; *Balabkins,* Not by Theory Alone, 91. For the limits of Carey's influence in the United States, see *S. Fine,* Laissez-Faire and the General-Welfare State (Ann Arbor, 1956), 47 n. 1.

69 Cf. *Dorfman,* German Historical School, 17 (identifying 1870s and 1880s as period of the height of German influence).

70 *Hovenkampf,* The Antitrust Movement, 112.

71 See the literature cited above, note 5.

72 Quoted in *Dorfman,* German Historical School, 22. See also *Hovenkamp,* The Antitrust Movement, 110.

73 Hadley was, however, a complex case, since he remained in essence a laissez-faire economist. See *Fine,* Laissez Faire and the General-Welfare State, 48 n. 4.

74 *Farnam,* Deutsche-Amerikanische Beziehungen, 29. Wagner's particular popularity is noted in *Herbst,* The German Historical School, 16.

What exactly was it that these mostly Yankee gentlemen brought home from their *Wanderjahre* in the Germany of Bismarck? As an example of the contours of high Germanophile scholarship in America, we may consider Richard T. Ely, probably the most influential Germanophile scholar of the era.[77] Ely, an American Christian Socialist,[78] worked hard to bring the German spirit both to his classroom and to his scholarship. He was particularly in the habit of assigning, to his students, Schmoller's *Grundfragen des Rechts und der Volkswirtschaft,* written in defense of state socialism against the attacks of Treitschke.[79] And he labored, with very considerable success, to bring a German institutionalist perspective to American social science, as well as to forge links between university scholars and state administrators.[80] Some of the ideas he promoted seem quaint or disturbing now: for example, he saw, in Germany, a salutary application of military spirit to the making of society; German universities, he believed, trained civil servants the way West Point and Annapolis trained American military officers.[81] But the main lesson he took from his German teachers was one still by and large

---

75 Following those three names came Sering, Roscher, Knies, Bücher, Brentano, and Cohn; and then a variety of others, including Simmel, Menger, Böhm-Bawerk, Held, Knapp, Stammler and Jhering. See *Farnam,* Deutsch-Amerikanische Beziehungen, 26. Fine's list of the most important of the German-influenced political economists includes Ely, H. C. Adams, Edmund J. James, Simon N. Patten, J. B. Clark, E. R. A. Seligman, and Richmond Mayo-Smith. *Fine,* Laissez Faire and the General-Welfare State, 199.

76 Landmarks: American attention was captured by a T. E. Cliffe Leslie article on the German historical school in 1875. (Cf. *J. Dorfman,* The Role of the German Historical School in American Enonomic Thought, 19); in 1876, C. F. Adams published an important German-influenced article on "The State and the Railroads" in the Atlantic Monthly. *Hovenkamp,* The Antitrust Movement, 109. Also significant was the establishment of Johns Hopkins Studies in Historical and Political Science by Herbert Baxter Adams in 1883; the report on German employment insurance by John Graham Brooks, published by Bureau of Labor (both discussed in *Farnam,* Deutsch-Amerikanische Beziehungen, 12-13); and the debate in Science, reprinted as Science Economic Discussion (1886). *Herbst,* German Historical School, 134 ff.

77 For Ely as particularly faithful to the teachings of the Germans, see *Herbst,* German Historical School, 161-62. On Ely as a disseminator of German ideas in America, see ibid., 18 ff.; *Dorfman,* German Historical School, 24 ff.

78 *Fine,* Laissez Faire and the General-Welfare State, 178; and the discussion in *J. T. Kloppenberg,* Uncertain Victory: Social Democracy and Progressivism in European and American Thought, 1870-1920 (Oxford, 1986), 207 ff.

79 *Farnam,* Deutsch-Amerikanische Beziehungen, 29.

80 It was to this decade that the beginnings of a very influential German-influenced school belong, the school of the socalled "Institutionalists," most prominent among whom were Ely, Thorstein Veblen, and John R. Commons. See most recently *H. Hovenkamp,* The First Great Law & Economics Movement, Stanford Law Review 42 (1990): 1013 ff. It was the Institutionalists, operating under German influence, who introduced concepts such as equalization of bargaining power (ibid., 1024) and "going concern" theory (ibid., 1025).

81 *Balabkins,* Not By Theory Alone, 50. Both Ely and H. C. Adams were convinced that a more activist state would attract the gifted grade of men who were going into industry. *Fine,* Laissez Faire and the General-Welfare State, 205-206.

current: the lesson that state interventionism can be a blessing. Ely took this lesson both from German theory and from German practice. As a student of Wagner's, he favored a program of "Verstaatlichung"; as an admirer of Bismarck's he believed the state should step in to aid "the weak and needy."[82]

In his emphasis on state interventionism, Ely was typical. From the 1870s onward, the lesson Americans carried home from Germany was, first und foremost, to look benevolently upon the activity of the state[83]; the rebellion against laissez-faire was the Germanophile style in American political economy.[84] The statism of American Germanophile scholarship showed, for example, in the event that marked the high tide of the movement: the founding of the American Economic Association in 1885. The A. E. A. was founded at the urging of Johannes Conrad,[85] who thought his students should found an American equivalent of the Verein für Socialpolitik.[86] Two of them, Simon Patten and Edmund James, following his advice, proposed a platform for a Society for the Study of National Economy, committed to the proposition that the state was "a positive factor in material production" with "legitimate claims to a share of the product."[87] This prospectus was toned down in the subsequent stages of planning for an American Economic Association,[88] and the A. E. A. soon abandoned its Germanophilic bent.[89] Nevertheless, the founding document of the Association was

---

82 *Herbst,* German Historical School, 190.

83 Also typical of German-influenced scholars, was, it should be added, an emphasis on historical and statistical method. Cf. *Dorfman,* German Historical School, 17-18; *Hovenkamp,* The Antitrust Movement, 109; and generally *Herbst,* German Historical School, 136 ff. But my focus here is on social and political programs, not scholarly ones.

84 Generally *Fine,* Laissez Faire and the General-Welfare State, 198-251. Cf. *Dorfman,* German Historical School, 20. If was, of course, *generally* true that American debate in the era of "laissez-faire constitutionalism" revolved almost exclusively around the question of the propriety of state intervention. See, e. g., *J. May,* Antitrust in the Formative Era: Political and Economic Theory in Constitutional and Antitrust Analysis, 1880-1918, Ohio State Law Journal 50 (1989): 257-395, here 262 ff. This deeply colored the American reading of German scholarship, as expressed, for example, in Ely's Property and Contract (1914). *Hovenkamp,* Law & Economics, 1022. There are, it should be noted, exceptions. Hadley is the most notable, but John W. Burgess, too, was not swayed by his German training from laissez-faire. *Fine,* Laissez Faire and the General-Welfare State, 92 ff.

85 *Farnam,* Deutsch-Amerikanische Beziehungen, 11. The principles of the A. E. A. are quoted in *Dorfman,* German Historical School, 27.

86 *Balabkins,* Not By Theory Alone, 98.

87 Quoted in *Fine,* Laissez Faire and the General-Welfare State, 213.

88 Ely's prospectus simply emphasized the inadequacy of laissez-faire, the need for historical and statistical study, and the value of social legislation, particularly in order to cope with the labor problem. *Fine,* Laissez Faire and the General-Welfare State, 216-17. The prospectus was toned down yet further when the association convened, partly in order to allay H. C. Adams' fear that the association would seem too Germanic.

89 The Germanic emphasis was stricken from the organic statute of the American Economic Association in 1888. *Fine,* Laissez Faire and the General-Welfare State, 221; *Dorfman,* German Historical School, 28.

quite Germanic indeed,[90] and for a few years at least there was something of an American Verein für Socialpolitik at work.

Germanophile scholarship remained, indeed, a powerful force throughout the decade of the 1880s, not only because the theory of the Verein für Socialpolitik was intellectually attractive, but also because Bismarck's state socialism had immense appeal to American meliorists.[91]

IV.

Yet, hard as we may look, we find that these Germanophile Americans stopped short of accepting the corporatist elements in the German work that they read so avidly.

To exemplify the failure of German corporatism in American thought, we may examine two figures influenced by Wagner's idea of "Verstaatlichung": H. C. Adams and Edward Bellamy. Wagner, to reiterate, favored "Verstaatlichung" of a wide range of enterprises, and also favored a society founded on "self-governing corporative bodies."[92] These two Wagnerite ideas had remarkably unequal fortunes in America. "Verstaatlichung" gained great support. It had, in fact, an entire association, the National League for Promoting the Public Ownership of Monopolies.[93] But the American who embraced this idea had startlingly little use for "self-governing corporative bodies," showing almost none of the German social yearning to transcend the individual.

The pattern shows, for example, in the most influential Germanophile pamphlet of the 1880s, H. C. Adams' *Relation of the State to Industrial Action.*[94] In his famous 1887 pamphlet, Adams, who had studied with Wagner and Held,[95] often echoed Wagner audibly. Indeed, Adams presented his argument as the consequence of an intellectual wrestling with German thought.[96] He described German

---

90 For the A. E. A.'s "echo" of the Verein für Socialpolitik, see, e. g., *Herbst,* German Historical School, 148.

91 *Herbst,* German Historical School, 191-92. Ely touted Bismarck's policies, "which made the state 'a benefactor and protector of the weak and needy.'" *Herbst,* German Historical School, 190.

92 Quoted and discussed above, text accompanying notes 53-54.

93 *Fine,* Laissez Faire and the General-Welfare State, 339. Figures for the success of the municipalization movement in ibid., 356. The demand for federal government ownership of railroads, telegraph and telephone also made its way into the Populists' Omaha platform of 1892.*Fine,* Laissez Faire and the General-Welfare State, 304.

94 *Herbst,* German Historical School, 149-50.

95 *J. Dorfman,* Henry Carter Adams: The Harmonizer of Liberty and Reform, in H. C. Adams, Relation of the State to Industrial Action *and* Economics and Jurisprudence (Dorfman, ed., New York, 1954), 11-12.

96 *Adams,* Relation of the State to Industrial Action, 98.

thought in terms that commingled Wagnerite "Verstaatlichung" with Schäffleän organicism. German thought, he wrote:

> ... proceeds from the assumption that some industries are from their nature "sovereign in character." Thus all businesses pertaining to transportation, as railroads, expressage, telegraphy, postal service and the like, pertain naturally to the state. These are the nerves and arteries of the body politic, and should be directed from a common center. It is indeed a litte ludicrous to notice the almost superstitious reverence with which a certain class of German writers trace out the analogy existing between the social organism and physical organisms. But the more rational thought seems to be that the government may properly take the initiative and control in all forms of business which possess what is termed "the collective interest", and since so many businesses are observed to fall into this class, German writers have cut the matter short by saying that presumption lies with the state, and by throwing upon individuals the burden of proof...[97]

Adams did not wish to see "blind subservience" to such German ideas.[98] Nevertheless in the end he liked German organicism, and he was quite willing to make it his own,[99] as part of a larger program of "Verstaatlichung." In pursuit of this program, Adams expounded three principles that should guide government in regulating industry. The first was to "raise the ethical plane of competition" without curtailing competition.[100] The second was, to reproduce Adam's emphatic capitals: *"The state may realize for society the benefits of monopoly"*[101]; the third: *"Social harmony may be restored by extending the duties of the state."*

---

97 *Adams,* Relation of the State to Industrial Action, 80-82.

98 *Adams,* Relation of the State to Industrial Action, 80-82: In England, where the philosophy of individualism permeates all thought, the presumption is in favor of private enterprise; in Germany, where the state is the center of all interests, the presumtion lies in the opposite direction. Yet the mental characteristic which leads to these diverse conclusions is the same for both peoples. Is it not, clear the philosophers of both schools condemn by their example any blind subservience to what they teach? And is it not absurd for American economists to array themselves in opposing schools as advocates of what Engish or what is German? I am not arguing for obstinacy but for independence ... Certainly not set of men should be so ready to maintain intellectual independence, in the domain of constructive economics, as they who, at the great universities of Germany, have learned how to read the true lessons from history.

According to Adams, there was a danger in the German model, for the great prestige of the state had attracted too many men of talent into public service. In consequence, "[a] German sewing machine is a very bungling affair, made after the abandoned models of American patterns; but German cities are well governed." *Adams,* Relation of the State to Industrial Action, 121.

99 *Adams,* Relation of the State to Industrial Action, 82: "*Society* is the organic entity about which all our reasoning should center. Both state action and the industrial activity of individuals are functions of complete social organism." In so saying, Adams was disagreeing with what he said was the German tendency to view the *state* as the critical organic entity: "The fundamental error of English political philosophy lies in regarding the state as a necessary evil: the fundamental error of German political philosophy lies in its conception of the state as an organism complete within itself. Neither the one nor the other of these views is correct." Ibid.

100 *Dorfman,* German Historical School, 26.

101 *Adams,* Relation of the State to Industrial Action, 98.

To that point, Adams sounded quite German, despite his protestations of independence from German thought. But once he explained *exactly which* monopolies should undergo "Verstaatlichung," and *exactly why,* the distinctively American character of Adam's thought became clear. The German thinkers, as we have seen, viewed industrial associations as "social organizations" — as "communal" in character, to use Wagner's language, the result of a need for supra-individual, "social" identity. Adams saw industrial concentration quite differently. To Adams, industrial concentration was the result, not of social needs, but of economic ones. There were, he said, "many industries which, from their nature, are monopolies, and cannot, therefore, be safely consigned to the guidance of the rule of private financiers."[102] Such industries would produce monopolies regardless, and if they were not public, they would be private, with consequent oppression to the public at large.[103] This drew, to be sure, in part on Wagner, who had recommended the nationalization of monopolies that earned monopoly profits. But Adams went well beyond Wagner in the sophistication of his economic reasoning. Indeed, it is fair to say that where Wagner approached his problem as a sociologist, Adams approached his as an economist, developing the technical theory of natural monopoly.[104] This emphasis on technical economic theory meant that Adams omitted a great deal — indeed the bulk — of what mattered to Wagner and his German colleagues. Nothing did Adams say about "status-based sense of honor"; nothing about the "crystallization" of "social forces." Organicist as he might occasionally be, Adam's strong tendency was to speak the language of economics. (Nothing, either, did he say about the inadequacies of parliamentary government.)

The pattern of Adams' thought was also, *mutatis mutandis,* the pattern of the novelist Edward Bellamy's. Bellamy spent a year in Germany before embarking on a brief legal career. Law proved alien to his tastes, however, and he turned to journalism.[105] Like others of this Germanophile era, he was captivated by Wagnerite ideas about nationalization; indeed, he produced a list of enterprises marked out for nationalization that followed almost verbatim that of Wagner: "railroads, telegraph and telephone, the express business, and the coal mines, [as well as] assumption by the state governments of the liquor business and the

---

102 *Adams,* Relation of the State to Industrial Action, 103.

103 *Adams,* Relation of the State to Industrial Action, 103 - 104. Adams, it should be noted, felt obliged to address considerable anxieties about monopolies, acknowledging that Americans ordinarily associated monopolies "with all that is odious, grasping and tyrannous." *Adams,* Relation of the State to Industrial Action, 98.

104 Adams propounded the theory of increasing returns. Relation of the State to Industrial action, 105 ff. For Adams as a pioneer of the technical theory of natural monopoly, see *Dorfman,* German Historical School, 26, and the discussion below note 112.

105 *J. Thomas,* Introduction, to E. Bellamy, Looking Backward, 2000 - 1887 (Cambridge, Mass., 1967), 4. On Bellamy, see also *Fine,* Laissez Faire and the General-Welfare State, 295 ff.

fire- and life-insurance business, and the municipalization of local public utilities."[106]

In his enthusiasm for such nationalization Bellamy was typical. But he was far from typical in the mode he chose for publicizing his beliefs: his famous utopian novel, *Looking Backward: 2000-1887*, published in the same year as Adams' tract. *Looking Backward* featured a hero who, upon awakening in the Boston of the year 2000, discovered a world in which all industry was state-owned. His benefactors explained to him how "[t]he epoch of trusts had ended in The Great Trust,"[107] and how the entire populace of the world had been transformed into the great Industrial Army. What had transpired? Industrial concentration had increased progressively until at last the state had stepped in, early in the twentieth century, to seize all industry. The result was a paradisiacal union of business and state, painted in detail in Bellamy's wildly popular work. Bellamy's novel, unfootnoted as it was, said little about German social thought. But it clearly bore, at the very least, an indirect German impress. Bismarckian in spirit, for example, was Bellamy's vision of the political ordering of his new Boston: the political leadership of his world was drawn from the industrial leadership. And in one rhapsodic moment, Bellamy made his admiration for one German leader clear. "The effectiveness of the working force of a nation, under the myriad-headed leadership of private capital, even if the leaders were not mutual enemies, as compared with that which it attains under single head, may be likened to the military efficiency of a mob, or a horde of barbarians with a thousand petty chiefs, as compared with that of a disciplined army under one general — such a fighting machine, for example, as the German army in the time of Von Moltke."[108]

Clearly enough there was a substantial German influence on Bellamy, just as there was on Adams. Indeed, in his eagerness to see industrial and political leadership coalesce, Bellamy was rather more Germanic than Adams. But, like Adams, Bellamy had resisted a critical corporatist belief. For, like Adams, Bellamy showed no discernible interest in "the lesser circles," in intermediate corporative bodies of the Wagnerite type.[109] However eagerly Bellamy may have rushed to claim the authority of Von Moltke, his writings stopped short of embracing German corporatist "social organizations." Indeed, Bellamy and Adams both seem simply to have lacked the ensemble of German yearnings for new associations that would transcend individual identity.

What was true of Adams and Bellamy was true of American social thought in general. Americans shared neither the characteristic German desire to transcend

---

106 *Fine*, Laissez Faire and the General-Welfare State, 299-300.

107 *Bellamy*, Looking Backward, 127.

108 *Bellamy*, Looking Backward, 253.

109 See the passage of Wagner's quoted above at note 53.

the individual, nor the characteristic German doubt about the legitimacy of representative government. To be sure, there were occasional mutterings consistent with anti-parliamentary views.[110] But even the most vigorous proponents of a political organization for industry did not argue for the abolition of Congress. And if the characteristically German suspicion of parliamentary government was generally absent, even more so was the characteristic German desire to identify new self-governing corporative bodies.

These were differences that seem to have expressed themselves in other social realms as well — for example, in the comparative weakness of the American co-operative movement.[111] These differences expressed themselves, too, in very considerable divergences in the style of American social science. What was true of Adams as contrasted with Wagner was generally true of Americans as contrasted with Germans: where Germans tended to speak the languages of sociology and political economy, Americans tended to speak the language of economics. Germans typically argued from a sociological need to form associative unions; Americans, almost to a man, used the reasoning of classical economics to show that competition led inevitably to consolidation.[112] Germans typically theorized

---

110 Thus Ely could favor proportional representation and like reforms. *Fine,* Laissez Faire and the General-Welfare State, 235. And numerous figures spoke of introducing political values into the industrial system. Again much was distilled in the motto of Bellamy's New Nation: "The industrial system of a nation, as well as its political system, ought to be a government of the people, by the people, for the people." Quoted in *Fine,* Laissez Faire and the General-Welfare State, 297 n. 24.

111 The German co-operative movement, like the German trade union movement, began with a striking initial inspiration from England. For a brief account, rich in Weimar social philosophizing, of the influence of the Rochdale Pioneers and the subsequent nineteenth-century history in Germany, see *K. Geiler,* Der genossenschaftliche Gedanke und seine stärkere Verwirklichung im heutigen Wirtschaftsrecht, in Beiträge zur Erläuterung des Deutschen Rechts 65 (1921): 136 ff. For a brief comparative account, noting the relative weakness of the cooperative movement in America, see *A. Williams,* Co-operation, in Encyclopedia Britannica, 11th ed. (1910), 7: 82 ff., esp. 89. My thanks to Professor K. W. Nörr for pointing out the importance of this movement for the subject of this contribution.

112 The American tendency was very much to speak of the economics of natural monopoly. For this theme in the work of a number of different figures, see generally *Fine,* Laissez Faire and the General-Welfare State, 221 - 32, 266; *Herbst,* German Historical School, 190; *May,* Antitrust in the Formative Era, 293 and note 311; and generally the discussion of *Hovenkamp,* First Great Law & Economics Movement, 999 ff.

The theory of natural monopoly predated German influence in America. It was perhaps as old as John Stuart Mill, writing in 1848 (see *Mill,* Principles of Political Economy 143 (W. Ashley rev. ed. 1923). Cited in *Hovenkamp,* Regulatory Conflict in the Gilded Age: Federalism and the Railroad Problem, 97 Yale L. J. 1017, 1017 n. 2 (1988)), and certainly as old as C. F. Adams, writing in 1871 (see *Adams,* The Railroad System, in Chapters of Erie (Boston, 1871)). Nevertheless, it became closely associated with the Germanic tradition. So much so, indeed, that when, in 1880, Ely reported on Railway regulation in Germany to the State Department, he cited neither Mill nor Adams, nor any writing on the German economy as such, but rather Gustav Cohn's Englische Eisenbahnpolitik. *Ely,* A Brief Sketch of the Railway History of Germany, in Papers Relating to the Foreign Relations of the United States (Washington, 1880), 420. Ely

about the need for some new form of "representation by occupational status" that would unite political and economic interests; such political economy was alien to Americans.[113] To state the point briefly, when the wide-ranging social theory of Germany entered America, it tended to become simply economics.[114]

Moreover, it tended to become *pure* economics. Americans showed a powerful inclination to separate economics from jurisprudence, in a way wholly alien to the German pattern. Where Germans like Schmoller and Roscher were reluctant to isolate economics from law,[115] the same rapidly showed itself not to be the case in America. By the early 1890s, Americans, with their economistic turn of mind, were abandoning German *Kathedersozialisten* for Austrian and English marginalists,[116] striking out on the path toward an American twentieth century in which economics would be the queen of the social sciences.

V.

Why were Americans so deaf to the corporatist strain — and indeed more broadly to the "social" and anti-parliamentary strains — in the Germans they so admired? A number of factors suggest themselves.

---

adopted German language, observing that "Russia, Turkey and Spain are the only important countries on the continent which have not already made important progress in the direction of the *Verstaatlichung* of the railways . . .," and added that it was "probable that the discontent in England will finally lead her to follow the example of the rest of Europe, and buy up the railways, as she already has the telegraph." *Ely*, Brief Sketch, 421.

One may perhaps surmise that Americans spoke solely in terms of the state seizure of natural monopolies because the terms of debate in America tended to be set by one question in particular: Railroad regulation. See *Hovenkamp*, Law & Economics, 997 (discussing C. F. Adams, H. C. Adams); *H. Hovenkamp*, The Sherman Act and the Classical Theory of Competition, Iowa Law Review 74 (1990) 1025 - 26; *Adams*, Relation of the State to Industrial Action, 111 ff.

113 The term "Political Economy" was in decline, in the United States, from 1883 onwards. *Farnam*, Deutsch-Amerikanische Beziehungen, 15 - 16.

114 All observers remark on this difference. In Hovenkamp's words:

"In spite of their German educations and their stated commitment to the historical method, Clark and Ely had generally analytic approached to the trust problem. They spoke in generalized terms, as the wastes of competition, economies of scale, and market dominance."

Hovenkamp, The Antitrust Movement, 118 - 20. See generally *Fine*, Laissez Faire and the General-Welfare State, 221 - 28, 290 - 91. Cf. also *Farnam*, Deutsch-Amerikanische Beziehungen, 24.

115 See, e. g., *Balabkins*, Not By Theory Alone, 53.

116 *Hovenkamp*, The Antitrust Movement, 109; *Fine*, Laissez Faire and the General-Welfare State, 274 ff. (discussing experience of J. B. Clark); *Dorfman*, Henry Carter Adams, 17. The economistic tendency showed in the argument of some figures that, despite concentration, potential competition would adequately discipline firms. *May*, Antitrust in the Formative Era, 285.

The least mysterious of the American differences was the absence of anti-parliamentarism. As a practical matter, representative government had a long history, and consequently great legitimacy, in America: the question of fundamental political ordering was not an open one.[117] What was political economy in Germany thus tended to become economics in America, in part simply because the basic political questions in America had been settled.[118]

As for the relative absence of interest in self-governing corporative bodies: in the end, that can only be explained by reference to factors far beyond the scope of this essay. For clearly enough, this absence was the result, in larger measure, of a much deeper individualism in America. As Robert Liefmann put it, speaking of France, "individualistic tendencies" and cartelization do not tend to go together.[119] An explanation of America's "individualistic tendencies" could come only through broad-gauged comparative sociological study much more ambitious than called for here. Question-begging though it may seem to say so, in the last analysis corporatism was weak in America because individualism was strong, and without an account of American individualism, the basic problem posed by this essay cannot be solved.

Nevertheless, one narrow point can be made without entering into the oceanic vastness of the comparative sociology of individualism. The lack of American interest in self-governing corporative bodies reflected a larger difference in the history of industrial concentration in the two countries: America was, notoriously, the land of trusts and big corporations, not of cartels. Let me quote again Liefmann's classic discussion of the difference between trusts and cartels:

> The term 'Cartels' we take to mean *voluntary agreements between* — or as we have called them, *associations of* — *independent enterprises of a similar type to secure a monopoly of the market*... They differ in this respect from the *monopolistic amalgamations*, in which *all* or nearly all the forms in a particular branch of trade are brought into one concern, thus abolishing completely the economic independence

---

117 Perhaps we can also see more complex differences in political assumptions in H. C. Adams' distaste for the police state measures associated with Bismarck's anti-socialist laws. See *Dorfman*, Henry Carter Adams, 32.

118 Related arguments are offered by Farnam: (a) that the presence of written constitutions meant that almost all social questions were defined as legal ones, not therefore amenable to the sort of social science reasoning characteristic of Germany; (b) the American assumption, embodied in the "Spoils System," that anyone could serve in government office — and indeed had a kind of native eligibility for office — made German-style bureaucratically-oriented social science impossible. *Farnam*, Deutsch-Amerikanische Beziehungen, 3 ff.

119 *Liefmann*, Cartels, Concerns and Trusts, 40. There is obviously much truth in the old proposition that the U. S. was simply irreducibly more individualistic than Germany. The tendency of scholars like Ely to "condemn alike that individualism which would allow the state no room for industrial activity, and that socialism which would absorb in the state the functions of the individual," or of H. C. Adams to denounce "the tyranny of German socialism" (both quoted in *Fine*, Laissez Faire and the General-Welfare State, 211), is testimony to the strength of that tradition among social thinkers.

> of former individual undertakings. The special form of amalgamation known in America as the trust has precisely the same effect ...[120]

The sort of industrial concentration German social thinkers witnessed was the cartel — a voluntary association of independent enterprises. American social thinkers, by contrast, witnessed trusts and big concerns. In America, unlike Germany, attempts at voluntary oligopolistic collusion rarely succeeded.[121]

To be sure, Americans of the later nineteenth century, largely under German influence, believed far and wide in the inevitability of industrial concentration.[122] But the kind of concentration they in fact observed was trustification, not cartelization. As a result, American scholars had less occasion than did German scholars had to wax poetic about associative values in industrial concentration. I have already suggested that German corporatism grew largely out of the experience of unionization and cartelization in Germany. Americans did not share that experience. Labor unions, to be sure, appeared in force in America. But cartels did not. And without cartels, American scholars could not easily build a theory of corporatism.[123]

The form of American social thought thus in part depended on the failure of cartelization in America — a failure for which we still lack any definitive explanation. Many explanations have, to be sure, been offered: that hostility from the courts prevented cartelization[124]; that in the absence of "salient" labor

---

120 *Liefman,* Cartels, Concerns and Trusts, 7, 10-11.

121 See *N. Lamoreaux,* The Great Merger Movement in American Business, 1895-1904 (Cambridge, 1985), 14-16 and often; *Hovenkamp,* Regulatory Conflict, 1042-43. Even where collusion took place, moreover, its aim (as in the case of trade associations) was to join in such causes as opposition to unfavorable tariff legislation, rather than to collude about prices or output. See id., 27; *L. Galambos,* Competition & Cooperation: The Emergence of a National Trade Association (Baltimore, 1966), 34.

122 See *G. Kolko,* The Triumph of Conservatism: A Reinterpretation of American History, 1900-1916 (Glencoe, 1963), 11 ff., esp. 15 (discussing Ely, H. C. Adams, A. T. Hadley, E. R. A. Seligman and others without discussing the German education that these men shared).

123 It is, to be sure, evident that some American scholars borrowed the German benevolent attitude toward cartels. Thus H. C. Adams concluded that pooling contracts should be legalized to deal with the problems of industrial concentration. *Dorfman,* Henry Carter Adams, 31. Seligman, Hadley and Jenks made similar arguments. *Hovenkamp,* Regulatory Conflict, 1040 n. 112 (1887 and 1890 respectively). (American industrialists too, could express admiration for European cartel cooperation. See *Kolko,* Triumph of Conservatism, 37). Nevertheless, this admiration could only be theoretical in the American context. Americans simply could not build their schemes on the presence of functioning cartels as their German contemporaries could.

124 See *A. Chandler,* The Visible Hand: The Managerial Revolution in American Business (Cambridge, Mass., 1977), 375: "Without the Sherman Act and ... judicial interpretations, the cartels of small family firms owning and operating single-function enterprises might well have continued into the twentieth century in the United States as they did in Europe." For the classic status of this view, see *M. Sklar,* The Corporate

political movement, businessman felt less pressure to organize.[125] One of the most interesting explanations proceeds from social causes: Where cartels did succeed in America, they succeeded in industries marked by geographic concentration, such as the fine-writing-paper industry, which was concentrated around Holyoke, Massachusetts,[126] and the Cotton manufacturing industry.[127] This data is striking in the comparative light of the German experience. In Germany, cartels tended to grow out of quasi-social gatherings: clubs and "breakfast cartels" founded in the associative traditions of mid-nineteenth-century German society.[128] "Breakfast cartels" did not have much hope of forming in America: American industry was, as a rule, simply too dispersed, and the American populace too heterogeneous, for such social-industrial groupings to form. In the North American vastness, "solidarity" was not a rallying-cry likely to stir Americans the way it stirred Germans; as a consequence, "solidarity" was unlikely to appear in the American language of analysis of industrial concentration. At any rate, whatever the reason, cartels of the kind that captivated German social theorists were little in evidence in America. On the contrary, American thinkers saw trusts, and had to build their theory around trusts.[129]

Reconstruction of American Capitalism, 1890-1916 (Cambridge, 1988), 154 ff. See also *Lamoreaux,* Great Merger Movement, 100.

There is, however, a substantial timing problem in attributing the failure of American cartelization to the Supreme Court. The leading case of *United States v. Addyston Pipe & Steel Co.,* 85 F. 271 (6th Cir. 1898), modified and affirmed 175 U. S. 211 (1899) was not place until 1899, after the tendency to consolidation had already appeared. *Lamoreaux,* The Great Merger Movement, 109 (discussing R. Nelson, Merger Movements in American Industry).

In part, it should be noted, American courts tended to avoid the whole question of cartelization by invalidating combination agreements as *ultra vires* under state corporation law. *Hovenkamp,* Sherman Act and the Classical Theory, 1021; *Lamoreaux,* Great Merger Movement, 162-63. It should also be noted that a number of common law courts and lower federal courts approved loose cartels until the early to mid-1890s. *May,* Antitrust in the Formative Era, 285.

125 *T. McGraw,* Rethinking the Trust Question, in McGraw, ed., Regulation in Perspective (1981), 5. See also *Wilson,* Why is there no Corporatism in the United States?, 232-35; *P. Schmitter,* Neo-Corporatism and the State, in The Political Economy of Corporatism, 32, 37-38 (W. Grant, ed., 1985).

126 See *Lamoreaux,* Great Merger Movement, 25.

127 See *Galambos,* Competition & Cooperation, 21. Lamoreaux argues, too, that collusion was more successful in industries that had not undergone rapid recent expansion. *Lamoreaux,* The Great Merger Movement, 62. This might profitably be compared with the German experience.

128 See *Pohl,* Entwicklung der Kartelle in Deutschland, 208-09 with further references.

To be sure, the famous German "Frühstückskartelle" had a kind of American counterpart in the famous Gary dinners, in which American steelmakers were convened by Judge Elbert H. Gary, Chairman of the United States Steel Corp. *Lamoreaux,* The Great Merger Movement, 118.

129 The image of society that confronted American thinkers can be discerned, for example, in the 1883 statement of the influential E. R. A. Seligman that the state must intervene "where free competition ends disastrously, and 'where the powers of the state

Whatever the relative weight of these (or other[130]) factors, they did their work. In the end, even before German influence began to fade in the 1890s,[131] it was clear that the German corporatist vision was not much at home in the United States. Electoral government was too secure; "social" alternatives to individualism struck too few responsive chords. The United States remained in the isolation that continues, for better or worse, to typify it. Perhaps by 1890 it was already possible to see what would certainly become clear by 1935: that corporatism was not likely to be a successful transplant in America.

themselves are threatened . . . by corporate monopolies.'" Quoted in *Dorfman,* German Historical School, 27. For Seligman's influence on the courts, see *Hovenkamp,* Law & Economics, 1004, 1008-1009.

130 Herbst points out that there may have been religious reasons for American hesitation before German thought. Part of the difficulty in the importation of German models may have arisen because of the link between the new political economy and the social gospel in America. "That German churches were state supported would, many Americans felt, necessarily vitiate their efforts toward social reform . . ." *Herbst,* German Historical School, 185 and generally 183 ff. Thus, to the extent that corporatism was associated with Christian Social reform, the comparatively weak link between state and church in America made it inhospitable to German influence.

131 E. g., *Farnam,* Deutsch-Amerikanische Beziehungen, 21. For the judgment that German-trained scholars showed themselves "notably ineffectual," see *Herbst,* German Historical School, 149.

Morton Horwitz, I should note, has discovered a different chronological pattern in his own studies of German influence: The associative theory of Gierke, he finds, was not yet influential in the 1880s, becoming influential only later. *Horwitz,* Santa Clara Revisited: The Development of Coroporate Theory, West Virginia Law Review 88 (1985): 173-224.

Verzeichnis der Mitarbeiter

Buxbaum, Richard, Professor Dr., University of California at Berkeley School of Law, Boalt Hall, Berkeley, CA 94720, USA

Clark, David S., Professor Dr., The University of Tulsa, College of Law, 3120 East Fourth Place, Tulsa, OK 74104, USA

Graziadei, Michele, Dr., Università di Trento, Facoltà di Giurispurdenza, Via Rosmini 33, 38100 Trento, Italia

Herget, James E., Professor Dr., University of Houston Law Center, 4800 Calhoun, Houston, TX 77204, USA

Hoeflich, Michael, Dean, Professor Dr., Syracuse University College of Law, Syracuse, NY 13244, USA

Reimann, Mathias, Professor Dr., University of Michigan Law School, Hutchins Hall, Ann Arbor, MI 48109-1215, USA

Riesenfeld, Stefan, Professor Dr., University of California at Berkeley School of Law, Boalt Hall, Berkeley, CA 94720, USA

Watson, Alan, Professor Dr., University of Georgia School of Law, Herty Drive, Athens, GA 30602, USA

Whitman, James Q., Professor Dr., Stanford Law School, Nathan Abbott Way at Alvarado Row, Stanford, CA 94305, USA

MIX
Papier aus verantwortungsvollen Quellen
Paper from responsible sources
FSC® C105338

Printed by Libri Plureos GmbH
in Hamburg, Germany